TRANSFORMING
SCHOOLS

GARLAND REFERENCE LIBRARY
OF SOCIAL SCIENCE
VOL. 888

TRANSFORMING SCHOOLS

edited by

Peter W. Cookson, Jr.
Barbara Schneider

GARLAND PUBLISHING, Inc.
New York & London / 1995

Library of Congress Cataloging-in-Publication Data

Transforming schools / edited by Peter W. Cookson, Jr.
and Barbara Schneider.
      p.   cm. — (Garland reference library of social
science ; v. 888)
    Includes bibliographical references and index.
    ISBN 0-8153-1257-1 (hardcover). —
    ISBN 0-8153-1533-3 (pbk.)
    1. Educational change—United States. 2. Educa-
tion—United States—Aims and objectives. 3. School
management and organization—United States.
I. Cookson, Peter W., Jr. II. Schneider, Barbara,
1946– . III. Series.
LA210.T74   1995
370'.973—dc20   94–36371
                                          CIP

Contents

Acknowledgments

This book is the expression of many people. The contributors have written essays that we believe capture some of the best thinking about the problems and possibilities of education. Each author has made a unique contribution, and collectively they have created a volume that we believe will have enduring significance; without their talents, patience, and intellects, *Transforming Schools* would not be a reality.

We have been helped by many people in the complex process of moving the book from its inception to its completion. The staff at NORC and The University of Chicago has been absolutely crucial in ensuring the efficiency and timeliness of the editorial process. In particular, Deborah Kulyukin took a leadership role and was indispensable to us. At Adelphi, Erin McKeon provided ongoing and invaluable assistance.

Garland Publishing has offered the kind of support that made working on this book a genuine pleasure. Helga McCue was very helpful in the preparation of the manuscript. We also owe considerable thanks to Barbara Anderson, whose editorial assistance ensured that the essays in the volume were cogent and literate.

Our patient and persistent editor, Marie Ellen Larcada, supported this project from its beginning, offered timely and useful advice, and was unstinting in her practical and intellectual support.

And finally, we wish to thank Joseph Conaty for showing us the error of our ways.

Introduction

For well over a decade the future of education in the United States has been the subject of intense debate. This conversation has seldom been polite; in fact, most of the time the level of discourse can be described as heated, intense, and often partisan. A sense of urgency infuses this debate because there is a general perception that the schools are failing. This sense of failure resonates deeply with American fears about chronic social inequality, a lack of national purpose, and the negative effects of international economic competition. Americans have an abiding faith in the efficacy of education that transcends its practical outcomes; for many Americans education is a secular religion. Strong and vibrant public schools are seen by most Americans as prerequisites to social progress. For this reason the debate over the future of American education touches deeply held beliefs that are only partially influenced by facts. But facts are essential if education is to be responsive to the profound cultural, social, political, and economic changes that are altering contemporary society. There is also an urgency to this debate because the condition of many children in the United States is tragic. One out of every four American children lives in poverty. According to the journalist Nancy Gibbs (1990, 42), "Every eight seconds of the school day a child drops out. Every 26 seconds, a child runs away from home. Every 47 seconds, a child is abused or neglected. Every 67 seconds, a teenager has a baby. Every seven minutes, a child is arrested for a drug offense. Every 36 minutes, a child is killed or injured by a gun. Every day 135,000 children bring their guns to school."

Proposals for redesigning education have been suggested by a great many policymakers, researchers, concerned advocates, educational interest groups, and business leaders. Whether the issue is the privatization of public education or the development of new curricula or the process of hiring and evaluating school administrators and teachers, nearly every aspect of the American educational system is being seriously considered for radical alteration. Critics believe that only major structural changes can reconfigure a sprawling public school system that seems out of touch with the economic, technological, and cultural changes that are now transforming the social and educational world. Some observers have noted that many of these major organizational changes have already begun, as evidenced by the Chicago School Reform Act (Bryk et al. 1993).

Educational reformers differ on how schools can be improved. Some reformers essentially want to start all over again; the privatization movement, which five years ago had few adherents, has acquired luster and respectability. If, for example, the voucher movement is successful, the public school system as it has been known for over a hundred years will be radically changed. Other reformers, while acknowledging public education's shortcomings, believe that schools can be improved by building on the past. According to this scenario, public schools should be reorganized but not deregulated. Between these two positions are countless other positions, each with its own vision, its own agenda, and even its own ax to grind.

This is a pivotal time in the history of American education. The dialogue about school reform cuts across social classes, political affiliations, and professional statuses. Today critics and reformers do not come primarily from the educational establishment but from a wide variety of other segments in society, such as government, business, and community organizations. These new voices question the fundamental organization of schools and entertain radically different ideas about the structures and purposes of American education.

The authors in this book address the issues that relate to the crisis in American education and review some of the proposed solutions. There is a need for rigorous scholarship and critical thinking about the problems facing American education; the purpose of this book is to address critical issues through the application of theory and data to policy. Thus, the title of this book, "Transforming Schools," reflects our perception about what schools are and can be. We use the term "transforming" because it implies a proactive strategy for merging innovative and new educational structures that maintain continuous links with the enduring issues of education's relationship to society and children. To transform education one must examine schools as social systems that are interrelated with families, communities, and the world of work.

The issues that unite these social systems include equity, learning, curriculum, pedagogy, and authority relations within schools and between schools and society. These issues are interconnected and create a conceptual web that requires data, theory, and application if it is to be untangled. We have organized these chapters in four thematic sections. Section 1, "Conditions for Educational Opportunities," has five chapters, each of which addresses critical issues of educational access from different perspectives. Section 2 is "Changing Definitions of Education," composed of five chapters that view education through new conceptual lenses. Section 3, "Learning and Assessment," is composed of four chapters that deal with the central issues related to the improvement of student learning. Section 4 has five chapters that examine "New Strategies for Solving Educational Problems." Each section is preceded by a review and discussion of its contents. While the topics covered in this book are wide-ranging, they are by no means exhaustive, and we have sought to find authors with a variety of theoretical frameworks and methodological approaches.

New Schools for the Twenty-First Century

Children born in 1994 will graduate from high school in 2013. If they have normal longevity, their work lives will last until the middle of the twenty-first century. The world they will live and work in will be fundamentally different from the world of their parents and teachers. While it is impossible to predict events in a world that is changing so rapidly, there are some trends that appear to be dynamic and capable of transforming society. Certainly the United States will become increasingly multicultural. If demographic trends continue, by the middle of the next century less than one-half of the American population will trace their family origins to Eastern or Western Europe. The explosion of electronic technology does not appear to be diminishing, and there may be technical revolutions waiting to be born. Because of the ongoing technological revolution, the nature of the workforce will be deeply and permanently transformed. Men and women who are not technologically literate will be essentially shut out from participation in the economy and society.

Also if demographic trends continue, the present-day concept of the family may evaporate, altering gender relations and relationships between parents and children. Because of biomedical breakthroughs, the very definition of parenthood is changing. If we look at these factors as a whole, it seems evident that the definition of community will be significantly different in the next century from what it was in the past. Affiliations will be formed less on the basis of family, religion, occupation, and neighborhood and more on the basis of shared lifestyles, peer groups, and values that transcend local institutions. Through computer networks it is increasingly easier to communicate with other computer users thousands of miles away than with the person next door.

Given this matrix of change, it seems inconceivable that schools can remain the same in terms of how educational problems are defined, how schools are organized, and how schools interact with the economy. For instance, the definition of literacy is now quite different from what it was in the past and will continue to change. The distinction between numeracy and literacy will be increasingly blurred as individuals will need to have quantitative skills and also be skilled in written and spoken language. Biomedical breakthroughs will change the way people think about their bodies and minds, the way they interact with one another, and their relationship to their physical and cultural environments. How will schools change their curricula to guide young people through these unprecedented alterations in society, culture, and economy? How will schools educate people to address the continuing ecological crisis? How will schools change so that traditional notions of nationality are replaced with an international consciousness capable of grappling with the problems of an interdependent world? Even today south Florida has closer cultural links to Latin America than to New England. In short, the very architecture of education is antiquated, a relic from a past century.

What is desperately needed at this time are new thought models about education and society and the relationship between the two. Our scientific and intellectual horizons are expanding at an exponential rate, or to change the metaphor, there is an explosion of knowledge that will surely alter society and the economy profoundly and as a consequence require that schooling be completely rethought. If schools of the twenty-first century are similar to those of the nineteenth century, the future prospects of humanity are diminished. We must not continue to exploit our environment as we have if future generations are to have productive lives. If the separation of the global haves from have-nots becomes wider, there is no social policy that will be able to bridge the chasm of anger and violence that will seethe and erupt throughout the globe. If we do not master technology it will master us, drying up creativity and producing a world of alienation unimagined by Karl Marx or Sigmund Freud.

The schools of the twenty-first century must be responsive, flexible, and dedicated to the life of the mind, and they also must be dedicated to the well-being of children. The society of the future will be the education society, and the very definition of what it is to be educated will be radically altered. Each of us has ideas about what schools should be like in the future. It is our hope that the chapters in this book will stimulate debate, inform judgments, and lead to imaginative speculation. Such activities are our best hope for "Transforming Schools."

Peter W. Cookson, Jr.
Barbara Schneider

REFERENCES

Bryk, A.S., J.Q. Easton, D. Kerbow, S.G. Rallow, and P.A. Sebring. 1993.
A View from the Elementary Schools: The State of Reform in Chicago.
Chicago: Consortium on Chicago School Research.

Gibbs, N. 1990. Shameful Bequests to the Next Generation. *Time*
(October 8): 42–46.

Tables and Figures

Transforming
Schools

Conditions for Educational Opportunities

This section examines the critically important question of how schools can bring about equality of educational opportunity. In the United States the concept of educational opportunity generally focuses on equality of fiscal and social resources for all children as they progress through formal schooling. The chapters in this section take the conventional assumptions about the relationship between educational opportunity and school policy and demonstrate why these assumptions have led to inadequate solutions for transforming schools. Moving beyond critiques of current discussions for achieving educational opportunity, the authors suggest new perspectives for improving the educational and work life chances of traditionally disadvantaged populations.

The authors strongly urge scholars to take a broader societal approach to understanding inequities in schooling by examining the social contexts in which students live, including the family, school, community, and workplace. Traditional analyses, which primarily examine individual attributes such as race and social class, are criticized as unsatisfactory, especially for addressing how educational inequities are sustained over time. The social processes of learning and the actions that teachers and families take are seen as more appropriate ways to gain a comprehensive view of how educational inequities become distributed in schools.

3

Social Institutions and Education Inequality

Aaron Pallas begins his chapter by reexamining the role of education in the processes of achievement. That is, does education equalize opportunity or does it diminish opportunity? Pallas argues that the expansion of educational opportunity has long been viewed as the key to the expansion of social opportunities for groups as well as individuals. He believes that traditional paradigms for examining this problem have been insufficient. One should approach the problem of inequality of educational opportunities by viewing opportunities as social goods.

Pallas frames his argument with an examination of the connection between inequality of educational opportunity and socioeconomic inequality. He contends that the relationship between the two is critical for the formation of social policy. If there is a weak relationship between educational opportunity and socioeconomic inequality, then policies designed to increase access to schooling for diverse groups in society may have little impact on the ways in which adult success is distributed among members of differing social groups.

Pallas demonstrates that individuals who attain more education are more successful in economic terms than those who obtain less schooling. However, he shows that there is no guarantee that a particular level of schooling will provide a constant economic return over time. The declining socioeconomic value of the high school diploma in today's labor market compared with its value over the last few decades illustrates this point. What this pattern implies, according to Pallas, is that attempts to upgrade the educational credentials of particular social groups, such as racial or ethnic minorities, the poor, or women, without taking into consideration the educational gains of more privileged groups can have unpredictable consequences. In order to improve the socioeconomic circumstances of traditionally disadvantaged groups, Pallas argues that we must broaden the relatively narrow prescriptions of increasing educational access and focus instead on a socioeconomic life cycle approach.

A life cycle approach, Pallas maintains, is one in which the roles of families, schools, and work experience are not viewed as static attributes of individuals but rather as dynamic social institutions that change over time. Pallas shows that earlier educational policies produced only moderate success because they attempted to ameliorate individual attributes rather than institutions. He concludes by reaffirming the need to learn more about how to transform institutions which, he explains, by definition resist change.

Maureen Hallinan looks specifically at the institutional practice of tracking, that is, the assignment of students to instructional groups on the basis of ability or achievement. Heatedly contested among educators and researchers, tracking is viewed by advocates as an instructional technique which enables teachers to gear their instruction to the ability level of their students. Critics on the other side question tracking policies, which they agree sort students on the basis of ascribed characteristics. Over the past two decades most research has shown that rather than promoting learning, tracking creates learning and social inequities.

Hallinan explains that, while learning may be related to a particular grouping arrangement, it need not be determined by it. The primary determinants of learning are cognitive and social processes, including students' access to the curriculum, the quantity and quality of instruction received, student and teacher expectations about student ability, and student self-confidence, motivation, and effort. It is these processes, not structural grouping arrangements, which ultimately determine student learning.

Arguing that educational debates have been consumed with discussions of the advantages or disadvantages of tracking rather than with issues related to process, Hallinan directs educators to focus more on creating a positive school culture which fosters both teacher competence and student motivation. Grouping arrangements are doomed to fail without a supportive, respectful democratic school culture where educators and parents are encouraged to plan and evaluate educational practices, support the professional staff in implementing these practices, and generate leadership which can motivate the community.

In the next chapter Chandra Muller argues that the actions parents take either in the home, community, or school are particularly important for improving the academic performance of adolescents. Muller contends that parent involvement is particularly interesting because it explains some of the mechanisms by which family background has its well-known influence on a child's achievement. It is also attractive from a policy standpoint because it represents a potentially low-cost effective resource that can be tapped by the schools.

There are many ways in which parents can be involved in their child's learning; however, certain factors are likely to constrain or facilitate such learning activities. For example, family economic resources, parents' knowledge, and the closeness of the community can create opportunities or barriers for parental involvement. Even though there are family and contextual differences, Muller maintains that there are some forms of parental involvement that successfully encourage academic achievement. These activities include talking about current school experiences, music classes, reduced television viewing, and the constructive use of free time. These non-academic activities are powerful predictors of relatively high test scores. Direct parental involvement in the school is strongly associated with higher grades.

Differences between test scores and grades suggest that the nature of parental involvement may have different consequences depending on the types of actions the families take. Parental involvement programs which encourage parent volunteerism may not be as effective as those that encourage parents to take a directive role in the educational decision-making process over the course of the child's education. These management skills may become increasingly important as the student progresses through formal schooling.

Consequences of Inequality of Educational Opportunities

Turning to the question of disparities in educational outcomes among minority populations, Roslyn Mickelson, Sumie Okazaki, and Dunchun Zheng ask why many Asian-American students succeed academically, while African-American, Latino, and White students who attend the same schools do not. Mickelson et al. offer a different perspective that accounts for the various achievement patterns observed among American adolescents of diverse class, racial, and ethnic backgrounds. The authors argue that it is not a question of expectation, because most adolescents share a positive belief in the value of education for achieving economic success. But at the same time, adolescents from different racial and ethnic backgrounds are keenly aware of the opportunities and barriers that they may encounter when they complete formal schooling. Knowing that they are likely to encounter blocked opportunities in the labor force, children from different minority groups develop distinctive educational strategies. For Asian-American students educational achievement continues to be a relatively functional strategy for upward mobility and success; for African-American students, this appears to be less true.

Relying on earlier work, Mickelson proposes that adolescent attitudes toward education are multidimensional. The first dimension is abstract and manifests itself in the attitude that education leads to success, whereas the second dimension is concrete, involving beliefs that educational credentials may or may not be fairly rewarded. It is the concrete attitudes rather than the abstract attitudes that vary significantly by race and class. African-Americans and Asian-Americans were significantly more pessimistic than White students about schooling and employment opportunities. These results are also consistent across social classes; middle- and lower-class African-Americans and Asian-Americans were significantly more pessimistic about schooling and employment opportunities than middle- and lower-class Whites.

Even though Asian-Americans share African-American attitudes toward education, they do not earn similar grades in school. Asian-American grades are equal to or better than those of White students in a similar social-class category. Mickelson et al. contend that despite acknowledged discrimination, school achievement among Asian-Americans may be explained by two complementary perspectives. First, Asian-American parents may compare themselves with adults from their country of origin who are relatively poor, rather than with White parents in the United States who are relatively affluent. This phenomenon may lead to the belief that despite real barriers to upward mobility, pursuing an education makes more sense than not pursuing one. Second, Asians may teach their children that they have an independent social identity in which studying hard in school and getting good grades are considered to be intrinsically important.

Conversely, the social identity of African-Americans may be different from that of Asian-Americans and may not support such positive values as getting good grades in school. The attitudes and values students have toward school not only can explain poor performance but can also lead to dropping out of school.

Next, Gary Natriello argues that the relationship between students' school performance and their confidence of future success are important determinants of continuing in school. When students perceive that their participation and performance in school is connected to a good future, they are more likely to continue in school. In order to persist in school, students need to perceive themselves as capable of completing school and to believe that completion of high school provides access to employment in good positions. Various environmental conditions make it difficult for some students to develop these attitudes and values. In certain communities, students may have little exposure to successful adults who gained their success through educational achievement. This problem is more likely to occur for racial and ethnic minorities who live in isolated communities that are severely disadvantaged economically .

Natriello focuses on general features of school organization, student experiences, and community factors that appear to be related to dropping out of school. Some schools may provide students with little chance for academic success because they fail to create opportunities for positive social relationships among students, staff, and families. The schools may also have difficulty in establishing an environment that is caring and supportive. Furthermore, teachers and administrators in such schools may be unable to counteract the negative messages peer groups and community members outside of the school send to students about the value of attending school regularly or graduating.

Many education strategies have been implemented in order to prevent students from leaving school before graduation from high school; such efforts occupy a central position in the school reform movement. Recent programs developed to solve the dropout problem take into consideration the negative conditions that students face in many schools and communities. Natriello discusses some of the new in-school and out-of-school programs and practices designed to enhance the students' prospects for academic success. He argues that the dropout problem can be eliminated only with a comprehensive effort that includes improved identification and enumeration of which students leave school early, more studies that address leaving school as a complex educational and social problem, and comprehensive assessments of programs and practices targeted at the prevention of dropping out.

1

Schooling, Achievement, and Mobility[1]

Aaron M. Pallas

Introduction

For more than a century, Americans have viewed education as the primary mechanism for redressing inequalities in social life. Our commitment to a capitalist economy virtually ensures the existence of winners and losers on the playing fields of American life, if only in a relative sense. But public explanations of social inequalities tend not to focus on the economic system which occupies a central position in American society; rather, we look to our special brand of individualism (Bellah et al. 1985) in interpreting individual differences. According to this philosophy, the characteristics of individuals account for their success, or lack thereof, in American society. In particular, individual differences in ability, effort, temperament, and tastes are seen as the source of individual differences in adult socioeconomic standing.

The collective understanding of how these individual characteristics are translated into adult achievement relies heavily on education as a key mediating mechanism. If you want a good job, the reasoning goes, get a good education. Good students who work hard will learn the skills that employers want and are willing to pay for. Thus individuals with more schooling will do better in the labor market, obtaining more prestigious, better-paying jobs than less-educated individuals.

Not getting a good education, according to this logic, is largely the fault of the student. The schools are open to everybody, and those who have the ability and put forth the effort will go as far as they like. Since schools operate on a principle of merit, those who don't succeed simply don't have what it takes to be successful. In this sense, schooling is seen as the great equalizer in American society. Because the schools are accessible to everyone, and because they select and sponsor individuals on the basis of talent and effort, schooling should cancel out the effects of social class, race or ethnicity, and gender factors that, according to the prevailing ideology, should be irrelevant to success.

How do these views conform to what we know about education, achievement, and mobility in American society? Just how much does adult success in U.S. society depend on an individual's social background—that is, social characteristics such as social-class origins, race, ethnicity, and gender? In particular, what role does education play in the process of achievement? Is education the great equalizer of opportunity, or is it more accurately characterized as the great *paralyzer* of opportunity?

These questions have an importance that transcends sterile academic debate. Throughout the course of American history, policymakers have demonstrated a concern with the extension of opportunities to traditionally disenfranchised groups. The expansion of educational opportunity has long been viewed as the key to the expansion of social opportunities for groups as well as individuals. But education is not the only possible route to the goal of "opening up" U.S. society to its historically downtrodden members; an array of policy instruments could be applied to this problem, and many of the weapons in the policymaking arsenal have nothing whatsoever to do with education.

Exploring our current understanding of the role of education in the process of social mobility and socioeconomic achievement thus provides a critical perspective for evaluating prevailing trends in U.S. educational policy. If reductions of inequalities in educational opportunities are clearly linked to how evenly social goods in American society are distributed, then strategies to reduce the dependence of education on background factors may result in a more equitable distribution of occupational prestige, income, and wealth. Conversely, if there is little connection between inequalities in educational opportunity and socioeconomic inequality, then policies designed to increase access to schooling for diverse groups in society may have little impact on the ways in which adult success is distributed among members of differing social groups.

This chapter is intended to provide a context for thinking about educational opportunity and school policy. I begin by describing recent evidence regarding the distribution of socioeconomic achievement and social mobility in U.S. society. Next I examine the components and sources of social mobility, focusing especially on the role of education in the mobility and achievement process. I conclude with an examination of the implications of these patterns for U.S. social and educational policy.

The Dependence of Adult Success in U.S. Society on Individual Social Background

Many studies of social stratification and mobility have examined the extent to which the achievements of the adult members of a society depend on their social origins. By comparing the occupational achievements of fathers and sons, measured through either a set of mutually exclusive occupational categories or the status or prestige associated with various occupations, researchers have sought to determine to what extent adult occupational attainments depend on social background.

Judging the "openness" of a society in this way requires distinguishing among the various forces that can shift the joint distribution of origins and destinations. In particular, a key problem has been to distinguish between circulation mobility (the extent to which children's occupational success depends on their social-class origins) and structural mobility (the extent to which children's occupational success is due to a change in the structure of occupations across generations). For example, the rise of industrialization led to a decrease in the proportion of farmers in the adult population and an increase in the proportion of individuals employed in manufacturing. Since the early decades of this century, the proportion of self-employed adults (including farmers) has declined, and the proportion of workers in white-collar occupations has increased (Hauser et al. 1975). More recently, the number of manufacturing jobs has waned while the number of service sector jobs has increased (Grusky and DiPrete 1990). When these changes result in a shift in the societal mix of highly rewarded and poorly rewarded jobs (with respect to either status or income or both), then a certain amount of mobility is likely to occur regardless of the relationship between origins and destinations. If the array of occupations available to a generation of children contains more high-status positions than the structure facing their parents, then a substantial number of children will achieve occupational positions that are of higher status than those of their parents. Conversely, if the occupational structure presented to a generation of children contains fewer desirable positions than the job market their parents entered, inevitably many of those children will wind up in positions that are of lower status than those of their parents. This kind of structural mobility can occur without regard to the amount of circulation mobility present or, for that matter, the extent to which occupational destinations depend on educational attainment.

Recent evidence on trends in the openness of the American occupational structure is provided by Hout (1988) and Grusky and DiPrete (1990). Hout (1988) used data from the General Social Survey to examine trends in U.S. occupational mobility between 1972 and 1985. He found evidence of declining structural mobility; in fact, there was little change in the distribution of occupations over this period and a growing convergence in the distributions of social-class origins and destinations, marked especially by an increase in the number of children with fathers in professional or managerial positions. But this decline in structural mobility was offset by an increase in circulation mobility, whose form differed by gender: The sons of high-status fathers had a declining likelihood of obtaining high-status jobs themselves, while the daughters of men with low-status positions had an increasing likelihood of high-status jobs.

In both cases, the association between origins and destinations declined over the period 1972 to 1985.

Of special interest for the current discussion, Hout (1988) examined the role of education in structuring the association between social origins and adult occupational achievements. His earlier work (Hout 1984) had indicated that the effect of social origins on men's destination status depends on their educational level. Among college graduates, origin status has no effect on occupational achievement, whereas origins have larger effects on the occupational status of individuals who obtain less education. This suggests that the decline in the dependence of occupational destinations on social origins observed over the period 1972 to 1985 may be due in part to the increase in the proportion of the labor force with college degrees.

Drawing on similar data spanning 1972 to 1987, Grusky and DiPrete (1990) conclude that the process of stratification has been changing over time. Their analysis shows that social origins have had less effect on the educational attainment of women in recent years than in the past, but that there is no similar trend among men. Conversely, the effects of education on occupational status have increased over time for men but remained stable among women.

These trends have a complex overall effect on gender differences in socioeconomic success. Gender-based trends in the effects of education on occupational status differ by level of education attained. Among college graduates, women in 1987 held a slight advantage over men in the status of their jobs, a reversal from the slight advantage held by men in 1972. But female high school graduates greatly extended their occupational status advantage over men during the period from 1972 to 1987. Grusky and DiPrete show that this pattern is not due to an increase in the labor market position of high school–educated women but rather to a decrease in the labor market position of high school–educated men.

The decline in the dependence of education on social background among women coupled with the increase in the dependence of occupational status on education among men provides some support for the claim that American society is becoming more universalistic in its criteria for allocating status and rewards to individuals. It is possible, however, that at least some of Grusky and DiPrete's findings may be attributable to structural mobility as much as circulation mobility; they document a decline in the share of the labor force in manufacturing jobs, and an expansion of the number and proportion of jobs in the service sector of the economy.

The Dependence of Adult Success on Educational Achievement

A discussion of origins and destinations may seem arcane. Are there other ways to examine the role of education in the process of achievement? One possibility is to describe the raw differences in socioeconomic rewards received by individuals with differing levels of education. One need not look very far to conclude that individuals who obtain more education are more likely to obtain jobs that convey greater social and economic rewards. Those who go farther through the American education system are more likely to have steady employment, to have higher incomes, and to work in positions that are more prestigious, have more opportunities for advancement, and allow for more autonomy and self-direction. Conversely, early-school-leavers have unstable employment histories and often wind up in dead-end jobs with low wages and few opportunities for getting ahead of their peers.

Figure 1.1 presents some evidence for the "education gap," that is, the gap in the socioeconomic rewards obtained by individuals with differing schooling histories.[2] This Figure shows the ratio of the average annual income of college and high school graduates aged 25–34 who were year-round full-time workers for the period 1975 to 1990. (For the sake of simplicity, college graduates here are defined as those who have completed exactly 16 years of schooling, and high school graduates, those who have completed exactly 12 years of schooling.) A ratio of 1.0 would imply that the incomes of college graduates were equal, on average, to those of high school graduates, while ratios greater than 1.0 imply that the incomes of college graduates are proportionally higher than those of high school graduates.

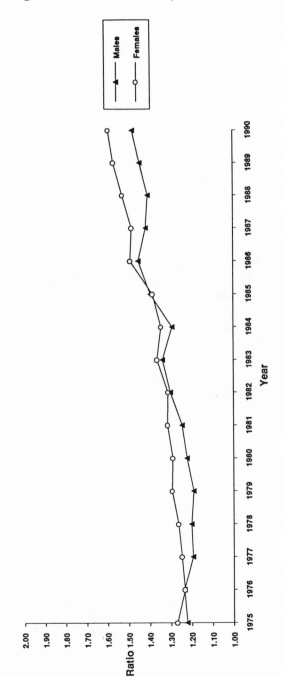

FIGURE 1.1. The Ratio of Average Annual Income of College and High School Graduates, 1975 to 1990, by Sex.

Note: Data pertain to year-round full-time workers aged 25–34. The source is Current Population Reports, ser. P-60, various years.

Figure 1.1 indicates that throughout the sixteen-year period covered, the annual incomes of college graduates substantially exceeded those of high school graduates, among both men and women. In the mid- to late 1970s, college graduates earned 20 percent to 25 percent more per year than high school graduates, even when we focus on year-round full-time workers. But the most striking implication of this Figure is the increase in the education gap in recent years. Over the last five years of the 1980s, the gap in the incomes of college-educated and high school–educated workers increased substantially, so that by 1990, male college graduates working full-time and year-round earned 48 percent more than male high school graduates, and female college graduates working year-round and full-time earned 59 percent more than female high school graduates.

A similar gap exists between high school–educated workers and those who did not complete high school. Over the last decade, both male and female high school graduates working year-round and full-time earned approximately 45 to 50 percent more than their peers who had not completed high school. Among men, this education gap also appears to have grown in recent years, while the pattern for women has been unstable.

Since individuals who obtain more education are more likely to be employed full-time and year-round, these comparisons probably underestimate the real gap in socioeconomic rewards between the more educated and the less educated. Including part-time workers and/or those who move in and out of the labor force sporadically would lower the estimated average annual incomes of both more- and less-educated workers, but the impact on average income levels would be greater for less-educated workers than for more-educated ones. In this sense, even the rather dramatic differences reported here can be viewed as somewhat conservative.

How much of this education gap really is due to differences in education? This is not a simple question, because individuals who obtain unequal amounts of education vary in ways that are related to, and perhaps antecedent to, their schooling experiences, and some of these other differences shape occupational rewards. Family background, cognitive skills, and personality factors are among the many simultaneous influences on both educational attainment and occupational rewards. Individuals from more advantaged backgrounds and with greater native ability choose, or are chosen, both to go further through school and to pursue more rewarding occupations. A failure to take account of these differences, which may be apparent prior to critical branching points in the education system, could result in attributing a larger share of the education gap to education than is really appropriate.

Estimates of the bias in the relationship between education and occupational rewards when family background and cognitive ability are not taken into account are provided by Olneck (1979). He found that about one-half of the education gap in occupational status among men who had not completed high school could be attributed to differences in family background and standardized test scores, but only about one-fifth of the education gap among men who went to college was really due to family background and cognitive ability. In contrast, about one-third of the education gap in income can be attributed to family background and measured ability. There is, however, no guarantee that Olneck's findings can be applied to current estimates of the education gap. The cohorts that he studied experienced labor market conditions that may differ substantially from those now in play, and there is good reason to believe that the current occupational structure has a great deal of influence on the occupational rewards associated with education.

Competing Explanations for the Linkages Between Education and Achievement

The persistent finding that individuals who go farther through school fare better in the labor market suggests that societies can use schools to shape the life chances of individuals and the society as a whole. But is this *necessarily* so? Not all of the competing explanations for the relationships between schooling and labor market success described here lead to this conclusion. Two of the most prominent explanations for the relationship between schooling and adult success are human capital theory and credentialism theory.

Human Capital Theory

Perhaps the most prominent explanation over the last quarter-century for the linkage between education and occupational success, human capital theory (Schultz 1961; Becker 1964) posits that employers reward workers in proportion to their marginal productivity. Marginal productivity is largely determined by an individual's stock of human capital, the reservoir of skills, knowledge, and values that a worker has acquired through education, training, and experience. Individuals will invest in the development of human capital as long as the marginal returns exceed the marginal costs (whether direct or opportunity costs) of the investment. Investment in education is thus conceived of as a rational decision based on a calculus weighing long-term costs and benefits. Individual workers, acting in a self-interested way, determine how much education (or other forms of human capital) to obtain in light of what they know about how employers will reward such education and of their knowledge about the costs of the investment. Employer demand for a skilled workforce thus drives individuals' demand for education and other means of building human capital.

Credentialism Theory

Human capital theory, a theory of *individual* investment decisions, has also been applied at the societal level. Human capital theorists have argued that collective increases in the educational credentials of the population should generate an aggregate increase in human capital, and thereby lead to overall increases in economic productivity. Critics of this viewpoint have questioned whether changes in the supply of education do in fact transform the structure of the economy, arguing instead that an aggregate increase in the educational credentials of the workforce may simply lead to a reshuffling of these better-educated workers into the same mix of jobs. If educational expansion does not lead to societal-level economic expansion, then it may be that an aggregate increase in educational credentials will have little effect on the process by which individuals are sorted into occupational positions, and hence little impact on the level of social mobility in a given system. At the same time, it may still be the case that individuals who obtain more education will be more successful in the labor market, because employers continue to reward better-educated workers more highly than less-educated ones (Walters and Rubinson 1983).

The theory that employers reward educational credentials, rather than the skills, knowledge, and values that they are said to represent, is frequently referred to as credentialism theory (e.g., Berg 1970; Collins 1979). According to this perspective, employers use educational credentials as a basis for allocating individuals to occupational positions, with the positions carrying the greatest rewards allocated to those individuals in the labor pool with the strongest educational credentials. The actual abilities of workers are never inspected directly, in this view; rather, educational credentials serve as a signaling or screening device (Spence 1973) to enable employers to make quick and cheap decisions about filling vacant positions.

Credentialism theory treats the occupational structure as fixed in the short run. This means that over short periods of time the expansion of educational enrollments and credentials may not necessarily result in an expansion of the economy. Put simply, obtaining a college degree instead of stopping with a high school diploma gives an individual a better chance at filling an existing position in the occupational structure, but does not create a new job for that individual. Increased educational credentials move individuals into a more favorable position in the labor queue so that when a high-status position becomes vacant, they have a better chance in the competition for that position (Thurow 1975).

Differing Predictions

These two approaches—human capital theory, which emphasizes individual decision making, and credentialism theory, which emphasizes the structure of the labor market—

make very different predictions about the likely consequences of upgrading the educational credentials of a society's members uniformly. Because human capital theory believes that the education system and the economy are tightly connected and very responsive to one another, it predicts that educational expansion should lead to economic expansion and the increased economic rewards that come from greater productivity, both for individuals and for society as a whole. Conversely, because credentialism theory believes that the education system and the economy are only loosely coupled, it predicts that educational expansion may not lead to economic expansion and need not result in greater aggregate economic productivity.

Since the United States has experienced a tremendous growth in education over this century, it is worth considering what effects educational expansion has had on economic growth in the United States. One prominent study (Walters and Rubinson 1983) suggests that, during the middle decades of this century, the expansion of secondary- and doctorate-level education led to increases in economic output, while increases in the proportion of individuals completing primary schooling or bachelor's or master's degrees had no apparent effect on economic output. Walters and Rubinson (1983) argue that this pattern of linkages between education and the economy must be interpreted in light of the changing meaning of education over the course of the twentieth century.

A technical-functional accounting views education as a process of augmenting productivity through upgrading individual skills and through fostering technological innovations that enable capital to be transformed into products more efficiently and is consistent with human capital theory. But education also may be viewed as a means for increasing economic output through a process of legitimating the existing social order by socializing individuals en masse, shifting the focus away from individual skills in a way consonant with credentialism. These differing interpretations of what education means yield contrasting predictions about when education might be likely to affect economic output. The latter theory, for example, suggests that education's effects on economic output might be observed most easily in the expansion of a level of schooling that is changing from an elite to a mass institution (Walters and Rubinson 1983).

Discussion

This analysis suggests a policy paradox within American society. While it remains true that, considered as a group at any point in time, individuals who attain more education are more successful in economic terms than those who obtain less schooling, there is no guarantee that a *particular* level of schooling will have a payoff that is constant over time. The results presented here indicate that a high school diploma generates lower socioeconomic rewards in today's labor market than in the past, at least in relative terms.

What this pattern implies is that attempts to upgrade the educational credentials of particular social groups, such as racial and ethnic minorities, the poor, or women, will have unpredictable consequences in the absence of knowledge of the educational credentials of the remainder of society. If the gains in educational attainments of traditionally disadvantaged groups are matched by gains among the more privileged members of society, the net effect of upgrading the credentials of minorities, the poor, and women may be simply to ratchet up the overall education distribution without increasing the relative chances of these groups to obtain more prestigious or higher-paying jobs.

A disciplined attempt to craft policies to improve the socioeconomic lot of traditionally disadvantaged groups must look beyond the relatively narrow goal of increasing access to education for these groups and focus on the socioeconomic life cycle (Duncan, Featherman, and Duncan 1972). A life-cycle approach to the role of education in the achievement process acknowledges that families, schooling, and jobs are not static attributes of individuals but rather dynamic institutions that change over time as individuals age and influence each other in important ways. Family background may influence whether or not a person graduates from high school in a different way than it affects whether or not that person graduates from college. Family influence on the characteristics of the first job may differ from family influence on the attributes of subsequent jobs. And while education may affect the choice of a first job, the characteristics of that job may determine whether an individual obtains further training or education, thereby influencing access to subsequent jobs.

A life-course perspective on education, mobility, and achievement (Featherman 1980) can provide the breadth of perspective needed to make sense out of these complex patterns. Such a perspective draws attention to the distinctive norms, institutional arrangements, and historical events that govern the life course of individuals within a society. Individuals' lives do not take place in a vacuum; rather, they are shaped by the distinctive features of time and place, including the culture and norms of their society, the specific features of the social institutions with which they come into contact and the linkages among them, and the array of demographic, social, and natural events that circumscribe a particular historical period. All of these forces contribute to the course of human lives, many in ways that we are only beginning to understand.

In particular, historical and cross-national evidence on education and work point to the lack of universals in understanding the role of education in the mobility and achievement process. Rather, the effect of education on socioeconomic achievement is conditioned by the nature of the educational system, the nature of the economy, and the linkages between schooling and the economy. Evidence also exists of the influence of specific historical events, such as sharp economic fluctuations (e.g., Elder 1974), wars (e.g., Mayer 1988), and the size of birth cohorts (Smith 1986), on the role education plays in achievement.

In order to clearly understand the role of education in the process of social mobility and socioeconomic achievement, one must consider the structure of the educational system, the structure of the economy, and the interactions between the two. In fact, Brinton (1988) adopts an even broader perspective, focusing on the structure of the human capital development system—that is, the system that develops the skills, knowledge, and values of individuals. This life-course-based view acknowledges explicitly the possibility that human capital may be developed after entry into the labor force, that is, in settings other than schools. On-the-job training, for example, is much more prominent in some countries than others, and even within a given country, on-the-job training is more prevalent in certain industries than in others. Since on-the-job training may substitute for education in allocating individuals to desirable positions, it is well-nigh impossible to understand the role of education in the achievement process without also understanding the role of training that is contemporaneous with or subsequent to participation in the schooling system.

A life-course approach to education, achievement, and mobility emphasizes both the temporal sequencing of key events in the life course and the interplay between individuals and institutions. This perspective entails much; among the more salient issues:

- *How rigid is the system?* Rigidity refers to the extent to which early decisions constrain later ones. In some societies, key career branching points come very early in an individual's lifetime and opportunities for second chances or getting back on track may be few. Other societies rely on later decision points and provide many opportunities to achieve. The United States is typically seen as less rigid than many other industrialized countries, in part because there is less age grading in access to education and occupational positions.

- *How closed or open is the system?* We can think of the openness of a system in terms of the mechanisms by which individuals obtain access to valued positions in the system. An open system is one in which individual chances of gaining access to a position are independent of the likelihood of others gaining access to a similar position. In contrast, a closed system is one in which a particular individual's gaining access to a position prevents others from gaining access to a similar position. Closed occupational structures place limits on the extent to which the knowledge and skills an individual develops through education can grant access to desirable jobs (Sørensen 1986).

- *How often does the system provide opportunities for investment in human capital?* Do opportunities exist throughout the socioeconomic life cycle, or are they concentrated into a particular period? Brinton (1988) and Kerckhoff (1990) give examples of contrasts between Japan, Great Britain, and the United States regarding when individuals have the opportunity to invest in human capital. Both Japan and Great Britain rely heavily on further education of adult workers in the form of employer-sponsored training within or outside the firm, whereas U.S. employers typically prefer to recruit workers from outside the firm who are already trained.

- *How are the linkages between education and the economy structured?* In particular, how do individuals negotiate the school-to-work transition? Rosenbaum and Kariya (Rosenbaum et al. 1990; Rosenbaum and Kariya 1990) have contrasted the dominant U.S. pattern of using markets to fill entry-level jobs with network-based approaches like those common in Japan. Institutional arrangements between schools and employers in Japan have essentially eliminated the floundering (Namboodiri 1987) that characterizes youth employment in the United States.

- *How is education used in making decisions about within-firm promotions?* Studies by Grandjean (1981) and Spilerman and Lunde (1991) have documented that education may have larger effects on access to desirable positions in some kinds of firms than others; even within firms, education may be more consequential for jobs requiring advanced skills. Conversely, though, obtaining more schooling may not affect promotion into lower-level positions in an organization (Spilerman and Lunde 1991).

- *How are schooling and work sequenced with family formation?* Are there norms that govern the timing and sequencing of marriage and parenthood that might affect how education influences socioeconomic success? Blossfeld and Huinink (1991) show that social norms in

Germany regarding the appropriate age for women to bear their first child influence the ability of these women to translate educational attainments into labor market success. Because prolonged participation in schooling frequently delays marriage and parenthood, highly educated women in Germany must accelerate childbearing after they leave school, which influences their occupational success.

Examples such as these show that while the individual decision-making mechanisms so central to human capital theory are relevant, they must be viewed in the context of larger, macrostructural forces, including culture, norms, institutional linkages, demographic trends, and historical events such as sharp economic turns for better or worse, natural disasters, and wars.

The Use of Policy Instruments to Influence Achievement and Mobility

In light of the complex role that education plays in mobility and achievement, how might policymakers use the resources available to them to promote a more equitable distribution of job-related rewards in American society? Surprisingly, the answer may have little to do with the attributes of individuals.

The key policies designed to address the problem of increasing the openness of U.S. society and reducing the inheritance of social-class privileges historically have emphasized increasing equality of educational opportunity as a means of increasing access to economic success for traditionally disadvantaged populations—the poor, racial and ethnic minorities, and women. Lyndon Johnson's Great Society, for example, spawned a raft of compensatory programs such as Title I/Chapter I, targeted primarily at the early elementary grades, and Upward Bound, designed both to enrich the academic skills of disadvantaged high school students and to facilitate their entry into institutions of postsecondary education. Implicit in such efforts to upgrade the skills of American youth was a faith in human capital theory as an explanation for the linkage between education and training and labor market success.

Most of these efforts were distinctive in that they typically attempted to transform *individuals*, not *institutions*. Compensatory programs attempted to make the poor more like the middle class (Natriello, McDill, and Pallas 1990), and programs like the Job Corps, the Comprehensive Employment and Training Act of 1973 (CETA), and the Job Training Partnership Act of 1982 (JTPA) generally tried to provide remedial training in basic academic skills as well as training in specific vocational skills to disadvantaged youth.

These programs can be judged only modestly successful. The evidence suggests that there has been a reduction in some inequalities in educational accomplishment among the major social groups in American society. For example, the high school completion rates of blacks are much closer to those of whites now than they were twenty years ago. But college-matriculation rates among blacks have actually declined in recent years, both in absolute terms and relative to those of whites (Hauser and Anderson 1991). Of course, many policies can influence the educational attainments of traditionally disadvantaged groups; in the case of minorities and the poor there is reason to believe that a decline in the availability of financial aid for college has also been influential in the drop in college attendance (Hauser and Anderson 1991; Karen 1991).

Nevertheless, history does not provide much reason to be optimistic that policymakers' attempts to transform the characteristics of individuals through education programs will have the desired effect of increasing the access of traditionally disenfranchised groups to desirable positions in society. What other strategies can be invoked to pursue this objective?

McDonnell and Grubb (1991) discuss four types of policy instruments by which federal and state policymakers address issues of education and training: (1) mandates, which consist of rules that govern the actions of individuals and institutions; (2) inducements, through which institutions receive valued goods (i.e., money) in exchange for particular actions; (3) capacity building, which consists of providing institutions with valued goods for the purpose of long-term investment in the institution's own resource system; and (4) system changing, which consists of changing existing institutional arrangements to alter the human resource development system. These policy instruments are often mixed or combined within a single policy, sometimes with unpredictable results, as each instrument has differing targets, costs, and contexts for implementation.

Of this array of policy instruments, system changing—the restructuring of existing institutional arrangements that compose the human resource development system in the United States—appears to be the policy strategy most likely to promote the goal of decreasing social inequality in American society. Packages of mandates and inducements have operated as blunt policy instruments insensitive to the scope and breadth of the human resource development system, particularly the processes by which individuals are matched with positions and move from an initial position to subsequent positions and organizations. Policies designed to promote institutional capacity building typically have not addressed the fact that institutions compete in markets, where increased capacity is not sufficient to ensure competitiveness.

Yet while system changing may hold the greatest promise for further opening American society to the disadvantaged, it is also the most difficult kind of policy instrument to implement successfully. The American traditions of decentralization and privatization run counter to attempts by federal and local governments to manipulate the processes by which employers acquire and develop human capital as manifested in the skills, knowledge, and values of individual workers. We simply don't have a great deal of experience in consciously transforming our institutions—institutions which, by definition, resist change.

Social institutions persist because they make sense to the members of a society. That is, the patterns of action that social institutions represent are taken for granted and legitimated as rational and purposive (Meyer and Rowan 1977). As long as legitimating myths (Kamens 1977) enable individuals to make sense out of the existing structures of the American education system and economy, these institutions are unlikely to change. To date, scientific evidence documenting nonrationality and unfairness in the working of such institutions has had little impact on the way most people view the schools, the economy, and the linkage between the two. The myths persist and will probably continue to do so.

Thus while remaining supportive of ongoing efforts to understand the human capital development system in the United States and the ways in which it is shaped by our distinctive culture, norms, history, and institutions, we cannot be sanguine about the capacity of such study to effect systemic change. While comparing current practices to those in other countries and earlier times may give us a sense of the possibilities, it is hard to believe that in the short run we can transform the possible into the probable. A more likely scenario is continued reliance on strategies that manipulate the human capital of individuals while ignoring the overall system, with only weak effects on the distribution of social opportunity in U.S. society.

NOTES

1. I am grateful to Anna Neumann for her comments on an earlier draft of this chapter.

2. For the format of this Figure I am indebted to a similar presentation in Smith (1986) that covers an earlier period of time.

REFERENCES

Becker, G. 1964. *Human Capital*. New York: Columbia University Press.

Bellah, R.N., R. Madsen, W.M. Sullivan, A. Swidler, and S.M. Tipton. 1985. *Habits of the Heart: Individualism and Commitment in American Life*. Berkeley: University of California Press.

Berg, I. 1970. *Education and Jobs: The Great Training Robbery*. Boston: Beacon.

Blossfeld, H.P., and J. Huinink. 1991. Human Capital Investments or Norms of Role Transition? How Women's Schooling and Career Affect the Process of Family Formation. *American Journal of Sociology* 97: 143–168.

Brinton, M.C. 1988. The Social-Institutional Bases of Gender Stratification: Japan as an Illustrative Case. *American Journal of Sociology* 94: 300–334.

Collins, R. 1979. *The Credential Society: An Historical Sociology of Education and Stratification*. New York: Academic Press.

Duncan, O.D., D.L. Featherman, and B. Duncan. 1972. *Socioeconomic Background and Achievement*. New York: Seminar Press.

Elder, G.H., Jr. 1974. *Children of the Great Depression: Social Change in Life Experience*. Chicago: University of Chicago Press.

Featherman, D.L. 1980. Schooling and Occupational Careers: Constancy and Change in Worldly Success. In *Constancy and Change in Human Development*, ed. Orville G. Brim, Jr. and Jerome Kagan, 675–738. Cambridge: Harvard University Press.

Grandjean, B.D. 1981. History and Career in a Bureaucratic Labor Market. *American Journal of Sociology* 86: 1057–1092.

Grusky, D.B., and T.A. DiPrete. 1990. Recent Trends in the Process of Stratification. *Demography* 27: 617–637.

Hauser, R.M., and D.K. Anderson. 1991. Post–High School Plans and Aspirations of Black and White High School Seniors: 1976–86. *Sociology of Education* 64: 263–277.

Hauser, R.M., P.J. Dickinson, H.P. Travis, and J.M. Koffel. 1975. Structural Changes in Occupational Mobility among Men in the United States. *American Sociological Review* 40: 585–598.

Hout, M. 1984. Status, Autonomy, and Training in Occupational Mobility. *American Journal of Sociology* 89: 1379–1409.

———. 1988. More Universalism, Less Structural Mobility: The American Occupational Structure in the 1980s. *American Journal of Sociology* 93: 1358–1400.

Kamens, D. 1977. Legitimating Myths and Educational Organization: The Relationship between Organizational Ideology and Formal Structure. *American Sociological Review* 42: 208–219.

Karen, D. 1991. The Politics of Class, Race, and Gender: Access to Higher Education in the United States, 1960–1986. *American Journal of Education* 99: 208–237.

Kerckhoff, A.C. 1990. *Getting Started: Transition to Adulthood in Great Britain*. Boulder, CO: Westview.

Mayer, K.U. 1988. German Survivors of World War II: The Impact on the Life Course of the Collective Experience of Birth Cohorts. In *Social Structure and Human Lives: Social Change and the Life Course*, vol. 1, ed. Matilda White Riley, 229–246. Newbury Park, CA: Sage.

McDonnell, L.M., and W.N. Grubb. 1991. *Education and Training for Work: The Policy Instruments and the Institutions*. Santa Monica, CA: RAND.

Meyer, J.W., and B. Rowan. 1977. Institutionalized Organizations: Formal Structure as Myth and Ceremony. *American Journal of Sociology* 83: 340–363.

Namboodiri, K. 1987. The Floundering Phase of the Life Course. In *Research in Sociology of Education and Socialization*, vol. 7, ed. Ronald G. Corwin, 59–86. Greenwich, CT: JAI.

Natriello, G., E.L. McDill, and A.M. Pallas. 1990. *Schooling Disadvantaged Children: Racing against Catastrophe*. New York: Teachers College Press.

Olneck, M. 1979. The Effects of Education. In *Who Gets Ahead? The Determinants of Economic Success in America* by Christopher S. Jencks, et al., 159–190. New York: Basic Books.

Rosenbaum, J.E., and T. Kariya. 1990. From High School to Work: Market and Institutional Mechanisms in Japan. *American Journal of Sociology* 94: 1334–1365.

Rosenbaum, J.E., T. Kariya, R. Settersten, and T. Maier. 1990. Market and Network Theories of the Transition from High School to Work: Their Application to Industrialized Societies. In *Annual Review of Sociology*, vol. 16, ed. W. Richard Scott and Judith Blake, 263–299. Palo Alto, CA: Annual Reviews.

Schultz, T.W. 1961. Investment in Human Capital. *American Economic Review* 51: 1–17.

Smith, H.L. 1986. Overeducation and Underemployment: An Agnostic Review. *Sociology of Education* 59: 85–99.

Sørensen, A.B. 1986. Social Structure and Mechanisms of Life-Course Processes. In *Human Development and the Life Course: Multidisciplinary Perspectives*, ed. Aage B. Sørensen, Franz E. Weinert, and Lonnie R. Sherrod, 177–197. Hillsdale, NJ: Lawrence Erlbaum Associates.

Spence, M. 1973. Job Market Signalling. *Quarterly Journal of Economics* 87: 355–374.

Spilerman, S., and T. Lunde. 1991. Features of Educational Attainment and Job Promotion Prospects. *American Journal of Sociology* 97: 689–720.

Thurow, L. 1975. *Generating Inequality: Mechanisms of Distribution in the U.S. Economy.* New York: Basic Books.

Walters, P.B., and R. Rubinson. 1983. Educational Expansion and Economic Output in the United States, 1890–1969: A Production Function Analysis. *American Sociological Review* 48: 480–493.

2

Tracking and Detracking Practices: Relevance for Learning

Maureen T. Hallinan

Tracking, the assignment of students to instructional groups on the basis of ability or academic achievement, attempts to facilitate instruction and promote learning by enabling teachers to gear instruction to the ability levels of their students. Advocates of tracking argue that when students are instructed in ability groups, educators can adapt the content and pace of instruction to meet their students' learning needs. As a result, the students do not become bored or discouraged but rather remain actively engaged in the instructional process.

Critics of tracking believe tracking creates inequities in the distribution of learning opportunities to students, because high-track pupils enjoy several advantages. They are exposed to a greater quantity of information and a more interesting curriculum than lower-track students (Barr and Dreeben 1983; Gamoran and Berends 1987), they receive higher-quality instruction (Nystrand and Gamoran 1987), and fewer disciplinary problems disrupt higher-track classes (Oakes 1985; Rosenbaum 1976). Moreover, track level is associated with social status. Higher-track students typically are more highly regarded by their peers and have stronger self-images than lower-track students, and teachers have high expectations for high-track students but low expectations for those in lower tracks (Oakes 1985). Finally, track assignment has been associated with background characteristics, particularly race. Black and Hispanic students are disproportionately assigned to lower tracks, and whites to upper tracks (Hallinan 1991), implying inequities in the assignment process and, consequently, in the distribution of learning opportunities.

Empirical research has not yet effectively resolved the tracking debate. A number of studies document the advantages of tracking for high-ability students, the negative effect of tracking on low-ability students, and the absence of an effect for average students (for a review, see Slavin 1987). However, few studies compare homogeneous grouping to heterogeneous grouping, primarily because not many heterogeneous groups are available for study. Existing research fails to detect a significant difference between the average achievement of students in tracked and untracked schools (Slavin 1990), leading to the general conclusion that the advantages of tracking for high-ability students are offset by its disadvantages for low-ability students; this results in the similar tracked and untracked school averages observed. These studies do not provide overwhelming evidence in favor of either homogeneous or heterogeneous grouping policies. More rigorous, longitudinal studies comparing student achievement in tracked and in heterogeneously grouped schools are needed to better evaluate the practice of tracking.

The debate on tracking frequently emerges as part of a more general discussion about school reform. Often, these discussions produce plans to restructure schools in any one of a variety of ways under the supposition that the new structure will lead to greater academic achievement. Typically, recommended changes include plans to reorganize schools by establishing different bases for assigning students to instructional groups. Recently, detracking (i.e., establishing groups heterogeneous with respect to ability) has been a popular recommendation.

Schools have several options when organizing students for instruction; the bases for group assignment include ability, age, gender, race or ethnicity, language, and curricular interests. The rationales for grouping students in each of these ways differ. In most cases, a grouping policy is implemented in the interests of promoting academic achievement. However, in some cases, a grouping practice is endorsed in the hope of fostering racial or cultural integration, improving social relations, or encouraging good citizenship, and some grouping practices aim to increase student interest or engagement in learning or to develop specific talents and academic skills.

What is frequently overlooked in plans to reorganize students for instruction is that each grouping practice has both advantages and disadvantages. While one grouping technique may indeed promote academic achievement, it may at the same time result in racial segregation. Another grouping practice might increase inclusiveness by better integrating special education students into the student body but make unreasonable demands on a teacher's instructional time. Some of the stated aims of education are de facto contradictory, such as reducing the variance in ability in a single class and at the same time maximizing diversity in student backgrounds. Consequently, no single grouping practice is more capable than others of attaining all the stated aims of education.

Each grouping practice also poses its own challenges to teachers. For example, grouping students by gender makes it necessary for a teacher to determine what methods of instruction are most conducive to learning for boys and for girls. Grouping students by ability requires that a teacher create different kinds of learning environments to engage and challenge students at different ability levels. How teachers respond to the demands imposed by a particular grouping practice has a major impact on its success.

The effectiveness of tracking or any other organizational arrangement of students is determined by the ability of teachers and students to create a positive learning experience for all students within the grouping. Assignment of students to an instructional group on whatever basis sets in motion certain instructional and social processes. These processes influence students' access to the curriculum, the quantity and quality of instruction received, student and teacher expectations about student ability, and students' self-confidence, motivation, and effort.

Learning may be related to a particular grouping arrangement but need not be determined by it. For example, when students are tracked, a teacher may be influenced by a student's track level to form higher or lower expectations of the student's achievement than indicated by the student's abilities and performance. However, if teachers are sensitive to the danger of labeling a student solely on the basis of track assignment, they may try to avoid doing so. Similarly, if students for whom English is a second language are grouped with native speakers of English, some of a teacher's instructional time may be spent on translation, effectively limiting the quantity of instruction provided for native speakers. Again, a principal's or teacher's awareness of this possibility may result in accommodations that avoid the loss of instructional time while maintaining the integrated language grouping policy.

In general, the primary determinant of learning is the set of instructional and social processes that occur within a grouping arrangement of students, not the arrangement itself. Regardless of how students are grouped, if the educational processes provide quality instruction, increase student motivation, and foster positive social experiences, students will learn. If these processes produce negative experiences, the academic outcomes will be negative. The important point is that instructional and social processes, not organizational arrangements, determine learning. Quality instruction and a high level of student involvement will produce learning regardless of grouping, if educators utilize the organizational arrangement effectively.

Since it is process, not structure, that ultimately determines student achievement, merely changing an organizational structure is unlikely to improve learning. In particular, plans to replace tracking by heterogeneous grouping or some other organizational scheme will not automatically produce higher achievement. Proposals to reorganize students for instruction must be built on a theoretical understanding of how a particular organizational structure affects the instructional and social processes that occur within it. Moreover, educators must be made aware of how an organizational arrangement may constrain learning in order to avoid the negative effects of the structure on the learning process while maximizing its positive effects. If a change in organizational structure is not accompanied by an improvement in the learning climate of the classroom, no increase in student achievement can be anticipated.

Teacher Commitment and Competence and Student Achievement

Newmann (1993) argues that, to be effective, a specific educational reform must increase either teacher commitment or teacher competence. If, for example, the reform involves detracking, then educators must be explicit about how teacher commitment and competence will increase in detracked classrooms. A proposed reform that in any way obstructs teacher improvement most likely will fail.

In describing a plan to reform schools by establishing local autonomy and control, Newmann (1993) shows how organizational change can have an impact on teachers. The rationale for the plan is that local control gives teachers and administrators a sense of responsibility for their school that leads to feelings of pride at success and culpability at failure. These feelings produce a commitment to greater excellence. Increased control also allows teachers to use the pedagogies with which they are most comfortable and which they have found from experience to be most effective. In this way, technical knowledge increases effectiveness and teachers become more likely to share their expertise with others, increasing the technical capacity of the entire faculty. In making explicit the links between local control and teacher commitment and competence, the plan provides a conceptual foundation for the proposed structural change, revealing how and why it would improve student outcomes.

That a restructuring plan increases teacher commitment and competence is a necessary but not a sufficient condition for its success. The plan must also take into account outside factors that affect teachers' commitments and competencies, including teacher training; national, state, and district policies governing the curriculum; policies for evaluating students; and teacher rewards and performance evaluation. If these factors support the teachers' role in a reorganization plan, the potential for the plan's success increases greatly.

On the other hand, restructuring a school may not improve student learning, either because the restructuring does not lead to greater commitment and competence on the part of teachers or because the external structures needed to support the plan are absent. For example, a restructuring plan currently under debate is school choice. The rationale for school choice is that allowing parents to select their children's school will increase competition among schools. Planners expect parents to select schools that will provide the highest-quality education for their children. Lower-quality schools would then become undersubscribed and eventually be forced to improve or close. As this process unfolds over time, the overall quality of schools should improve. However, the multiple interests and various political and social agendas brought to the school choice debate suggest that factors may intervene to lessen the effectiveness of school choice. School personnel may not provide parents with the kinds of information they need to select a high-quality school for their child. Teachers may resent pressure to compete and lose commitment to teaching and to their students. In an effort to promote their schools, administrators may impose technological innovations on their staff with which the teachers are not comfortable or in which they are not competent. This will likely lead to lower teacher commitment and competence, resulting in the failure of the school choice plan.

While attention to the effects of organizational structure on teacher commitment and competence is critical to a valid evaluation of an organizational practice, teacher variables are not the only determinants of student learning. Of equal importance is the impact of the reorganization on student motivation and effort. Changing a grouping structure does not, in and of itself, lead to greater student engagement in learning, although an effective structure permits the evolution of processes that foster student involvement in learning by increasing student motivation and effort. Usually, this occurs when students have experiences of success; an increased sense of control over their environment; an accessible, interesting, and challenging curriculum, and a decrease in negative attitudes, interactions, and behaviors.

In the ongoing debate over tracking, discussions rarely have focused explicitly on how an organizational arrangement affects teacher commitment and competence or student motivation and effort. An increasing number of schools are simply abandoning tracking and replacing it by heterogeneous grouping. In some schools this has been successful, at least in the short term. In other schools detracking has not improved educational outcomes and has been abandoned. Examination of detracking plans is likely to show that unsuccessful programs did not have the expected outcomes because they did not increase teacher competence and commitment or because the plans did not enhance student confidence or increase student motivation and effort. In short, whether the educational reform plan involves ability grouping or detracking, its effectiveness will be determined by the extent to which the plan increases teacher competence and commitment, on the one hand, and student motivation and effort, on the other.

The Culture of a Successful School Program

Once educators have linked the effects of a proposed educational program on teacher competence and commitment and student motivation and effort, they must gain community support for the program and obtain assistance in implementing it in the school. The success of the program depends on the climate of the school community in which the plan is established.

In examining recent efforts to detrack schools, Oakes and Lipton (1992) conclude that a detracking "culture" in schools that detrack accounts for the success of this organizational innovation. They identify five components of this culture: an understanding that powerful norms supporting tracking must be taken into account; a willingness to make detracking part of a larger plan to change school practice; a politically and socially sensitive involvement in inquiry and experimentation; an ability to change teachers' roles and responsibilities; and a long-term commitment to innovation by leaders who prioritize student achievement and democratic values. While Oakes and Lipton (1992) attribute the success of detracking plans to their culture, the five components of this culture actually are requisite conditions for the success of any educational program or practice, including tracking.

The first component of a positive educational culture is awareness of the powerful norms underlying either an existing educational practice or a proposed change in an educational practice. In the case of tracking, Oakes and Lipton (1992) claim that the basis of ability grouping is a belief that intelligence is a global characteristic that encompasses all facets of a person's understanding and ability, that it is probably fixed from the beginning of a person's life, and that learning is a linear accumulation of facts and skills. Consistent with this perspective, tracked schools set specific curricula, employ a fairly standard pedagogy, and emphasize skills and memorization as well as comprehension and higher-order thinking processes.

Heterogeneous grouping, in contrast, is supported by a norm that defines intelligence as multidimensional and developmental (Gardner 1983; Sternberg 1990) and sees learning more as a process of constructing meaning than accumulating information. Detracked schools promote diverse educational experiences, allow flexibility in the curriculum, and stress learning skills.

Both conceptualizations of intelligence point to recognizable features of a complex intangible characteristic. At times intelligence appears fixed, at other times dynamic; under certain conditions, intelligence seems to be global, under other conditions, multidimensional. No single model can describe intelligence fully. At best, any model of intelligence or learning stresses certain characteristics and pays less attention to others.

Given the complexity of intelligence, it is naive to point to either tracking or detracking practices as more consistent with the way people learn. Both methods of organizing instruction can facilitate student learning if teachers recognize that intelligence is manifested in a variety of ways and that students have diverse learning styles. The belief that intelligence is an innate quality and learning a linear process can provide a rationale for either tracked or detracked classrooms. Similarly, the view that learning is multidimensional and meaning based provides a justification for either homogeneous or heterogeneous ability grouping practices as a way of fostering learning. What is critical is not how educators conceptualize intelligence but rather how they translate their conceptualization of intelligence into a curriculum and pedagogy consistent with their students' learning styles. No single model of intelligence can capture all of its dimensions, but any reasonable model of intelligence is broad enough to support various pedagogies and organizational practices consistent with current understanding of how students learn.

A different set of norms relates to the purpose of schooling. Many believe that the aim of schooling is to prepare students for the workforce, while others think that schooling exists to create good citizens. A commitment to the task of preparing a productive workforce seems to support the differentiated curriculum of a tracking structure. A commitment to preparing students to live and work in a multicultural environment in a democratic society appears to support heterogeneous grouping. However, these goals are not necessarily contradictory; successful school practices should evolve from efforts to balance both of these educational goals and to provide a learning environment that fosters cognitive, technical, and social skills. Again, both tracking and detracking practices are consistent with efforts to prepare students for the workforce and for life in a pluralistic and culturally diverse society.

The second way a school culture supports an educational practice is by incorporating the practice into an overall plan for helping students to learn better. The organization of students for instruction has little impact on learning unless it is part of an overall educational plan aimed at increasing the achievement of all students. For tracking to succeed, other pedagogical practices in the school must be consistent with the goals and methods of tracking. For example, the school's reward structure must be adapted to compensate for differences in curricular coverage across tracks and must provide opportunities for students in lower tracks to receive recognition. An incentive system must be established that rewards teachers for effort and creativity regardless of the ability level of the students they teach.

Similarly, if a detracking plan is to be successful, provisions must be made for the diverse learning styles and capabilities of students in a heterogeneous classroom. The most academically able students need learning challenges, while the lower-ability students require extra support. A sufficient number of teachers and aides must be available to provide instructional assistance to students of diverse abilities in a single classroom, and teachers should be rewarded for efforts to make the curriculum accessible to a diversity of students. Administrators must allow teachers to use time flexibly in order to cover appropriate topics in depth (under the assumption that students learn more when provided with more information).

In addition to providing classroom support, educators must ensure ongoing teacher training in order to bring about the successful adaptation of an educational plan. In terms of grouping policies, tracked schools need to address such issues as teacher expectations of student performance, creative approaches to teaching gifted or low-ability students, bases for assignment of teachers to tracks, and norms governing teacher status in the social hierarchy of the school. In detracked schools, ongoing education is needed to help teachers restructure the curriculum, to facilitate various rates of progress, to support different interests, and to use new methods of evaluation, such as student portfolios. Provisions must be made for students with special needs, whether they be academically gifted or learning disabled. Regardless of the educational practice, communication with parents and other interested community members is essential in order to obtain and maintain community support for the educational plan.

In fact, the third way a school culture can support an educational practice is by ensuring the involvement of interested parents and other community members in discussion of the practice and its place in the overall educational mission of the school. A successful organizational practice rests on dialogue among the relevant parties regarding underlying educational assumptions, roles, and responsibilities. Educators and concerned community members should agree on school goals and determine how an educational practice will help attain those goals. While consensus about an educational practice may not result from such open discussions, a compromise usually can be negotiated. The compromise will likely result in a level of support that will sustain the educational plan.

In discussions of tracking or detracking policies and practices, the particular concerns of certain members of the community need to be taken into account. If a tracking plan is proposed, school administrators must be sensitive to the realistic concerns of parents of students in low-ability tracks, as considerable empirical evidence documents the educational disadvantages of tracking for these students. Rather than equating these disadvantages with tracking itself, examination and discussion might focus on how instruction and student engagement can be improved in the basic tracks and how the status hierarchy and reward structure of the school can be modified to counter the stigma of a low-track assignment. Likewise, if a detracking plan is proposed, administrators should acknowledge and take seriously the concerns of parents of gifted students and students with special learning needs. Parents' fear that detracking will disadvantage students with special learning needs or abilities will be decreased if administrators construct detracking plans in such a way as to reduce or eliminate anticipated inequities. In addition, the parties involved should be encouraged to experiment with and evaluate educational practices continuously to make them more responsive to students' learning needs. This kind of inclusive and democratic involvement in educational theory, practice, and policy should maximize the effectiveness of an established organizational structure and counteract efforts of dissatisfied school and community members to sabotage a program.

The fourth way a school culture can support efforts to attain academic excellence through restructuring is by building an educational plan or practice on a realistic and appropriate definition of the teacher's role in implementing the plan. Traditionally, teachers in a teacher-centered classroom are responsible for choosing pedagogical strategies based on experience and advice from administrative experts. An expanded role here might encourage teachers to familiarize themselves with research findings, educational theories, and pedagogical innovations to improve their teaching. Team teaching may be another organizational option. Whatever the definition of the teacher's role, it needs to be supported by an administration that provides adequate time and resources.

In schools where students are tracked for instruction, teachers traditionally have been allowed little influence in determining the content of the curriculum but considerable discretion in determining its presentation to students. New roles that can be defined for teachers within a tracked structure to better support their efforts and increase their competence and commitment could include a greater voice in curriculum content, textbook selection, course prerequisites and requirements, and graduation requirements, as well as greater flexibility in allocating instructional time throughout the day and week. Teacher representation on district-level committees could be expanded, and teacher recommendations should be made a significant factor in track placement. Improved pedagogical technology and training in its use should be provided. Workshops, in-service programs, lectures, and liaisons with institutions of higher education and community businesses would all promote greater teacher involvement and effort and have a positive effect on the success of the program.

Similarly, if a school opts to detrack students for instruction, the teacher's role must be examined and supported. In detracked classes, teachers are given a number of new responsibilities and new roles, including those of instructional coach, team teacher, student advisor, and curriculum planner. They also are asked to participate to a significant extent in organizational decision making. Most importantly, they are expected to challenge and engage students having a wide variety of learning needs. A critical examination of these new roles is needed in order to provide the resources and support that teachers require to carry out their added responsibilities.

Finally, a supportive culture will ensure the presence of an effective leadership continually defining the purpose of an educational plan or practice and the educational goals it aims to attain and sustaining the commitment of educators and community members to the success of the plan. At times, this requires a leadership willing to resist entrenched school and community groups. Political expediency may tempt educators to consider a particular organizational structure or to alter the design of the curriculum in a way that could be detrimental to the aims of the school. For example, political considerations may lead an administrator to set aside additional resources for gifted students or those with special needs to the detriment of the core program or vice versa. However, effective leaders should be able to remind key decision makers that their highest priority is to improve the educational opportunities of all students. Even if compromise is necessary, an overall commitment to this end should avoid jeopardizing a carefully designed and implemented educational plan.

In summary, for any organizational plan or practice to be effective, it must be proposed and implemented within a school culture that supports the plan. The components of a school culture are far-reaching, involving the attitudes and behaviors of district-level personnel, school administrators, teachers, staff, parents, and community members. In a supportive culture, these various groups will discuss a particular educational plan or practice, determine how it fits into their shared vision of education, and become involved in its design, implementation, and evaluation. When a new educational policy or practice is proposed in a supportive school culture, the likelihood of its success greatly increases.

Characteristics of Effective Instruction

The most critical component of a successful educational practice is effective instruction. The way students are organized for instruction matters only to the extent that it facilitates or constrains the instructional process. Effective instruction based on a rich curriculum and appropriate pedagogical techniques can be found in both tracked and detracked classrooms.

Educators have identified four basic properties of instruction that lead to successful learning outcomes (Steinberg and Wheelock 1992). These properties pertain to the nature of the curriculum, pedagogical practices, methods of evaluation, and the use of time. The process of effective instruction primarily involves teachers and students but also relies heavily on the commitment of administrators and the support of the community.

Typically, the curriculum is designed around a body of information that educators determine in advance to be appropriate for a particular grade. All students at that grade level are exposed to the subject matter and are expected to learn it. Facts are presented in a sequential manner; most of the material is in an assigned textbook and there is little reliance on supplementary sources. The syllabus does not change significantly from year to year, from one school to another within a school district, or even from one school district to another within or between states.

Recently educators have argued that a curriculum would be more effective if it were organized around themes and practical applications. The ideal curriculum would include problem solving, higher-order thinking skills, and contextual analysis and would incorporate multiple student perspectives and allow multidimensional answers. Teachers would encourage students to expand the curriculum based on their own interests and in response to topics that emerged from reading and group discussions. Less uniformity of material would exist across classes at the same grade level or from one year to the next.

A more extensive curriculum would appeal to a broader array of students, allow students to participate in the curriculum at the level of their own cognitive abilities, facilitate teacher-student interaction, recognize a variety of talents, and stress concepts and meaning rather than rote response. Long-term projects would be encouraged, allowing students to pursue a topic in greater depth if they wished.

A theme-based curriculum is consistent with a variety of organizational practices. While a theme-based approach is frequently found in a heterogeneous classroom, it can be implemented equally well in a homogeneous classroom. All students, regardless of how they are grouped for instruction, should benefit from a curriculum that encourages individual research, student-initiated learning, and students' interest in topics related to the basic curriculum.

A second feature of successful instruction is related to pedagogical techniques. The traditional pedagogical model is teacher-centered instruction. The teacher presents the curriculum to the students using a pedagogy characterized by teacher lectures, extensive note taking, and seatwork. Students learn the material through listening, reading, memorization, responding to the teacher's questions and taking uniformly administered tests. What little discussion occurs is directed by the teacher.

An alternative pedagogical model that focuses on students as key agents in the instructional process is gaining in popularity. Students are encouraged to learn from their peers and on their own as well as from the teacher, and to use the library, newspapers, and other resources to supplement themes discussed in the classroom and in their texts. They select and complete projects at whatever level of intellectual complexity is appropriate for them, working in cooperative groups and assisting each other in completing a group product. The teacher's role, to a large degree, is one of facilitator, encourager, and director, enabling students to develop thinking skills, creativity, responsibility, and curiosity.

Both teacher-centered pedagogical techniques and student-centered instruction can occur in either homogeneous or heterogeneous classrooms and it is inappropriate to associate one or the other pedagogical model with a particular method of organizing students for instruction. If student-centered instruction is indeed found to be more effective in motivating and engaging students in the learning process, then it can and should be adopted, regardless of school policy governing the organization of students for instruction. Nevertheless, it should be noted that student-centered instruction appears particularly suited to the diversity of student ability that is found in a detracked classroom and is one of the ways teachers can be freed to respond to the individual learning needs of a diverse body of students.

A third characteristic of effective instruction involves methods of assessing student learning. Typically, teachers use competition as a primary method of motivating students, assessing students' progress relative to that of their peers. Self-mastery or progress toward some objective standard is not counted unless it results in a change in rank. The widespread use of grade point averages to measure high school achievement and the practice of normalizing test scores illustrate the relative nature of grading. Being evaluated solely on the basis of rank particularly discourages low-ability students, since their efforts seldom change their rank in class. Consequently, relative assessment can act as a deterrent to achievement for many students because it dampens their motivation and effort.

The competitive model of instruction leads to a formal and standard method of assessment. The most common way of assessing students' progress is by use of uniformly administered standardized and nonstandardized tests. Students in the same class are given the same examinations regardless of their cognitive abilities and learning skills, and their progress in a course is judged in terms of their scores on those tests.

Educators and researchers often criticize formal tests, arguing that they are biased against particular subsets of students, such as minority groups, low-income students, or students who experience test anxiety. To the extent that these criticisms are valid, formal tests are faulty measures of student progress. Moreover, test results often are based on true-false and multiple-choice questions, which allow guesswork and luck to play a role in determining a student's score.

An increasingly popular alternative pedagogical technique motivates students through the use of cooperation rather than competition. Many teachers now divide classes into cooperative work groups for at least a part of each day. Small groups of students work together, helping each other with assigned tasks and producing either individual or group products. Greater emphasis on cooperation increases the likelihood that every child who participates will experience some success. Cooperative learning methods also broaden the learning task by providing opportunities for students to explain their understanding of the curriculum to their peers and to develop at least minimal teaching skills. The result is likely to be greater engagement and learning for all students.

Alternative methods of assessment include teacher evaluation of student projects, portfolios, and other displays of student work. Written appraisals of a student's work by teachers and, if appropriate, by other students, can provide a more meaningful form of student assessment.

When test results are de-emphasized and student evaluations are based on a wide variety of products, it becomes easier for teachers to judge student accomplishments relative to earlier work rather than based on the accomplishments of peers. This gives students a sense of control over the evaluation, because it is determined by their own efforts rather than by the progress of their classmates. Furthermore, measuring student progress rather than objective achievement greatly increases the likelihood that students will experience success in at least some areas of the curriculum. Success, in turn, motivates students to expend more effort in learning. Consequently, employing a number of more personal methods of evaluating student work and measuring progress as well as accomplishment should improve student achievement.

New assessment techniques can be implemented within any organizational structure. Students in both tracked and detracked classes benefit from the implementation of a greater variety of evaluation methods. Creative ways of measuring student achievement that attach value to student effort and progress as well as to student accomplishments tend to increase students' confidence and sense of control over their learning efforts, strengthen motivation and effort, and increase involvement in the instructional process regardless of how students are grouped.

Finally, successful instruction is characterized by creative use of teacher and student time. Most schools schedule classroom instruction in time slots that do not change over the school day, week, and year, except under special circumstances. Fixed instructional periods require that lessons be structured to accommodate the time frame, regardless of the pedagogical value of such a practice. Fifty-minute periods leave little time for long-range projects, spontaneous student discussion, creative involvement in assignments, and unanticipated questions, concerns, and contributions of students.

A more flexible time schedule accommodates a wider variety of instructional methods. A school day, week, or year can be arranged into periods of different length to adjust to the requirements of a particular subject and the instructional methods of different teachers. The school year can be divided into quarters or trimesters instead of the traditional semesters, and can accommodate modules, minicourses, workshops, study days, project days, and other instructional arrangements. The school day and week can be organized in ways that permit theme-driven instruction, projects, experiments, field trips, and various other instructional methods. Flexible use of time provides greater opportunities for students with diverse skills to become involved in curriculum-related tasks and allows students with differing abilities to take the time they need to finish a project. It avoids an artificial segmentation of the curriculum that dampens students' curiosity and limits their involvement with the subject matter.

The flexibility of a school's time schedule operates independently of the way students are grouped for instruction; consequently, flexible scheduling is possible in both tracked and detracked classes. In tracked schools it is possible to arrange different schedules for different tracks, thus allowing more instructional time for lower-track students. For example, fewer courses but longer or more frequent class periods could be provided for some students, and more individual study time could be made available for others. In detracked schools, a flexible time schedule should permit teachers to be more responsive to the learning needs of individual students. In general, students are likely to have greater opportunities for meaningful learning under a system that permits and encourages flexible scheduling.

In general, educators provide more effective instruction when they adopt a rich, wide-ranging curriculum, employ effective pedagogical strategies, utilize a wide range of assessment techniques, and use instructional time creatively and flexibly. Attitudes toward improving instruction must be built on the premise that all students can learn and must be challenged to do the best work of which they are capable.

Finally, the harshest criticism that can be leveled against any educational reform or practice is that it fails to provide equal learning opportunities for students who differ from the mainstream in background or ability. A fear that gifted or special-needs students, low-income students, or minorities will be disadvantaged by an educational practice lies at the root of much of the resistance to educational change and reform. Accommodation to the needs of special populations of students must be an integral component of the planning and implementation of any educational program.

Conclusions

Students learn best in a school climate and culture that fosters both teacher commitment and competence and student motivation and effort. Moreover, both teacher and student engagement in the learning process must be supported by school and community resources, attitudes, and norms. The way students are organized for instruction does not determine the learning climate of a school.

In an open, respectful, and democratic culture, educators and parents plan and evaluate educational practices, define and support the role of the teacher in implementing these practices, and generate leadership to involve and motivate the community in support of a school program. When the question is whether to group students homogeneously or heterogeneously for instruction, it is important to recognize that either of these organizational plans can be consistent with a productive learning environment.

When administrators or teachers decide to track or detrack students without also creating the atmosphere or mobilizing the resources to support the grouping practice they select, they jeopardize the likelihood of a successful outcome. Tracking and detracking policies fail when educators try to implement them in the absence of a supportive culture. Ensuring that support for an organizational practice is in place before it is adopted greatly increases the likelihood of its success.

In general, no organizational structure or pedagogical practice is inherently superior to any other. There is no best way to group students for instruction, although the organizational arrangement of students does influence student outcomes indirectly through its effect on the cognitive and social processes of teachers and students in the classroom. Whether tracking or detracking leads to an improvement in student achievement depends on whether the practice facilitates or constrains the instructional processes that occur in the classroom. The success of any grouping practice increases significantly if the practice is well conceptualized and widely discussed beforehand, and if educators and parents are involved in the implementation and evaluation of the program. Researchers and educators who criticize tracking or detracking plans without taking into account the context in which those plans are implemented do a serious disservice to efforts at educational reform.

NOTES

The author expresses appreciation to the agencies that funded this work: the National Science Foundation and the United States Department of Education, Office of Educational Research and Improvement.

REFERENCES

Barr, R., and R. Dreeben. 1983. *How Schools Work.* Chicago: University of Chicago Press.

Eder, D. 1981. Ability Grouping as a Self-fullfilling Prophecy: A Micro-Analysis of Teacher-Student Interaction. *Sociology of Education* 54: 151–162.

Gamoran, A., and M. Berends. 1987. The Effects of Stratification in Secondary Schools: Synthesis of Survey and Ethnographic Research. *Review of Educational Research* 57: 415–435.

Gardner, H. 1983. *Frames of Mind: The Theory of Multiple Intelligences.* New York: Basic Books.

Hallinan, M.T. 1991. School Differences in Tracking Structures and Track Assignments. *Journal of Research on Adolescence* 1(3): 251–275.

Newmann, F.M. 1993. Beyond Common Sense in Educational Restructuring: The Issues of Content and Linkage. *Educational Researcher* 22(2): 4–13.

Nystrand, M., and A. Gamoran. 1987. A Study of Instruction as Discourse. Paper presented at the annual meeting of the American Educational Research Association.

Oakes, J. 1985. *Keeping Track: How Schools Structure Inequality.* New Haven: Yale University Press.

Oakes, J., and M. Lipton. 1992. Detracking Schools: Early Lessons from the Field. *Phi Delta Kappan* 73(6): 448–454.

Rosenbaum, J.E. 1976. *Making Inequality: The Hidden Curriculum of High School Tracking.* New York: John Wiley and Sons.

Slavin, R. 1987. Ability Grouping and Student Achievement in Elementary Schools: A Best-Evidence Synthesis. *Review of Educational Research* 57: 293–336.

———. 1990. Ability Grouping in Secondary Schools: A Best-Evidence Synthesis. *Review of Educational Research* 60(3): 471–499.

Steinberg, A., and A. Wheelock. 1992. *The Harvard Education Letter* 8(5): 1–4.

Sternberg, R.J. 1990. *Metaphors of Mind: Conceptions of the Nature of Intelligence.* New York: Cambridge University Press.

3

Parental Ties to the School and Community and Mathematics Achievement

Chandra Muller

Recently there has been an emphasis among policymakers and educators on encouraging parental involvement in the schooling of children. Most large school districts have programs designed to increase parent involvement, including teaching parents skills so that they can better help their children at home (e.g., Epstein 1991). Parental participation in parent-teacher organizations (PTO) and volunteering are also encouraged. Parental involvement in a child's schooling is nearly universally accepted as having a positive influence on the performance of the child; indeed, many studies document this.

Parental involvement is attractive conceptually for several reasons. From an academic standpoint it is interesting because it explains some of the mechanisms by which family background has its well-known influence on a child's achievement. From a policy perspective it is attractive because it represents a potentially low-cost effective resource to be tapped by schools.

Few researchers have questioned whether all forms of involvement are equally beneficial to a child's learning, and if not, which kinds of parental actions are best. This chapter focuses on that question by examining ten different forms of involvement and their associations with achievement test scores and rates of gain in achievement test scores from eighth grade to tenth grade in order to address two main questions. First, are there measurable differences in the association between parental involvement and mathematics achievement? And second, what kinds of parental actions are associated with higher performance? While there has been research on parental involvement, most has centered not on involvement in education but rather involvement with the school. The positive relationship of parental involvement with the school and evaluations of students by teachers has been documented. Stevenson and Baker (1987) found that parental involvement, as measured by teacher reports of parental attendance at PTO meetings and parent-teacher conferences, is positively associated with teacher evaluations of students. Fehrmann, Keith, and Reimers (1987), using the High School and Beyond database, found that a parental involvement composite (including both involvement in home-based activities not directly related to school and involvement at school) is positively related to student grades. Lareau (1989) also found that teacher's evaluations of students are improved when their parents are involved in school activities. And Epstein (1991) found that children of parents who engage in school-initiated, structured activities at home designed to complement the school program have reading achievement test scores that improve at a faster rate over the course of the school year. Dornbusch et al. (1987) examined parenting styles (which include actions having to do with involvement in education) and found that parents with an authoritative style have children with higher grades.

In conceptualizing parental involvement in education, one might imagine that there is no one right way for a parent to become involved because too many factors constrain and facilitate involvement. For instance, attributes associated with socioeconomic status (SES) such as money and parents' education restrict access, as does the context in which the parent is raising the child, including community and school characteristics. The child's gender also makes a difference in the way parents become involved. With so many preexisting conditions to consider, along with the particular needs of the child, one might expect great variation in the involvement strategies adopted by parents and one might also expect that parental action might have a differential impact depending upon the circumstances and needs of the child. Yet there are also similarities among the consequences for student involvement. The focus of this chapter is on involvement that encourages academic achievement despite differences among students.

Dimensions of Involvement

Locus of Action

It is useful to consider several dimensions which may affect parental involvement and its consequences. The first dimension is the context or locus of action, either the home, the community, or the school. Action in the home will likely be subject to fewer systematic constraints than action outside the home. For example, talking with the child about school is a form of home-based involvement, compared with talking with the child's teacher about the child or attending a parent-teacher organization meeting, each of which is based in the school. Talking with the child may vary depending on the interest the parent takes in the child's school and on the parent-child relationship. It is not likely to depend directly on such characteristics of the school as whether parents are encouraged to become involved in school activities, although some might argue that if parents are more involved at school they are more likely to talk with their child about the school.

Studies of parental involvement with respect to younger children have been almost entirely concentrated on involvement inside the home. For example, the Home Observation for the Measurement of the Environment (HOME) measures the nature of the interaction between mother and child (Bradley and Caldwell 1984). Research on adolescents includes the analysis of home-based involvement as well; for instance, Rumberger et al. (1990) examine parenting style and the extent to which parents talk with their children, demand specific (and responsible) behavior, and structure the child's environment. Among school-age children, parental involvement with the school is often emphasized by researchers. For example, Epstein (1986) examined differences among parents in activities ranging from playing games with the child to encourage learning to signing a child's homework.

Involvement in the community may take a variety of forms. Parents may form friendships with the parents of their children's friends, creating an intergenerational network or community. Coleman (1988) discusses the potential importance of these ties and of the "closure of intergenerational ties." Coleman and Hoffer (1987), and more recently, Bryk, Lee, and Holland (1993), document the power of "value" or "functional" communities, composed of parents and their children. Involvement in the community may take other forms as well. Parents may make use of community resources such as the library (e.g., Epstein 1986), enrichment classes, or after-school programs.

In general, involvement outside the home is more likely to be subject to external constraints, and involvement inside the home will vary according to internal factors (like interests and values and the relationship between parents and child) and parental resources. Consequently, involvement inside the home, at least that which is most influenced by parental values and attitudes, is likely to represent the kind of behavior in which parents have engaged historically, since it is least likely to change when external constraints change.

Purpose of Action

Parental action is also likely to vary according to intended purpose. As discussed above, some forms of involvement may come about because of the parent's interest in engaging in a particular action. For instance, talking with the child about school activities may depend on the interest of the parent (and perhaps the child) in school and on the relationship between parent and child, but the discussion is not targeted at a particular consequence. Other actions of parents are likely to be more instrumental or goal-directed, designed for a particular consequence. For example, when a parent checks a child's homework it is probably because the parent wants to make sure it is complete and perhaps is interested in assuring its quality. Affective involvement, like involvement in the home, is likely to represent the ways parents have historically been involved with their children. Instrumental involvement is likely to be a response to a particular circumstance of the child, perhaps as an intervention in a problem or as an effort to influence a particular decision. Many attempts of teachers and schools to increase involvement encourage instrumental forms of action, like helping with school assignments and checking homework (e.g., Epstein 1986).

Authority of Action

The third dimension in which involvement is likely to vary is the position of the parent in relation to the school and the process of educating the child. Parents may play a supportive role, as is often the case when they volunteer at school, or they may play a more authoritative or managerial role, as they might when selecting a school or attempting to influence decisions about what courses the child should take. Baker and Stevenson (1986) and Lareau (1989) have documented differences in involvement style of parents depending upon their level of education. Parents with higher levels of education act as leaders or managers in shaping the school activities and opportunities of their children, whereas parents with lower levels of education take on a more subordinate position relative to school personnel.

Each of the above dimensions may affect when and why parents are likely to get involved and the possible consequences of their actions. Education is a complex process in which a child's ability and preparation interact with decisions that influence the child's opportunity to learn (which is influenced by the school's evaluation of the child). Parental involvement may play a role at each point, but different forms of involvement may be relevant depending on the step of the process. This chapter compares the associations of different forms of involvement with different forms of academic performance so we may understand better which kinds of involvement are associated with each behavior.

First we will look at the associations between background and involvement with test scores and with grades. Differences in the associations will allow for comparison with how involvement is related to an objective measure of the student's performance (at least, one that is comparable across all students in this sample) compared with an evaluation of each student which is made by the teacher, probably in relation to the other students in the class. Second is an examination of the relationship that background and parental involvement have with gains in test scores from eighth to tenth grade. Performance gain measures the extent to which students use available resources and opportunities to increase knowledge.

Method

Data

The database upon which this analysis draws is the base year and first follow-up of the National Education Longitudinal Study of 1988 (NELS: 88). As eighth graders, students were asked to complete an interview questionnaire about their background, schoolwork and activities, home life, attitudes, and social relationships. In addition, each student was administered a series of curriculum-based cognitive tests prepared by Educational Testing Service to measure ability in reading, mathematics, science, and social studies. Parents of each student were asked to complete a questionnaire asking about family characteristics, involvement with the educational process, commitment of family resources to education, and attitudes of the parents about the child's school and education. Students were followed up two years later and were administered a new test battery and interview. A complete description may be found in NCES (1992).

Native Americans are excluded from all analyses because they are a unique racial and ethnic group and thus should not be categorized with any other group, yet they are too small a group to be examined separately. For the first analyses, of the relationships of parental involvement with grades and test scores for eighth grade, only base year data are used and analyses include all students in the sample (except Native Americans). The second analysis, of test score gains, includes only students in the panel.

Variables

Parental Involvement

Ten measures of parental involvement have been selected for analysis here. The measures are briefly summarized in the Appendix, and a detailed expository summary of each measure may be found in Muller and Kerbow (1993). They include four measures which originate in the home and which vary primarily according to individual characteristics of the family and student: (1) discussion with parents about current school experiences; (2) discussion about high school program planning; (3) parental checking of homework; and (4) parental restriction of television on weekdays. Two measures originate in the home but may include the use of community resources. The (5) amount of after-school supervision provided for the child and (6) enrollment of the child in extra music classes may vary according to the availability of community alternatives as well as parent resources. Parental ties to the social community of the child are measured by (7) the number of parents of the child's friends who are known by the parent. Links between parents and the school are measured by (8) the frequency of parental contact with the school; (9) the level of parental participation in a PTO, and (10) whether the parent volunteers at the school. The forms of involvement that demand an interaction with actors outside the family, especially other parents and the school, are likely to be forms of involvement which are most subject to additional constraints and therefore may be less stable or reflective of individual characteristics of the family, including its values and priorities.

Background and Achievement Test Scores and Grades

Achievement test scores and grades are the two most common measures of academic outcomes. The NELS: 88 data base includes four achievement tests, in reading, mathematics, science, and social studies (history and government). The measures used here are the base year and first follow-up IRT mathematics compiled by NCES. Students in NELS: 88 were asked to report their grades "from sixth grade up till now" in four subject areas (English, mathematics, science, and social studies); this analysis used student mathematics grades. Since the grades measure has a historical and cumulative component, because students were asked about their grades over almost a three-year period, it is conceivable that the students' grades affect their score on the achievement test administered for NELS: 88. This could come about when a student has been tracked according to grades received in sixth or seventh grade, on the basis of which the student would have been provided with different opportunities for learning material relevant to test performance. For this reason, when predicting test scores, grades are controlled.

The background variables used throughout the analysis are derived directly from NCES variables. They include family income, parents' highest education, sex of student, family structure (single mother, stepparent, or intact family), race and ethnicity, and urbanicity.

Analysis Results

Recall that the forms of parental involvement may be categorized along several dimensions. First, one can consider the context or locus of action, in the home, community, or school. Whether a child is enrolled in music classes and the amount of after-school supervision are usually determined by parents, who may utilize available services in the community. While the actions are constrained by regional availability, they are not constrained by the willingness of others to engage in a relationship in the way that knowing other parents and forming relationships with the school would be. For instance, how much parents talk with their children about school experiences or whether a child takes music lessons outside of school probably has less to do with the cohesiveness of the neighborhood or the extent to which the school tries to foster parental involvement than with the measures classified as external to the home.

A second important distinction to make is between action that is instrumental, that is, action designed to influence a particular circumstance, and affective action motivated by more general concerns. For example, one could contrast talking with the child about school experiences to parents contacting the school about a child's academic problem. The first, talking about school experiences, has probably become a habit in many families; some parents and children have always talked about school. Compare this to contacting the school, which parents usually do for fairly specific reasons, like a child's less-than-perfect grades.

Many home-based actions, particularly those that are affective, are likely to reflect ways that parents and their children have interacted for a long time. The best example is parent-child discussion of everyday school activities, but television restriction, extra music classes, and after-school supervision also fall into this category. Parental acquaintance networks may also be classified as affective—parents do not usually belong to them for a particular purpose; however, they are outside the home, and they imply the acceptance of a relationship by other parents.

Activities that are instrumental are more likely to take place outside the home, or at least to be motivated by outside factors. Contacting the school about academic behavior and participation in PTO are likely to be largely instrumental activities. The former is usually motivated by the child's poor performance and the latter by an interest in managing an aspect of the child's education. Checking homework and talking about high school program planning, while they take place in the home, are probably also instrumental. Checking homework is usually an effort to improve the child's homework performance (in response to poor performance). Talking about high school program planning may indicate that parents are thinking more actively about programming questions (perhaps because of their options). Evidence also suggests that program planning may contain an element of intervention; parents are more likely to discuss programming when the child has poor grades (Muller 1991).

Finally, parental action may be authoritative or supportive in relation to the school. Authoritative action is that in which the parent is a leader or manager, compared with action that supports the initiative and leadership of the school and school personnel.

Base Year Test Scores and Grades Compared

Table 3.1 shows standardized coefficients for separate regressions of test scores and grades on background and parent involvement variables.[1] Since grades and test scores affect one another when grades are predicted, test scores are controlled and in models predicting test scores grades are controlled.

Not surprisingly, home-based, affective actions are the forms of involvement most closely associated with eighth grade test scores. This is probably because test scores are a measure of preparation and readiness, which are taught from an early age. Table 3.1 indicates that talking about current school experiences is a powerful predictor of eighth grade test scores; its coefficient is nearly as large as that of family income. Whether the child takes extra music classes and how much a child is supervised after school are strongly associated with achievement test scores. To a lesser extent parental acquaintance networks and restricting television predict eighth-grade math test scores. These forms of involvement may all measure the extent to which parents regulate and direct the child's activities outside of school. Extra music classes demand that the child use free time to practice, and parental friendship networks may allow values and norms to be more easily enforced.

Two forms of involvement, parental checking of homework and the frequency with which parents contact the school, are negatively associated with achievement test performance. Almost certainly these actions do not make the child's performance lower—more likely they are a response of parents to poor performance. These two actions are probably the most clearly instrumental forms of involvement measured. They are forms of parental intervention, and they are important predictors of grades, as well; however, contacting the school is more important than homework checking (which is home-based) for predicting grades. Each form of intervention is usually a response on the part of parents to poor performance by the student.

In general, the forms of involvement which best predict grades appear to be more instrumental and more closely associated with the school. Talking about high school program planning, a directed or instrumental form of action, is strongly

TABLE 3.1. Standardized Coefficients for Regression of Base Year Mathematics Achievement Test Scores and Mathematics Grades.

	Test Scores		Grades	
Family income	.146***	.130***	.004	-.010
Parents' highest education	.219***	.187***	.013	.001
Sex of student (male = 1, female = 0)	.012	.047***	-.047***	-.027***
Single mother	.042***	.041***	-.047***	-.047***
Mother, stepfather	-.007	-.001	-.047***	-.039***
Asian-American	.013*	.017**	.036***	.039***
Hispanic	-.082***	.074***	.020**	.022**
African-American	-.166***	-.152***	.080***	.073***
Urban	-.001	.008	-.001	-.015
Suburban	.021**	.027***	-.034***	-.033***
8th-grade grades	.340***	.302***		
8th-grade test score			.409***	.376***
Talk about current school experiences		.114***		.046***
Talk about high school program		.009		.058***
Parents check homework		-.090***		-.034***
Frequency parents restrict television		.044***		.006
Child enrolled in extra music class		.070***		.016*
Amount of after-school supervision		-.061***		-.028***
Number of friends' parents known		.044***		.022**
Frequency parents contact school		-.078***		-.068***
PTO participation		-.013		.056***
Parent volunteers at school		.010		.005
R²	.319	.354	.174	.190

* p < .05   ** p < .01   *** p < .001

associated with grades. Its coefficient is larger than that for talking about current school activities, which may be less focused on intended purpose. Notice also that parent participation in a PTO, a school-based action, does not predict test scores but is strongly associated with grades.

The way parents regulate the child's time outside of school may be more directly related to test scores than grades. Enrollment in extra music classes and restricting television are highly associated with test scores and have little or no relationship to grades. Two other activities that may measure ways parents regulate the out-of-school activities, after school supervision and parental acquaintance networks, predict test scores better than grades.

Notice that while family income and parents' highest education are the best predictors of student test performance (aside from grades), they are not associated with grades when test scores are controlled. The relationship between income and parents' highest education can be explained by variation in student test performance. These two SES-related measures are more important for predicting test scores, perhaps in part because of their importance in the preparation of the child for school. Likewise, involvement not directly related to school and that which is not goal-directed is more important for predicting test scores. Grades, on the other hand, are associated with parental interaction with the school.

Comparing background coefficients when parental involvement is and is not in the model shows how background measures are associated with each performance measure and how involvement either explains background-associated differences in performance or accentuates differences. First, however, notice that the amount of variance explained by the addition of parental involvement is greater when predicting test scores than when predicting grades (.035 for test scores compared with .016 for grades). The parental involvement measured in this study appears to have more to do with test scores, and possibly with preparation, than with grades.

When only other background variables are controlled, males do not achieve significantly higher mathematics test scores than females. However, when parental involvement is added to the model, test scores of males are markedly higher than that of females. For the same level of parental involvement and background, males achieve higher test scores than females. Gender differences with respect to grades indicate that males receive lower grades than females, but some of that difference is explained by parental involvement. When parental involvement is controlled, males still receive lower grades than females; however, the difference is smaller.[2] Previous results indicate that parents are more involved with female children in home-based activities and are more involved with male children in school-based activities; despite this difference, the mechanisms by which involvement is associated with grades and with test scores is much the same for both males and females (Muller 1991).

The other background measures are differentially associated with grades and with test scores, but involvement does not matter in their association with performance. Income and parents' highest education are strongly related to mathematics test scores and grades; once test scores are controlled, these factors are not associated with math grades. Students of single mothers tend to get higher test scores and lower grades, probably because income is controlled. These mothers have especially low incomes when income is compared with other SES-related factors, some of which are unmeasured in the model. Children of a single mother or of stepfather and natural mother receive lower grades.

Test Score Gains

Table 3.2 shows standardized coefficients for regressions of background controls and parental involvement in mathematics achievement test scores in eighth and tenth grades. When tenth-grade scores are predicted, eighth-grade scores are controlled; thus, test score gain is estimated. Regressions of tenth-grade scores control for eighth-grade test scores (and other variables mentioned above), so that factors associated with test score gain can be examined. These models are estimated only using the panel sample, whereas the models in Table 3.1 were estimated for the entire base year cohort (excluding Native Americans).[3]

At first glance the patterns of involvement associated with growth as measured in the tenth grade appear similar to those associated with eighth-grade test scores; nonetheless, some important differences exist. While talking about school experiences is still a good predictor of test score gain, it is less important than some of the other measures of involvement and the background measures of family income and parents' highest level of education. Talking about current school experiences probably reflects the way parents and their children have been interacting for a long time. It may also reflect the extent to which the child's school life is integrated with everyday family activities. These kinds of factors are probably associated with preparation for schoolwork and for test taking. The results of the regressions shown in Table 3.2 suggest that they are less important for the child's achievement gains than for preparation. Notice also that the coefficients for income and education are essentially equal in the model of test score gain, while parents' highest education is a better predictor of eighth-grade test scores than parents' income. Parents' education may also be more important for a child's preparation. For test score gain, however, parents' income plays as important a role as education, perhaps indicating the benefit from having resources ready to mobilize.

The most directed forms of involvement measured, and those that are probably a response to a child's poor performance, have negative coefficients. Contacting the school retains its strong association with growth. If it were truly effective in promoting test score growth, then it would be smaller in absolute size or positive. Checking homework diminishes in importance for predicting negative growth. It may be that parents respond to problems by checking homework and that it is somewhat effective. In each of these cases of intervention, without a way to control for the reasons parents engage in the activity it is impossible to understand the process by which involvement is associated with gains in test scores.

Taken together, these models suggest that for gains in test scores a broad-based strategy of parental management of the child's environment is important. Notice especially that involvement outside the home, in particular parental acquaintance networks and parental participation in a PTO,

TABLE 3.2. Standardized Coefficients for Regression of Base Year Mathematics Achievement Test Scores and Gains in Mathematics Grades Achievement Test Scores. (Includes Panel Sample Only)

	Grade 8	Grade 10
Family income	.122***	.047***
Parents' highest education	.196***	.058***
Sex of student (male = 1, female = 0)	.056***	.007
Single mother	.049***	.011*
Mother, stepfather	.007	-.003
Asian-American	.021**	.009*
Hispanic	-.073***	-.003
African-American	-.149***	-.027***
Urban	.026***	.006
Suburban	.038***	.017***
8th-grade grades	.303***	.098***
Talk about current school experiences	.121***	.028***
Talk about high school program	.011	-.009
Parents check homework	-.095***	-.014**
Frequency parents restrict television	.046***	.021***
Child enrolled in extra music class	.061***	.007
Amount of after-school supervision	-.060***	-.021***
Number of friends' parents known	.035***	.015**
Frequency parents contact school	-.076***	-.035***
PTO participation	-.017*	.017***
Parent volunteers at school	.008	-.011*
Base year test score		.734***
R^2	.350	.721

*p < .05   **p < .01   ***p < .001

predict gains in test scores better than they predict eighth-grade scores.

Parental friendship networks may exert normative pressure on students. For instance, Coleman, Hoffer, and Kilgore (1982) hypothesized that this was one facet of Catholic schools that might account for their success. Also, parental friendship networks may provide parents with information about opportunities or about the child's behavior. PTO participation is likely to be the best measure of a forum available to parents to learn about opportunities in the school. It is also a place to influence school policy.

Restricting television and after-school supervision are also important predictors of mathematics test score gains and may measure something about parental management of the child's environment. Children whose parents restrict the amount of television they watch probably watch less television than they would otherwise, but more importantly, they are probably also affecting how conducive the child's environment is to learning. Likewise, after-school supervision may be measuring the extent to which a parent is in a position to manage a child's environment outside of school, even if the parent is not directly providing the supervision. It probably also reflects the amount of supervision the child had before eighth grade.

Discussion

In this analysis I examine the relationship of family background, student characteristics, and parental involvement to student mathematics achievement test scores, mathematics grades and gain in test scores.[4] A student's eighth-grade test scores are assumed to be, in part, a measure of the student's preparation for schoolwork, and indeed, the forms of involvement associated with eighth-grade test scores are largely those that have to do with home environment.

Regressions on gain in mathematics test scores control for the child's earlier test performance and therefore for the child's earlier preparation. Gain, then, is influenced by, among other factors, the child's opportunity to learn. Effective parental involvement is likely to be involvement that maximizes this opportunity.

In conceptualizing parental involvement of this sort, it is useful to consider the work of Dornbusch and his colleagues (see Dornbusch et al. 1987; Rumberger et al. 1990; Baker and Stevenson 1986). Dornbusch and his colleagues studied the relationship of parenting style to adolescent behavior and found that authoritative parenting is related to academic success as measured by grades (Dornbusch et al. 1987) and not dropping out (Rumberger et al. 1990). Authoritative parents at once have high expectations, tend to encourage their child and talk with the child. They take the child's needs into account, and also provide a structured and directed environment in which behavioral standards are maintained and they give clear parental guidance in decision making.

The framework of Dornbusch and his colleagues relies heavily on work by Baumrind and others who study younger children. One of the useful insights of the work of Dornbusch is that parenting style, which is probably similar to the style used by parents when the child was younger, is also important when the child reaches adolescence.

Many of the results in this chapter are consistent with the work of Dornbusch and his colleagues. In particular, the variables measuring parent-child discussion of current school activities, restriction of television watching, and enrollment in music classes when combined in a model, probably measure aspects of authoritative parenting. We see the importance of communication with the child as well as of a structured and directed environment.

It is especially in the results for test score gain that the work of Baker and Stevenson (1986) becomes useful. Rumberger et al. (1990) focus almost exclusively on parenting practices within the home. Baker and Stevenson suggest that academic success can also be linked to the way parents interact with schools. They examine involvement indicating active management of the child's transition from eighth grade to high school, reasoning that a child's school career should be thought of as a management problem: "parents must . . . help [their child] move skillfully through the [school] organization" (Baker and

Stevenson 1986: 157). Thus this management component should be especially important for the student's achievement, and they show that such actions are positively associated with a student's grades.

Their work is not inconsistent with that of Dornbusch and his colleagues; rather they each focus on a different task of parenting. Dornbusch and his colleagues are concerned with parenting style within the home, and Baker and Stevenson focus on the relationship between parent and school. The results here suggest that for base-year test scores the factors related to parental involvement (and probably parenting style) in the home are most important.

The importance of parental ties to the school and community (especially actions suggesting that parents are in a position to manage the child's environment and probably school career) for predicting test score gains suggests that the needs of students may change as the child faces an increasing complexity of school options. Parenting that includes reaching out to schools and communities in an authoritative way may take on increasing importance. This is distinct from supportive activities like volunteering. The kind of parental involvement which is more closely associated with academic success is that in which the parent uses the school as a support to actively manage the student's environment.

Conclusion

Parents are involved with their children in different ways, and different forms of involvement are related to different measures of performance. Involvement in the home, especially in activities that do not have an obvious direct purpose, is most closely associated with initial test performance, possibly because of its relation to preparation. Involvement in school activities and in more directed, instrumental activities is associated with grades, especially when test scores are controlled. Involvement that has to do with managing the child's environment and school decisions appears to be related to gains in test scores.

In all cases, there is a strong association between involvement that is probably intervention in a problem and performance; however, the strongest relationships (relative to other variables in the models) are with student grades. Student grades may best reflect behavior problems to which parents respond, and parents may be most likely to respond to poor grades.

The differences between test scores, grades, and test score gains suggest the multifaceted nature of parent involvement. It may have different consequences depending on the kind of action taken; policy to encourage parental involvement should take these differences into account. If policymakers and educators wish to encourage gains in test performance by means of parental involvement programs, then a plan of action that encourages parent volunteerism may not be as effective as one that encourages parents to take a leadership role in decisions and problem solving over the course of the child's education.

NOTES

This research was supported by a Spencer Foundation Postdoctoral Fellowship from the National Academy of Education. The opinions expressed herein are those of the author and not of the sponsoring agency. An earlier version was presented at the annual meeting of the Sociology of Education Association in Asilomar, California, in February 1993.

1. Pairwise deletion was used to estimate all models, and all statistics are weighted. The weight and design effect are adjusted according to the recommendations in NCES (1992: 56–58).

2. In each of these models a performance measure (either grades or test scores) is controlled, but the results related to these gender differences remain essentially the same regardless of the control for performance.

3. Comparison of the regressions on eighth-grade test scores for the eighth-grade cohort and the panel sample show that the estimations are similar. The two main differences are that the coefficients for

attending an urban school and for PTO participation are each significant for the panel but not the entire sample.

   4. An important qualification of these results is that they are strongest for whites. Lamborn et al. (1991) find that the relationship of parenting style to academic success is not the same for nonwhite racial and ethnic groups. Baker and Stevenson's study included mothers from only one school; thus they had a homogeneous sample. Furthermore, others have found that parenting style is associated with SES and that the parenting described as actively authoritative and managing is associated with more highly educated professional parents (e.g. Lareau 1989).

REFERENCES

Baker, D.P., and D.L. Stevenson. 1986. Mother's Strategies for School Achievement: Managing the Transition to High School. *Sociology of Education* 59: 156–167.

Baumrind, D. 1978. Parental Disciplinary Patterns and Social Competence in Children. *Youth and Society* 9: 239–276.

Bradley, R.H., and B.M. Caldwell. 1984. The Relation of Infants' Home Environments to Achievement Test Performance in First Grade: A Follow-up Study. *Child Development* 55: 803–809.

Bryk, A., V. Lee, and P. Holland. 1993. *Catholic Schools and the Common Good*. Cambridge: Harvard University Press.

Coleman, J.S. 1988. Social Capital in the Creation of Human Capital. *American Journal of Sociology* 94: S95–S120.

Coleman, J.S., and T. Hoffer. 1987. *Public and Private Schools: The Impact of Communities*. New York: Basic Books.

Coleman, J.S., T. Hoffer, and S. Kilgore. 1982. *High School Achievement: Public, Catholic, and Private Schools Compared*. New York: Basic Books.

Dornbusch, S. et al. 1991. Community Influences on the Relation of Family Statuses to Adolescent School Performance: Differences between African Americans and non-Hispanic Whites. *American Journal of Education* 99: 543–567.

Dornbusch, S.M., P.L. Ritter, P.H. Leiderman, D.F. Roberts, and M.J. Fraleigh. 1987. The Relation of Parenting Style to Adolescent School Performance. *Child Development* 58: 1244–1257.

Epstein, J.L. 1986. Parents' Reactions to Teacher Practices of Parent Involvement. *Elementary School Journal* 86: 277–294.

———. 1991. Effects on Student Achievement of Teachers' Practices of Parent Involvement. In *Advances in Readings/Language Research*, vol. 5, ed. Steven B. Silvern. Greenwich, CT: JAI.

Fehrmann, P.G., T.Z. Keith, and T.M. Reimers. 1987. Home Influence on School Learning: Direct and Indirect Effects of Parental Involvement on High School Grades. *Journal of Educational Research* 80: 330–337.

Lamborn, S.D., N.S. Mounts, L. Steinberg, and S.M. Dornbusch. 1991. Patterns of Competence and Adjustment among Adolescents from Authoritative, Authoritarian, Indulgent, and Neglectful Families. *Child Development* 62: 1049–1066.

Lareau, A. 1989. *Home Advantage: Social Class and Parental Intervention in Elementary Education*. New York: Falmer.

Muller, C. 1991. Parental Involvement in the Education Process: An Analysis of Family Resources and Academic Achievement. Ph.D. Diss., University of Chicago.

Muller, C., and D. Kerbow. 1993. Parent Involvement in the Home, School, and Community. In *Parents, Their Children, and Schools*, ed. Barbara Schneider and James S. Coleman. Boulder, CO: Westview.

National Center for Educational Statistics (NCES). 1992. *National Education Longitudinal Study of 1988 First Follow-up: Data File User's Manual* (NCES 92–030). Washington, DC: U.S. Department of Education.

Rumberger, R.W., R. Ghatak, G. Poulos, P.L. Ritter, and S. Dornbusch. 1990. Family Influences on Dropout Behavior in One California High School. *Sociology of Education* 63: 283–299.

Stevenson, D.L., and D.P. Baker. 1987. The Family-School Relation and the Child's School Performance. *Child Development* 58: 1348–1357.

Appendix A:
Description of Parental Involvement Variables

Talk about current school experiences	Constructed from student responses to the questions "Since the beginning of the school year, how often have you discussed the following with either or both of your parents or guardians?" (1) "school activities," and (2) "things you've studied in class." Responses were summed to range from 0 to 4 and divided by two; thus the variable construct ranges from 0 to 2. The category for a single variable with the value of 0 represents a response category of "not at all," and a 2 represents "three or more times."
Talk about high school program	Constructed from student responses about the frequency with which the student has talked with the (1) father or (2) mother "about planning your high school program." If the student's response to the question about talking with the father was greater than zero, then the value for that response was used. Otherwise the response for talking with the mother was used. The range is 0 to 2, with 0 = "not at all" and 2 = "three or more times."
Frequency that parent checks homework	Student response to the question "How often do your parents or guardian check your homework?" Responses were coded so that a zero represents "never" and 3 represents "often."
Frequency that parents restrict TV	Student response to the question "How often do your parents or guardian limit the amount of time you can spend watching TV?" Responses were coded so that a zero represents "never" and 3 represents "often."
After-school supervision	Constructed from the student response to the question "On average, how much time do you spend after school each day at home with no adult present?" The variable is coded 4 = "more than three hours" and 0 = "none—never happens."

Extra music class	Parental response to the question "Has your eighth-grader attended classes outside of his or her regular school to study any of the following?—music" 1 = attended, 0 = not attended.
Friends' parents known	Summation of the parents of the child's friends known. Parents were first asked to identify the first names of up to five of the child's friends. Then parents were asked "whether you know the parents of that child." The variable was coded "yes" = 1, "no" = 0. Responses of "yes" were summed so range is 0 to 5.
Frequency that parents contact school	Constructed from parental responses to two questions: "Since your eighth-grader's school opened last fall, how many times have you or your spouse/partner contacted the school about each of the following?" (1) "Your eighth-grader's academic performance"; and (2) "Your eighth-grader's academic program for this year." Two response categories, "Three or four times" and "More than four times," are combined and the variables rescaled to range from 0 to 2, where 0 = none. The two responses are then summed to produce a variable ranging from 0 to 4.
PTO participation	Constructed from parental responses to the questions: "Do you and your spouse/partner do any of the following at your eighth-grader's school?" (1) "Belong to a parent-teacher organization"; (2) "Attend meetings of a parent-teacher organization"; and (3) "Take part in the activities of a parent-teacher organization." Responses are 1 = yes, 0 = no and summed for a variable ranging from 0 to 3.
Parent volunteers at school	Parental response to "Do you and your spouse/partner do any of the following at your eighth-grader's school?—Act as a volunteer at the school." Responses are 1 = yes, 0 = no.

4

Reading Reality More Carefully Than Books: A Structural Approach to Race and Class Differences in Adolescent Educational Performance

Roslyn Arlin Mickelson
Sumie Okazaki
Dunchun Zheng

During the past few years a great deal of media and scholarly attention has been directed at the educational achievements of Asian and Asian-American students. Cross-national comparisons report Asians excel far beyond their American counterparts. The academic feats of Asian-American students are said to surpass those of other minorities and Whites in the United States (Barringer, Takeuchi, and Xenos 1990; Caplan, Choy, and Whitmore 1991, 1992; Hirschman and Wong 1986; Stevenson and Stigler 1992). Stereotypical images of minority children abound in the popular and scholarly literature. Asian-Americans are considered "model minorities" (Kitano and Sue 1973). In contrast, minority children from African-American, Native-American, and Latino backgrounds are stereotyped as school failures. These stereotypes rarely differentiate among the various ethnic groups within Latino, African-American or Asian-American minority groups (Slaughter-Dafoe, Nakagawa, Takanishi, and Johnson 1990) nor are the important social-class differences within groups (Mickelson 1990; College Board 1993) systematically considered.

Putting aside for the moment the question of the accuracy of these depictions, it is indisputable that many Asian-American students excel in school, while African-American, Latino, and American-Indian youth are disproportionately found in the ranks of dropouts and lower achievers. One of the more intriguing questions to arise from these patterns is why so many Asian-American students who attend the same public schools as African-American, Latino, and White students succeed, while many of the other minority students do not. Explanations for diverse educational outcomes by race and ethnicity are wide-ranging. Until quite recently (Gibson and Ogbu 1991; Steinberg, Dornbusch, and Brown 1992) explanations advanced for the successes of Asian-American students were often quite different from those used to account for the success of Whites or the failures of African-Americans, thereby making systematic comparisons among various racial and ethnic groups difficult.

In this chapter we offer an approach that begins to account for the various achievement patterns observed among American adolescents of diverse class, racial, and ethnic backgrounds. We start with the notion that perceptions of the opportunity structure influence adolescents' achievement attitudes and behaviors. All adolescents share beliefs about the ideal role of education in achieving the American Dream. At the same time, all adolescents perceive more or less realistically the nature of the opportunities and barriers that await people like them once they leave school. This is to say, adolescents from racial and ethnic minority groups are aware that they will face barriers to success. These perceptions, then, are refracted through the prism of different worldviews. Parents, older siblings, and neighbors impart an ethnic group's received collective wisdom and lived experiences within the opportunity structure to children over the years of their childhood. This historically contingent worldview channels and shapes adolescents' educational attitudes and school performance.

We will try to explain how children from different minority groups who experience various forms of blocked opportunity can develop cultural frameworks with quite different educational strategies. For Asian-American students educational achievement continues to be a relatively functional strategy for upward mobility and success. For African-Americans, this is less true. Our approach, moreover, permits an exploration of class variation within each racial and ethnic group as well. As a result, we move toward a parsimonious theory which explains class, racial, and ethnic variations in school outcomes.

The Myth of the Amazing Asian-American

The topic of educational achievement among persons of Asian descent continues to captivate the interest of parents, policymakers, and academics. Comparative studies of American and overseas Asian educational practices and student achievement have been the basis for recommendations for reforming U.S. schools (e.g., Stevenson and Stigler 1992). Moreover, a host of studies have reported the extraordinary achievements of Asian-American students, particularly those of recent Asian immigrants to this country (Caplan, Choy, and Whitmore 1992; Gibson 1988; Hirschman and Wong 1986; Steinberg, Dornbusch, and Brown 1992; Walker-Moffat 1992). Because Asian-Americans have high levels of educational achievement and low rates of crime, mental health-seeking, and reliance on social services, they have earned the label of "model minority."

While noting the overall patterns of high achievement, it is important to note the heterogeneity among Asian-Americans in this country. Asian-American populations vary with respect to country of origin, social class, religion, language, generational status in the United States, cultural background, immigration status, and group history in this country. For example, while Japanese and Chinese immigrants began to arrive in this country in the 1800s (Takaki 1987, 1989), Korean laborers came to Hawaii at the turn of the century (Takaki 1993), and immigrants from Southeast Asia and the Pacific islands have accounted for a large part of the growth in the Asian-American population within the past decade (O'Hare and Felt 1991).

The diversity in the backgrounds of Asian-Americans is reflected in the variability in their income, employment status, and the educational level of adults (Barringer, Takeuchi, and Xenos 1990). For example, Southeast Asian households tend to have less than one-third of Filipino and Asian-Indian annual incomes (United States General Accounting Office 1990; United States Department of Commerce 1992a). Recent immigrant adults from Southeast Asia have been relatively uneducated; some are even illiterate in their own language (United States General Accounting Office 1990). As Barringer, Takeuchi, and Xenos point out, research indicates that although some Asian-Americans are better educated and better paid than many other American minorities, there still may be a gap between their relatively high educational levels and their resultant occupations and incomes. The literature suggests that compared to Whites, most Asian-Americans seem to be overeducated for the occupations they hold (p. 29). Asian-Americans receive 21 percent less income than Whites for each additional year of schooling (O'Hare and Felt 1991). The relatively weaker return from education is particularly true for Asian-American women. Barringer, Takeuchi, and Xenos (1990) caution that any assessment of "Asian success" requires consideration of national origin, recency of arrival for immigrants, nativity, gender, actual occupations, and sector of employment.

The model minority stereotype of Asian-Americans is, of course, a myth. Studies of Asian-American students' mental health have shown that Asian-Americans, particularly those who are foreign-born immigrants, tend to have higher rates of depression and other psychological adjustment difficulties than White students (Abe and Zane 1990; Gong-Guy 1987; Kuo 1984). Asian-American youth gangs have recently gained the attention of parents, the law enforcement system, and criminologists (Chen 1993; Walker-Moffat 1992).

The model minority myth also results from a popular misconception that all Asian-Americans are well educated. Educational attainment varies widely among Asian-Americans of different ethnic groups and generations in the United States (United States Department of Commerce 1992a; Schmidt 1992). Although the overall educational level of Asian-Americans is high, recent census data reveal that 20 percent of Asian-Americans over the age of twenty-five have less than a high school diploma (O'Hare and Felt 1991; United States Department of Commerce 1992a).

Myths even pervade teachers' perceptions of their Asian-American students, whom they describe as exemplary, delightful pupils, or model students (Caplan, Choy, and Whitmore 1991, 1992; Gibson 1988; Lee 1991). Nevertheless, not all Asian-American students do well in school, many struggle to achieve, and certain ethnic groups and recent immigrants have high rates of school failure and dropping out. Walker-Moffat (1992) points to the case of Hmong teenage girls, who often drop out of school in order to have children because of the crucial importance of bearing children to Hmong women's status. Furthermore, Walker-Moffat (1992) notes that one reason Hmong students get high grades is that they are placed in ESL and low-level, non-college-bound classes. Sue and Zane (1985) found that immigrant Asian-American college students study longer hours and take fewer classes in order to compensate for their lack of expertise with English. Moreover, they found that among foreign-born Asian-American students who get high grades, many also appear to suffer from the stress of immigration and other emotional distresses.

In addition, Asian-American students also face many of the same obstacles to school success that other minority students encounter. These may include racial and ethnic hostility from other students and teachers, overcrowded classrooms, and limited proficiency in English.

Despite these difficulties, recent comparisons of students from four ethnic groups showed that Asian-Americans excel academically not only in comparison to African-Americans and Latinos but also in comparison to Whites (Steinberg, Dornbusch, and Brown 1992). Similarly, Asian-American students are more likely to persist in school than students from other racial and ethnic groups (Gibson 1988, p. 360; United States Department of Commerce 1992a, 1992b). Recent College Board results indicate Asian-American students are more likely than students from any other ethnic group to score well on college entrance exams (1993).

Because the patterns of African-American and White adolescent education have been thoroughly explicated elsewhere, they need not be reviewed here. We now turn to various explanations that have been advanced for Asian-American high educational performance relative to both White and other minority students.

Explanations for Asian-American Achievement

Heredity

Genetic approaches to explaining the ethnic differences in academic achievement continue to be advanced by scholars like R. Lynn (1987) and J. P. Rushton (1988). Lynn (1987) compared IQ test scores of various racial groups to advance a genetic-evolutionary theory that Asians are superior to Europeans in intelligence, who are, in turn, superior to Africans. Rushton (1988) argued that selective evolutionary processes have resulted in differential reproductive strategies for human racial groups, which in turn are manifested in racial differences in brain size and intelligence. These works have been criticized for falling short in scientific methodology and for assuming that academic achievement can be largely explained by genetic factors in intelligence (Cain and Vanderwolf 1990; Sue and Okazaki 1990, 1991).

Even if genetic-evolutionary arguments for racial and ethnic differences in achievement are refuted, few scholars deny that heredity plays some part in individual differences in intelligence, which in turn may be reflected in academic achievement. However, evidence is not sufficient to conclude that the observed achievement differences among various ethnic groups in the United States are due to racial variations in intelligence. Moreover, the documented variations in performance within a particular ethnic group in different social contexts (Gibson 1988; Lee 1991) suggest social-structural factors have as powerful an influence as either culture or intelligence.

Cultural Values

The tension between the tendency to lump together all Asian-Americans and the tendency to recognize historical, linguistic, social-class, and cultural variability among them is reflected in cultural arguments advanced to explain their academic achievements. Undergirding the claim of commonalities in culture is the influence of Chinese culture and Confucianism on Japanese, Vietnamese, and Korean cultures (Lee 1991). For example, Nathan Caplan and his colleagues describe education and achievement, a cohesive family, and hard work as the "core" values that constitute the bedrock of refugees' culturally derived beliefs (Caplan, Choy, and Whitmore 1991). Uichol Kim and Maria B. J. Chun (1993) cite the commonalities across East Asian cultures which share a Confucian and Buddhist core. In a related vein, Harold Stevenson and James Stigler (1992) argue that Japanese and Chinese parents share certain assumptions that differ from those of other American parents about child development, the respective roles of schools and families in children's education, the influence of effort versus ability in school achievement, and the malleability of children.

The flip side of the cultural values coin is the claim that the values associated with the culture of poverty, which many poor African-Americans, Latinos, and American Indians allegedly share, undermine their children's achievement (Lewis 1966; Valentine 1971). While this older explanation of minority groups' underachievement has been soundly debunked, it has reappeared in a modern form as the current rhetoric about "at-risk" youth, whose parents ostensibly fail to provide them with the wherewithal to succeed in school. Both the claim of superior Asian cultural values which innoculate children against school failure and that of inferior values of children at-risk require greater empirical scrutiny.

Cultural values as explanations for Asian achievement are not new. Caudill and DeVos (1956) argued that the successful adaptation of Japanese immigrants to the United States was due to the compatibility between traditional Japanese and middle-class American values. Similarly, Sung (1967) argued that the Chinese values of hard work and scholarship enabled their children to succeed in American schools. John Ogbu (1983) notes that such explanations make no distinction between the behavior and values of peasants and those of higher classes within Chinese society, nor do they explain why children of immigrant peasants succeeded in their new countries while their peers in China did not. Stanley Sue and Sumie Okazaki (1990) also point out that cultural values do not operate in a vacuum. Similarly, Ogbu (1987) cautions that any microcultural analysis which fails to include the wider societal structure cannot show how educational performance is linked with the wider economy and polity. Moreover, different members of the same cultural groups have vastly different educational outcomes across diverse societal conditions; for example, Koreans in Japan are not noted for their academic achievement while those in the United States frequently excel in school (Gibson and Ogbu 1991; Lee 1991). Finally, it is not clear that the educational or family values of ethnic minorities who are less likely to succeed in school (e.g., African-Americans or Latinos) are, in fact, essentially different from those of ethnic minorities who do (e.g., Chinese-Americans).

Our approach to the central question of class, racial, and ethnic differences in school outcomes draws heavily from three recent conceptualizations of minority achievement. Although these models are grounded in different disciplines, they have in common the view that what adolescents do in school is influenced by their perceptions of the social world in which they live. The first has been proposed by cultural anthropologists, the second by psychologists, and the third by a sociologist. We turn to a description of each of these.

Cultural Model

John U. Ogbu (1991) begins with the proposition that all groups in society, minorities as well as the majority, have a cultural model or folk theory that serves as a framework for interpreting the world. His conception of a cultural model links an ethnic group's educational orientation to specific historical conditions of the group's incorporation into a majority society and the group members' lived experiences once in it. Importantly, each group's cultural model is connected to some degree with the historical record of relative academic success or failure of its members in the host society. Ogbu argues that what distinguishes educationally successful minority groups from less successful ones is the cultural model guiding their adolescents' school behavior. More successful minorities tend to be immigrant groups who compare returns from education and opportunities for advancement in the United States to those in their country of origin, or they look within the group and compare the social positions of group members with and without educational credentials. This within-group comparison supports a view of education as a credible strategy for advancement. In contrast, less successful students tend to be involuntary minorities who compare their returns from education to those of the majority group—a between-group comparison—find themselves wanting, and develop cultural models where, quite reasonably, education does not serve as a strategy for advancement.

Psychological Explanations

Psychologists Stanley Sue and Sumie Okazaki (1990) offer an approach to explain how differences in structures of opportunity contribute to high achievement among Asian-Americans and lower levels of educational success among other minorities. Their relative functionalism explanation posits that Asian-American students work harder and achieve academically because they regard educational achievement as the best means to success in this country for people like themselves. For Asian-Americans, compared to other ethnic minority and majority groups, other means to success are perceived as relatively less functional. Unlike African-Americans and Latinos, Asian-Americans in this country have very few models in political leadership roles, professional sports, or entertainment. Even in business, there may be a glass ceiling effect, whereby Asian-Americans are disproportionately underrepresented in management and other high-status positions within organizations. Therefore, education (and the professional opportunities it opens up) may be the most viable means of achieving success.

One problem with this explanation is that it presumes that a rational-choice model underlies Asian achievement but an irrational one shapes the behavior of other ethnic minorities like African-Americans and Latinos. In reality, education is also the most viable route to success for all ethnic and minority people. Medical school is still a relatively more functional route to success for African-Americans than is the National Basketball Association or Capitol Records. Far fewer African-Americans and Latinos will become upwardly mobile through sports and entertainment than through the professions and business. The question that remains unanswered by the relative functionalism hypothesis is why Asian-Americans continue to pursue education despite discrimination and limited opportunity while African-Americans and Latinos do not. Why are members of certain minority groups more likely to pursue education than others? Relative functionalism explanations tend to be circular: Those who pursue education believe it will work; those who don't believe it do not pursue education. Why some minorities believe education will work and others have lost faith in it as a strategy for success remains unclear.

Abstract and Concrete Attitudes

Roslyn Mickelson's (1990) investigation of the relationship between perceptions of various barriers and opportunities in the occupational structure and high school achievement of adolescents from diverse racial and ethnic backgrounds begins to answer these questions. She compared the attitudes toward education and school performance of about 1,200 African-American and White adolescents and proposes that all adolescents' attitudes toward education are multidimensional. The first dimension is composed of abstract attitudes that reflect the American Dream's account of the role of education and opportunities. An example of one of the beliefs which comprise the abstract attitude scale is: "Education is the key to success in the future." The second dimension is composed of concrete attitudes rooted in the material realities in which educational credentials may or may not be fairly rewarded. Unlike abstract attitudes, concrete attitudes actually channel and shape achievement behavior. An example of one of the beliefs which form the concrete attitudes scale is the statement, "Based on their experiences, my parents say people like us are not always paid or promoted according to our education."

Mickelson (1990) demonstrated that all students simultaneously hold abstract and concrete attitudes toward education, and that concrete, not abstract, attitudes vary by students' race and class. Importantly, she showed that concrete attitudes, but not abstract attitudes, contribute significantly to the explained variance in achievement among all students. Substantively, the study illustrated how perceptions of race and class stratification in the opportunity structure, which are, along with gender, large components of the social context of achievement, influence school outcomes.

Dunchun Zheng (1991) later analyzed the data from the Asian-American sample in Mickelson's (1990) study and compared them with those of the African-American students. He demonstrated that, like African-Americans and Whites, Asian-American students hold dual attitudes toward education. Asian-Americans' abstract attitudes were uniformly very positive and reflected the dominant ideology's account of education and opportunity, but did not correlate with their high school achievement. Similarly, their concrete attitudes correlated with high school achievement.

Mickelson, Okazaki, and Zheng (1993) reanalyzed her original data, this time including Asian-American, African-American, and White adolescents in the sample. The newly included Asian-American sample of approximately one hundred students is comprised predominantly of Japanese, Chinese, and Korean youth. Using the model of achievement Mickelson proposed in her earlier work (Mickelson 1990), they first submitted student attitude and achievement measures to three-way analyses of variance to test for mean differences by race, class, and gender. The second step of their analysis used a multiple regression analysis to determine the relative contribution of various social forces (abstract and concrete attitudes, parental education and occupation, gender, peer influence) to the prediction of achievement.

TABLE 4.1. Means of Attitudes and Achievement by Race, Ethnic, Class, and Gender Cohort.

Class	MALES			FEMALES		
	Black	Asian	White	Black	Asian	White
MIDDLE						
GPA	2.19	2.98	2.71	2.36	2.94	2.81****
Ascore	5.48	5.19	5.02	5.22	5.33	5.07*
Cscore	4.39	4.39	4.90	4.43	4.54	5.00****
(N)	56	37	224	84	34	241
WORKING						
GPA	2.10	2.72	2.42	2.29	2.94	2.74
Ascore	5.23	5.37	4.93	5.29	5.22	5.18
Cscore	4.20	4.23	4.55	4.19	4.10	4.81
(N)	138	18	109	140	15	93

* p <.05   **** p <.0001.

Note: Ascore and Cscore ranged from 1 to 7 where 1 indicated high and 7 indicated low endorsement of the relationship of education and opportunity.

The results of the analyses of variance of students' attitudes by their race-by-gender-by-class groups indicated all students hold very positive abstract attitudes toward education. Whites, African-Americans, and Asian-Americans share extremely positive beliefs about the role of education in achieving the American Dream. Moreover, both African-Americans' and Asian-Americans' abstract attitudes toward education were significantly more optimistic than those of Whites in similar class and gender cohorts (see Mickelson, Okazaki, and Zheng 1993 for details).

All held concrete attitudes toward achievement that reflected racial, ethnic, and class differences in opportunity. Middle-class Asian-Americans' concrete attitudes were almost identical to those of African-Americans; that is, the attitudes of both ethnic groups were significantly more pessimistic about schooling and opportunity than those of middle-class White students. Similarly, working-class Asian-Americans' concrete attitudes were virtually identical to those of working-class African-Americans, and both were significantly more pessimistic than those of working-class Whites about the value of education with respect to the opportunity structure.

The ANOVAS reveal significant racial, ethnic, and class differences in grade-point averages as well. In all comparisons Asians' grades exceeded those of Whites and African-Americans in comparable classes. With the exception of working-class Asian women, whose average grades were identical to those of their middle-class counterparts, the grades of all middle-class students exceeded those of students of the same race and gender in the working class.

The results of multiple regression analysis indicate that, as hypothesized, abstract attitudes do not contribute to the explained variance in achievement for individuals from any ethnic group. Concrete attitudes contribute significantly to the explained variance in all students' achievement, suggesting that the effects of family background and the opportunity structure are expressed through students' concrete attitudes. Those with more positive perceptions of the role of education in their future received higher grades. Not surprisingly, students whose friends plan to attend college achieved higher grades. Comparisons among the three racial and ethnic groups indicate that gender is an important factor in achievement among Blacks and Whites, but not among Asian-American students (see Mickelson, Okazaki, and Zheng 1993 for details).

Mickelson, Okazaki, and Zheng's (1993) finding that all students have both concrete and abstract attitudes indicates that while all youth are well socialized into the dominant ideology's account of education and opportunity, simultaneously all students are keenly aware of their place in the opportunity structure. Students from different classes and ethnic groups read reality more carefully than their textbooks, and what they learn shapes their school performance.

The abstract attitudes of both Asian-American and African-American students are higher than those of Whites in comparable gender and class cohorts. This comparability of abstract attitudes suggests Asian-American and African-American youth embrace, at least in theory, the optimistic account of the role of schooling in achieving the American Dream. As members of oppressed racial and ethnic minorities, it is not surprising that Asian-Americans and African-Americans hold concrete attitudes toward education that reflect the realities of racism in employment opportunities, pay, glass ceilings, and short career ladders. But while Asian-Americans' concrete attitudes are almost identical to those of African-Americans in their assessment of the racial, ethnic, and class barriers to realizing the American Dream, the grades of Asian-Americans are equal to or better than those of Whites of similar class and gender cohorts who ostensibly do not face comparable barriers. This pattern of school achievement among Asian-Americans in the face of likely discrimination is precisely what we wish to understand and explain. Why do Asian-Americans recognize job ceilings, limited career ladders, (and) the many extra hurdles they must face, yet continue to achieve in school? Why does knowledge of the limitations of the opportunity structure depress the achievement of many African-Americans? For possible explanations, we revisit Ogbu's (1991) conceptualization of cultural models, and Sue and Okazaki's (1990) relative functionalism.

Linking Cultural Frameworks and the Structure of Opportunity

In this section we will formulate a parsimonious explanation of the differences in school outcomes we and others have observed among Asian-Americans in comparison with African-Americans. The question is extremely important because both minorities are oppressed in American society. The nature of each group's oppression is historically contingent and varies with region, social class, and length of time in this society. Mickelson, Okazaki, and Zheng's data show Asian-American and African-

American youth are keenly aware of the racism and lesser opportunities they are likely to face once they leave school. Both groups are markedly different (as reflected in their concrete attitudes) in this regard from White students of the same social class. But the behavior of Asian-Americans and African-Americans in school is quite disparate, as evidenced by their grade point averages. On the whole, Asian-American youth much more often than African-American youth vigorously pursue education as the solution to this problem and work very hard in school, while African-American youth are much less likely to do the same.

We start with the concept of cultural model, which Ogbu (1991) describes as a group's understanding of how their society works and their respective place in that working order. Cultural models are influenced by two historical forces: (1) the group's initial terms of incorporation and (2) subsequent discriminatory treatment. Because of immigrant minorities' voluntary incorporation into the host society, they possess a dual frame of reference that allows them to develop or maintain an optimistic view of their future possibilities. They compare their current situation, not with that of the dominant group, but with that of kinfolk in their country of origin or that of other members of their group in the host society. In both contrasts, members of their group with more education fare relatively better than those with less. This leads them to the conclusion that, despite real barriers to opportunity, pursuing an education makes sense—at least more sense than not pursuing one.

Involuntary minorities, like African-Americans, Chicanos, and American-Indians, in contrast, have as a frame of reference only the dominant group of their society. The reasons for this lie in their long history of subordination and their collective memory of discriminatory treatment. They are more cynical about the promise of opportunity through education because they accurately perceive that, relative to the dominant group, they do not receive comparable (e.g., fair and equitable) returns for their hard work in school. This assessment, rooted in their material reality, leads to disillusionment, cynicism about schooling, and the reasonable conclusion that investing time, effort, and hopes for the future in education may not be the most rational choice (Mickelson 1993; Ogbu 1991).

Another aspect of immigrant minorities' responses to discrimination is their explanations for why they face ethnic barriers. They attribute the barriers to their newness, their language difficulties, and cultural traits that set them apart from the majority, as well as to racism and ethnic prejudice. Acquisition of educational credentials appears to be a rational response to unequal returns to education because voluntary minorities can continue to believe in the overall societal rules for advancement while they place the onus on themselves to acquire the cultural traits (such as standard English and educational credentials) perceived as necessary to compete in what they still believe to be an essentially meritocratic system. Involuntary minorities, like African-Americans, in contrast, perceive labor market discrimination as a relatively permanent barrier. They are more skeptical regarding the relative function of schooling, and of meritocratic assumptions of the links between education and status attainment alleged to underlie the opportunity structure (Mickelson 1993; Ogbu 1991).

Divergent cultural models provide an explanation of why education may be treated as relatively more functional to Asian-Americans than to African-Americans. Asian-American students in the sample studied by Mickelson, Okazaki, and Zheng (1993) share with African-American students concrete attitudes which reflect their awareness of the job ceiling, the glass ceiling, and other barriers to opportunity that members of oppressed minorities face in American society. However, significant differences in the groups' achievement suggest that each group interprets these barriers through a different cultural model. In the case of Asian-American youth, comparisons with uneducated Asian-Americans or with Asians in their country of origin likely reveal educational achievement to be a relatively more functional response to their future given the lack of alternatives. The cultural model of African-American youth refracts perceptions of their future through a lens littered with a history of broken promises and poor returns to education even for those who have education comparable to that of majority Whites. A rational response by African-Americans to perceptions of their place in the social order does not necessarily lead them to believe that education is relatively functional for them. Their assessment, rooted in their material reality, may lead to disillusionment, cynicism about schooling, and the reasonable conclusion that investing time, effort, and hopes for the future in the pursuit of education may not necessarily bring the promised rewards.

A final element in a group's cultural model is its social identity. Immigrants come to their host society with an identity forged prior to their immigration. They teach their children that they are different from the dominant group and that what sets them apart is valuable and worthwhile. Ogbu (1991) argues, therefore, that learning the host society's language and norms does not diminish the positive identity immigrants possess; it is additive rather than subtractive of their identity. In Margaret Gibson's (1988) words, voluntary minorities can accommodate themselves to the dominant culture without assimilating or losing their identity. The identities of involuntary minorities develop in opposition to the dominant group's culture under terms of subordination. For many involuntary minority youth an oppositional identity constitutes a way of believing and acting which affirms one as a bona fide member of a group which is different, indeed, in opposition to the cultural identity of the dominant group or the "oppressors." If studying hard in school is a dominant cultural norm, subordinate members may reject it. The work of Signithia Fordham and John U. Ogbu (1986) suggests how the oppositional identity of some adolescent African-Americans leads them to ridicule high achievers as "acting White."

The concept of an oppositional identity is hauntingly reminiscent of Paul Willis's (1977) description of working-class White "lads," whose identity centered around their resistance to schooling. In contrast to "earholes," who passively acquiesced to the school and its demands, the lads undermine and resist education. In his account of how English working-class White males end up with working-class jobs, Willis described how the lads' resistance to education is both fundamental to their social identity and rooted in the material realities of their male working-class culture, which, for example, considered books and reading to be "feminine" and, thus, to be avoided. But this behavior sealed their fate. Once they resisted schooling they consigned themselves to never rising above the factory floor if they were lucky enough to find a job in the deindustrialized English economy. Their resistance, just like the oppositional identity of African-Americans who refuse to study in order to avoid "acting White," forecloses any possibility that they will attain jobs other than low-wage, low-skill dead-end service jobs in the restructured, "information age" economy (Ray and Mickelson 1993).

The following story about a working-class African-American male illustrates how his understanding of the function of education was shaped by the barriers to success faced by his sister. Al Boswell was interviewed by the first author several years after he graduated from a Los Angeles area high school. He was selected to be interviewed because he had participated in Mickelson's (1990) survey of student attitudes several years earlier. Although highly intelligent, articulate, and hard working, he had, nonetheless, dropped out of college after three semesters and taken a job as a clerk in a truck rental agency. When asked, Al could not give a reason for dropping out of college. Twenty minutes later in the interview, he described how at the time he dropped out of college his older sister, who had graduated from college with a social work degree, had not been able to find work for two years. Discouraged, she applied abroad and eventually found a job in the Virgin Islands at much less pay than she would have received in Los Angeles and at a considerable distance from her family. At first Al did not connect his decision to drop out of school with his sister's difficulties in the labor market. Later in the interview he reflected upon the two events and speculated that, indeed, the two may well have been connected. That is to say, until the interview he had not been conscious of the effects of his sister's struggles on the cultural model through which he understood the meaning of education for people like him. When asked again how he understood his decision to leave college, Al responded with a shrug of resignation, "Why bother?"

If our conceptualization of the relationship between achievement and the dynamics of class, race, and opportunity is correct, we can expect voluntary minority students to begin to redefine the relative function of education with each succeeding generation in the United States. The longer an immigrant group has been in the United States, the longer will be its history of racial barriers and diminished returns for education, and the weaker will be its collective memory of education and opportunity in their country of origin. Over time, the cultural model of voluntary minorities may begin to resemble those of involuntary ones, and this may result in declining academic achievement for voluntary minorities.

While the evidence is far from complete, there appear to be some data on Japanese-Americans which lend support to this hypothesis. Barbara Schneider and her colleagues note that Japanese-Americans represent a unique group among East Asians (Schneider, Hieshima, and Lee 1994). Because of reduced immigration in the last five decades, Japanese-Americans are primarily an American-born English-speaking ethnic group; 72 percent of them are either third (Sansei) or fourth (Yonsei) generation (Takaki 1989). In their comparisons of middle-school Japanese, Chinese, Korean, and White student performance and parental attitudes toward education, Schneider, Hieshima, and Lee find evidence of acculturation among the Japanese. Japanese and White American parents shared similar attitudes toward education and Japanese student grades were lower than those of Korean or Chinese students but comparable to those of White youths. The researchers speculate that continued discrimination experienced by Japanese-American families in the labor force and by their children in school may undermine their commitment to education. Repeated incidents of racism may erode their confidence in the instrumental value, or relative functionalism, of education (Schneider, Hieshima, and Lee 1994).

Similarly, Alan Shoho (1992) reports that because of growing economic pressures among Hawaiians of Japanese descent, third-generation Japanese have reduced involvement in their children's education (compared to first- and second-generation parents). He notes that the ramifications of decreased parental involvement in the education of Yonsei (fourth-generation) youth has resulted in greater levels of social misbehavior and educational underachievement among them.

Conclusions

Most Asian-American youth, while keenly aware of limitations and discrimination they face, continue to believe that perseverance in school will bring more rewards than resisting education, albeit fewer than for Whites but certainly more than they could hope for without educational credentials. Aewon Park, a Korean-American high school senior in an advanced placement Chemistry class, explained her academic achievements. "My mom tells me that, yes, I'll have to be three times as good as Whites to become a doctor." This statement suggests that she knows she will face racism and discrimination, but she believes that eventually her hard work will compensate for them, and she can become a physician. Unlike African-American Al Boswell, she still has reasons to bother to acquire an education.

We have not answered the question of why immigrant cultural models develop differently from those of involuntary minorities. Is the reason purely historical? Is it because immigrant minorities have been here long enough for several generations of youth to be battered by blocked opportunity? How do immigrant minorities come to perceive education as a relatively more functional strategy than other approaches? To put it differently, why do numerous involuntary minorities depend on noneducational avenues like sports, entertainment, and politics more often than schooling as a relatively more functional strategy for success when education is a far more likely route to mobility? Any definitive explanation for racial and ethnic differences in school outcomes must begin to answer these questions.

A final set of questions that arises from the notion that cultural models are historically contingent concerns the future children of the young Korean woman, Aewon Park, who plans to be a physician despite the racial barriers she knows she will encounter. In thirty years, will her daughter think and act in a similar fashion? Or will her generation become cynical realists actively resisting schooling like so many Latino, American-Indian, and African-American adolescents today, who, after many generations, have come to doubt the value of education for achieving the American Dream?

NOTES

This research was supported by grants to the first author from the Social Science Research Council, the Foundation of the University of North Carolina at Charlotte, and the State of North Carolina. Preparation of this article was supported in part by the National Research Center on Asian American Mental Health and the National Institute of Mental Health.

REFERENCES

Abe, J.S., and N.W.S. Zane. 1990. Psychological Maladjustment among Asian and White American College Students: Controlling for Confounds. *Journal of Counseling Psychology* 37: 437–444.

Barringer, H.R., D.T. Takeuchi, and P. Xenos. 1990. Education, Occupational Prestige, and Income of Asian Americans. *Sociology of Education* 63: 27–43.

Cain, D.P., and C.H. Vanderwolf. 1990. A Critique of Rushton on Race, Brainsize, and Intelligence. *Personality and Individual Differences* 11: 777–784.

Caplan, N., M.H. Choy, and J.K. Whitmore. 1991. *Children of the Boat People: A Study of Educational Success.* Ann Arbor: University of Michigan Press.

———. 1992. Indochinese Refugee Families and Academic Achievement. *Scientific American* 266: 36–42.

Caudill, W., and G. DeVos. 1956. Achievement, Culture, and Personality: The Case of the Japanese American. *American Anthropologist* 58: 1112–1126.

Chen, Q. 1993. Homicide, Guns, Extortion, Theft Have Become Problems among "Model Minority Students"—Chinese Parents Should No Longer Focus on Report Cards Alone. *Chinese Daily News* (March 10): B2.

College Board, 1993. *1993 Profile of SAT and Achievement Test Takers.* New York: College Board.

Fordham, S., and J.U. Ogbu. 1986. Black Students' School Success: Coping with the Burden of "Acting White." *Urban Review* 18: 161–176.

Gibson, M.A. 1988. *Accommodation without Assimilation. Sikh Immigrants in an American High School.* Ithaca: Cornell University Press.

Gibson, M.A., and J.U. Ogbu. 1991. *Minority Status and Schooling: A Comparative Study of Immigrant and Involuntary Minorities.* New York: Garland.

Gong-Guy, E. 1987. *California Southeast Asian Mental Health Needs Assessment.* Oakland, CA: Asian Community Mental Health Services.

Hirschman, C., and M.G. Wong. 1986. The Extraordinary Educational Attainment of Asian Americans: A Search for Historical Evidence and Explanations. *Social Forces* 65: 1–27.

Kim, U., and M.B.J. Chun. 1993. Educational "Success" of Asian Americans: An Indigenous Perspective. Unpublished manuscript, Department of Psychology, University of Hawaii.

Kitano, H.H.T., and S. Sue. 1973. The Model Minority. *Journal of Social Issues* 29: 1–9.

Kuo, W.H. 1984. Prevalence of Depression among Asian Americans. *Journal of Nervous and Mental Disease* 172: 449–457.

Lee, Y. 1991. Koreans in Japan and the United States. In *Minority Status and Schooling: A Comparative Study of Immigrant and Involuntary Minorities,* ed. M. Gibson and J. Ogbu, 131–168. New York: Garland.

Lewis, O. 1966. The Culture of Poverty. *Scientific American* 215: 16–25.

Lynn, R. 1987. The Intelligence of the Mongoloids: A Psychometric, Evolutionary, and Neurological Theory. *Personality and Individual Differences* 8: 813–844.

Mickelson, R.A. 1990. The Attitude-Achievement Paradox among Black Adolescents. *Sociology of Education* 63: 44–61.

———. 1993. Minorities and Education in Plural Societies. *Anthropology and Education Quarterly* 24: 269–276.

———, S. Okazaki, and D. Zheng. 1993. Different Tales Told at the Dinner Table. Paper presented at the annual meeting of the American Educational Research Association, Atlanta, GA.

Ogbu, J.U. 1983. Minority Status and Schooling in Plural Societies. *Comparative Education Review* 27: 168–199.

———. 1987. Variability in Minority School Performance: A Problem in Search of an Explanation. *Anthropology and Education Quarterly* 18: 312–334.

———. 1991. "Immigrant and Involuntary Minorities in Comparative Perspective." In *Minority Status and Schooling: A Comparative Study of Immigrant and Involuntary Minorities*, ed. M.A. Gibson and J.U. Ogbu. New York: Garland.

O'Hare, W.P., and J.C. Felt. 1991. Asian Americans: America's Fastest Growing Minority Group. *Population Trends and Public Policy Report Number 19*. Washington, DC: Population Reference Bureau.

Ray, C.A., and R.A. Mickelson. 1993. Restructuring Students for Restructured Work: The Economy, School Reform, and Noncollege Bound Youth. *Sociology of Education* 66: 1–23.

Rushton, J.P. 1988. Race Differences in Behavior: A Review and Evolutionary Analysis. *Personality and Individual Differences* 9: 1009–1024.

Schmidt, P. 1992. Report Details Education and Income of Asian-Americans. *Education Week* (September 30): 11.

Schneider, B., J.A. Hieshima, and S. Lee. 1994. East Asian Academic Success: Family, School, and Community Explanations. In *The Development of the Minority Child: Culture In and Out of Context*, ed. P. Greenfield and R. Cocking. Hillsdale, NJ: Lawrence Erlbaum Associates.

Shoho, A.R. 1992. A Historical Comparison of Parental Involvement of Three Generations of Japanese-Americans (Isseis, Niseis, Sanseis) in the Education of their Children. Paper presented at the meeting of the American Educational Research Association, San Francisco, CA.

Slaughter-Dafoe, D., K. Nakagawa, R. Takanishi, and D. Johnson. 1990. Toward Cultural/Ecological Perspectives on Schooling and

Achievement in African- and Asian-American Children. *Child Development* 61: 363–383.

Steinberg, L., S.M. Dornbusch, and B.B. Brown. 1992. Ethnic Differences in Adolescent Achievement: An Ecological Perspective. *American Psychologist* 47: 723–729.

Stevenson, H.W., and J.W. Stigler. 1992. *The Learning Gap: Why Our Schools Are Failing and What We Can Learn From Japanese and Chinese Education.* New York: Summit Books.

Sue, S., and S. Okazaki. 1990. Asian-American Educational Achievements: A Phenomenon in Search of an Explanation. *American Psychologist* 45: 913–920.

———. 1991. Explanations for Asian-American Achievement: A Reply. *American Psychologist* 46: 878–880.

Sue, S., and N.W.S. Zane. 1985. Academic Achievement and Socioemotional Adjustment among Chinese University Students. *Journal of Counseling Psychology* 32: 570–579.

Sung, B.L. 1967. *Mountain of Gold: The Story of the Chinese in America.* New York: Macmillan.

Takaki, R. 1989. *Strangers from a Different Shore: A History of Asian Americans.* New York: Penguin Books.

———. 1993. *A Different Mirror: A History of Multicultural America.* Boston: Little, Brown.

———, ed. 1987. *From Different Shores: Perspectives on Race and Ethnicity in America.* New York: Oxford University Press.

United States Department of Commerce. 1992a. *The Asian and Pacific Islander Population in the United States: March 1991 and 1990.* Current Population Reports. Population Characteristics P20–459.

———. 1992b. *The Black Population in the United States: March 1991.* Current Population Reports. Population Characteristics P20–464.

United States General Accounting Office. 1990. Asian Americans: A Status Report HRD-90–36FS. Washington, DC: U.S General Accounting Office.

Valentine, C. 1971. *Culture and Poverty.* New York: Basic Books.

Walker-Moffat, W. 1992. The Hmong Paradigm: Why Asian Americans Succeed Academically, or Do They? Paper presented at the annual meeting of the American Educational Research Association, San Francisco, CA.

Willis, P. 1977. *Learning to Labor.* New York: Columbia University Press.

Zheng, D. 1991. Race and Gender Differences in Attitudes and Behaviors Related to Academic Achievement. Master's Thesis, Department of Asian American Studies, University of California, Los Angeles.

5

Dropouts: Definitions, Causes, Consequences, and Remedies

Gary Natriello

After more than a decade of neglect by policymakers, educators, and social scientists, culminating in its omission from consideration in the 1983 report *A Nation at Risk*, the problem of dropouts or early school leavers enjoyed renewed attention in the late 1980s and early 1990s. This was capped by the inclusion of "increasing the high school completion rate to 90 percent" as one of six national education goals (Bush 1991). Although the reasons for this revival of attention are no doubt many and varied (Rumberger 1987), three stand out in contemporary discussions of the problems of the U.S. educational system.

First and foremost, there is a growing realization that completion of high school is the absolute minimal educational level necessary to prepare youngsters for the vast majority of jobs in the modern economy. The extent to which this is true at present or will be in the future is still being debated (Ray and Mickelson 1993; Bailey 1991; Burke and Rumberger 1987), but the widespread belief that it is or shortly will be true focuses greater attention on the dropout problem.

Second, the increased pressure on U.S. schools to produce excellent performance in their students has been accompanied by a wary scrutiny of possible strategies for enhancing school performance measures that will exclude those students who will depress aggregate scores (McDill, Natriello, and Pallas 1986).

Thus there has been renewed interest in studying dropping out as a safety valve by which the educational system will respond to the growing pressure to produce only top-caliber graduates.

Third, the overrepresentation of students from some minority groups among school dropouts has contributed to the growing concern that large segments of the U.S. population may be isolated from mainstream social, political, and economic life if they fail to attain the basic education represented by the high school diploma. Even those who argue that we should expect some proportion of students to fail to complete high school are troubled by the fact that such failure is disproportionately distributed among racial and ethnic groups.

The renewed attention to the problem of students' dropping out of school before receiving a high school diploma has taken various forms as policymakers and educators have sought to understand the dropout problem and to reduce the numbers of students leaving school early. Efforts have been most vigorous in four areas: defining and enumerating dropouts, identifying those factors associated with early school leaving, understanding the consequences of dropping out for both individual students and the society at large, and developing and assessing programmatic efforts to reduce the numbers of students who leave school prior to graduation.

Defining and Counting Dropouts

Defining and counting dropouts appear to be rather straightforward tasks; indeed, laymen looking at the dropout problem typically assume that we have solid data on the number and nature of early school leavers. However, the problem of establishing a common definition and measurement strategy for identifying these students and calculating dropout rates may have received more attention from policymakers than any other, and while progress has been made, we still do not have procedures in place in all jurisdictions that permit us to count dropouts and compare dropping out rates across localities and states. A look at the problems inherent in this process reveals why this is still the case.

Definitions

There is no universally agreed upon definition of dropping out. Formulating one involves decisions about a number of factors, as evidenced by the definition offered by Morrow (1987: 49).

> A dropout is any student, previously enrolled in a school, who is no longer actively enrolled as indicated by fifteen days of consecutive unexcused absence, who has not satisfied local standards for graduation, and for whom no formal request has been received signifying enrollment in another state-licensed educational institution. A student death is not tallied as a dropout. The designation of dropout can be removed by proof of enrollment in a state-licensed educational institution or by presentation of an approved high school graduation certificate.

As is obvious from the elements of this definition, standards for designating dropouts may differ in terms of the period of absence required before classifying a student as a dropout, the standards for school completion, the nature of other educational institutions deemed acceptable for continuing one's education, and the procedures by which the institution the student leaves may be informed about subsequent enrollment in another acceptable institution. Perhaps less obviously, the process of classifying dropouts also depends on the school's procedures for adding students to the roll and the time in the student's life when the dropout count is taken. Jurisdictions which have more demanding criteria for adding students to the permanent roll may have lower enrollment and consequently lower dropout rates than those with less demanding enrollment criteria. Similarly, assessing dropout status when students are eighteen will produce larger numbers of dropouts than assessing dropout status at twenty-five, after students who left school have had opportunities to return either to regular high school programs or to alternatives such as GED programs. Thus the seemingly clear-cut notion of a dropout is anything but clear and consistent in practice.

Calculating Dropout Rates

The calculations used to discover dropout rates can be even more varied than the definitions used to classify a dropout. During the 1980s U.S. government statistics were used to generate several quite different dropout rates (Pallas and Verdugo 1986; Pallas 1989). Morrow (1987: 43) notes that three factors influence the mathematical computation of a dropout rate: the time frame during which the number of students who drop out is counted, the range of grade levels selected to represent a pool of possible dropouts, and the method of student accounting used—Average Daily Attendance or Average Daily Membership. Extending the time frame, limiting the range of grade levels to those in which school leaving is likely to occur (e.g., seventh to twelfth grades), and calculating the pool of students served by the school using Average Daily Attendance will all increase the dropout rate.

There are at least three distinctly different types of dropout rates reported in the literature (National Education Goals Panel 1991: 219). Event rates provide a measure of the proportion of students who drop out in a single year without completing a certain level of schooling. Status rates provide a measure of the proportion of the entire population of a given age who have not completed a certain level of schooling and are not currently enrolled. Because status rates include all those who have quit school at any time, they are much higher than event dropout rates for any one year. Finally, cohort rates provide a measure of dropping out among a single group or cohort of students over a given period of time.

Each of these rates offers advantages to particular decision makers at particular times. Event rates allow educational managers to monitor the tendency of students to leave school before graduation in a single year. Such rates might be useful in signaling changes in educational programs, and outside forces affecting the needs of a student population. Status rates can provide policymakers with a cumulative understanding of the impact of the set of educational opportunities available to a total population over a somewhat longer period of time. These rates might capture the effects not only of students leaving particular schools and programs at one point in their educational careers, but also the effects of their pursuit of alternative means of completing their high school education. Cohort rates allow educators to determine how many students leave school over a specified period of time, as well as how many seek alternate means of securing a diploma. These rates can provide insight into the stability of the group of students that schools and systems enroll.

The most recent movement to standardize the collection of data pertaining to dropouts has been prompted by the inclusion in the national education goals of the goal of a United States high school graduation rate of at least 90 percent by the year 2000 (Bush 1991). This has focused attention on the indicators used to assess the dropout rate, and the technical planning subgroup working in this area has recommended the development of a Voluntary State/Local Student Record System based on standard definitions of "high school completer" and "dropout" that would permit the tracking of students who transfer from one school district to another (National Education Goals Panel 1992). A key feature of this approach is the collection of data on all students in the system in order to fully understand the dropout problem. Moreover, an investigation into the current state of automated student information systems in individual states has highlighted the considerable problems of moving toward a reporting system based on uniform definitions and data-gathering methods and has stressed the need to develop an approach more closely tailored to the needs of individual states than to a single national mode (Pallas 1992). The National Education Goals Panel, along with the National Center for Education Statistics and the Council of Chief State School Officers, continues to work on the challenge of developing a sound indicator system for monitoring the dropout problem nationwide.

The Incidence of Dropping Out

The reported rates of dropping out vary widely, as do the methods used to develop such rates, making it difficult to compare rates from different systems. Policymakers interested in comparing dropout rates from two or more jurisdictions must be aware of system differences in defining early school leavers, in time periods during the school year when dropout data are collected, in data collection methods, in procedures for tracking youth no longer in school to determine whether they complete their education elsewhere, and in the methods used to calculate the dropout rate (U.S. General Accounting Office 1987). With these problems in mind, the rates considered here are best treated as illustrative.

For the United States as a whole, in 1990 about 347,000 students dropped out of grades ten to twelve, resulting in an event dropout rate of 4.1 percent of all high school students between the ages of fifteen and twenty-four. Event dropout rates for the United States have fallen from more than 6 percent in the 1970s to just above 4 percent in 1990 (Kaufman and McMillen 1991).

In 1990 about 3.8 million individuals between the ages of sixteen and twenty-four had left high school before completing their programs, about 12.1 percent of all individuals in this age group. Examination of the long-term trend in status dropout figures reveals that this rate is down slightly from that of about 14 percent that prevailed in 1973 (Kaufman and McMillen 1991).

Cohort rates for the United States are available from the two most recent national longitudinal studies of secondary school students, the High School and Beyond study and the National Educational Longitudinal Study of 1988. Data from the High School and Beyond (HS&B) study of the high school sophomore class of 1980 indicate that 17.3 percent of these students dropped out of high school by their senior year; by 1986 about 46 percent of these dropouts (8 percent of the original cohort) had returned to school. Data from the National Educational Longitudinal Study of 1988 show that 6.8 percent of the eighth-grade class of 1988 had dropped out between the eighth and tenth grades (Kaufman and McMillen 1991).

Of course there is considerable variation in dropout rates among different student groups and among different geographic areas. In 1990 the event dropout rate for the United States was 3.4 percent for White non-Hispanic students, 5.1 percent for Black non-Hispanic students, and 8.1 percent for Hispanic students. The rates for White and Black non-Hispanic students have declined in recent years; in 1980 the event dropout rate for White non-Hispanic students was more than 6 percent; that for Black non-Hispanic students was 8.4 percent. The Hispanic rate has shown no such improvement (Kaufman and McMillen 1991).

These racial and ethnic differences in the event rates are also reflected in the status rates. In 1990 the status dropout rate was 9.0 percent for White non-Hispanic students, 13.2 percent for Black non-Hispanic students, and 32.4 percent for Hispanic students. The White status rate had decreased from 12 percent and the Black rate from 22 percent in 1973; the Hispanic rate has shown no similar trend toward improvement.

There is also variation in dropout rates among urban and nonurban areas. In 1990 the event dropout rate for the United States was 5.7 percent in central cities, 3.2 percent in suburban areas, and 3.5 percent in nonmetropolitan areas. The corresponding status dropout rates were 15.5 percent, 9.9 percent, and 11.7 percent in the same year (Kaufman and McMillen 1991).

In New York City, the nation's largest school system, the systemwide event dropout rate is calculated for the population of students aged fourteen and over, including those in ninth grade in middle schools and in citywide special education programs. For the 1991–92 school year the systemwide event dropout rate was 6.2 percent, continuing a downward trend from 8.7 percent in 1988–89, 7.8 percent in 1989–90, and 6.8 percent in 1990–91 (Office of Research, Evaluation, and Assessment 1993).

The method of calculating cohort dropout rates adopted by the New York City schools assigns students to a particular graduating class based on their date of first-time entry into ninth grade. A cohort of 71,028 students was assigned to the class of 1992 based on their first-time enrollment in the ninth grade during the 1988–89 school year. As of June 30, 1992, analyses revealed that 16.2 percent of this cohort had dropped out of school. Another 29.7 percent of the class of 1992 was still enrolled in high school; these individuals had high school careers extending beyond the traditional four-year time frame. Those graduating constituted 35.5 percent of the class of 1992, and those obtaining the GED represented 3.2 percent of the class.

The remaining members of the cohort were either legitimately discharged (15.3 percent) or of unknown status (0.1 percent).

The cohort approach adopted in New York City permits the system to follow the school careers of students beyond the traditional four-year period following entry into high school and allows analyses which include students whose high school careers extend beyond four years. Dropout rates are calculated for the fourth, fifth, sixth, and seventh years since high school entry.

Considering only those students who are not legitimately discharged, the fourth-year dropout rates for the classes of 1989, 1990, 1991, and 1992 were 24.8 percent, 22.7 percent, 20.5 percent, and 19.1 percent, respectively. The declining trend in dropout rates is not mirrored in the fourth-year graduation rates. For these same classes, the fourth-year graduation rates were 45.1 percent, 44.4 percent, 46.4 percent, and 45.7 percent, respectively. These rates do not mirror the fourth-year dropout rates, largely because increasing percentages of each class remain enrolled at the end of four years.

Both dropout rates and graduation rates are higher after the fourth year. For the class of 1989 the dropout rate for those not legitimately discharged rises in the fifth year to 30.0 percent and then declines to 29.7 percent in the sixth year and 28.7 percent in the seventh year. For this same class the graduation rate rises to 61.5 percent in the fifth year, 63.5 percent in the sixth year, and 66.7 percent in the seventh year, as more students complete high school (Office of Research, Evaluation, and Assessment 1993, p. 41).

These rates indicate that the proportions of students leaving high school prior to graduation in an urban area such as New York City are declining, but that significant numbers of students continue to leave early. In addition, the lower dropout rates unaccompanied by higher graduation rates indicate that some students that remain are taking longer to complete high school. Finally, the analysis of graduation and dropout rates beyond the traditional four-year high school period reveals that graduation rates continue to climb as more students complete high school, and that dropout rates are higher beyond the fourth year as some of these students finally leave without a diploma.

Factors Associated with Dropping Out of School

The apparent causes of dropping out are many. At least three different classes of antecedents have been cited: characteristics of individual students, characteristics of their schools, and the wider environments in which both the students and the schools exist. Early efforts to identify the student characteristics associated with leaving school before graduation have been joined by more recent efforts to understand the role of schools in exacerbating or ameliorating the dropout problem, and by efforts to appreciate the impact of factors outside of schools.

Individual Student and Family Characteristics

Research on dropping out has often focused on individual student characteristics that can be linked to nonattendance at school. Among those identified have been racial and ethnic minority status, low socioeconomic status, poor school performance, low self-esteem, delinquency, a history of substance abuse, pregnancy, non-English-speaking families, single-parent families, and families that are less involved in the educational process (Ekstrom et al. 1986; Rumberger 1983, 1987).

More recent analyses have revealed interactions among these characteristics. For example, Ensminger and Slusarcick (1992) find that for males who performed poorly in first grade, having a mother with at least a high school education decreased the likelihood of their dropping out, while among females the presence of an intact mother-father family decreased the likelihood of dropping out. Forste and Tienda (1992) find that although childbearing during the teen years reduced the likelihood of high school completion, the impact of teenage pregnancy varied by ethnic group, with the graduation rates of Hispanic mothers being most negatively affected and those of black teen mothers being least negatively affected.

Several theories have been offered to explain the relationships between student characteristics and dropping out. Some investigators have argued that accelerated role transitions or the earlier-than-normal assumption of new adult roles such as worker or parent lead to increased likelihood of dropping out

(Pallas 1986). Such new roles are seen as conflicting with the individual's ability to fulfill the responsibilities associated with the role of student. This would explain the negative effects of individual factors such as teen pregnancy, teen marriage, early employment, and substance abuse.

Other investigators have suggested that the degree of perceived articulation between school participation and performance and student futures is an important determinant of school continuation. Students who believe that their participation and performance in school is connected to adult futures that they value are more likely to continue in school (Stinchcombe 1964; Natriello and Dornbusch 1984). For students to perceive such articulation they must both view completion of high school as necessary for access to certain adult positions and consider those adult positions valuable. In addition, for students to remain in school they must envision themselves as being capable of completing school. When students have no exposure to adult positions that they deem valuable, when the adult positions that they value do not have educational requirements, or when they do not perceive themselves as capable of completing school, they are less likely to persist. Students who are isolated in racial or ethnic minority groups and in low socioeconomic status groups or who are from single-parent families may have less exposure to desirable adult positions with educational requirements. Students with histories of poor academic performance or low self-esteem may not view themselves as capable of completing school. Of course, when more than one of these factors is present the articulation between completion of school and desirable adult futures becomes even weaker.

School Characteristics

In recent years there has been increased interest in determining which characteristics of schools and school programs lead students to drop out. Some analysts argue that an overemphasis on the relationships between individual characteristics and dropping out in effect places blame for early school leaving on students who may be victims of educational systems which do not meet their needs (Wehlage and Rutter 1986).

One aspect of school operations that has a clear and conscious relation to the dropout problem is the degree to which school personnel act to remove students from school. Early examinations of the issue revealed that large numbers of students are expelled or suspended from school (Children's Defense Fund 1974). More recently, researchers have observed personnel in crowded urban schools pushing students out (Fine 1991). A more broad-based examination of this issue in New York City high schools has revealed that although discharge practices do vary across schools as the result of school-level policies and variation in staff behavior, the discharge process is rational; that is, students with poor attendance and performance in courses are more likely to be discharged, as are older students who have been retained in grade (Riehl 1993). Nonetheless, some schools more actively push students out than others.

Dropping out has been linked to more general features of school organization and student experience within schools. Such features may be considered along two dimensions. First, it has been observed that schools often present students with limited opportunities for academic success. Indeed, studies have found that one of the factors most strongly correlated with early school leaving is lack of academic success in school (Wagenaar 1987). Students who more often get low grades, fail subjects, and are retained in grade have a much greater chance of leaving school before completing high school. Students who have difficulty meeting the academic demands of the school tend to leave early rather than continue in the face of the frustration they often experience in trying to obtain good grades. Among the reasons most often given for dropping out of school by students in the National Educational Longitudinal Survey who left between the eighth and tenth grades were "failing in school," noted by 40 percent, and "could not keep up with schoolwork," noted by 31 percent (McMillen et al. 1992).

A second dimension of school organization and student experience in school associated with dropping out is the limited availability of positive social relationships and the lack of a caring, supportive climate. Positive supportive relationships between teachers and students and among students and a climate of shared purpose and concern have been identified as key elements of efforts to hold students in schools (Wehlage et al. 1989). Among the reasons for dropping out noted by students in the National Educational Longitudinal Survey who dropped out between the eighth and tenth grades, 51 percent reported that they did not like school and 23 percent reported that they did not belong (McMillen et al. 1992).

Schools differ in the degree to which they provide welcoming and supportive social environments for students, and these differences are often related to structural characteristics of schools. Bryk and Thum (1989) find that high levels of structural differentiation and weak normative environments in schools lead to higher dropout levels. As Legters et al. (1992) point out, organizational features conducive to positive relations, such as small school size, a limited number of different teachers assigned to each student, and teachers who have been trained to focus on the needs of students, are found more often in elementary schools than in middle and high schools. The latter often feature larger size, departmentalized structures which expose students to different teachers for each subject, teaching roles defined in terms of subject matter expertise as opposed to interest in students, low levels of involvement with students' families and communities, and tracking of students on the basis of academic preparation—all attributes which present barriers to the establishment and maintenance of positive social relationships and a climate of shared purpose and concern.

Environmental Aspects

In addition to the characteristics of students and the conditions which they encounter in school organizations, the larger environment in which students and schools are embedded affects dropout rates. Such environmental aspects may be considered from two perspectives: the degree to which schooling is perceived as relevant to students' lives outside of school, and the degree to which external conditions are supportive of students' continued participation in school.

The relevance of schooling to the lives of students is a product of both the content of schooling and the nature of students' lives outside of school. Schooling may be perceived as less relevant when students see no connection between the curriculum of the school and the culture of their families and neighborhoods, or when the values presented and demanded by the school are at variance with those of their peer groups (Legters et al. 1992).

Conditions outside of school may fail to provide support for regular school attendance and continuance in school. Conditions which contribute to leaving school early include a variety of personal, familial, and community problems, such as teenage pregnancy, alcohol and drug abuse, delinquent gang membership, family violence and child abuse, family social or financial needs requiring students to be at home or to work, and socially disorganized communities with high rates of crime (Natriello et al. 1990). Fourteen percent of students who dropped out between the eighth and tenth grades in the National Educational Longitudinal Survey reported that they dropped out because they could not work and go to school at the same time, 9 percent dropped out because they had to support a family, and 14 percent reported dropping out because they became a parent (McMillen et al. 1992).

Consequences of Dropping Out of School

The consequences of dropping out of school vary depending on a number of factors, including the nature of the activities students engage in after leaving school and the nature of their social and economic environment. At one time in our nation's history, there were attractive positions in the workforce open to individuals who had not completed high school. Such positions are less common today, and there is, moreover, a growing perception that dropouts will increasingly be at a disadvantage in the future job market (National Academy of Sciences 1984).

Cognitive Consequences

Although appropriately controlled studies of the impact of dropping out on cognitive growth are rare, some evidence exists that leaving school early has a negative impact. Alexander, Natriello, and Pallas (1985) examined the performance of sophomores in the High School and Beyond Study who stayed in school until the twelfth grade and of those who dropped out before the twelfth grade. When they controlled for prior achievement differences, they found that the cognitive skills of youngsters who stayed in school improved more than those of dropouts over this period of time. Moreover, the advantage for those who stayed accrued across a rather broad range of skills.

Economic and Social Consequences

The lower levels of cognitive growth experienced by dropouts appear to be reflected in less success in the job market. Dropouts are more likely than those who complete high school both to be unemployed and to earn less when they are employed. In October 1990, 67.5 percent of recent high school graduates who did not enroll in college were employed, while only 46.7 percent of recent high school dropouts had jobs. This gap between employment rates for graduates and dropouts has grown slightly over the past thirty years (U.S. Department of Education 1992), lending support to the claim that dropouts face an increasing disadvantage in the U.S. labor market.

The earnings of dropouts continue to lag behind those of high school graduates. In 1990 White male dropouts earned 27 percent less than White male high school graduates, and Black male dropouts earned 28 percent less than Black male high school graduates. The income disadvantage for females was even greater: In 1990 White female dropouts earned 44 percent less than White female high school graduates, and Black female dropouts earned 56 percent less than Black female graduates. These disparities in earnings have increased over the past twenty years (U.S. Department of Education 1992).

This pattern of relatively less success in the job market results in reductions in personal income as well as reductions in national income and government revenues. Moreover, individuals who leave school early are more likely to engage in criminal activity, have poorer health and lower rates of political participation, and simultaneously require more government services such as welfare and health care assistance (Rumberger 1987).

Programmatic Remedies to Prevent Dropping Out

The recognition of the human and economic costs of early school leaving have led to the development of a range of efforts designed to prevent students from dropping out before completing school, efforts that have intensified over the past decade as the dropout problem has come to occupy a more central position in the school reform movement. Dropout prevention programs make use of the growing base of knowledge about the individual characteristics associated with leaving school early to identify potential dropouts and target them for special services. Programs to ameliorate the dropout problem are typically designed with the multiple causes of dropping out in mind, both those associated with schools and those associated with the larger environments in which schools and students function.

School-Based Remedies

School-based remedies have included programs and practices designed to enhance the prospects for academic success as well as those designed to strengthen the positive social relationships and climate of support and concern students will find in school. Approaches to the former have included improving diagnosis of student's skills and abilities and tailoring instruction to the needs of individual students, altering evaluation processes to recognize student effort, restructuring school tasks to draw on a wider range of human abilities, enhancing remediation programs to use more time for instruction during the school year and during the summer, and increasing the use of tutoring and technology to deliver instruction to students whose needs are not met by regular classroom instruction (Natriello et al. 1990). Examples of programs designed to promote the academic success of students in schools include the federal Chapter I program designed to provide additional assistance to disadvantaged students, early childhood programs such as preschools and kindergartens which aim to give at-risk students an academic boost, and the Summer Training and Education Program (STEP), which furnishes underachieving fourteen- and fifteen-year-old students from low-income families extra academic help, life skills, and work experience during two consecutive summers (Legters et al. 1992).

Efforts to improve prospects for positive social relationships and a shared climate of concern for students have included mentoring programs to link adults and students, house plans in large schools to create smaller environments in which a limited number of students and teachers work on the entire academic program, and the use of older students as peer mentors for younger students (Natriello et al. 1990). Mentoring programs involve adult volunteers from the community and institute homeroom advisory periods in which teachers meet with students several times each week to discuss educational, career, and personal issues. House plans such as the "schools within schools" created in New York City, the "house" systems involving groups of 250 high school students in Columbus, Ohio, and the "academic units" with special vocational-academic emphases in Philadelphia high schools are becoming more prevalent. Programs which use peer support often assign older students to serve as advisors to younger students, either in the same school or in assisting with the transition from a lower school to the new school (Legters et al. 1992).

Environmental Remedies

Programs have also been developed to ameliorate some of the negative environmental factors affecting persistence in school. Attempts to solve the problem of the lack of relevance of school to the current and future lives of students have included revising the curriculum to relate it more clearly to real world experience, updating vocational education programs in order to integrate academic and vocational skills with clear links to the world of work, creating multicultural curricula with materials and role models from the students' own ethnic or cultural backgrounds, and instituting programs which make more salient the link between schooling and work. Examples of curriculum projects that focus on real world experiences are the Action Learning Projects in Minnesota's Project Together, the Foxfire student publishing experience, and community service projects (Kakassy 1980; Wigginton 1989; Nettles 1991; Legters et al. 1992). The thirty-three-school project of the Vocational Education Consortium of the Southern Regional Education Board is a prominent effort to integrate academic and vocational skills (Bottoms and Presson 1989). States and local school districts around the country are moving toward multicultural curricula, though not without controversy. Career Passport, one example of recent efforts to make more salient and meaningful the links between performance in school and success in the workplace, assists students in documenting their skills in work-related areas (Charner 1988; Legters et al. 1992).

Strategies dealing with unsupportive environmental conditions have attempted to develop new relationships between families and schools and to integrate educational and human services to address the social and economic problems which impede progress through school (Legters et al. 1992). Epstein (1992) notes that efforts to strengthen the relationships between families and schools can take a variety of forms—school assistance for families, school communication with families about school programs and student progress, the use of parent volunteers in the school, the involvement of parents in learning activities at home, and the involvement of parents in various school governance activities. For example, New Jersey's School-Based Youth Services Program, an integrated services approach, offers a wide array of human and educational services such as employment counseling, training, and placement, drug and alcohol abuse counseling, family crisis counseling, academic counseling, health services, recreational opportunities, summer and part-time job development, and referrals to other health and social service providers (Legters et al. 1992).

Prospects for Educational Policy on School Dropouts

In the years ahead, policymakers, educators, and social scientists will likely continue to center policy, practice, and research around the four areas of activity identified in this chapter. Not only do questions remain in each area, but progress in each is necessary if we are to address the dropout problem comprehensively and effectively. Improved identification and enumeration of dropouts are essential to development of more fine-grained understandings of the reasons why students leave early. Better understanding may lead to more success in early identification of potential dropouts and more careful monitoring of their progress in school.

Recent advances in our knowledge of the consequences of dropping out have served primarily to fuel concerns about leaving school early as an educational and social problem. Better understanding of these consequences will continue to have this effect but may also lead to a greater appreciation of those situations in which dropping out is likely to have less pernicious effects for individuals and for society, providing insights that will help us to design paths and opportunities for dropouts to continue their education and participate more fully in the social, political, and economic mainstream.

Finally, advances in our understanding of the impact of efforts to prevent dropping out are necessary not only to guide us in the refinement of such programs but also to suggest approaches that are unlikely to be successful even if refined. Moreover, the limited success of targeted dropout prevention efforts together with the growing pressure to rethink the fundamental nature of schools is likely to lead to programmatic efforts more integrated with the overall school program. Just as researchers attempting to develop indicators of the extent of the dropout problem have discovered a need for more broad-based data collection on the performance and persistence of all students, so too educators are concluding that broad-based efforts to make schools better for all students may mitigate the need for special efforts to prevent dropping out.

REFERENCES

Alexander, K., G. Natriello, and A. Pallas. 1985. For Whom the School Bell Tolls: The Impact of Dropping Out on Cognitive Performance. *American Sociological Review* 50: 409–420.

Bailey, T. 1991. Jobs of the Future and the Education They Will Require: Evidence from Occupational Forecasts. *Educational Researcher* 20: 11–20.

Bottoms, G., and A. Presson. 1989. *Improving General and Vocational Education in the High Schools*. Atlanta, GA: Southern Regional Education Board.

Bryk, A.S., and Y.M. Thum. 1989. The Effects of High School Organization on Dropping Out: An Exploratory Investigation. *American Educational Research Journal* 26: 353–383.

Burke, G., and R.W. Rumberger. 1987. Introduction. In *The Future Impact of Technology on Work and Education*, ed. Gerald Burke and Russell W. Rumberger, 1–12. London: Falmer.

Bush, G. 1991. *American 2000: An Education Strategy*. Washington, DC: U.S. Department of Education.

Charner, I. 1988. Employability Credentials: A Key to Successful Youth Transition to Work. *Journal of Career Development* 15: 30–40.

Children's Defense Fund. 1974. *Children Out of School in America*. Washington, DC: Washington Research Project.

Ekstrom, R.B., M.E. Goertz, J.M. Pollack, and D.A. Rock. 1986. Who Drops Out of High School and Why? Findings from a National Study. *Teachers College Record* 87: 356–373.

Ensminger, M.E., and A.L. Slusarcick. 1992. Paths to High School Graduation or Dropout: A Longitudinal Study of a First-Grade Cohort. *Sociology of Education* 65: 95–113.

Epstein, J.L. 1992. School and Family Partnerships. In *Encyclopedia of Educational Research*, ed. Marvin C. Alkin, 6th ed., 1139–1151. New York: Macmillan.

Fine, M. 1991. *Framing Dropouts: Notes on the Politics of an Urban High School*. Albany: State University of New York Press.

Forste, R., and M. Tienda. 1992. Race and Ethnic Variation in the Schooling Consequences of Female Adolescent Sexual Activity. *Social Science Quarterly* 73: 12–30.

Kakassy, A. 1980. Project Together: An Opportunity for Positive Student Involvement, Influence, and Change. *Social Studies Review* 20: 13–19.

Kaufman, P., and M.M. McMillen. 1991. *Dropout Rates in the United States: 1990.* Washington, DC: National Center for Education Statistics, U.S. Department of Education.

Legters, N., E.L. McDill, and J. McPartland. 1992. *Responses to the Challenge of Educating At-Risk Youth.* Center for Research on Effective Schooling for Disadvantaged Students, The Johns Hopkins University, Baltimore, MD.

McDill, E.L., G. Natriello, and A.M. Pallas. 1986. A Population at Risk: Potential Consequences of Tougher School Standards for Student Dropouts. *American Journal of Education* 94: 135–181.

McMillen, M.M., P. Kaufman, E. Hausken, and D. Bradby. 1992. *Dropout Rates in the United States, 1991.* Washington, DC: National Center for Education Statistics, U.S. Department of Education.

Morrow, G. 1987. Standardizing Practice in the Analysis of School Dropouts. In *School Dropouts: Patterns and Policies,* ed. Gary Natriello, 38–52. New York: Teachers College Press.

National Academy of Sciences. 1984. *High Schools and the Changing Workplace: The Employers' View.* Report of the Panel on Secondary School Education for the Changing Workplace. Washington, DC: National Academy Press.

National Education Goals Panel. 1991. *The National Education Goals Report: Building a Nation of Learners.* Washington, DC: U.S. Government Printing Office.

——. 1992. *The National Education Goals Report: Building a Nation of Learners.* Washington, DC: U.S. Government Printing Office.

Natriello, G., E.L. McDill, and A.M. Pallas. 1990. *Schooling Disadvantaged Children: Racing Against Catastrophe.* New York: Teachers College Press.

Natriello, G., and S. Dornbusch. 1984. *Teacher Evaluative Standards and Student Effort.* New York: Longman.

Nettles, S.M. 1991. Community Involvement and Disadvantaged Students: A Review. *Review of Educational Research* 61: 379–406.

Office of Research, Evaluation, and Assessment. 1993. *The Cohort Report: Four-Year Results for the Class of 1992 and Follow-Ups of the Classes of 1989, 1990, and 1991 and the 1991–92 Annual Dropout Rate.* New York: New York City Board of Education.

Pallas, A.M. 1986. *The Determinants of High School Dropout.* Baltimore, MD: Center for the Social Organization of Schools, The Johns Hopkins University.

———. 1989. Conceptual and Measurement Problems in the Study of School Dropouts. In *Research in the Sociology of Education and Socialization,* vol. 8, ed. R. Corwin and K. Namboodiri, 87–116, Greenwich, CT: JAI.

———. 1992. *Statewide Student Record Systems: Current Status and Future Trends.* Washington, DC: National Education Goals Panel.

Pallas, A.M., and R.R. Verdugo. 1986. *Measuring the High School Dropout Problem.* Washington, DC: Center for Statistics, U.S. Department of Education.

Ray, C.A., and R.A. Mickelson. 1993. Restructuring Students for Restructured Work: The Economy, School Reform, and Non-college-bound Youths. *Sociology of Education* 66: 1–20.

Riehl, C. 1993. Determinants of Student Discharge from High School: The Effects of Organizational Environment and Student Performance. Ph.D. Dissertation, Teachers College, Columbia University.

Rumberger, R.W. 1983. Dropping Out of High School: The Influences of Race, Sex, and Family Background. *American Educational Research Journal* 20: 199–220.

———. 1987. High School Dropouts: A Review of Issues and Evidence. *Review of Educational Research* 57: 101–121.

Rumberger, R., G. Poulos, R. Ghatak, P.L. Ritter, and S.M. Dornbusch. 1990. Family Influences on Dropout Behavior in One California High School. *Sociology of Education* 63: 283–299.

Stinchcombe, A. 1964. *Rebellion in a High School.* Chicago: Quadrangle Books.

U.S. Department of Education, National Center for Education Statistics. 1992. *The Condition of Education, 1992.* Washington, DC: U.S. Government Printing Office.

U.S. General Accounting Office. 1987. *School Dropouts: Survey of Local Programs.* Washington, DC: U.S. Government Printing Office.

Wagenaar, T. 1987. What Do We Know about Dropping Out of High School? In *Research in the Sociology of Education and Socialization,* vol. 7, ed. R. Corwin, 161–190. Greenwich, CT: JAI.

Wehlage, G.G., and R.A. Rutter. 1986. Dropping Out: How Much Do Schools Contribute to the Problem? *Teachers College Record* 87: 374–392.

Wehlage, G.G., R.A. Rutter, G.A. Smith, N. Lesko, and R. Fernandez. 1989. *Reducing the Risk: Schools as Communities of Support.* London: Falmer.

Wigginton, E. 1989. Foxfire Grows Up. *Harvard Educational Review* 59: 24–29.

Changing Definitions of Education

The educational system is fairly uniform in its structure and function; across the United States there are clearly identifiable school buildings organized by grades where certified teachers teach standardized curricular topics to registered students. This prevailing model of education is frequently dismissed by scholars and policymakers as irrelevant for society's needs in the twenty-first century. In fact, there are increasing calls for a total reorganization of American elementary and secondary education. The authors in this section critique several different theoretical approaches and programs designed to radically alter the goals, assumptions, and conventional definitions of education and its relation to society. Focusing on a variety of theories about how schools can be improved, the authors in this section assess the connections between theoretical concepts and practical applications. Particular attention is given to the recent suggestions that families, neighborhood associations, businesses, and child advocacy groups should have broader authority and control in local decision making about education.

Theory and Educational Change

Rolland Paulston begins this section with an extensive review of educational theories typically used to analyze educational change. Employing a new analytic method, which he terms "perspectivism," he critiques and analyzes the differences these studies have made in promoting new knowledge and practice. Paulston argues that new ways of examining text are needed to accommodate the seemingly incomprehensible research

129

languages that scientific communities create in order to infuse new ideas and educational practices into scholarly and public debates. The increasing size and scope of the educational enterprise has resulted in a lack of consensus about basic notions of reality and knowledge. Given the widespread ontological and epistemological pluralism evident in scholarly work since the 1950s, Paulston believes that it is imperative that we translate cultural codes and modernist vocabularies to postmodern ways of seeing and representing educational change.

To accomplish this objective, Paulston uses discourse analysis and phenomenographic methods to examine how educational change is defined in comparative and international education texts. Paulston relies on Barthes's concept of text (1979), which interprets text in relation to other texts rather than in relation to their authors. Rather than linking authors to their work, he links writing to field, which allows relating written works from one intercultural field to another. Paulston's approach to this process is phenomenographic, that is, a text or body of work is condensed into points and then placed in relation to other points. These points are then mapped at both macro and meso levels of social reality.

Applying these procedures, Paulston examines sixty exemplary studies that have been used to explain educational change theory and practice over the last thirty years. Paulston categorizes textual knowledge into three periods: (1) the 1950s and 1960s, when functionalist and positivist perspectives dominated the discourse; (2) the 1970s and 1980s, when radical functionalists and radical humanists challenged earlier approaches; and (3) the 1990s, when heterogeneous paradigms of competing cultural clusters are proliferating. These periods are then placed in topological maps which contrast two interdependent planes of reality—the form of text orientations within the field and the genealogy and direction of knowledge relations. Such methods, he maintains, allow for greater clarity and understanding of differences and a greater contribution of ideas to general discourse than do more traditional modes of text analysis.

A new theory that has gained prominence among scholars and practitioners is a theory of how intelligence is conceptualized. The classic view is that intelligence represents a single underlying capacity which enables abstract reasoning. Today this perspective is widely discredited among psychologists and others interested in the development of cognitive thinking. Rejecting the unitary view of intelligence, Howard Gardner, a developmental psychologist, defines intelligence as the ability to solve problems or fashion products valued in a particular cultural setting (Gardner 1993). Gardner maintains that there are seven relatively autonomous intelligences: linguistic, musical, logical-mathematics, spatial, bodily-kinesthetic, interpersonal, and intrapersonal. Each individual has all of these intelligences and combines and blends them in different ways when solving problems and learning new knowledge.

Gardner's theory appears to have considerable allure for school districts intent on revamping their existing curriculum to accommodate newer conceptions of learning. Several of these districts have attempted to incorporate some of Gardner's concepts of intelligence into their schools' curricula and teacher instructional practices. These grassroots efforts are quite different from other school reform efforts. They do not have the standard technical and social supports, including established models for implementation, pedagogical guidelines, or specially trained key field staff, to help the schools adopt principles of multiple intelligence (MI) in classrooms. Instead, school staff who independently decide to use Gardner's theory chart their own course for reform. Why his theory is especially attractive to schools and how school staff proceed to act on their interpretation of the theory is the focus of the chapter by Mindy Kornhaber and Mara Krechevsky.

In their investigation of nine school sites that adopted Gardner's theory, Kornhaber and Krechevsky sought to gain an understanding of how schools and their clients viewed the use of MI theory in their schools. They interviewed administrators, teachers, students, and parents. They also visited schools, made classroom observations, participated in lessons, and reviewed the new materials. On the basis of this information, the authors compared the nine schools with respect to three issues: why and how the schools adopted the theory, how they implemented it, and what forms of assessment they used to determine success.

Their preliminary findings are that MI is commonly used as an organizing framework for new activities in schools. As such, it provides a language that enables teachers to be more conscious of their work and validate their practices. To enhance staff knowledge of MI, conventional professional training methods are employed—study groups, in-service training, and outside consultants. Implementation is primarily in two areas: (1) changes in school curriculum (i.e., various tasks that rely on several different intelligences are incorporated into traditional subject areas), and (2) changes in organizational structure (i.e., team teaching and expanded roles for specialists). With respect to assessment, formal program evaluation is limited to informal interviews and observations. The minimal nature of this evaluation is understandable as the programs are relatively new. Student assessment seems somewhat more developed, and in some schools student reporting measures are altered to accommodate the new emphasis on diverse intelligences. Several of the sites are also experimenting with portfolios which document a student's actual work products in various subjects.

In several of the sites the adoption of MI involved not only training for the staff but also activities for the parents. The schools in the Kornhaber and Krechevsky study recognized the importance of educating parents about changes in the school curriculum as a consequence of taking an MI approach. Several of the schools actively sought input from parents in determining how extensive the commitment to MI should be. The involvement of parents in the study schools is not unusual; increasingly researchers and policymakers seek to involve parents more directly in their children's education.

Mary Driscoll explores why schools need to create stronger bonds with their students' families. She defines schools as dynamic and complex interactive wholes—as communities that embody history, change, process, and experience. This "wholeness" gives shape and meaning to the lives of those who teach and learn in a particular school. Envisioning the school as a community means retaining an emphasis on the interconnections of individuals to one another. Looking back to Dewey (1970), Driscoll points out that the original function of schooling was not a private one; schools were not designed to measure individual accomplishment or success, but to develop students into citizens capable of leading productive lives and taking social responsibility for others. For Dewey, ineffective schools were ones that were separated from the family with distinct activities and events that were unfamiliar to the child.

Driscoll argues that contemporary work on effective schools has basically reversed Dewey's conception of schools. Now schools operate autonomously from the home and take as a measure of their success students' performance on standardized tests. She maintains that the concept of an effective school needs to be defined on grounds other than test scores. Schools need to be assessed on general, schoolwide expectations and consistent values.

By examining the school context and community, one gains a better understanding of how and why students learn not only knowledge assessed on standardized tests but also values and attitudes toward work, political participation, and family formation. Viewing the school as a community means taking into account the school's role in sustaining tradition and memory, implicit and explicit values, activities that bind the community's members to each other and the school, and the management of social and academic tasks. Community is the entity which provides the context from which individuals derive shared meanings and memories.

According to Driscoll, there are at least three important implications of thinking about schools as holistic communities. First, parents must be seen as important and vital participants in the school community. Second, having accepted parents as members of the school community, educators must think more creatively about how families can become engaged in the core work of the institution. To illustrate this point, Driscoll describes three innovative programs designed to strengthen connections between families and the core mission of the school. And finally, parents have an important role in perpetuating the cultural narrative of the school and helping to orient the school's staff and students toward the future. Implicit in her definition of a school community is the concept that schools should not mirror the values of the families but rather that the families and schools must work together to prepare students for a better future society. A genuine school community speaks with the united voice of students, staff, administrators, and parents.

Community Influence and School Reform

The last two chapters in this section examine the role other groups—neighborhood associations, the business community, and the judicial community—are expected to play in achieving educational reform. Kathryn Borman, Debra Martinson, Louis Castenell, Karen Gallagher, and Sally Kilgore discuss how local neighborhood groups and large-scale businesses have become involved in designing local school curricula and offering experiences aimed at improving student performance and aspirations.

Borman et al. conclude that local neighborhoods have generally been ignored in fashioning programs for school change. Local groups often lack the power, influence, and experience to be considered real players in school reform plans. Despite guidelines which encourage participation of neighborhoods in school reform efforts, local population myths, folklore, group political history, and social experience have made community-based alliances difficult. Exclusion of particular groups from the school decision-making processes has, in many instances, reinforced resistance to change at the local level. Even though local community groups are not often perceived as desirable collaborators by some schools, most schools recognize that without their support change will be difficult, if not impossible, to achieve. Borman et al. review the efforts of several exemplary programs designed to actively involve neighborhoods in the school decision-making process. The authors contend that while the programs are admirable in that they attempt to meet local needs and national goals, oftentimes the individuals in charge of them lack the technical knowledge and management skills that are needed to break existing barriers and redirect activities toward change.

In contrast to local groups, businesses have the requisite power, influence, and management expertise, but they have run into difficulty because they lack the necessary knowledge of particular community needs and the sensitivity to local diversity which is crucial to the success of reform. Examining business programs that aim to improve the technical skills of young workers so they can become more competitive in the labor force, Borman et al. remain quite skeptical about the likelihood of their success. They argue that American businesses, which hire low-skilled dutiful workers, do not have a vested interest in training more skilled workers. Thus, the potential for reform is seriously undermined. For school reforms to succeed, businesses have to recognize their own motives and work with local neighborhood groups to create more real jobs for young workers that have opportunities for advancement.

Social service organizations and child advocacy groups also have become involved in the daily life of schools. Judith Cohen discusses the new roles of schools in areas that were once the sole province of the family or community. Concentrating on the role of social service agencies in the schools, Cohen describes various health care and social service programs currently operating in many urban schools. Some of these initiatives require the full-time services of child abuse prevention workers, probation officers, and welfare administrators at the school site. The presence and activities of the nonteacher staff, she concludes, fundamentally change the function of schooling.

Cohen maintains that schools are the best structure to provide child welfare services. The systems of family, neighborhood, church, judiciary, and social services that traditionally provided such services are fragmented, underresourced, and ill equipped to meet the growing emotional, physical, and social needs of today's children. Schools, rather than courts or other social systems, are the most appropriate structure for child advocacy because they are the one stable existing social institution in many communities. School personnel have many more opportunities to closely interact with families and communities than any other social service provider, often have a moral commitment to children, and are keenly aware of the diversity of social and economic resources available to the children they serve.

Recognizing some of the obstacles to creating schools as centers for child advocacy, Cohen details how these barriers can be overcome through better teacher training, greater coordination with social services, and more direct funding at local sites for social services. She maintains that this is feasible only if the scope and mission of schools is rethought and the schools have the broad support of state and national policymakers. The role of the federal and state governments in improving the quality of education is examined in Section 3, "Learning and Assessment."

6

Mapping Knowledge Perspectives in Studies of Educational Change

Rolland G. Paulston

> Aporia is a figure whereby a Speaker sheweth that he doubteth either where to begin for the multitude of matters, or what to do or say in some strange or ambiguous thing.[1]

> Only metaphysicians [i.e., those who argue for a privileged final vocabulary] think that our genres and criteria exhaust the realm of possibility. Ironists continue to expand that realm.[2]

> In the 1990s post-modernism has become a mature and multifarious movement that cannot be ignored by practitioners of the human studies. It is situated throughout the reaches of discursive space. The point is to domesticate it by selective appropriation rather than take it whole or attempt to wish it away.[3]

Today long-dominant goals and assumptions underlying modern theories of education and society are undergoing a ravaging subversion. Poststructuralist, postmodernist, postpatriarchal, post-Marxist—yea, posteverything it would seem—theories push forth new ways of seeing and being grounded in, paradoxically, antiessentialist and antifoundationalist ideas. Social relations and basic notions of reality and knowledge undergo fragmentation, and many educators find themselves confused and disoriented in a shifting intellectual landscape with new knowledge communities speaking seemingly incomprehensible research languages. Surprisingly swift and unexpected, this rupture is also imploding the study of educational change. Now no metanarrative, or grand theory, be it positivism or humanism, functionalism or Marxism, can credibly claim hegemonic privilege and the right to fill all the space of truth. Given this spread of ontological and epistemological pluralism, how are we as educators and scholars to move past our present unsettling aporia into a postmodern space of more heterogeneous knowledge relations appropriate to our time?

In this chapter I argue for the utility of mapping knowledge perspectives as a kind of cognitive art, or "play of figuration," to help orient educators to knowledge communities and their cultural codes, and to reinscribe modernist vocabularies into postmodern ways of seeing and representing educational change. To do this, I use a "perspectivist" approach to examine educational change discourse in comparative and international education studies since the 1950s, and suggest how the diverse ways of seeing that were discovered using textual exegesis may be mapped at macro and meso levels of social reality. Here I am guided by Bourdieu's notion of "habitus," where intellectual fields are viewed as systems of "durable, transposable dispositions" produced by a dialectical interaction with objective structures and actors' views of the world. [4]

To reveal such dispositions I use Barthes's notion of text, as an arrangement in a certain order, [5] as "that social space that leaves no language safe or untouched, that allows no enunciative subject to hold the position of judge, teacher, analysis confessor, or decoder" (p. 51). This interpretive approach is used to compare educational texts intertextually—i.e., in relation to other texts—rather than in relation to their authors. A distinction between the work and the text should also, perhaps, be noted. Where literary works are concrete and visible, the text reveals and articulates itself according to and against certain rules. Where the work is held in the hand, the text is held in language. Here the original modernist linking of subject (author) and object (work) is replaced with practices (writing) and the intertextual (field). This relationship of the text to its intercultural field, as illustrated in Figures 6.1–6.3 following, is creative, active, and practical. Texts are seen to interact continuously in an open field which they produce and by which they are produced, and in which they may be interpreted, typed, and mapped. The guiding idea here is phenomenographic. It is well expressed by Olsson's argument that "To understand is to condense a thought-position into a point and then place it in relation to other points."[6] In this chapter I use a phenomenographic analysis to enter into texts and type points, or thought positions, in some sixty exemplary studies that seek to explain educational change theory and practice. These positions, once discovered, are then transferred to a two-dimensional space. The ensuing cognitive map of disparate yet interrelated points is, accordingly, a provisional construct, one social mapper's unique contribution to understanding difference.

Changing Representations of Educational Change Knowledge

While comparative educators only recently began to discuss explicitly their theoretical framing dispositions following the appearance of Thomas Kuhn's magnum opus, *The Structure of Scientific Revolutions* (1962), implicit knowledge perspectives can be identified in the field's early discourse. The eighteenth- and nineteenth-century foundational texts of Berchtold, Jullien, and Basset, for example, all advocate encyclopedic description and macro comparisons of public instruction in order to generalize on its efficiency in the then-emergent project of individual and social modernity. With the ensuing construction of national systems of education in the industrial, or modern, world and their transfer in part to the colonized world, comparative educators shifted their attention to the study of the effects of social forces and contexts in the shaping and differentiation of these systems. By 1950, the stories of Sadler, Kandel, and Hans, among others, helped to consolidate the paradigm of modernity (see fig. 3) as the dominant, even if implicit and unspoken, way of representing or modeling national and cross-national educational phenomena.

Figure 6.1 seeks to capture changing textual knowledge orientations in exemplary comparative education scholarship during three major periods: i.e., in the 1950s and 1960s, when an orthodoxy of functionalist and positivist ways of seeing dominated discourse; in the contentious 1970s and 1980s, when the radical functionalist, humanist, and radical humanist paradigms challenged positivist and functionalist hegemony, and unresolved heterodox struggles to replace one master narrative with another prevailed; and in the emergence of a more heterogeneous postparadigmatic period of competing cultural clusters and proliferating mininarratives as we move through the 1990s.[7] To facilitate comparison, Figure 6.1 identifies eight kinds—or directions—of hermeneutic, or discursive, reference within the texts noted, i.e., the representation of knowledge control and organization; of knowledge and ontology, framing, and style; of knowledge, gender, and emotions; and of knowledge products. As Gottlieb points out, formal methods of discourse analysis are relatively new in educational studies. From this perspective, knowledge is not "found" using positivist procedures, but is constructed in and through the discourses of distinct and specifiable cultural clusters, or knowledge communities. Discourse analysis seeks to identify patterns of language that both shape and reflect what is called "thinking," i.e., the basic intellectual commitments held in language.[8] These commitments, or characteristic dispositions, are presented in Figure 6.1 as a "bricolage," i.e., an assemblage of cultural odds and ends. Bricolage, as a juxtaposition of disparate ideas, serves as a metaphor for the systems of thought through which texts are seen to classify the components of the world and the myths through which texts explain themselves. These myths and systems are not united by logical continuity nor are they totalizing. Bricolage, as a nonhegemonic alternative to Western rationalism—which seeks to unify totality according to a system patterned after deductive logic—is revealed in constructed cultural complexes without reference to some ulterior reality.

FIGURE 6.1. A "bricolage," or assemblage, of changing representations of educational change knowledge in comparative and international education texts, 1950s–1990s.

Characteristics of Textual Representations	Linear 1950s - 1960s	Branching 1970s - 1980s	Intertwined 1990s -
Knowledge Control and Organization:	Orthodoxy; hierarchial and centralized	Heterodoxy: Emergence of "neo-" variants and new inquiry perspectives	Heterogeneity: Disputatious yet complementary knowledge communities
Knowledge Relations:	Hegemonic and totalizing	Paradigm clash -- i.e., "either/or" competition of incommensurable world views	Emergent post-paradigmatic -- i.e., rhizomatic and interactive
Knowledge Ontology:	Realist views predominate	Realist and relativist views contest reality	More perspectivist views encompass multiple realities & perspectives
Knowledge Framing:	Functionalism and positivism dominant	Functionalist, critical and interpretive views compete and decenter	More eclectic, reflexive and pragmatic
Knowledge Style:	Parsimonious and value-free	Agonistic and partisan	Increasingly intertextual, ecologistic, & contingent
Knowledge/Gender:	Maleness: Logic dominant	Feminist ideas emerge, compete, decenter	Gender issues more open and indeterminate
Knowledge/Emotions:	Optimism and confidence	Disdain, incredulity, or exhilaration	Ambivalence -- i.e., nostalgia for certainty; delight in diversity
Knowledge Products:	Law-like crossnational statements the ideal	Competing Ideologies	Explanation, interpretation, simulation, translation and mapping
Illustrative Texts:	Adams & Farrell (1969); Anderson (1961); Bereday (1964); Husén (1967); Noah & Eckstein (1969); Schultz (1961)	Anderson (1977); Bourdieu & Passeron (1977); Bowles & Gintis (1976); Carnoy (1984); Clignet (1981); Epstein (1983); Heyman (1979); Husén (1988); Karabel & Halsey (1977); Kelly & Nihlen (1982); Paulston (1977)	Altbach (1991); Cowen (1990); Lather (1991); Masemann (1990); Paulston (1990; 1993); Paulston & Tidwell (1992); Rust (1991); Stromquist (1990); von Recum (1990)

Orthodoxy

Following World War II, with the crises of decolonization and cold war competition, comparative education studies—and especially those in North America—continued to be framed in evolutionary and functionalist perspectives while moving closer to the social sciences and their concerns to secure progress through social and economic development. Using the vocabulary, if not the experimental rigor, of the natural sciences, comparative and international education studies flourished during those decades of functionalist and positivist orthodoxy and drew strength from the creation of scholarly journals in the field, an increase in governmental and foundation support, and the founding of numerous comparative education centers in leading U.S. and European universities.

At the University of Chicago's prestigious Comparative Education Center, for example, the first director, C. Arnold Anderson, argued in a foundational text (1961) that the ultimate aim of comparative education must be—as with the social sciences—systematic knowledge of causation, i.e., the shaping of the results of analysis into lawlike generalizations. Where half a century earlier educational research and educational psychology programs had gained entrance and eventual methodological respectability in major European and North American universities by using statistics and experimental methods, Anderson argued that comparative education should seek acceptance with a strategy of (1) integration with the social sciences, (2) the use of the natural sciences model of hypothesis testing and analysis of covariation, and (3) a commitment to theoretical explanation and generalization. [9]

To this end, Anderson proposed a strengthening of two broad yet complementary approaches to comparative education and their integration into social science research. The first, intraeducational analysis generating strictly educational data, viewed education as if it were an autonomous social system. This strand would generate the statistical correlations and "hard" data seen as indispensable for comparing educational systems and practice. The second approach, interdisciplinary research on educational-societal relations, would examine the social, political, and economic functions and tasks laid upon the schools by a society. Anderson's strategy for the creation of a more systematic and social scientific comparative education found strong support in related efforts to establish the field both in the United States and in Western Europe. Anderson saw only hypothesis testing using nomothetic and functional approaches as suitable for knowledge framing if comparative education aspired to capture relevant aspects of "the concrete reality" (p. 11).

Bereday also proposed a comparative methodology that built upon positivist and evolutionist assumptions, yet chose instead to stress the need for an inductive non-social-science comparative methodology capable of simultaneous analysis of educational practice across national frontiers. Ideally, hypothesis testing to advance the identification of laws in comparative education might also follow. Bereday's methodology-driven approach sought to develop an increasingly analytical but dispassionate field akin to comparative politics and comparative religion, i.e., a field "unhampered by ethical or pragmatic considerations." [10]

In a closely related text, Noah and Eckstein argued that a more scientific comparative education would not be found in comparative method alone, as advocated by their teacher Bereday, but in a more rigorous inductive method as proposed by Cohen and Nagel in their *Introduction to Logic and Scientific Method*. Noah and Eckstein saw the attainment of rigorous scientific explanation in comparative education as a difficult goal, but one most likely to result from a methodological empiricism grounded in functionalist assumptions that avoided reflection on ideology and theory. Their research-framing choices focused on testing low-level propositions about the relationship of education to society. Questions about the form and function of schooling would be restricted to matters of pedagogical efficiency and correlational analysis of educational relations with more complex systems. Here the correlational method was seen as a defining, if imperfect, substitute for experimentation. Explanation in comparative education is presented as progressive, i.e., as an evolutionary process proceeding sequentially from (1) curiosity, description, and primitive quantification; to (2) qualitative interpretation examining forces and factors; to (3) sophisticated quantification offering a means of rigorous scientific testing to support policy and planning; to (4) "scientific prediction."[11] The empirical science model would, Noah and Eckstein contended, bring comparative education into a condition of epistemological modernity at a time when, ironically, not only scientism but the very foundations of modernity were coming under serious attack in the social sciences and the humanities as well.[12]

The International Evaluation of Educational Achievement Project (IEA), widely reported by Husén and others, brought to fruition these antecedent calls for a more scientific comparison of educational practice in schools around the world. Driven in part by U.S. fears following Sputnik and Western European concerns with the emergence of mass secondary education, the IEA project drew most heavily on empirical and quantitative traditions of measurement as developed in educational psychology. For the first time, comparative educators would measure international differences in school achievement using internationally developed objective tests in what was claimed to be a pathbreaking effort to account for variations in test results. In time, Husén suggested, a more scientific understanding of intellectual functioning and curriculum would produce efficient and predictable instructional practices.[13] The project also provided a working model of a new comparative education seeking causal explanations grounded in correlational studies rather than the narrative description and moral exhortation commonly found in earlier studies. With the involvement of comparative educators from Teachers College, Columbia University, the Universities of Chicago and Stockholm, and numerous ministries of education around the world, the project optimistically sought to validate the scientific aspirations of the field in the 1950s and 1960s. Viewing the world as an educational laboratory and using comparative and correlational methods, the IEA project initially expressed the aim of discovering a wide range of cognitive, pedagogical, and curricular universals. After decades of testing, considerably less grand findings pointed to

the importance of unintended outcomes of schooling, and the
dangers of too many data and too little conceptual modeling.
Both comparison and policy implications remained problematic,
given the Project's dependence on precoded, forced-choice
survey questions and a near total lack of attention to questions of
meaning and context, i.e., to the consequences of embedding
education in complex webs of cultural, economic, and political
relations.

By the late 1960s a number of international funding
agencies and comparative educators turned their attention to
educational change efforts in Third World settings, a new branch
of comparative education that addressed problems of
educational planning, development, and theory construction in
largely macro studies of education and social change. In what
might be seen as a canonical text representing this structural-
functional variant of the prevailing orthodoxy, Adams and
Farrell proposed that the primary purpose of comparative and
development studies should be the generalization and
specification of testable propositions, or statements of relations
across objective variables.[14] Scholars in comparative education
were seen to have been most reluctant to undertake this task;
thus "our knowledge remains scattered and unsystematic." The
authors' corrective advocated a structuring of knowledge within
and across educational systems according to Parsonian notions
of unilineal differentiation, a process that "will follow an
approximately similar sequence in all societies" undergoing
modernization.[15]

Heterodoxy

By the early 1970s, the modernist project had achieved regnant
status in comparative and international education studies at the
same time that it came under widespread attack in the social
sciences and in development studies from a combination of
emergent critical and interpretive knowledge communities.[16]
Reasons for the vulnerability and eventual decentering of
functionalism are suggested in the shift from a segregated to a
plural society in the United States. With cultural pluralism came

new advocates of epistemological and ontological pluralism. Functionalist theory, moreover, proved unable to adequately predict, control, or explain frequent development failures.[17] Equally important, the rise of a global field with numerous new scholars and comparative education programs in Europe, Asia, and in the Third World saw an increased recognition of antithetical neo-Marxist, critical theory, feminist, hermeneutic, and dependency perspectives. Third World critics especially came forth to challenge what they saw as a self-serving, elitist, and patriarchal Northern functionalist discourse.[18]

Decentering of the structural-functionalist worldview with its positivist epistemological vision also followed from the publication of Berger and Luckmann's influential text, *The Social Construction of Reality*, in 1966. Here the humanist paradigm— and its support of the intersubjective or social origin of all ideas—branched into ethnomethodological and phenomenological camps (see fig. 3) and strengthened the arrival of a new hermeneutic or ethnographic approach in comparative education studies.

The radical functionalist worldview first elaborated to explain how education functions to reproduce capitalist structures by Althusser,[19] and later by Bowles and Gintis,[20] also rather quickly and effectively mounted a telling critique of structural-functionalist explanations of educational change and modernization efforts. Carnoy documents the subsequent appearance in the early 1970s of a variety of neo-Marxist texts rooted in the historical materialist worldview as an early example of such a clash of paradigms.[21]

During the 1970s and 1980s texts drawing on Marxist radical functionalist counterorthodoxy greatly increased in number and influence and produced a powerful critique—if not a successor paradigm—to entrenched Durkheimian and Parsonian structural functionalism and its variants in modernization and human capital theories. But because earlier traditional Marxist-Leninist texts portray education as a repressive state apparatus, they pay little attention to how education might contribute to a revolutionary socialist strategy. By the 1970s, as Carnoy has shown, neo-Marxist researchers gave this latter question their highest priority.

In France, Althusser's 1960s interpretation of Marx has the superstructure—including education—determined by the relations of production. The hegemony of the dominant class was seen to lie in the very relations of the means of production and to directly define the purposes and functioning of the educational system. Thus Althusser saw the educational system hyperfunctionally—i.e., it necessarily reproduced the relations of production and precluded any counterhegemonic response from educators or students.

In the United States, Bowles and Gintis applied Althusser's theory of structural correspondence and construed the reality of American education as a direct reflection of the values and relationships of capitalist production. Attempts to reform schools without corresponding changes in the structure of production, they argued, would always fail.

In Britain, Basil Bernstein along with the new sociology of education school elaborated an eclectic neo-Marxist project, combining perspectives from Durkheim, Marx, and sociolinguistics to study educational institutions as agents of cultural transmission and reproduction. While Bernstein's story of social-class influence in the classification and framing of educational knowledge is clearly tied to the radical wing of the "old" sociology of education, he also draws widely upon both the humanist—or interpretive—and functionalist worldviews. In a perceptive assessment, Karabel and Halsey conclude that the macro-sociological conflict approach of the American neo-Marxists and the essentially micro-sociological interpretive studies of the British were highly complementary. Both "waged war" against the common enemies of structural-functionalist theory and methodological empiricism without ever coordinating their critiques.[22]

By the early 1980s a more humanistic Marxism, or radical humanism, gained prominence in critical studies. Texts framed in this knowledge orientation drew on the earlier critical theory of the Frankfurt School led in Germany by Jürgen Habermas, in North America by Henry Giroux, and in the Third World by Paulo Freire. As a branch of this intellectual movement, numerous radical feminist texts also began to draw upon critical theory's agenda for the liberation of consciousness. Here critical theory texts use a negative dialectical argument to expose education's role in the patriarchal domination of women, much as capitalists are seen to dominate workers in Marxist texts. Kelly and Nihlen, for example, critique all existing comparative education texts for their silence on education's role in the reproduction of gender inequality.[23] They also present a reflective critique of their own rigid reproduction framework and find that it too "fails both to deal with 'deviations' and to chart how and when they occur or become significant." The answers, they argue, will not come from deterministic functionalist or radical functionalist analysis of structure or history, but from interpretive research rooted in the humanist and radical humanist paradigms. These worldviews will reveal how women experience and interpret education in their everyday lives, and will show how they come to see and resist domination by making the invisible visible.[24]

With the spread of ontological pluralism and the decentering of positivist dominance in the social sciences over the 1970s and 1980s, humanistic or interpretive research also began to appear in comparative education texts. An illustrative text by Heyman, for example, lays out an alternative ethnomethodological knowledge orientation, a rationale to replace narrow functionalist and positivist approaches with an agenda for ethnographic inquiry in the field.[25] Heyman's 1979 text contends that comparative education has not provided useful knowledge to educational planners, policymakers, and reformers because of its decontextualized commitment to social "facts" (i.e., the IEA study), its narrow sole interest in functional and structural relationships (i.e., modernization and Marxist research), and its focus on reified social science indicators rather than on interaction among participants in everyday social and educational environments. Research based on the measurement of indicators as a proxy for theoretically related concepts results, according to Heyman, is a gross distortion of the very social reality that comparativists seek to reveal and understand. His heterodox argument builds upon Garfinkel's work of the 1960s and calls for the replacement of all positivist and materialist methods with interpretive approaches claimed to be better for observing, describing, and interpreting the "reality" of our daily existence. Ethnomethodology, i.e., the study of how individuals engage in reality-making processes, is suggested because it promises to capture more of the continuous production of social reality in human interaction than do correlational studies. Correlational studies assume that objects cannot be two things at once and that objects have stable, discreet, and permanent properties—assumptions more appropriate for inquiry in the physical sciences. For Heyman, the level of analysis in comparative studies must shift from macro to micro, from an objectivist-realist to a subjectivist-relativist ontology, and to the study of everyday life. Comparative education research must stop "pretending to be scientific" and instead become microscopic, steer a heuristic course, and build its comparative interpretations and theories through replication.

In a related paradigmatic study, Clignet also rejects both functionalist and radical functionalist, or Marxist, worldviews. Despite their apparent differences, Clignet demonstrates that both paradigms share a number of weaknesses.[26] Both use effects to explain events and both stress vertical hierarchical relations at the expense of horizontal interactive relations. With their unwavering focus on structure, both ignore the way assimilation and replication processes performed by schools are contingent on critical sets of interaction among individuals and social groups located within the same layers of social reality. Both perspectives prevent researchers from analyzing the various mechanisms used by schools in assimilation and replication functions, and both prevent researchers from differentiating between educational interactions and their outcomes in students' life chances. Instead, Clignet looks to behavioral science and proposes a biological or psychological framework that distinguishes the perspective of each individual organism and differentiates its modes of adaptation to the environment—in this case, the school environment of teachers and students. This ecologistic approach rejects the notion of universal viability found in functionalist and critical arguments. Instead, it starts at the micro level with biographies of individual actors and analyzes the relationship between educational structures and actions. It sees local adaptation and differentiation as an integral part of social reality and as necessary to historically and culturally contingent strategies if attempts to change are to be effective. Accordingly, Clignet argues, the failure of most policies for educational change follow from their rigid and uniform top-down pedagogical treatments that "reflect ideological rather than scientific principles." By the mid-1980s all claims to foundational knowledge in the field had become vulnerable to this attack. [27]

The first summary examination of texts seeking to reveal and map paradigmatic and theoretical perspectives in the field of comparative education appeared in 1977. My phenomenographic typing of how the international educational reform literature explained   national reform efforts and outcomes produced a heterodox, or bipolar, juxtaposition of texts framed in either equilibrium or conflict worldviews. [28] Reform explanations linked: (1) the evolutionary, functionalist, and systems ways of seeing with the equilibrium pole; and (2) the Marxist, cultural revitalization, and anarchistic/utopian ways of seeing educational reform with the conflict pole. As texts offering interpretivist, feminist, or problem-approach explanations of educational reform process and outcomes had yet to appear in this reform discourse, they were absent from the summary Figure. Such would not be the case today. As may be seen in Figures 6.1 and 6.2, the consequences of subsequent branching and pragmatic entwinement of functionalist, critical, and interpretivist knowledge perspectives and the emergence of radical hermeneutic critique and explanation, as evidenced especially in many feminist texts, is clearly apparent and burgeoning. [29]

By the mid 1970s, Anderson somewhat qualified his earlier strong advocacy of a totalizing and hegemonic structural-functionalist approach to comparative education. In response to attacks from advocates of competing holistic-interpretive and critical perspectives, he cautioned that confusion and "vulgar functionalism" indeed arise when investigators "too readily infer ostensible functions of schools from putative societal needs" rather than from strict adherence to "confirmation of many a priori hypotheses" concerning complex matrices of variables explaining functional equivalents among the educational practices of different systems. Despite some pessimism about the state of the art in comparative education, Anderson predicted continued progress in the identification of "functional equivalents for the basic structures and functions of educational systems." He admonished, however, that the price of "progress" would require the exclusion of competing paradigms: "Perhaps, we should cease to speak of society as a 'seamless web' and see it rather as a matrix of .5 correlation coefficients. Accordingly, holistic conceptions of society should be espoused with heavy qualifications, even when we would not put conflict at the center of our conceptual scheme."[30]

Emergent Heterogeneity

Representations of knowledge in comparative education texts began a shift away from heterodoxy and paradigm clash in the late 1980s.[31] While a few researchers still claim orthodox purity and remain within their exclusive paradigmatic utopias—and some continue unsuccessful partisan efforts to replace one worldview with another—the collapse of grand theory in the social sciences means that no one knowledge community can now claim a monopoly of vision.[32] Rather, a growing number of researchers see all claims to universal, foundational knowledge—be they positivist "science" or interpretivist "science" or Marxist "science"—as incomplete and problematic.[33]

Husén pointed the way past heterodoxy with his recognition that no one paradigm can answer all questions, that all serve to complement disparate worldviews.[34] I too see the field moving from heterodox paradigm wars to a global terrain of disputatious yet interactive and often complementary communities as the use of knowledge becomes more eclectic and is reoriented by new ideas and new knowledge constructs flowing from a variety of cultural study approaches in, for example, interpretations, simulations, translations, probes, and conceptual mapping.[35] Knowledge has become more "textual." It is increasingly seen as construction employing a conventional sign system where even nonbook texts such as architectural structures, musical compositions, or graphic texts such as maps are seen to "presuppose a signifying consciousness that it is our business to uncover."[36] With the appearance of poststructural and postmodern studies, comparative education discourse has also begun this excavation[37] with a shift in knowledge framing from traditional social science and Marxist science models to perspectives of the interpretive humanities and linguistics.[38]

Discourse Communities Today

Functionalist/Neofunctionalist

Neofunctionalist theory has seen the growth of numerous vital new branches, while the traditional structural-functional root paradigm continues to come under heavy attack from all quarters. Humanist texts, for example, critique functionalism's "anti-individualism" and "downward conflation," where a supposedly integrated cultural system is seen to create a consensus that engulfs the social and personality systems. Radical functionalist texts attack functionalism's "conservatism," "idealism," and willingness to accept structured inequality and human misery as the price of social order, efficiency, and homeostasis, or moving equilibrium. Neofunctionalist texts seek to address and move beyond these problems by synthesizing core paradigmatic assumptions with opposing paradigms and other theoretical traditions.

Modernization theory also has several branches. The evolutionary functionalist branch draws heavily on Durkheim and Parsons to explain how increasingly complex and differentiated societies and educational systems create a need for mass schooling. Interventionist attempts to modernize Third World educational systems using top-down planning and innovation based on idealized Western economic models and applied science are in deepening crises[39] despite efforts by the World Bank and other international agencies to improve efficiency and productivity.[40] Texts here have for the most part remained closed for decades to the many lessons of an often-failed practice.[41]

Neofunctionalists retain Parsons's unflinching logo-centrism (i.e., a belief in reason as the controlling principle in the universe) and general social system perspective while opening their texts somewhat to rational-actor approaches and interpretive perspectives; to conflicting social and cultural factors in educational planning and reform projects (but only at the project level),[42] and to a recognition of the centrality of structured inequality and interest-group conflict in explanations of failed educational reform.[43] In Germany, Luhmann argues that the Western type of modern society differentiates subsystems to produce both scientific theories and theories of systemic self-reflection.[44] Framing their story of national educational knowledge patterns in Germany and France in this post-Parsonian perspective, Schriewer and Keiner find a marked "German" preference, or a consensus favoring a "hermeneutic-reflective style." The "French," they contend, prefer a "science of education style." Today, these two research orientations have begun, but only barely, to converge. Perspectives that are outside of their gross either-or dichotomy are ignored and thus made invisible, a continuing acceptable practice in functionalist discourse.

Rational-choice theory seeks to move action theory away from the macrosystem level and back toward the actor and possibilities for human agency and more contingent understanding. The leading branch draws upon game theory and empirical analysis to explain how actors predictably act in social change situations.[45] Rational-choice theory is undergoing rapid growth as both neofunctionalists and neo-Marxists now seek to put into place a positive foundation of rational-choice microtheory to support a diverse variety of macrotheoretical constructs. Coleman especially has contributed to the development of a broader action theory which synthesizes interests in actors and systems to clarify the meaning of voluntaristic action.[46] Analytical Marxists, as well, now freely borrow from rather conservative rational-choice and game theory—and even from general equilibrium theory and neoclassical economics—to elaborate the microgrounding of what their radical texts see as macrosocial historical materialist processes.[47]

Conflict theory examines symbolic codes and culture-mediated power relations. It draws on both functionalist and macrohistorical sociological theory to explain education in contexts of privilege, domination, and cultural reproduction. Building on paradigmatic texts by Weber, Simmel, Dahrendorf, and Collins, conflict theory focuses on the structure and consequences of conflict within social and educational systems. In Europe the cognitive focus is most often on structuralist theories that treat symbolic codes largely as classification systems. These texts emphasize the rationality of symbolic codes within formal systems of knowledge and, as with Bourdieu and Passeron, often attempt to "de-center" the agency of code production. American and British approaches, in contrast, tend to focus more on the codes themselves.[48] Archer, for example, presents a "morphogenetic" explanation, where mutual causal processes are seen to counteract systemic stress and to facilitate structural differentiation and increased information flow.[49] Texts emphasizing conflict theory willingly incorporate Marxist ideas,[50] yet reject historicism and see only continued conflict into the future.[51] With its predilection for methodological eclecticism and micro-macro interaction, conflict theory, as in the work of Pierre Bourdieu and Randall Collins, is becoming increasingly attractive as a perspective to study how changing stratification and organization are grounded in the interactions, structures, and intersubjectivity of everyday life.

Radical Functionalist/Neo-Marxist

While the sort of traditional Marxist structural determinism associated with the 1970s texts of Althusser and of Bowles and Gintis has now largely disappeared, neo-Marxist and post-Marxist theory continues—though in something of a state of shock following the collapse of socialist theory and practice in Eastern Europe, in the former USSR, and in much of the Third World. Anticipating this change to some extent, a text by Bowles and Gintis in 1986 moved far beyond the earlier radical functionalist model of social class reproduction and argued a new post-Marxist theoretical discourse, or "postliberal democracy," combining features of liberalism and Marxism.[52] Carnoy and Samoff have also rid their Marxist analysis of its hyperfunctionalist features.[53] They now break with orthodox

Marxist social class theory and present a less deterministic neo-Marxist "transition-state theory" that emphasizes the role of the state and de-emphasizes the influence of productive forces and class conflict in an explanation of what they see as Third World "transitions to socialism." Yet their perspective's inability to recognize—let alone to explain—reverse transitions from socialism to market economies in, for example, the former USSR, Nicaragua, Eastern Europe, and elsewhere gives their text a somewhat teleological cast seemingly at odds with both their findings and recent historical events.

Radical Humanist/Critical Theory

Cultural rationalization theory also draws upon a number of what were earlier viewed as ideologically incommensurable perspectives.[54] Habermas, a leading theorist in this community, has proposed an ambitious reconstruction of Marx's grand emancipatory narrative. Rejecting both utopian historicism and the endless negative dialectics of the earlier Frankfurt School—while continuing to wear his logocentrism on his sleeve—Habermas now idealistically seeks a neonormative foundation in undistorted language communication. Moving toward the pragmatic center, he finds useful bases for his cultural reconstruction project in linguistic theory, in Mead's intersubjective theory of communicative democracy, in Weber's theories of bureaucracy and progressive cultural rationalization, and in Parsons's action theory.[55]

Critical theory, the main branch growing out of radical humanism, has in its many forms been a leading contender over the past several decades of paradigm conflict. It is closely related to cultural rationalization theory but is more normative and directly attacks the repressive character of Western reason, culture, and society. Marcuse and Freire have, perhaps, most directly influenced comparative educators' use of this perspective in their advocacy of emancipatory modernity and a revolutionary subject variously resisting domination by the world capitalist system,[56] distorted knowledge relations,[57] or, among the feminists, oppressive gender relations.[58] A vital and growing variation of this theoretical framing perspective drawing upon Horkheimer's negative dialectics is also found in several recent critical ethnographic studies. They offer thick descriptions of cultural and economic domination and examine prospects for resistance—supposedly from the actor's viewpoint.[59]

Examples of poststructuralist and postmodernist theory in comparative education texts are as yet few in number. With their variety and resistance to representation, texts infused with postmodern sensibility are also the most difficult to categorize and map. For the most part related to the humanist and radical humanist paradigms (see fig. 2) they focus on space and cultural codes and reject all metanarratives (i.e., grand theories), determinism, and universals. They also reject the truth claims of positivist science, of history, and of classical rationalism (i.e., the notion that one can rank knowledge claims according to intuitive truth standards).[60] Instead the social world is usually portrayed as a collage of blurred genres, of multiple narratives—or, if you will, language games and traces tied to specific forms of empowerment as suggested in Figure 6.2. The time of total relativity is seen to be present everywhere. Postmodern texts attack everything that claims to be free of contradiction, closed, uniform, or unequivocal. These claims are usurped by paradox, diversity, ambiguity, and chance.[61] Postmodern deconstruction annihilates stable spaces and permanent boundaries at all levels of reality in a continuous circulation of information. Space is no longer in geography, as in modernist views, but now is in electronic hyperspace. And unity is only in the terminals, or nodes. From this perspective's extreme relativism, both the subject and society tend to disintegrate into spatial and social confusion. According to Jamison, our ability to grasp our positions as individual and collective subjects and to locate ourselves so as to be able to act and struggle is undermined. Science shifts from attempts to discover universal truth to the creation of provisional and parochial new ideas and a preference for paralogy—i.e., a type of counterlogical analysis. In redefining educational goals, the postmodern perspective avoids the imposition of normative decisions and looks instead to a better understanding of the power relations between various information grids in which education occurs, to local knowledge, to "decentralized small units," and to making the invisible visible.[62]

From the postmodern perspective, the electronic and telecommunication revolutions give a new prominence to language, and postmodern science turns to language games as the minimum relation required for society to exist. Where modernist science permits only the single linear language game of denotation and progress, postmodern science favors a pragmatics of language games. As in traditional or premodern narrative, the positions of speaker, listener, and referent of the narratives are more fluid and interchangeable. Society is seen to be reproduced in a circular, face-to-face fashion. From the postmodern perspective, the once dominant discourses of positivist and Marxist science become, for example, just more language games incapable of legitimating, or delegitimating, the other language games. The postmodern perspective rejects the modern belief that theory mirrors or corresponds to reality. From its perspectivist and relativist positions it contends that, at best, theories provide only fleeting, partial perspectives on their objects, that all cognitive representations are mediated by language, culture, and history. The notion of totalizing macroperspectives, i.e. paradigms, is rejected in favor of microtheory and a micropolitics that challenges modern discourse and institutionalized forms of power.[63]

It seems likely that postmodern theory, with its difficult and provocative new ideas, has the potential to occupy some of the space vacated by the collapse of modernist grand theories, especially structural-functionalism, with its notions of consensus and causality, and Marxist structuralism, with its tired global philosophy of the subject and its vision of social evolution as destiny. Instead, postmodern perspectives reject modernity as a historical movement toward control based on foundational knowledge and replace notions of rationality and logic with paralogy, or counterlogic, and a concern to allow all to speak and enter the terrain of social agonistics. Its de-centering and antifoundational perspective links power with knowledge and, reflexively, even views emancipatory moral rhetoric as merely another of the forms assumed by power.[64]

Since the beginning of the nineteenth century, comparative education texts have made valuable contributions to our understanding of educational relations in earlier stories of transformations to capitalism, urbanism, and political democracy. Today, with the transformation of modernity, poststructural and postmodern ways of seeing offer comparative educators timely yet challenging new metaphors and perspectives in their attempts to theorize the present into as yet unknown educational and cultural constructs.

Humanist/Interpretivist

The pragmatic-interactionist orientation in comparative education texts also rejects totalizing theory and favors interpretive method in attempts to understand how social actors come to consciousness within social structures. It has sought to determine, through a better understanding of knowledge in practice and community, which perspectives have pragmatic, i.e., operational and heuristic value. [65] Drawing upon Dewey and Mead—and more recently on neopragmatic texts by Rorty— pragmatic interactionism offers an intersubjective central space where all paradigmatic perspectives may overlap (see fig. 2), where all worldviews and ways of seeing may interact in the context of a contingent educational change practice, and a pragmatism that claims to be open to difference. [66]

Equally central to the humanist paradigm, the ethno-graphic perspective favors local knowledge and interpretation over totalizing paradigmatic constructs and modernization agendas for progressive change. In comparative education, this perspective has, for example, been used to describe participant perception of classroom experiences among poor Latin American students [67] and patterns of academic persistence and achievement among immigrant and "involuntary minority" children. [68] While the ethnographic perspective claims to provide description of how ethnic groups and others view and interpret educational practice, ethnographic data as "thick description" have little if any comparative value without the imposition of an ethnological or ideological comparative overlay. [69]

Accordingly, neither Heyman's proposal to replace positivism with ethnomethodological method nor Clignet's call for an exclusive phenomenological approach to comparative education has as yet garnered much support. But with the field now entering a time of eclectic critical post-positivism, the humanist paradigm, with its focus on culture, creativity, and emotion, is combining with other perspectives in the void left by the deconstruction of the scientific functionalist and the emancipatory grand metanarratives. Here, phenomenography, or narrative-dependent content, also shows promise in recent efforts to map increasingly diverse cultural clusters and knowledge communities now interacting within the dynamic intellectual field of comparative and international education texts.[70]

Phenomenography is about the qualitatively different ways in which people experience or think about various phenomena, about the relations between human beings and their world. In comparative education, phenomenographic studies have sought, as in this work, to characterize how researchers see, apprehend, and think about knowledge constructs such as paradigms and theories at different times and in different knowledge cultures and subcultures. Through empirical studies as well as textual analysis, phenomenographic studies seek not to describe things as they are but to show how they have been presented as sedimentations of ways of thinking about the world.[71] Categories of description identified in phenomenographic research are seen as a form of discovery and as the main outcomes of such inquiry. Comparison of alternative perspectives seeks to identify distinctive characteristics or essential structures of each conceptualization, as in this discourse analysis, so they may be made visible, described, and mapped.[72]

Mapping Knowledge Perspectives

Earlier examples of mapping knowledge perspectives in comparative and international education texts can be seen in Anderson, where implicitly structural functionalism orthodoxy occupied all space; in Paulston, where polarized equilibrium and conflict paradigms enclosed equal space; in Epstein, where three distinct and supposedly incommensurable and irreconcilable paradigms labeled "neopositivist," "neo-Marxist," and "neo-relativist" contested for space; in Adams's presentation of a multidimensional typology; and in the more open and interactive maps presented in this study.[73] Maps are a distinct mode of visual representation that use space to represent space. They offer, when combined with discourse analysis, a system of possibility for new knowledge. All maps contrast two interdependent planes of reality—the ground or the territory. Accordingly, any map is a construct, a conceptual configuration that has been thematized, abstracted, and lifted from the ground to another plane of meaning. Topographic maps, for example, reinscribe a place, or "analysis situs," of geological features on a flat map surface. In similar fashion, conceptual maps—as presented here—reinscribe and structure ways of seeing social and educational phenomena embedded in the semiotic space of literary texts and the intertextual space of educational practice.

In Figure 6.2, paradigms and theories in the field of comparative education have been identified with the use of textual analysis and are presented in a metadiscourse field with four paradigmatic "nodes" and four theory "basins." Textual dispositions regarding social and educational change (the verticle dimension) and characterization of reality (the horizontal dimension) are the coordinates used to topologize, or give form—albeit fuzzy—to textual orientations, or genres within the field. Arrows are used to indicate genealogy and the directions of knowledge relations. Several advantages of the Figure may be noted. It facilitates, for example, a reinscription and resituation of meanings, events, and knowledge communities in an open field. It suggests a dynamic and rhizomatic field of tangled roots and tendrils. Comparative education is now portrayed as a mapping of the intertextual weavings of diverse discourse communities rather than the objectified images presented to the world in earlier foundational texts. The strength of social theory in the field today is in fact firmly grounded in the very multiplicity of its perspectives and tools known through intertextual composition. Simultaneously, in the shaping and

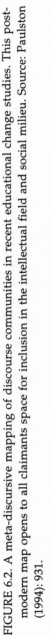

FIGURE 6.2. A meta-discursive mapping of discourse communities in recent educational change studies. This post-modern map opens to all claimants space for inclusion in the intellectual field and social milieu. Source: Paulston (1994): 931.

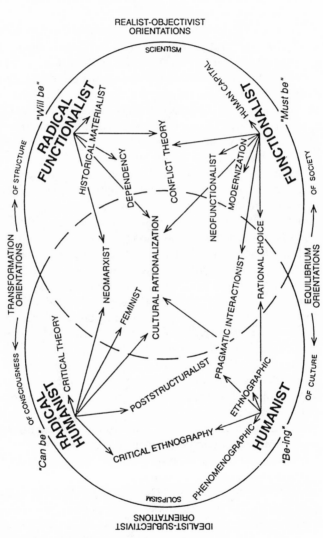

interrelating of knowledge communities and relations, Figures 6.1, 6.2, and 6.3 introduce into complex systems a fleeting representation of their own complexity and help new discourse communities find space and voice both on the map and in the agonistic field.[74]

The paradox here is that conceptual mapping can create both distorted authoritarian images and new tools to challenge orthodox boundaries and the epistemological myth of cumulative scientific progress. Maps also will vary depending on the mapper's textual orientation and the topological format chosen. With computer technology, cognitive mapping becomes an ongoing, rapidly changing process. Flows of information "can now stake out claims on expanses of pure space in which bodies of knowledge have displaced human bodies and on which all boundaries are tenuous."[75] Today, social cartography offers comparative educators a valuable tool to capture text and context, to transfer the rhetoric and metaphor of texts on to maps, and to open a way for intertextuality among competing discourses.[76] And when needed, maps can also provide a way to see all knowledge communities thoroughly enmeshed in the larger boundary disputes that constitute our world. Here postmodern social cartography is a critical practice as it questions all exclusions and boundaries, demystifies rhetoric (including its own), and interprets discourse as a site and object of struggle where different groups strive for hegemony in the production of meaning and ideology. Fox-Genovese contends that by giving structure to new ideas, cognitive mapping can serve as a means of counterhegemonic boundary setting needed to break down unjust established boundaries. In contrast, another postmodern argument sees all boundary setting as leading to hierarchy and eventual oppression. Deluze and Guttari, for example, suggest that boundaries must be constantly contested by what they call "nomads," i.e., militants who advocate partial perspectives and resist all demands to globalize or hierarcize.[77] I come down somewhere in between these opposing arguments and favor a contingent and provisional use of boundary making as a basis for critical postmodern cartography. In this way, maps can also be practical. They can provide individual and community orientation to and in practice, and they can help us see and juxtapose proliferating knowledge communities producing an ever-expanding textual discourse.[78]

Figure 6.3 presents a textually derived mesomapping of paradigmatic worldviews and theoretical perspectives entering into and intertwined in a specific educational reform practice. This visual representation, in contrast to Figure 6.2, describes a specific national educational change practice at a particular time and place—i.e., in Nicaraguan higher-educational reform efforts in the early 1980s. It begins to suggest how ideas and social practices interconnect. Here practice is viewed as a hermeneutic circle where four major stakeholder groups in the reform practice bring their guiding worldviews, theoretical perspectives, and purposes into a goal-oriented interactive educational change process.[79] Where Figure 6.3 suggests actors, behavior, and accomplishments within the context of everyday life, Figure 6.2 offers a systemic juxtaposition of the sources of intellectual energy identified in paradigmatic exemplars and the interaction of theoretical perspectives. With such perspectivist maps of various levels of the micro-meso-macro continuum, educational policy researchers can now move beyond modernism's arbitrary dichotomies and absurd oppositions to situate themselves within the multiple levels of reality in which they are players. And by becoming mappers, they will help to make educational studies a more reflexive and spatial field whose subject matter increasingly encompasses itself. They can also gain what Bourdieu sees as "an extraordinary autonomy, especially when you don't use it [i.e., cognitive mapping] as a weapon against others, or as an instrument of defense, but rather as a weapon against yourself, as an instrument of vigilance."[80]

Conclusion

This study has used discourse analysis and the phenomenographic method to examine the weave of discourses and practices about educational change in comparative and international education texts over time as bricolage—i.e., as historically locatable assemblages of cultural codes and practices, and as cognitive maps spacing discursive formations and their ways of

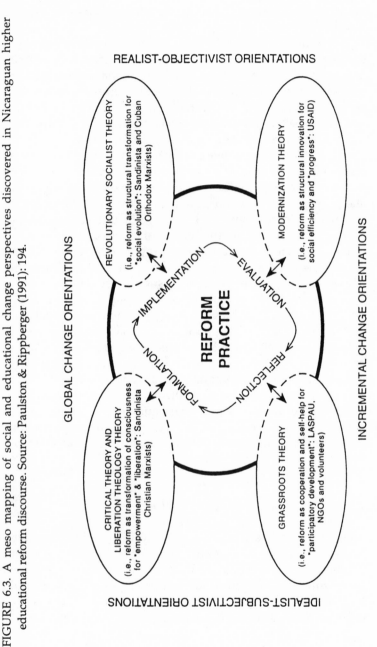

FIGURE 6.3. A meso mapping of social and educational change perspectives discovered in Nicaraguan higher educational reform discourse. Source: Paulston & Rippberger (1991): 194.

seeing at macro and meso levels of social reality. Three major orientations to knowledge in the field over time are identified as the orthodox, the heterodox, and the emerging heterogeneous. Relations between discourse communities today are also identified and discussed. We note that comparative educators and their texts are becoming more reflexive and eclectic, thus allowing new ways of seeing and new mapping opportunities to emerge from the reinscription of earlier theories and the changing spatial relations of our time.

NOTES

1. J. Smith, *Mystical Rhetoric* (London, 1657): 150.

2. R. Rorty, *Contingency, Irony, and Solidarity* (Cambridge: Cambridge University Press, 1989): 135.

3. D. Weinstein and M. A. Weinstein, "Postmodernizing (Macro) Sociology." *Sociological Inquiry* 63 (1993): 224–225.

4. For an explanation of Bourdieu's interactive field of power, see his "Social and Symbolic Power," *Sociological Theory* 7 (1989): 14–25. Bourdieu in his mapping rationale argues that social and intellectual worlds may be uttered and constructed in different ways according to different principles of vision and division, that failing to construct the space of positions leaves you no chance of seeing the point from which you see what you see. And because the struggle over boundaries and classifications such as maps is a fundamental dimension of class struggle, "to change the world one has to change the ways of world making, that is, the vision of the world and the practical operations by which groups are produced and reproduced" (p. 23).

5. R. Barthes, "From Work to Text," in *Textual Strategies: Perspectives in Poststructural Criticism*, ed. J. Hariri (Ithaca: Cornell University Press, 1979): 48–63. Barthes argues that textual understanding is related to social and political understanding. Where modernist science has traditionally viewed language as a transparent instrument or tool devoid of ideational or practical content, literary theory sees language as opaque and seeks to penetrate this opacity in order to recover the commitments and practices contained in language. My choice has been to see this reading as mythic. See P. Ricoeur, "The

Model of the Text: Meaningful Action Considered as a Text," in *Interpretive Social Science*, ed. R. Rabinow and W. Sullivan (Berkeley: University of California Press, 1979): 73–102. Others have seen readings as "violent" (Foucault), "social" (Brown), "political" (Jameson), "rhetorical" (Gadamer), or "ludic" (Baudrillard). These and other orientations to textual exegesis are examined in M. Shapiro, "Literary Production as a Politicizing Practice," in *Language and Politics*, ed. M. Shapiro (New York: New York University Press, 1984): 215–254.

6. G. Olsson, "Invisible Maps: A Prospectus," *Geografiska Annaler* 73 (1991): 91.

7. Illustrative texts of the 1950s and 1960s subjected to analysis are D. Adams and J. Farrell, "Societal Differentiation and Educational Differentiation," *Comparative Education* 5 (1959): 249–262; C. A. Anderson, "The Methodology of Comparative Education," *International Review of Education* 7 (1961): 1–23; G. Bereday, *Comparative Method in Education* (New York: Holt, Rinehart and Winston, 1964); T. Husén, ed., *International Study of Achievement in Education: A Comparison of Twelve Countries* (Stockholm: Almqvist and Wiksell, 1967); H. Noah and M. Eckstein, *Toward a Science of Comparative Education* (New York: Macmillan, 1969); and T. Schultz, "Education and Economic Growth," in *Social Forces Influencing American Education*, ed. N. Henry (Chicago: University of Chicago Press, 1961): 46–88.

Texts from the 1970s and 1980s are C. A. Anderson, "Comparative Education over a Quarter of a Century: Maturity and Challenges," *Comparative Education Review* 21 (1977): 405–416; P. Bourdieu and J. Passeron, *Reproduction: In Culture, Education, Society* (Beverly Hills: Sage, 1977); S. Bowles and H. Gintis, *Schooling in Capitalist America* (New York: Basic Books, 1976); M. Carnoy, "Marxism and Education," in *The Left Academy: Marxism on American Campuses*, ed. B. Ollman and E. Vernoff (New York: Praeger, 1984): 79–98; R. Clignet, "The Double Natural History of Educational Interactions: Implications for Educational Reforms," *Comparative Education Review* 25 (1981): 330–352; E. Epstein, "Currents Left and Right: Ideology in Comparative Education," *Comparative Education Review* 27 (1983): 3–29; R. Heyman, "Comparative Education from an Ethnomethodological Perspective," *Comparative Education* 15 (1979): 241–249; T. Husén, "Research Paradigms in Education," *Interchange* 19 (1988): 2–13; J. Karabel and A. Halsey, ed., *Power and Ideology in Education* (London: Oxford University Press, 1977); G. Kelly and A. Nihlen, "Schooling and the Reproduction of Patriarchy," in *Cultural and Economic Reproduction in Education*, ed. M. Apple (London: Routledge and Kegan Paul, 1982): 162–180; and R.

Paulston, "Social and Educational Change: Conceptual Frameworks,"
Comparative Education Review 21 (1977): 370–395.

   Texts from the 1990s are P. Altbach, "Trends in Comparative
Education," *Comparative Education Review* 35 (1991): 491–507; R. Cowen,
"The National and International Impact of Comparative Education
Infrastructures," in *Comparative Education: Contemporary Issues and
Trends*, ed. W. Halls (Paris: UNESCO, 1990); P. Lather, *Getting Smart:
Feminist Research and Pedagogy within the Post-Modern* (London:
Routledge, 1991); V. Masemann, "Ways of Knowing: Implications for
Comparative Education," *Comparative Education Review* 34 (1990): 465–
473; R. Paulston, "Comparative and International Education: Paradigms
and Theories," in *International Encyclopedia of Education* (Oxford:
Pergamon Press, 1994); R. Paulston and M. Tidwell, "Latin American
Education—Comparative," in *Encyclopedia of Educational Research* (New
York: Macmillan, 1992); V. Rust, "Postmodernism and Its Comparative
Education Implications," *Comparative Education Review* 35 (1991): 610–
626; N. Stromquist, "Gender Inequality in Education: Accounting for
Women's Subordination," *British Journal of Sociology of Education* 11
(1990): 137–154; H. von Recum, "Erziehung in der Post-moderne"
(Education in the postmodern period), *Die politesche Meinung* 237 (1990):
76–93.

   8. E. Gottlieb, "The Discursive Construction of Knowledge,"
International Journal of Qualitative Studies in Education 2 (1989): 131–132.

   9. Anderson, "Methodology of Comparative Education," p. 11.

   10. Bereday, *Comparative Method*, pp. 4–9.

   11. Noah and Eckstein argue for a combination of E. Nagel's logical
positivism and K. Popper's hypothesis-testing approaches. See their
chap. 10, "Scientific Method and Comparative Education," pp. 112–122.

   12. See, for example, Rorty, *Contingency*, chap. 3, where he argues
that thinkers such as Nietzsche, Freud, and Wittgenstein have, along
with Dewey, enabled societies to see themselves ironically, as historical
contingencies rather than as expressions of underlying, ahistorical
human nature or as realizations of suprahistorical goals. For an
influential critique of positivism by Rorty, see his *Philosophy and the
Mirror of Nature* (Princeton: Princeton University Press, 1979).

   13. T. Husén, *International Study of Achievement in Mathematics: A
Comparison of Twelve Countries* (Stockholm: Almqvist and Wiksell, 1967),
pp. 2, 71–72.

   14. Adams and Farrell, "Societal Differentiation and Educational
Differentiation," *Comparative Education* 5 (1959), p. 257.

15. *Ibid,* p. 261.

16. N. Wiley, "The History and Politics of Recent Sociological Theory," in *Frontiers of Social Theory: The New Syntheses,* ed. G. Ritzer (New York: Columbia University Press, 1990): 392–416.

17. S. Klees, "The Economics of Education: Is That All There Is?" *Comparative Education Review* 35 (1991): 721–734.

18. The emergence of a global comparative-education field is well documented in *Emergent Issues in Education: Comparative Perspectives,* ed. R. Arnove, P. Altbach, and G. Kelly (Albany: State University of New York Press, 1992).

19. L. Althusser, *Philosophy and the Spontaneous Philosophy of the Scientists* (London: Verso, 1990). See especially pp. 1–42, "Theory, Theoretical Practice, and Theoretical Formation," where Althusser's deterministic structural reproduction arguments from the 1960s are reprinted.

20. Bowles and Gintis, *Capitalist America,* pp. 132–134, 195–199, and 208–211.

21. Carnoy, "Marxism," pp. 83–87.

22. Karabel and Halsey, *Power and Ideology,* p. 71.

23. Kelly and Nihlen, "Reproduction of Patriarchy," pp. 162–163.

24. See, for example, S. Star, "The Sociology of the Invisible," in *Social Organization and Social Process,* ed. D. Maines (New York: Aldine De Gruyter, 1991): 265–283.

25. Heyman, "Comparative Education," pp. 241–243.

26. Clignet, "Double Natural History," pp. 331–334.

27. Paulston, *Social and Educational Change,* pp. 371–374; and Epstein, "Currents," pp. 3–6.

28. See Paulston, *Ibid,* pp. 372–373.

29. See Masemann, "Ways of Knowing"; Lather, "Getting Smart"; and inter alia, N. Stromquist, "Determinants of Educational Achievement of Women in the Third World," *Review of Educational Research* 59 (1989): 143–183.

30. Anderson, "Comparative Education over a Quarter of a Century," p. 413. R. Lawson made the first major pluralist counterattack on attempts by Anderson and his students to enclose the field in functionalist logic and scientistic methods—i.e., the "Chicago Orthodoxy." In his 1975 presidential address, "Free-Form Comparative Education," *Comparative Education Review* 19 (1975): 345–353, Lawson opposed "the application of a political religion to social science," the

denial of legitimate opposition, and the enclosure of all scholarly activity within an orthodoxy of narrow political parameters (pp. 345–346).

31. Altbach, "Trends in Comparative Education," *Comparative Education Review* 35 (1991): 491–507. For a continuation of this movement, see Paulston, "Ways of Seeing," pp. 177–202.

32. See the debate in "Colloquy on Comparative Theory," *Comparative Education Review* 34(3) (1990): 369–404.

33. See also Rust, "Postmodernism," pp. 614–616.

34. Husén, *Achievement in Education*, pp. 10–12.

35. Rust, "Postmodernism," pp. 623–626.

36. R. Barthes, "Work to Text," p. 61. M. de Certeau claims, in this regard, that "narrative structures have the status of spatial syntaxes," that all discourse suggests a positioning in space, and that such imaginary spatial trajectories invite comparison. I would also argue for a conceptual mapping that links the concept-metaphor of textuality with the provisional structure of topography. From this view, texts communicate not only an order of signs (i.e., semiology) but have validity for a more philosophical portrayal of the "experience of space" (i.e., in cognitive mapping) as well. See M. de Certeau, *The Practice of Everyday Life* (Berkeley: University of California Press, 1984); and B. Bartolovich, "Boundary Disputes: Textuality and the Flows of Transnational Capital," *Meditations* 17 (1992): 27.

37. See C. Cherryholms, *Power and Criticism: Post-Structural Investigations in Education* (New York: Teachers College Press, 1988); von Recum, pp. 82–86; Rust, "Postmodernism," pp. 622–624; and M. Liebman and R. Paulston, "Social Cartography: A New Methodology for Comparative Studies." *Compare* 25 (1994): 233–245.

38. For influential examples of earlier postmodern turns in anthropology and cultural geography, respectively, see J. Clifford and G. Marcus, eds., *Writing Culture: The Poetics and Politics of Ethnography* (Berkeley: University of California Press, 1986); and T. Barnes and J. Duncan, eds., *Writing Worlds: Discourse, Text, and Metaphor in Representations of Landscape* (London: Routledge, 1992).

39. For an argument that economists and their "crassly materialistic view of education" and "treatment of schools as manpower factories" helped to produce development education failures, see P. Coombs, *The World Crisis in Education* (London: Oxford University Press, 1985), pp. 14–20.

40. See T. Schultz, "Investing in People," *Economics of Education Review* 8 (1989): 219–240.

41. Klees, "Economics of Education," pp. 731–733; and J. Lauglo, "Vocational Training and the Bankers' Faith in the Private Sector," *Comparative Education Review* 36 (1992): 227–236. From a critical pragmatic perspective, Lauglo critiques World Bank efforts to train human resources for modernization projects as biased in favor of neoclassical economics and the private sector and as "too narrow to suit changing conditions." In the Bank's operational work "They come in and . . . tell you what you need." Their view of change is evolutionary and unilinear. Their theoretical orientation is Eurocentric, lacking in cultural sensitivity, and comes across "as ideological (or as aloof economic theorizing) rather than rooted in experience" (p. 232).

42. Rondinelli et al., *Planning Educational Reforms in Developing Countries* (Durham: Duke University Press, 1990), pp. 53–63.

43. See, for example, D. Plank, "The Politics of Basic Education Reform in Brazil." *Comparative Education Review* 34 (1990), 538–560.

44. See N. Luhmann, "The Paradox of Systems Differentiation and the Evolution of Society," in *Differentiation Theory and Social Change: Comparative and Historical Perspectives*, ed. J. Alexander and P. Colony (New York: Columbia University Press, 1990): 63–91; and J. Schriewer and E. Keiner, "Communication Patterns and Intellectual Traditions," *Comparative Education Review* 36 (1992): 25–51. Luhmann's objectification of the subjective realm expands reality to include both realist and relativist worldviews, as communication required by "autopoiesis" or self-referential, systems. From this totalizing perspective, actions are seen not to be produced by an actor's subjective motives but by the needs of complex systems to manage their own reproduction, i.e., to transform noise into information which keeps in motion the self-referential network of internal processes. Luhmann claims that his logocentric story of complex systems can fill all the space of knowledge and that it will put an end to controversies between positivists and dialecticians and between scientists and humanists. See his "Insistence on Systems Theory: Perspectives from Germany," *Social Forces* 61(4) (1983): 987–998.

45. D. Turner, "Problem Solving in Comparative Education," *Compare* 17 (1987), pp. 110–121, 158–163.

46. J. Coleman, "Micro-foundations and Macrosocial Behavior," in *The Micro-Macro Link*, ed. J. Alexander et al. (Berkeley: University of California Press, 1987): 153–173.

47. *See* J. Elster, "Further Thoughts on Marxism, Functionalism, and Game Theory," in *Analytic Marxism*, ed. J. Roemer (Cambridge: Cambridge University Press, 1986): 36–59.

48. For an excellent review, see R. Collins, "Conflict Theory and the Advance of Macro-Historical Sociology," in Ritzer, "Frontiers of Social Theory," pp. 68–87.

49. See M. Archer, chaps. 6, 7, and 8. *Social Origins of Educational Systems* (London: Sage, 1984).

50. Bourdieu and Passeron, *Reproduction*, pp. 4–5, 141, and 217.

51. See, for example, R. Paulston, "Education as Antistructure: Nonformal Education in Social and Ethnic Movements," *Comparative Education* 16 (1980): 64–65.

52. S. Bowles and H. Gintis, *Democracy and Capitalism* (New York: Basic Books, 1986): 176–213.

53. M. Carnoy and J. Samoff, *Education and Social Transition in the Third World* (Princeton: Princeton University Press, 1990), pp. 3–13, 377–380. For a sympathetic yet rigorous critique of Marxist theories of schooling, see D. Liston, *Capitalist Schools: Explanation of Ethics in Radical Studies of Schooling* (New York: Routledge, 1988). Liston sees traditional Marxist explanations as trapped within a functionalist view of schools — i.e., they use effects to explain events, they lack researchable propositions, and they lack empirical assessments of radical functionalist claims. Instead, Liston advocates a plurality of methodological approaches to study educational change efforts, considering "the empirical scientific" orientation appropriate for questions of causality within structural relations and the "hermeneutic-interpretive" orientation appropriate to questions of cultural and personal meaning. F. Jamison has also proposed an ambitious reconceptualization of the radical structuralist perspective. His "cognitive mapping" strategy provides a conception of social totality that includes both the micro view of decentered individual experience and the macro view of saturated and enormously complex new international space now thoroughly penetrated by what he calls hypercapitalism. Such maps—yet to be created—would, he claims, have "the great merit of stressing the gap between the local positioning of the individual subject and the totality of class structures in which he or she is situated, a gap between phenomenological perception and a reality that transcends all individual thinking or experience. This ideology attempts to span or coordinate, to map, by means of conscious and unconscious representations" (p. 353). See his highly original chapter, "Cognitive Mapping," in *Marxism and the Interpretation of Culture*, ed. L.

Grossberg and C. Nelson (Urbana: University of Illinois Press, 1988): 347–357.

54. See, for example, H. Weiler, "Why Reforms Fail." *Journal of Curriculum Studies* 21 (1989): 291–305; and A. Welsh, "Knowledge and Legitimation," *Comparative Education Review* 35 (1991): 508–531. In his characterization of comparative education texts, Welsh notes the choice of a "broadly functionalist, positivistic perspective" from 1930–1970; the addition of critical and interpretive views during the 1970s; and after 1980, the use of neo-Weberian and micro-macro knowledge perspectives as well. See his "mapping" study, "Class, Culture, and the State in Comparative Education," *Comparative Education* 29 (1993): 7–27.

55. For an explanation of how Habermas sees Mead's social psychology as clearing "the way for a communication concept of rationality," see J. Habermas, "The Paradigm Shift in Mead: The Foundations of Social Science in the Theory of Communication," in *Philosophy, Social Theory, and the Thought of George Herbert Mead*, ed. M. Aboulafia (Albany: State University of New York Press, 1991): 137–168.

56. R. Arnove, "Comparative Education and World Systems." *Comparative Education Review* 24 (1980): 48–62.

57. See P. Altbach, *The Knowledge Context: Comparative Perspectives on the Distribution of Knowledge* (Albany: SUNY Press, 1987).

58. See for example, N. Stromquist's "Educating Women: The Political Economy of Patriarchal States," *International Studies in Sociology of Education* 1 (1991): 111–128; and "Women and Literacy: Promises and Constraints," *Annals, AAPSS* 520 (March, 1992): 54–65. Here feminist perspectives are brought to bear on problems of structured inequality to help make the invisible visible, and to produce valuable new knowledge.

59. D. Foley, "Rethinking School Ethnographies of Colonial Settings: A Performance Perspective of Reproduction and Resistance." *Comparative Education Review* 35 (1991): 532–551; and L. Weis, *Working Class Without Work: Highschool Students in a De-industrializing Economy* (New York: Routledge, 1990): pp. 11, 14–15, and 214.

60. See Cherryholms, *Power and Criticism*, chaps. 1 and 8; and Rust, "Postmodernism," pp. 614–616.

61. J. Derrida, *Speech and Phenomena* (Evanston: Northwestern University Press, 1973). The postmodern political agenda evidences a stoic bias and a paradoxical irresolution of things in the world. See, for example, the brilliant, if deeply nihilistic, theoretical narrative by J. Baudrillard, *Revenge of the Crystal: Selected Writings on the Modern Object*

and Its Destiny, 1968–1983 (London: Pluto Press, 1990), and especially his nightmare vision "Mass Media Culture," on pp. 63–98.

62. J. F. Lyotard, *The Differend: Phrases in Dispute* (Minneapolis: University of Minnesota Press, 1988): 20–38. Here, foundationalist discourse seeking to establish universals or to provide true accounts of phenomena in the world is viewed from a postmodernist perspective as nostalgia. Postmodern texts reject all totalizing ambitions of modernist social science. All knowledge, both personal and communal, is to be critically examined and continually undermined through paralogical deconstruction. While postmodernism in the abstract is unescapably relativistic and nihilistic, in practice growing numbers of academics have selectively appropriated new ideas from this perspective to question our fragmenting cultural order and to retheorize modernist theories of resistance, i.e., feminism, critical theory, Marxism, dependency theory, and the like. Above all, postmodernism directs our attention to problems of difference, and to the Other in a global electronic society. Ironically, it welcomes new ways of seeing, as in this chapter, and then deconstructs or undermines them. For a penetrating yet fairminded critique of contradictions and absences embedded in the postmodern perspective, see J. Duncan and T. Barnes, eds., *Writing Worlds: Discourse, Text, and Metaphor in the Representation of Landscape* (London: Routledge, 1992): 248–253.

63. S. Best and D. Kellner, *Postmodern Theory: Critical Interrogations* (New York: Guilford Press, 1991): 4–5, 170. See also R. Paulston and M. Liebman, "An Invitation to Post-Modern Social Cartography," *Comparative Education Review* 38 (1994): 215–232.

64. M. Foucault, *Power/Knowledge* (New York: Pantheon, 1980).

65. Examples may be seen in E. King, "The Expanding Frontier of Pluralism," *Comparative Education* 19 (1983): 227–230; in his earlier study of practice, *Other Schools and Ours*, 5th ed. (London: Holt, Rinehart, and Winston, 1979); and "Commentary: Observations from Outside and Decisions Inside," *Comparative Education Review* 34 (1990): 392–394. For an outstanding presentation of how critical pragmatism views educational change problems, see C. Cherryholms, "Modernity, Pragmatism, and Educational Change," in *Discourse and Power in Educational Administration*, ed. D. Corson and A. Hargreaves. Forthcoming.

66. See A. Neiman, "Ironic Schooling: Socrates, Pragmatism, and the Higher Learning," *Educational Theory* 41 (1991): 371–384.

67. B. Avalos, *Teaching Children of the Poor: An Ethnographic Study in Latin America* (Ottawa: International Development Research Centre, 1989), pp. 9–12, 158–164.

68. M. Gibson and J. Ogbu, see chap. 1. *Minority Status and Schooling: A Comparative Study of Immigrant and Involuntary Minorities* (New York: Garland, 1991).

69. As in G. Spindler and L. Spindler, see chaps. 1 and 2. *Interpretive Ethnography of Education* (Hillsdale: Erlbaum, 1987).

70. H. Ross et al., "On Shifting Ground: The Post Paradigmatic Identity of U.S. Comparative Education," *Comparative Education* 22 (1992): 113–131, where changing ways of seeing the field of comparative education are presented.

71. G. Helmstad and F. Marton, "Conceptions of Understanding." Paper presented at the American Educational Research Association Annual Meeting, San Francisco, CA, April 20–24, 1992.

72. See F. Marton, "'Phenomenography' and the Art of Teaching All Things to All Men," *Qualitative Studies in Education* 5 (1992): 253–268; and my study, "Ways of Seeing Education and Social Change in Latin America: A Phenomenographic Perspective," *Latin American Research Review* 27 (1992): 177–202. Drawing the boundaries of textual dispositions or genre categories is, of course, controversial. The anti-interpretive textualists argue for "system, interconnection and seamlessness." The structuralists call for at least provisional boundaries so as to confront those who draw boundaries of superordination in the social milieu. James Clifford concedes that "the free play of readings may in theory be infinite . . . [but] there are at any historical moment [only] a limited range of allegories available." See Bartolovich, "Boundary Disputes," p. 29.

73. See Anderson, *The Methodology of Comparative Education*, pp. 20–21; Paulston, *Social and Educational Change*, pp. 372–373; Epstein, "Current Left and Right," pp. 5 and 6; and D. Adams. "Expanding the Educational Planning Discourse: Conceptual and Paradigmatic Explorations." *Comparative Education Review* 32 (1988): 400–415.

74. For a discussion of maps as socially embedded discourse see J. B. Harley's highly original essay, "Maps, Knowledge, and Power," in *The Iconography of Landscape: Essays on the Symbolic Representation, Design, and Use of Past Environments*, ed. D. Cosgrove and S. Daniels (New York: Cambridge University Press, 1988): 123–138.

75. Bartolovich, "Boundary Disputes," p. 23.

76. For related attempts using figural space to map cognitive constructs, see for example, C. Hampden-Turner, *Maps of the Mind* (New York: Macmillan, 1982), with sixty provocative maps that combine text and visuospatial imagery; K. W. McCain, "Mapping Authors in Intellectual Space: A Technical Overview," *Journal of the American Society for Information Science* 41 (1990): 433–443, where superficial author cocitation analysis (ACA) using computers produces three-dimensional maps of clusters claiming to interrelate "subject areas, research specialties, schools of thought, shared intellectual styles, or temporal or geographic ties"; and M. Lynch, "Pictures of Nothing? Visual Construals in Social Theory," *Sociological Theory* 9 (1991): 1–21, where the author draws upon ethnomethodological and social constructivist studies of representation in the natural sciences. He finds that labels, geometric boundaries, vectors, and symmetries may be used as a sort of "rhetorical mathematics" to convey the impression of rationality. While such "theory pictures" show little beyond what a text says in its writing, they are valuable in their ability to simulate a hermeneutic passage from written ideas to an independent representational or mathematical space. Here maps can provide an independent "work space" that reflexively informs a reading and makes possible, as in this chapter, the representation of intellectual fields as theoretical landscapes.

77. See Bartolovich, "Boundary Disputes," p. 30.

78. See J. B. Harley, "Deconstructing the Map," *Cartographica* 26 (1989): 1–20; and S. S. Hall, *Mapping the Next Millennium: The Discovery of the New Geographies* (New York: Random House, 1992). I view the emergence of new theory as a local process that takes place in competing intellectual communities. Differences between communities are primarily between the "facts," i.e., the cultural code that each emphasizes and the metaphors each employs. The application of old beliefs to new circumstances may accordingly be seen as an attempt to identify similarities and differences, making the acquisition of new theory an inherently metaphorical process. Here the task for policy analysis shifts to interpretation of discourse and to new ways or metaphors—such as conceptual mapping—in which the representation of difference may be presented. From this perspective, Arib and Hesse argue that "to make explicit the ramifications of metaphor [mapping] is to engage in critique, evaluation, and perhaps replacement. Metaphor [mapping] is potentially revolutionary." See M. Arib and M. Hesse, *The Construction of Reality* (Cambridge: Cambridge University Press, 1986): 156. For help in using internal grounds rather than an absolute benchmark assessment to evaluate metaphors in context, Hesse has provided a useful formal framework to assess the suitability of

metaphor in identifying similarity. See M. Hesse, "The Explanatory
Function of Metaphor," in *Revolutions and Reconstructions in the
Philosophy of Science* (Brighton: Harvester, 1980): 111–124.

79. See Paulston and Rippberger, pp. 193–194.

80. P. Bourdieu, *In Other Words: Essays towards a Reflexive Sociology*
(Stanford: Stanford University Press, 1990): 27.

REFERENCES

Bachelard, G. 1964. *The Poetics of Space*. Translated by M. Jolas. New
York: Orion.

Barnes, T., and J.S. Duncan. 1992. *Writing Worlds*. New York: Routledge.

Barthes, R. 1992. *Mythologies*. London: Jonathan Cape.

Battersby, J. 1991. *Paradigms Regained: Pluralism and the Practice of
Criticism*. Philadelphia: University of Pennsylvania Press.

Berger, P., and T. Luckmann. 1967. *The Social Construction of Reality*.
New York: Anchor Books.

Berman, M. 1982. *All That Is Solid Melts Into Air: The Experience of
Modernity*. New York: Simon and Schuster.

Booth, W.C. 1979. *Critical Understanding: The Powers and Limits of
Pluralism*. Chicago: The University of Chicago Press.

Brown, R.H. 1989. *A Poetic for Sociology: Towards a Logic of Discovery For
the Human Sciences*. Chicago: The University of Chicago Press.

Burns, R., and A. Welch. 1992. *Contemporary Perspectives in Comparative
Education*. New York: Garland.

Carnoy, M., et al. 1993. *The New Global Economy in the Information Age*.
University Park: Penn State Press.

Downs, R.M. 1985. "The Representations of Space: Its Development in
Children and Cartography." In *Development of Spatial Cognition*,
ed. R. Cohen, 323–345. Hillsdale: Lawrence Erlbaum.

Fox-Genovese, E. 1989. "Literary Criticism and the Politics of the New
Historicism." In *The New Historicism*, ed. H. Veeser, 213–224. New
York: Routledge.

Gardner, H. 1983. *Frames of Mind: The Theory of Multiple Intelligences*.
New York: Basic Books.

Garfinkel, H. 1967. *Studies in Ethnomethodology.* Englewood Cliffs: Prentice-Hall.

Geertz, C. 1973. *The Interpretation of Cultures.* New York: Basic Books.

Ginsburg, M., ed. 1991. *Understanding Educational Reform in Global Context: Economy, Ideology and the State.* New York: Garland.

Goodman, N. 1978. *Ways of Worldmaking.* Indianapolis: Hackett.

Gore, J.M. 1993. *The Struggle for Pedagogies: Critical and Feminist Discourses as Regimes of Truth.* New York: Routledge.

Gregory, D., and J. Urry, eds. 1985. *Social Relations and Spatial Structures.* London: Macmillan.

Guillen, C. 1968. "On the Conceptual Metaphor of Perspective." In *Comparatists at Work*, ed. R.B. Vowles, 28–90. Waltham: Blairsdell.

Habermas, J. 1981. "New Social Movements." *Telos* 49: 33–37.

———. 1975. *The Legitimation Crisis.* T. McCarthy, trans. Boston: Beacon Press.

Harding, S. 1991. *Whose Science, Whose Knowledge?* Ithaca: Cornell University Press.

Harley, J.B. 1989. "Deconstructing the Map." *Cartographica 26*: 1–20.

Hawley, E.W. 1979. *The Great War and the Search for a Modern Order.* New York: St. Martin's.

Huyssen, A. 1986. "Mapping the Postmodern." In *After the Great Divide: Modernism, Mass Culture, Postmodernism* 179–222. Bloomington: Indiana University Press.

Jackson, P. 1989. *Maps of Meaning.* London: Unwin Hyman.

Jamison, F. 1988. "Cognitive Mapping." In *Marxism and the Interpretation of Culture*, ed. C. Nelson and L. Grossberg, 347–360. Urbana: University of Illinois Press.

———. 1984. "Postmodern, Or the Cultural Logic of Late Capitalism." *New Left Review* 146: 53–92.

Kuhn, T. 1962. *The Structure of Scientific Revolutions.* Chicago: University of Chicago Press.

Lemmert, C. 1992. "General Social Theory, Irony, Postmodernism." In *Postmodernism and Social Theory: The Debate Over General Theory*, ed. S. Seidman and D. Wagner, 17–46. Oxford: Blackwell.

Little, D. 1991. "Towards Methodological Pluralism." In *Varieties of Social Explanation.* San Francisco: Westview Press.

Lyotard, J.F. 1984. *The Postmodern Condition: A Report on Knowledge.* Minneapolis: The University of Minnesota Press.

Maxcy, S.J., ed. 1994. *Postmodern School Leadership.* Westport: Praeger.

Megrowitz, J. 1985. *No Sense of Place: The Impact of Electronic Media on Social Behavior.* New York: Oxford University Press.

Meinig, D.W. 1976. "The Beholding Eye: Ten Versions of the Same Scene." *Landscape Architecture* (January): 47–64.

Meyer, J., and M. Hannan, eds. 1979. *National Development and the World System: Educational, Economic and Political Change, 1950-1970.* Chicago: University of Chicago Press.

Morrow, R., and C. Torres. 1994. "Education and the Reproduction of Class, Gender, and Race: Responding to the Postmodern Challenge." *Educational Theory* 44: 43–61.

————. 1994. *Social Theory and Education: A Critique of Theories of Social and Cultural Reproduction.* New York: SUNY Press.

Nicholson, L. 1990. *Feminism/Postmodernism.* New York: Routledge.

Parsons, T. 1966. *Societies: Evolutionary and Comparative Perspectives.* Englewood Cliffs: Prentice-Hall.

Paulston, R. 1983. "Conflicting Theories of Educational Reform." In *Better Schools: International Lessons for Reform,* ed. J. Simmons, 21–70. New York: Praeger.

Pieterse, J. 1988. "A Critique of World System Theory." *International Sociology* 3: 251–266.

Poster, M. 1990. *The Mode of Information: Poststructuralism and Social Context.* Chicago: University of Chicago Press.

Pred, A., and M. Watts. 1992. *Reworking Modernity.* New Brunswick: Rutgers University Press.

Ricoeur, P. 1980. "Existence and Hermeneutics." In *Contemporary Hermeneutics: Hermeneutics as Method, Philosophy and Critique* 236–256. London: Routledge.

Rorty, R. 1989. *Contingency, Irony and Solidarity.* Cambridge: Cambridge University Press.

Rust, V. 1977. *Alternatives in Education: Theoretical and Historical Perspectives.* London: Russell Sage.

Sack, R. 1980. *Conceptions of Space In Social Thought: A Geographical Perspective.* Minneapolis: University of Minnesota Press.

————. 1981. "A Typology of Educational Reforms." *Prospects* 11: 39–59.

Schrag, F. 1986. "Education and Historical Materialism." *Interchange* 7: 42–52.

Smith, C.D. 1982. "The Emergence of 'Maps' in European Rock Art: A Prehistoric Preoccupation with Place." *Imago Mundi* 34: 9–25.

Smith, N. 1981. "Degeneracy in Theory and Practice: Spatial Interactionism and Radical Eclecticism." *Progress in Human Geography* 5: 111–118.

Soja, E. 1989. *Postmodern Geographies: The Reassertion of Space in Critical Social Theory.* New York: Verso.

Turner, J. 1922. "The Promise of Positivism." In *Postmodernism and Social Theory*, ed. S. Seidman and D. Wagner, 156–178. London: Blackwell.

Wallerstein, I. 1991. *Unthinking Social Science: The Limits of Nineteenth-Century Paradigms.* Cambridge: Polity Press.

Wittgenstein, L. 1958. *Philosophical Investigations.* Oxford: Blackwell.

Woods, D. 1992. *The Power of Maps.* New York: The Guilford Press.

Wright, J. 1966. "Terrae Incognitae: The Place of the Imagination in Geography." In *Human Nature in Geography*. Cambridge: Harvard University Press.

7

Expanding Definitions of Learning and Teaching: Notes from the MI Underground

Mindy Kornhaber
Mara Krechevsky[1]

Introduction

Overview

In this paper, we report on an initial study of teachers and schools using Howard Gardner's Theory of Multiple Intelligences (MI). We conducted telephone interviews and later visited nine sites. The sites ranged from one classroom within a school to several schools within a district. Our goals were to uncover (1) the bases on which an MI approach was adopted, (2) the different ways in which the theory was being implemented, and (3) any formal or informal evaluations that suggested that MI was working.

In 1983 Howard Gardner published *Frames of Mind: The Theory of Multiple Intelligences*. Gardner, a developmental psychologist at the Harvard Graduate School of Education and the Boston Veterans Administration Medical Center, argued against the "classical" or "unitary" view of intelligence (Gardner 1983). This classical view holds that intelligence is a single underlying capacity enabling the kind of abstract reasoning embodied by the scientist, mathematician, and logician (Gardner 1983).

The classical view of intelligence was bolstered by Charles Spearman's early and influential work in psychometric testing. According to Spearman (1904, 1927), intelligence is an ability to detect relations and correlates. This ability is fueled by some sort of "mental energy," which he called general intelligence or g. Despite the warnings of Alfred Binet (Binet and Simon 1916), the father of intelligence testing in the schools, Binet's invention, mental age scores, lent credence to the idea that intelligence was one "thing." The conversion of mental age scores to IQ scores (Stern 1912) also helped to support a unitary notion of intelligence.

To challenge the unitary view of intelligence, Gardner drew upon findings from evolutionary biology, anthropology, developmental and cognitive psychology, neuropsychology, and psychometrics. He studied patterns of development in normal children and adults and patterns of abilities found in special populations, such as brain-damaged patients, child prodigies, and idiots savants. Defining an intelligence as the ability to solve problems or fashion products valued in particular cultural settings, Gardner posited seven relatively autonomous intelligences: linguistic, musical, logical-mathematical, spatial, bodily-kinesthetic, interpersonal, and intrapersonal (Gardner 1983, 1993). In Gardner's framework each person possesses all the intelligences; however, individuals combine and blend them in various ways in the course of solving problems and learning within domains of knowledge. (See Gardner 1983 and 1993 for a complete account of the theory's development.)

In its challenge of a unitary view, MI theory also calls into question conventional assessments of intelligence. Traditional intelligence tests address primarily linguistic and logical-mathematical abilities using paper-and-pencil measures. However, according to MI theory, such assessments not only overlook other intelligences, such as musical or interpersonal, they are not "intelligence fair." They do not ask people to draw upon the media and materials of different domains. Test subjects are not asked, for example, to perform a dance, moderate an argument, or compose a tune. Traditional programs for the gifted admit children on the basis of IQ test scores. However, MI theory implies that children possess gifts in a wider range of areas. These gifts cannot adequately be assessed by traditional IQ tests with their narrow focus on language and logic (Gardner 1993).

Although Gardner's theory was aimed primarily at his fellow psychologists, its impact was felt largely among educators (Gardner 1993). One year after the publication of *Frames of Mind*, a group of public school teachers in Indianapolis began meeting to discuss how to apply Gardner's theory. Three years later they started "The Key School," an elementary magnet school based on MI. Within a few more years, there were many private and public schools either based on or drawing upon MI theory. Few of the schools adopting the theory had any association with Gardner or his research group, Harvard Project Zero, and most of these associations were quite informal.

The adoption of MI theory by schools is unlike the adoption of several other recent reforms. Gardner, unlike founders of other reform efforts, does not propose a particular method of implementation or model of school organization. Thus, MI stands in marked contrast to such reforms as James Comer's School Development Program at Yale University. Comer sets forth a model for restructuring schools around three teams: a management team, a parent team, and a mental health team. Along with promoting organizational changes to enhance school climate, Comer trains district and school staff to become "change agents." Similarly, Henry Levin's Accelerated Schools program, based at Stanford University, emphasizes school-based governance committees. Participating schools are encouraged to design a reform program in conjunction with their district and to craft a clear set of goals. These efforts are aimed at bringing elementary children in largely disadvantaged schools up to grade level by the end of the sixth grade (Levin 1988).

Nor does Gardner advocate a particular approach to pedagogy. For example, he does not advise either teaching to students' intellectual strengths, or teaching to the separate intelligences every day, or integrating the intelligences in disciplinary or interdisciplinary curricula. This stance is unlike that of Ted Sizer's Coalition of Essential Schools. The Coalition, housed at Brown University, sets forth nine principles which can serve as guides to pedagogy as well as to curriculum and school organization at the high school level. For instance, teachers should act as coaches, coach no more than eighty students, and focus on "essential questions" (Sizer 1984, 1992).

Another difference between MI theory and other reforms mentioned above is that Harvard Project Zero does not provide a field staff to visit schools, collect information, and provide feedback. The Comer Program has field staff who gather data from the schools and whom people in the school and district can consult (Comer 1980, 1988a, 1988b). Similar staff exist for Sizer and Levin.

Though Gardner is interested in applications of his theory, he has focused more on research activity within Project Zero than on creating a framework for schools using MI (Gardner, personal communication). These unique features—the absence of field staff, pedagogical guidelines, and models for implementation and school structure—provoked an investigation of why schools adopted the theory, how they adapted it, and whether they attempted to evaluate their programs. This chapter presents the results of this study.

Methods

The data analyzed came primarily from two sources: interviews and site visits. The initial information was gathered from interviews with principals or program directors. Most of these were conducted by phone during the spring of 1992, although one was conducted in person. In the interviews, we asked for background information about the site and the surrounding school district, about issues concerning the schools' adoption of MI, how the theory was actually implemented, parents' reactions to the use of MI, and what, if any, evaluations had been conducted of their MI program. In addition to visits and interviews, we gathered written materials from most of the schools, either before or after our visits. Among these were program descriptions, newspaper clippings, grant proposals, and report card forms.

The sites in the study were not chosen on a random basis. Several had already had some contact with Project Zero personnel. Others were ones we had heard about through an informal network of people interested in the application of MI theory in schools. None were schools with which personnel from Project Zero had any ongoing discussions. Rather, they formed part of an MI Underground: places where teachers or administrators had decided on their own to implement the theory and where Gardner and other Project Zero personnel provided little, if any, direct input.

The only "hard" criterion for inclusion of a site was that MI implementation be in at least its second year.[2] As it turned out, all of the sites were elementary schools except for one (Poseidon), and all save one (Mercury) were public schools. In other respects, the sample was quite heterogeneous. One site consisted of a single elementary teacher in a small town in the Northwest (Dionysus). Another consisted of several schools within a large northeastern urban school district (Apollo). The rest were single schools in which either the whole staff or a cluster of teachers was implementing the theory. Our sample includes schools from all parts of the country except the Southwest. Table 7.1 summarizes key aspects of this sample.

After the initial interviews, we visited the schools and programs to observe classes and interview teachers. The visits all took place in the spring of 1992 and ranged in length from half a day (Poseidon) to two days (Apollo and Mercury). Visits to Venus, Athena, Neptune, and Dionysus each lasted one day; visits to Aphrodite and Diana each lasted one and one-half days. In the classroom sessions, we observed and sometimes participated in lessons given by teachers using the theory. We also interviewed some of these teachers as well as others implementing MI whose classroom practices we were not able to observe directly. In an attempt to triangulate the data, teacher interviews covered the same topics as those with the administrators. The visits also included many informal conversations with faculty, administrators, and students which provided a sense of how the faculty viewed the use of MI in their schools.

TABLE 7.1. School characteristics by site.

Site	Grades	Community	Geographic Location	SES	Racial/Ethnic Composition	School Size
Aphrodite	pre-K–5	urban/suburban	Southeast	mostly low and middle income	25% African-American, 25% other racial minorities; c. 25% linguistic minorities	600 students
Apollo	pre-K–5	urban	Mid-Atlantic	mostly low income	c. 95% minority, mostly African-American & Caribbean	800–1,000 students/school
Athena	pre-K–1	suburban/rural	Mid-Atlantic	mostly middle income	c. 99% white	170 students
Diana	pre-K–5	suburban/rural	South	varied SES	23% minority, mostly African-American	c. 500 students

Dionysus	K–5	suburban/rural	Northwest	primarily low and middle income	10% minority, mostly Native American	550 students
Mercury	pre-K–5	urban	Midwest	mostly middle income	26% minority, mostly African-American	355 students
Neptune	pre-K–5	suburban/small city	New England	varied SES	c. 95% white	780 students
Poseidon	7–8	urban/subrural	New England	varied SES	all white	340 students
Venus	pre-K–2	suburban	Mid-Atlantic	mostly low and middle income	70% minority, 34% African-American, 20% Hispanic, 10% Asian	450 students

As our discussion of sample and methods indicates, this initial study has several limitations. First, we did not have equal access to all the schools in terms of time and were not always able to observe classes in depth. Some visits included many short observations; others consisted of a few long observations. Interviews with teachers were occasionally cut short—not surprisingly, since they often occurred during teacher preparation periods or even during classes. Furthermore, the interviews did not always follow a set protocol. Some interviews were conversational, with teachers speaking at length about what they were doing and why; others more closely followed a guided interview format. Finally, very few conversations or meetings with parents were possible. Nevertheless, over the course of the visits and interviews, a number of similar themes emerged, providing what we think is a fairly accurate snapshot of life in the MI Underground.

Findings

The discussion of findings consists of three parts. The first is devoted to the issues of why and how schools adopted MI. The second deals with issues of implementation. Finally, we discuss program and student assessment.

Adoption

MI theory was not adopted in a vacuum. It is important to note that all the study sites drew on a variety of educational reform ideas, ranging from whole language, thematic curriculum, and cooperative learning to Foxfire, the Megaskills social curriculum, and Bloom's Taxonomy. In many but not all cases, multiple intelligences formed an overarching organizational framework into which these other reform ideas fit. In other cases, MI coexisted side by side with ideas considered equally compelling. Sometimes the role of MI in the school varied with the sources consulted. For example, one program administrator at the Venus School described the reforms in her school as "a tapestry of programs" headed by MI. However, a diagram showing the relationship among the strands of the tapestry put MI on an equal footing with thematic curriculum and "independent/small group investigations." In many instances schools seemed to have adopted MI in order to create or lend a framework to the activities in their school.

Creating or Lending a Framework

One of the first questions we asked the principals was why their schools decided to adopt the theory. Their answers fell into two rough categories. In the first, MI created a framework for *newly formed programs*. For instance, in District Apollo and the Venus School, MI served as the basis for programs to identify a larger number of gifted children than had previously been included in such programs. Similarly, the principal of the Aphrodite School used MI as a new school theme to attract diverse students within her district's desegregation program. Finally, MI served as the basis for creating a school within a school at the Neptune site.

In the second category, MI was used as a philosophical framework for activities *already taking place* in the school. For example, in the Mercury School, the principal said that "a lot of what I think MI is about—and a lot of the manifestations—we were doing, so it fits us really, really well." The Mercury first-grade teacher echoed this sentiment, saying she thought the main value of MI lies in heightening the teachers' awareness of, and giving labels to, what they were already doing. After hearing Gardner speak, the principal of the Poseidon School reports thinking, "Aha! This is the research that supports what we're doing. . . ."

Validation

Regardless of the school's stated motivation for using MI, the theory also served to validate teachers' practices. One Poseidon School teacher's reaction to *Frames of Mind* was: "I finally read somebody who's done something that validates what I've always believed." A K-1 teacher at the Athena School who had been teaching for thirty-two years commented:

> What goes around comes around. I heard about it [MI] as
> 'different learning styles [years ago].' . . . [Gardner made

these ideas] newsworthy. People in the public read about it, it gives more validity to what we do. . . . I don't think there was anything about the theory that led me to do things differently, but it gives a lot of credence to what I do.

A program administrator in District Apollo also commented that

I think teachers—good teachers anyway—have been making provisions for those kids [children weak in language and math], but feeling a great sense of guilt. If they took time away from the program to allow the youngster to do more music, to do art, to do dance, to interpret more through the nontraditional method, they had to do it with a closed door. Now they can keep the door open, now they can celebrate what youngsters can do and I think that's why it's been so appealing to people all over. It's gotten them to open their doors, and to yell, loud and clear, "This child is special."

Vocabulary

One way in which MI encouraged this flexibility was by providing a language that helped people to be more conscious of their work. As one teacher in the Aphrodite School put it, teaching for various intelligences feels right "intuitively . . . [but] unless you put things into [theoretical] terms, you aren't necessarily going to be able to do as much effective work on it." Vocabulary associated with MI helped him in "considering the areas that I don't emphasize, naming those areas—that does help. Studying those helps—because then I can make notes and say something about it and not take it for granted." The director of the Mercury School said MI influenced his school by "providing us with an intellectual framework and common language." The faculty found this common language useful not just among themselves but also useful for students, parents, and new teachers. As one teacher said, "By exposing all of the kids to the language, . . . they all knew what they were good in. . . . We spent a lot of time with the language . . . and I think [it helped] children . . . with self-esteem and confidence . . ." Teachers at the Poseidon School also felt that MI language aided communication with parents and students.

As these quotes indicate, for some people the language of MI fit naturally with their intuitive practices. However, for others, mapping practices onto MI theory entailed a fair amount of work, a process aided by staff development efforts.

Staff Development

One issue that arises when educators try to adopt MI-based approaches is how to go beyond teaching the linguistic and logical-mathematical intelligences and challenge all the intelligences. At the schools we visited, a variety of staff development activities addressed this issue. These included organized study groups among the teaching staff, visits to other schools, and seminars with hired consultants.

Study Groups

To help implement and adapt Gardner's theory to their settings, teachers at the Aphrodite, Diana, Mercury, and Poseidon Schools got together to read and discuss *Frames of Mind* and related articles. The Mercury School study group conducted experiential workshops on different ways to implement the theory. Since it did not seem appropriate to learn about MI solely in linguistic ways, the teachers experimented with various approaches. For example, they used jump ropes to demonstrate bodily-kinesthetic intelligence and took apart and put together tools from the turn of the century to learn about spatial and logical-mathematical intelligences.

Visits to the Key School

Personnel of all nine sites had heard about the Key School and were somewhat familiar with its approaches, which use thematic curricula and projects to draw on children's diverse strengths. In addition to traditional academic subject areas, children learn music, bodily kinesthetics, and visual arts four days a week. The Key School also has a "Flow Room" that allows students to choose from a range of activities in line with their interests. "Pods" or special-interest classes are taught to mixed-age groups throughout the year.

Five of the sites either visited the Key School or brought Key School teachers to talk at their own schools. Some of the five schools consciously adopted certain elements of the Key School's model while rejecting others. For example, the Diana and Poseidon Schools created rooms similar to the Key School's Flow Room, and the Aphrodite School was planning to implement such a room in the future. In addition, the Diana and the Mercury Schools were experimenting with pods. Like the Key School, other schools were also testing video portfolios as a method of visually documenting students' strengths and interests, and others had implemented sustained, theme-based projects.

While these features transplanted from the Key School were useful starting points to begin implementing MI theory, a number of educators at the five sites felt that the Key School model isolated intelligences into different subject areas and classes. An administrator at the Athena School commented, "What we found at the Key School was . . . that they've broken their day into these little segments [around each intelligence]." So rather than following the Key School model, the Athena School preferred to use interdisciplinary projects. A number of teachers and administrators at the Mercury and Diana Schools also said the Key School had not sufficiently integrated and expanded on MI *within* the classroom.

Again, there is no one right answer. Gardner himself does not advocate either that the intelligences be taught in separate classes or units or that they be integrated within classes and units. Nevertheless, it makes some sense for teachers and administrators to feel that teaching the intelligences in isolation is not entirely consonant with MI. The theory states that normal individuals always use intelligences in combination (Gardner 1983). For example, a musician needs intra- and interpersonal intelligences to infuse music with feeling and communicate with an audience. It apparently seemed artificial to some educators to teach the intelligences individually; however, objections to the Key School approach may be based more on the degree to which intelligences were isolated from each other rather than on the concept of attending to each in itself. To some extent all sites attended to the intelligences individually.

Outside Consultants

Along with looking to the Key School for a model, the schools brought in outside experts. Some of these specialized in MI theory. Other consultants were experts in areas associated with particular intelligences. In the latter category, a number of workshops related to individual intelligences were given for teachers at the Venus School. Practitioners in music, movement, and art led workshops on how to design activities that both met county curricular objectives and addressed a particular intelligence. At District Apollo, after teachers explored their own intelligences, they worked with outside experts who trained them in their areas of expertise. For instance, teachers worked with professional artists, examining children's work in music, dance, and visual arts and learning how to identify characteristics of unusual ability in children.

In the category of specialists in MI theory, the Athena and Venus Schools and District Apollo had occasional consultations with Project Zero about devising alternative ways to assess children's intelligences. The Mercury School hired a professor from a nearby college to teach an optional seminar in MI. A few schools hired specialists in MI theory who had no formal affiliation with Gardner or Project Zero.

In sum, schools decided to adopt MI theory for several reasons, including offering a framework for existing or new programs, offering a language to help educators develop and express what they do, and providing validation to already-existing practices. Although many sites used similar routes to develop programs making use of the theory, such as study groups, consideration of the Key School model, and outside consultants, implementation of the theory took different forms across the nine sites.

Implementation: How Schools and Programs Adapted MI

An exploration of how the theory was actually implemented in classrooms includes two interweaving themes: changes in curriculum and organization.

Changes in Curriculum

Curriculum changes in the majority of the nine sites encompassed attempts both to enhance individual intelligences that were not already adequately represented in the classroom and to integrate the intelligences in the context of meaningful work. The sites varied in the extent to which they emphasized one approach or the other.

Enhancing Individual Intelligences

Every site tried to develop the different intelligences: methods included implementing learning centers in the different intelligences, asking children to reflect on and sometimes label the intelligences required by a task teaching key aspects of different intelligences, and bringing in outside experts. As an example of the latter, each school in District Apollo hosted four artistic residencies, consisting of ten sessions with the children. We observed lessons by a choreographer, a painter, and a storyteller. Each of these highlighted separate intelligences: bodily-kinesthetic, spatial, and linguistic.

The program administrator also brought in a mathematician to work with three classrooms. In one session in a first-grade class the mathematician held up two books: a large, thin, flat book and a slightly thicker, small book, and asked, "Which book is bigger?" After several children identified the large, thin book, he said "A mathematician would say, 'I don't know which book is bigger.' And he would not be fooling around. Why would he say that? Do some quiet thinking to figure out why the smart mathematician would say 'I don't know which book is bigger.'"

The mathematician then engaged the children in a discussion emphasizing the importance of posing the question, "What do you mean?" He extended this to other examples so that children could practice asking, "What do you mean?" (Who is bigger, Michael Jordan or Roseanne Barr? The Little Prince or Little Red Riding Hood?) In this lesson, the mathematician encouraged the children to use their logical-mathematical intelligence to make distinctions in categories such as "big" and to understand that precise terms were needed to answer the problems he posed.

The teacher at the Dionysus School typically presented a topic related to a theme using one or more intelligences. After this, children rotated through seven different learning centers, each of which emphasized a particular intelligence. Teachers in both the Venus and the Mercury Schools also developed a range of learning centers to reflect the different intelligences. For example, two of the kindergarten teachers at the Mercury School categorized the twenty-five learning centers in their huge classroom according to the intelligences emphasized in each. While many of these centers were likely in place before the schools adopted MI, a special effort was also made to address areas that had been overlooked in the past, e.g., introducing centers that were explicitly "bodily-kinesthetic" or "musical."

The Neptune School also made an effort to enhance individual intelligences. There, a fourth-grade teacher organized the classroom into various centers, where we observed children taking their own fingerprints and categorizing them, using colored wood blocks as part of a math game, writing poetry together in a designated corner, and building constructions out of toothpicks.

Integration of Intelligences into the Curriculum

Accompanying activities designed to enhance individual intelligences were efforts to integrate the intelligences into lessons. This took place in three somewhat overlapping ways: creation of a project-based curriculum, use of MI to foster learning within a discipline, and integration of the arts into the curriculum.

(1) *Projects*. Projects appear to be a common route for integrating the intelligences. The use of projects, advocated by Gardner in later writings (Gardner 1993), is in keeping with his definition of intelligence—good projects address problems or yield products of importance in a culture. Furthermore, in group projects, children with strengths in different intelligences can each make a contribution.

We saw several good examples of group projects. The Aphrodite School involved students in a nine-week-long effort known as "the City of the Future." The city was a collection of two-by-two-foot squares of painted corrugated cardboard. On each square were constructed buildings, landscaping, and other features one would find in a city. These squares were then organized into residential, commercial, industrial, and historical areas. The massive project involved all the children in two large fourth- and fifth-grade classrooms. After dividing into pairs, children were asked to plan a two-by-two-foot site and to construct a small initial model of it. Then they were asked to build a larger model making use of a math unit in which they had built geometric shapes. This effort drew on a number of intelligences: logical-mathematical, spatial, bodily-kinesthetic, and interpersonal. One classroom teacher who was involved in this project told us that he would have used such projects without having read about MI. However, MI enabled him to address more consciously children's diverse abilities.

(2) MI: *Fostering learning within disciplines.* In all of the schools, teaching in particular curricular areas—for example, language, music, or math—drew on different intelligences. Since according to MI we all possess diverse intelligences, it makes sense to teach and learn disciplinary information by drawing on more than language and logic. At the Dionysus School, the teacher presented a lesson on architectural forms through the ages. After the lesson, children moved to learning centers where they worked on composing a song about architecture and setting it to music, drew impressionistic sketches of different parts of the school building, wrote about buildings they would like to design, and built three-dimensional geometric shapes of increasing complexity. At the Diana School, a math teacher taught fractions through woodworking, leather working, gardening, and mechanical and architectural drawing, which engage a range of intelligences.

Perhaps the most striking example of the use of multiple intelligences within a discipline was at the Athena School. During a music activity, the teacher tapped different intelligences in order to engage children in the lesson. Pairs of children sat in a circle with the teacher; one child in each pair held a tambourine. The teacher began the lesson by asking, "What's it called when people play in groups of two?" After discussing a wrong answer, "quartet," one child from each duet

stood up and got ready to play the tambourine to a recording of
"Popcorn." The teacher conducted the children, asking them to
shake the tambourine with one hand or two, to tap it in front of
themselves, and to tap it in different patterns: four taps against
their hip, four against their hands, and then similar patterns of
twos and ones.

The teacher described her approach later:

> I have some children who come into school already with a
> real full, complete sense of this intelligence [music]. It's
> well developed already in all ways. Now I have a lot of
> children that . . . [musical intelligence] can be developed.
> And in order to help them develop *that* intelligence, I'm
> trying to be aware of using the other intelligences. . . . for
> some children, they'll get to use their interpersonal skills
> . . . there's the kinesthetic [hitting the tambourines]. We
> did the patterning, we did some patterns. So, if there are
> some logical-mathematical kids I can pull them into music
> that way. . . . I'm trying to look at my one intelligence
> [music], but then also to help the kids experience more, I
> want to incorporate the other intelligences into the class.

(3) *Integration of arts into the curriculum.* In addition to the
traditionally emphasized linguistic and logical-mathematical
intelligences, MI theory posits others—musical, bodily-
kinesthetic, spatial—which are frequently used for problem
solving in the arts. Thus, providing students with regular
opportunities for problem solving in artistic disciplines is
consistent with the theory. Classroom teachers in all nine sites
used various art forms in their curriculum.

Although one might speculate that the prevalence of art in
these classrooms was due to the fact that the sample included
mostly elementary schools, evidence exists to link the use of the
arts to the presence of MI theory. First, the arts are often the first
"frills" to be cut in budget squeezes. Yet in three of the schools
budgets were being threatened at the same time that the arts
were prevalent. Second, the use of art in regular classrooms
appeared most prominent in the one middle school we visited,
probably because of a teaming of arts and academic teachers.
Furthermore, at a K–12 MI steering committee meeting at the

Athena School, high school teachers described many lessons and projects incorporating the arts.

In the Venus School, there was a district-wide interrelated arts team in place that worked with teachers on integrating the arts into their classrooms. A second-grade teacher described a member of the team who used dance and movement activities to assess children's understanding of place value. Children were asked to generate movement patterns to represent the ones, tens, and hundreds places and then to represent them physically. A primary teacher at the Diana School described inventing "math raps" and songs about money in math, as well as using theme-based songs, skits, and dances in social studies. In District Apollo, a first-grade teacher spoke of teaching a child to read through music. She excerpted words from a Whitney Houston song, set books to music, and danced out different parts of books.

Gardner speculates, though we have no direct evidence from our sample, that MI theory may be useful as a "way to protect otherwise threatened programs" (personal communication). That is, the theory can be used to justify breadth when the prevailing winds shift toward budget cuts or back-to-basics.

Organizational Issues

Coinciding with changes in the curriculum were organizational efforts that facilitated the implementation of MI theory. We touch on two of these: teaming and the changing role of specialists. In addition, we also consider how the use of MI theory affected the climate of the school.

Teaming

According to MI theory, while each one of us has a full array of intelligences, relative strengths and weaknesses of these intelligences vary within and among individuals. One implication of this theory is that not every teacher will be equally adept at addressing students' different intelligences. Although the sample included one school (Dionysus) in which a single teacher worked in isolation to teach and develop all the intelligences, in all the other sites various collaborative efforts seemed to be needed to apply MI. We noted earlier that outside consultants helped students and teachers to address the different intelligences; however, they were not a regular part of the school organization. In addition to, or instead of, using these outside experts, teachers in some of the schools served as resources for each other. Sometimes the teams predated the application of MI, and in other instances they were spurred by it. In both cases, teaming enabled teachers to complement their own strengths and foster the diverse strengths of their students.

The Poseidon School had teamed its academic and art teachers together prior to adopting MI. However, once MI theory was brought in, teaming helped teachers to focus on various intelligences. For example, one art teacher was working with a language arts teacher, and together they addressed what the language teacher said was "visual, spatial, and . . . [other intelligences] that play into that."

At the Neptune School, teaming began with the adoption of MI. The school's three kindergarten teachers each assumed responsibility for two different intelligences and developed units to highlight these. Students rotated among the teachers two days a week. On the day we visited, the kindergarten students spent time with each of the three teachers, allowing all the students a special lesson focusing on logical-mathematical, spatial, and bodily-kinesthetic intelligence.

Changing Roles of Specialists

Related to teaming was the stretching of roles that occurred among special-area teachers. For example, at the Mercury School, the librarian had traditionally focused on reading stories and other fiction. But after her introduction to MI, she realized she could interest children in language and books in ways that were not purely linguistic. She devoted four to six weeks to each intelligence, starting each unit with a book or story relevant to that intelligence. For example, with music, she used stories set to music; for art, she focused on book illustrations; and for bodily kinesthetics, she used books about sports and games as well as miming and acting out stories and role playing. Children were offered a choice of activities in line with the diversity of intelligences and learned that they could use the resources in the library to support their interests. Nonfiction books about chess, sports, dance, and other subjects appealed to children who were previously uninterested in books.

At the Athena School, specialists and classroom teachers were already co-teaching a number of classes before the introduction of MI, an interaction that helped foster the use of MI in the classroom. For example, a first-grade teacher, realizing that she herself could not engage children's musical intelligence, teamed with the music teacher. The physical education teacher at the Neptune School tried to incorporate the intelligences into her activities by asking children to draw diagrams of athletic games, write instructions for games, and move to music.

Impact of MI on Climate

The impact of MI on school climate varied from site to site. The extent to which MI fit happily into the school organization seemed to depend on a number of factors that also affect other reform efforts: the actions of administrators, whether MI was adopted by an entire school or just a few teachers, and whether it had been "ordered in" from the top.

At three sites, the impulse for adopting MI came in a top-down fashion. At Aphrodite, an enthusiastic new principal assigned to the school three weeks prior to a new school year secured funding to make the school into an MI school. With little experience as principal and little time to lobby for using the theory, she not surprisingly met with a great deal of resistance. Similarly, at Neptune the superintendent had drafted a new principal to help him make one of the district's schools into an MI school. At the time of the study only a few teachers were voluntarily applying the theory. Two of these volunteers reported problems brewing among other teachers in reaction to news that the application of MI might become schoolwide. Some of them reportedly said they would quit rather than adapt their teaching. Part of the difficulty raised by MI in the Neptune School may have stemmed from its status as a special program (see, e.g., McQuillan and Muncey 1991)—the MI teachers had both extra classroom resources and a significant amount of publicity.

Similarly, in the Dionysus School, where only one teacher was using MI, the teacher's colleagues expressed some understandable ambivalence toward his Herculean efforts. This teacher ran a one-person show, and his colleagues (who were all veteran teachers) demonstrated only mild interest in modifying their teaching to be more in line with MI. The teacher said that he found this sentiment perfectly understandable ("we all have to do what we know best"), but thought MI would be a great way for new teachers to start.

In sum, to accommodate the diversity of intelligences posited in MI theory, the sites we visited had to make changes in both curriculum and organization. In most schools, curriculum was adapted by teachers to highlight various intelligences rather than being totally reworked. This was accomplished through the use of learning centers and expert consultants, the integration into the curriculum of projects and the arts, and the use of intelligences to teach within a discipline. At least two organizational changes accompanied these curricular changes: teaming and expanding the roles of specialists.

The impact of MI implementation on schools' climates varied depending in part on the actions of administrators, the status of the MI program within the school, and whether a whole school or only part of the school was involved. Such effects are not specific to MI theory, but attend many educational reform efforts (Comer 1980; McQuillan and Muncey 1991).

Assessment

Although the main goal of our field study was to see what was being done in schools using MI, we also wanted to know if and how the sites evaluated the efficacy of MI programs. We also wanted to learn if and how MI had affected student assessment practices. It is worth emphasizing that neither program evaluation nor student assessment are tests of MI theory per se. To conduct such a test, one would want to question the existence and number of intelligences and their independence. (See Gardner 1993 for information on testing of the theory itself.) We will now describe how schools evaluated their interpretations and adaptations of the theory.

Program Assessment

Formal program evaluation in the schools we visited was very
limited. About half the schools were using some kind of evaluation techniques, ranging from observations to interviews to
questionnaires. However, in most cases the evaluations applied
only to limited areas of their MI programs—for example, teacher
use of MI or parent satisfaction with MI. The minimal nature of
these efforts at program assessment was understandable, since
most of the sites had only recently put the theory into place.

District Apollo conducted the most formal evaluation,
although plans for a formal evaluation were also under way in
the Venus School. The use of MI at both of these sites was
supported by a federal grant requiring evaluation. In District
Apollo, an outside evaluator conducted seven focus-group
interviews with teachers, students, and parents. Preliminary
findings suggested that those interviewed had overwhelmingly
positive feelings about the MI program and that program
objectives were being achieved. For example, children in the
program reported they improved in "reading, spelling, art,
music, and math." On the negative side, some of the teachers
identified a lack of knowledge of child development and
classroom routines among the artists as one problem with artistic
residencies. A limitation of District Apollo's evaluation was its
exclusive reliance on group interviews and its lack of control
groups.

In the Neptune School, a questionnaire sent home to
parents resulted in "very, very favorable" responses to the
program, according to the principal. An administrator said that
parents noticed "their children were taking risks, [were] very,
very happy to go to school, [and] didn't want to stay home from
school." Again, the usefulness of this evaluation is limited by the
lack of a control group.

The Dionysus School teacher conducted his own research
by keeping a daily journal and tracking the daily progress of
three students with behavior problems. He also administered
three different inventories: an MI/learning centers inventory, a
classroom climate survey, and a small group attitudinal survey.
His results showed that behavior problems diminished rapidly,
students developed increased responsibility and independence

throughout the year, cooperative learning skills improved, and students established and applied skills in new areas. His class, more ethnically and racially diverse than those of other teachers in the school, also consistently outperforms the rest of the school on state and national achievement tests.

Despite the lack of formal evaluation, the majority of teachers and administrators interviewed said MI programs worked well and identified several areas they believed were improved by the application of MI theory. The principal of the Poseidon School described the positive effects she attributes to MI:

> The most dramatic impact has come through the conversations that we've had with children and their parents. We spend far too much time as educators trying to figure out what children and parents already know, if they can tell us. And again, that structure [e.g., MI language] provides them with a wonderful format for talking about strengths. And when you focus on strengths, people are willing to share a whole lot more and take a risk.

Similarly, teachers and administrators at the Venus and Mercury Schools also said they felt that MI had enhanced discourse within the school.

Along with discourse, teachers felt classroom practices had been improved. When a kindergarten teacher at the Venus School was asked how her classroom practices differed from what she did before MI, she identified several changes. Before MI she had conducted the same follow-up activities after each lesson. Now, when planning a lesson, she tries to think of a related activity for each of the intelligences. In addition, she now conducts her whole-class instruction using skills from the different intelligences, like music or movement. A primary teacher at the Diana School said she is teaching more in line with her own intelligences (musical, bodily-kinesthetic, and linguistic), as well as trying to shore up some of her weaker areas (spatial and intrapersonal) in the classroom. For instance, in math she includes more spatial activities like using geoboards and other geometric problem-solving tools.

A teacher at the Aphrodite School said he thought his use of projects and MI was effective, based on what he saw among his students. He said that his students want to tell the rest of the school about their accomplishments. They asked questions like "When are we going to get a chance to present?" and "Can we do a poster about it?"

Student Assessment

MI has affected, either formally or informally, the way students are evaluated at all the sites we surveyed. In four of the sites, formal evaluations have been modified as a result of MI.

Formal Evaluation

Report cards have been changed to reflect an emphasis on diverse intelligences at three sites; at a fourth, an observational checklist was developed. District Apollo and the Neptune School now use alternative report cards divided among the seven intelligences. District Apollo also created a set of kindergarten assessments based on MI theory in order to identify children for their program. Teachers and administrators at the Mercury School have begun to revise their students' progress reports. After two years discussing dimensions of the personal intelligences, they have now devoted an extensive section of their progress reports to these intelligences. At the Venus School, the teachers and grant staff developed a behavioral checklist to identify the dominant intelligences for each child from kindergarten to grade two.

Five of the sites we visited were also experimenting with portfolios. Portfolios are efforts to collect and document children's work in various subjects or projects, a method advocated by Gardner, among others (Gardner 1993; Wolf 1990; Wolf, LeMahieu, and Eresh 1992). Portfolios help to show children's strengths in diverse intelligences. Teachers at the Poseidon School were experimenting with a range of formats for portfolios. One team used photographs and audio- and videotape to capture students' different strengths.

Along with portfolios, teachers and administrators at the Poseidon School are using MI theory to acquaint themselves more fully with students from the elementary school who will enter the following year. Since the spring of 1989, they have visited sixth-grade classrooms to introduce the idea of MI, brainstorming with the children about "how you would know if you had a strength in an area." They also leave journals for students to write their reflections on areas in which they see themselves as being expert. Later the teachers visit again to meet with students individually and learn more about their strengths, inviting students to "tell us, show us, or involve us." These journals and interviews allow the school to schedule every child with that child's range of strengths and needs in mind.

Informal Assessment

Informal assessment of children within classrooms appears to be affected by MI in all the sites we visited. For instance, a primary teacher at the Diana School reported that MI has changed her assessment practices, not just in terms of the report card but in realizing that children have different intelligences. She no longer downgrades projects in which children sing a song or perform a dance. A second-grade teacher at the Venus School reported that she sees MI as:

> a way to look at kids more broadly, and yet more specifically at the same time. The breadth is that there are more options, and the specificity comes in looking at individuals, and how you can reach that individual, and what ways might work for that kid and trying to provide multiple ways within a day, a week, a lesson.

While assessment may become both broader and more specific under MI, at the schools we visited MI-related approaches to student assessment coexisted with the formal and informal practices already in place. For example, following the presentation by students at the Aphrodite School of their City of the Future, several children stayed to talk informally about their work. One boy said he and his partner put in elevators *and* stairs "for people who are paranoid" about elevators. He also included "two sets of stairs, one that doesn't move and one that does, for elders." An administrator of the district's gifted and talented program was impressed by what the child said. He reviewed the boy's file, but found his IQ score was not close to the required cutoff point for admission to the gifted program, although the student was clearly demonstrating unusual thoughtfulness—at least in this particular project.

As one special education teacher at District Apollo noted:

> when you talk about assessing a child, you're talking about seeing how they're functioning, you still tend to think in certain traditional ways, . . . how is the child doing in reading or in phonics, or letter recognition or sound recognition, and math concepts, you know, readiness skills. You're not always thinking in terms of the other intelligences, which really should be as important.

It is not surprising that given the short period of time in which MI was being used, formal evaluation was scanty and traditional assessment practices were still in place. Of course, for accountability reasons, many sites were still obligated to administer standardized tests. Nevertheless, in many cases, MI made a significant difference in student assessment: Teachers were focusing more on students' strengths, looking at a broader range of abilities, and many schools were altering formal reporting methods to capture these diverse strengths.

Conclusion

In this chapter, we describe an initial effort to document the ways in which multiple intelligences theory is being used in school reform. Further research needs to be conducted on some of the questions not addressed here, e.g., how to reconcile the goal of exposing all children to all of the intelligences and tailoring teaching and curriculum to suit individuals' needs, how to strike a balance between disciplinary and interdisciplinary learning, and how to deal with issues of accountability. We intend to conduct research in the near future involving a more in-depth look at several of the schools in the survey.

Nevertheless, these preliminary findings may be of use to individuals or organizations currently applying MI or considering applying MI. Beyond that, this survey may be of interest to those who are studying broader issues of school reform. Clearly, many good ideas relevant to education are not accompanied by an implementation model. Understanding the ways in which these ideas can be adopted and implemented may enhance efforts toward school reform.

NOTES

Project Zero's work on the application of MI in classrooms has been generously supported by the Spencer Foundation, the William T. Grant Foundation, and the Rockefeller Brothers Fund. We are grateful to the teachers, administrators, and students who so graciously allowed us to visit their schools. We are also indebted to Barbara Neufeld, who helped us develop our interview guides. Finally, this work would not have been possible without the ideas and support of Howard Gardner, our mentor and friend.

1. Order of authors was determined by a coin toss.

2. We date implementation from the time the theory was first applied in classrooms rather than from the time teachers or administrators began talking about using the theory.

REFERENCES

Binet, A., and T. Simon. 1973. *The Development of Intelligence in Children.* Elizabeth S. Kite, trans. Baltimore: Williams and Wilkins, 1916. Reprint New York: Arno Press.

Gardner, H. 1983. *Frames of Mind: The Theory of Multiple Intelligences.* New York: Basic Books.

———.1993. *Multiple Intelligences: The Theory in Practice.* New York: Basic Books.

McQuillan, P.E., and D.E. Muncey. 1991. School-Within-a-School Restructuring and Faculty Divisiveness: Examples from a Study of the Coalition of Essential Schools. Unpublished Working Paper no. 6.

Sizer, T.R. 1984. *Horace's Compromise: The Dilemma of the American High School.* Boston: Houghton Mifflin.

208   *Transforming Schools*

————. 1992. *Horace's School: Redesigning the American High School.* Boston: Houghton Mifflin.

Spearman, C. 1904. The Proof and Measurement of Association between Two Things. *The American Journal of Psychology* 15: 201–292. Excerpted in J.J. Jenkins and D.G. Patterson, eds., *Studies in Individual Differences: The Search for Intelligence* (1961): 59–73. New York: Appleton-Century-Crofts.

————. 1927. *The Nature of Intelligence and the Principles of Cognition.* London: Macmillan.

Stern, W. [1912]. 1914. *The Psychological Methods of Testing Intelligence.* G.M. Whipple, trans. Baltimore: Warwick and York.

Wolf, D. 1990. Assessment as an Episode of Learning. In *Construction vs. Choice in Cognitive Measurement,* ed. R. Bennett and W. Ward. Hillsdale, NJ: Lawrence Erlbaum.

Wolf, D., P. LeMahieu, and J. Eresh. 1992. Good Measure: Assessment as a Tool for Education Reform. *Educational Leadership* 49 (8): 8–13.

8

Thinking Like a Fish: The Implications of the Image of School Community for Connections between Parents and Schools

Mary Erina Driscoll

The concept of the school community has implications for the way in which researchers, practitioners, and policymakers think about parents and schools. After a call for the development of a holistic perspective of school organizations, I review some recent work that embodies a communal vision of schools. Finally, I discuss the implications of this vision of community for the ways in which we think about parental engagement in the school and the contributions parents can make to their children's education.

Thinking Like a Fish, or the Development of Integrated Perspectives

Late in Norman Maclean's story of a Montana family, *A River Runs through It* (Maclean 1976), a striking incident occurs. The narrator, Norman, describes the afternoon when he, his brother Paul, and his father return to the Blackfoot River where they fly-fished often during the youth of the boys. As an adult, Norman has become an occasional fisherman at best, but Paul has pursued the craft of fly-fishing until he is recognized in the region as an expert.

The two brothers are quite different when it comes to their fly-fishing technique. The essence of the task for both men is to catch fish by luring them with dead flies (or facsimiles thereof); depending on the season and the weather, however, the fish are attracted by different kinds of lures. Norman prides himself on his wide assortment of flies, including the exotic Bunyan Bug No. 2 Yellow Stone Fly. Paul's philosophy is quite different and the fishing flies that line his hatband are far fewer in number. As Norman observes, "He thought that with four or five generals in different sizes he could imitate the action of nearly any aquatic or terrestrial insect in any stage from larval to winged."

Nowhere is the stylistic and philosophical difference between the two brothers on the finer points of fishing more evident than on this last afternoon they fish together. At first, it is Norman who appears to be the better fisherman. Luckily, he realizes early that the fish are feeding on stone flies and meets with much success when he uses his exotic Bunyan Bug to attract them. His brother looks on glumly, catching nothing, until finally he moves to another part of the river. Soon, to Norman's surprise, Paul is catching fish fast and furiously even as Norman's luck is running out. Knowing Paul does not have the specialized lure that brought Norman early success, he asks Paul over a shared cigarette how he has managed to catch more fish.

> He thought back on what had happened like a reporter. He started to answer, shook his head when he found he was wrong, and then started out again. "All there is to thinking," he said, "is seeing something noticeable which makes you see something you weren't noticing which makes you see something that isn't even visible."

What he has noticed, Paul explains, is that stone flies are hatching in the sunlit hole just above where his brother was catching fish. But he has also seen that the fish are biting only in the shadow, a little farther down the stream, where no flies are hatching. "After that, I should have seen [the flies] dead in the water. Since I couldn't see them dead in the water, I knew they had to be at least six or seven inches under the water where I couldn't see them. So that's where I fished," Paul tells him.

In short, he has improvised, using a large fly that he believes will appear to be yet another drowned stone fly to the

fish which encounter it. When his father terms him "a fine
fisherman," Paul acknowledges the importance of this imagined
perspective by replying : "I'm pretty good with a rod, but I need
three more years before I can think like a fish."

An Integrated View of Educational Practice and Inquiry

Knowledge of shadow, light, and the flow of the river; the
capacity to imagine the perspectives of others; keen and
informed intuition; and even sleight-of-hand—all of these, Paul
reports, played a part in his choices and his success in "catching
his limit." These are his true tools. What becomes more and more
evident to his brother is that Paul brings to bear on the task at
hand a wealth of knowledge that apprehends the river as it exists
this afternoon, in this weather, at this place.

The heart of this wisdom at which we marvel with
Maclean is the imagined perspective of the insiders, the
participants, filtered through the informed and practiced eye of
the fisherman. Paul's talent depends on intimate knowledge of a
complex living system, nurtured and sustained by experience,
intuition, and even luck. He understands the intricacies of a
living reality. Unlike his brother, who thinks about catching fish
as a linear transaction that requires a perfect match among skills,
tools, and opportunity, Paul sees the moment as a rare occasion
in which nature and knowledge combine, a textured and
patterned whole of shifting elements that are constantly in flux.
The knowledge he seeks and uses is not simple, and must be
built up in layers over time with his experience. With his brother,
we realize that Paul's true gift is his rare capacity for multidimensional vision.

The richness of this integrated perspective and its utility
for understanding virtually every element of the river is no less
helpful when we turn our attention to educational practice and
policy. The sharp delineation between these two perspectives on
fishing is instructive when we view our field of educational
research and the lessons for practice that are generated from it.
Like the narrator, we have taken a linear perspective: schools are
the occasions where resources, raw materials, and processes are
aggregated, and in this meeting raw materials are transformed

into educated individuals. Moreover, we have come to count on certain predictable and limited relationships to guide our understanding, just as Maclean knows the fish will bite the fly. And in trying to improve practice and set policy, we have engaged in a good deal of research that is the equivalent of trying to find the right fly to catch the fish under a set of conditions we predict. Like Norman with his boxful of exotic lures, our belief in the importance of the right tools and skills transmitted to the right people is virtually boundless. Thus much of our research has tried to capture yet another rational-technical fix that will improve the production process and guarantee more effective education.

But in this effort to isolate critical relationships and to understand the teaching and learning skills that promote effective education, we have on occasion reduced our vision so drastically that we have lost sight of the whole. Our perspective is sharpened and limited to include only detailed knowledge of some element of the school organization. In looking for hard and fast rules of prediction, we have imagined that all educational institutions will share and model for us some lawful, regular reality. Translating the results of such inquiry into meaningful insights that will improve practice has been difficult whenever we fail to take into account the complex living entity that is a school.

In short, much of our thinking about schools has focused on the whole as merely the sum of its parts. In the worst cases, those parts are taken apart and carefully examined, counted, and reassembled into something that vaguely resembles the original educational process but which no fish would recognize as a river.

The School as a Community

In contrast to this rational-technical vision of schools, it is useful to redirect attention toward educational inquiry and practice that construes schools as dynamic and complex interactive wholes, as communities that embody history, change, process, and experience and shape and give meaning to the lives of those who teach and learn there. Two general caveats are in order.

First, echoes of this call toward a renewed vision of community may be heard in the debate among educational researchers about the relative merits of quantitative versus qualitative methods of inquiry. But here the argument is that this is not *fundamentally* a methodological critique. Although it may be true that the conventions within methodological traditions can encourage a piecemeal or reductionist measure of the school, replacing with measurement and quantification the thick description found in participant-observer research or more narrative accounts, the essential elements of the vision described here are philosophical. Envisioning the school as a community means retaining an emphasis on the interconnections of individuals to one another and committing oneself to an attempt to reconstruct the whole even if the parts are examined separately. Thus some of the work described below (e.g., Rutter et al. 1979; Driscoll 1989; Bryk and Driscoll 1988; Bryk, Lee, and Holland 1993) employs quantitative methods that combine multiple perspectives in an attempt to present an integrated vision of the school community. Although this methodological debate is not irrelevant to this discussion, it should be cast in somewhat different terms.

Second, it is vital to note that the call for a renewed communal vision of school is by no means new. Although it may be found in contemporary discussions of educational research, as will be noted in detail below, the idea of an holistic vision of the school as a guiding metaphor is a far from recent creation. Almost a century ago John Dewey wrote of the importance of a communal perspective on education and referred to the school as a "small society."

It makes sense, then, to begin this selected overview of research and writing embodying a communal perspective with Dewey, recalling some of the seminal constructs that animated his thinking about schools in the early part of the twentieth century.

Dewey and the School as Community

In *My Pedagogic Creed* (Dewey [1897] 1970), Dewey spoke of the importance of the school's function in society and the necessity for schools to be construed as communities. Schools were the mechanisms through which a democratic society fostered and supported the development of citizens who were equipped to take care of one another. The school's function, then, was not a private one; its measure was not individual accomplishment or success, although it might be the place where individuals grew and developed their own gifts and talents. The school, he argued, was "primarily a social institution. Education being a social process, the school is simply that form of community life in which all those agencies are concentrated that will be most effective in bringing the child to share in the inherited resources of the race, and to use his own powers for social ends" (Dewey 1970, p. 237). In much of his writing, he expanded further on these ideas, noting in 1916, for example:

> The school must itself be a community life in all which that implies. Social perceptions and interests can be developed only in a genuinely social medium—one where there is give and take in the building up of common experience. (Dewey 1966, p. 358)

Dewey's perspectives, even in his own time, challenged common conceptions of what schools and education should be. The factory model of education, born in the last century and surviving until our own time, was particularly guilty of ignoring the idea of community in schools. Education which neglected this "fundamental principle of the school as a form of community life," he warned, was doomed to failure; such education "conceives of the school as a place where certain information is to be given, where certain lessons are to be learned, and where certain habits are to be formed" (Dewey 1970, p. 238). But when the school represented what he termed "an embryonic community life" (Dewey 1956, pp. 28–29), then both social and individual purposes of education could be joined:

> When the school introduces and trains each child of society into membership within such a little community,

saturating him with the spirit of service, and providing
him with the instrument of effective self-direction, we
shall have the deepest and best guaranty [sic] of a larger
society which is worthy, lovely and harmonious. (Dewey
1956, pp. 28–29)

Dewey's call for a communal vision of education, then,
saw the child as a central element in a living and changing
system, a "small society," membership in which schooled the
child for his eventual role as a full-fledged member of a
democratic society.

Contemporary Research on Effective Schools

Dewey would have found it difficult to imagine an effective
school that was not predicated on connections between school
and home life or which did not embody the idea of school
community. The only true measure of the worth of a school was
the child's ability to use what the school provided throughout
his life. Thus an ineffective school was by definition an
institution that stood separate from home life, distinct from the
round of daily events so familiar to the child before he ever
encountered formal education. (Dewey [1900] 1956, p. 75)

But unlike Dewey's work, a stream in contemporary
research on schools has employed on occasion a restricted notion
of what constitutes effectiveness, defining as its sole measure of
goodness a relatively narrow range of abilities that are measured
by standardized tests. Ever since the first "Coleman Report"
twenty-five years ago (Coleman et al. 1966), quantitative
investigations of what have become known as the "outcomes" of
schooling, using an economically inspired "input-output"
model, have proliferated. But as "effective schools" research has
grown, so have critiques of the unduly reductionist models
sometimes embodied in these studies. Coleman himself is among
those who have sought to expand this econometric model into a
richer picture of the school setting (e.g., Coleman and Hoffer
1987; Schneider and Coleman 1993). In a particularly cogent
piece, for example, Bossert (1988), while acknowledging the
importance of studying the "products" of schooling, notes some

of the problems in using a model that focuses only on predicting achievement:

> The rationale for many studies in educational administration rests on an assumed but indirect link between certain organizational characteristics and student learning. For example, many researchers have studied the determinants of school climate because climate factors are supposed to be related to student achievement (Brookover, Beady, Flood, Schweitzer, & Wisenbaker 1979; Miskel, Feverly & Stewart, 1979; Sergiovanni & Starratt 1979). Yet climate effects on student learning, although statistically robust, are loosely defined and have no clear basis in a theory of schooling or few identifiable links to children's learning experiences (Anderson 1982). It is important to identify frameworks that can assess directly the relationships among organizational factors that affect what students accomplish in school. (Bossert 1988, p. 341)

In other words, what Bossert calls "statistically robust" predictive models do not always provide legible or coherent organizational mirrors that illuminate for policymakers and educators what represents the best practice in education; they identify the right tools but give us no sense of the river. Thus a new generation of research on "effective" schools has worked to broaden the definition of that term. Some of this work has attempted new definitions of "goodness" in schools and "successful" school effects; other research, by no means unrelated, attempts to explain or understand students' overall academic performance—however measured—in light of school characteristics, interpersonal relationships, beliefs, and values that help to promote good teaching and learning. This research endeavors to focus on the ways these characteristics are combined in a good school, animated by the belief that the whole of a good school is indeed more than the sum of its parts. (See Rowan 1990 for amplification.)

Two Examples: Research on School Ethos and Professional Community

For example, the concept of school ethos developed in work on school effects (Rutter et al. 1979) is far more than an aggregate collection of individual variables. Rutter et al. recognize that it is the *interaction* of social processes and not merely their sum that explains the variance in the performance outcomes measured. As Rossman, Corbett and Firestone indicate (1985, p. 6) Rutter et al. "suggest a way to synthesize the research findings on discrete practices and more implicit cultural values. . . . The specific practices themselves were not as important as the way they came together to form a school ethos of culture that coalesced practices, beliefs, values, and norms into a caring community that fostered positive development and growth in the adolescents who passed through the school's doors."

In other words, the "ethos" of an effective school is in large measure a reflection of general, schoolwide expectations of consistent values and norms that permeate the institution. The ethos of an effective school is characterized by generally shared high expectations of teachers and respect for them; positive models of administrators and other teachers for teacher behavior that reflects concern for one another; and some system of feedback through which teachers can evaluate their work. Context and school community are the critical backdrops for understanding how and why students learn.

Similarly, a substantial body of research has emerged that looks at the context of teachers' work and the professional community within the school as it affects what teachers do. As McLaughlin and Talbert indicate, a complex and reflective vision of teaching has at times been overshadowed by what they term "relatively mechanistic" ideas of the tasks of teaching that "spawned an industry of teacher-proof curricula" (McLaughlin and Talbert 1990, p. 2).

In the past decade, the vision of teaching as a complex enterprise framed in significant ways by the context in which teachers work has become more widespread. McLaughlin and Talbert note an increasing "recognition of teaching as a professional enterprise requiring individual judgment," which, in turn, has led to an increased understanding that "effective teaching depends on more than just teachers' subject-matter knowledge and general pedagogical skills or even pedagogical content knowledge. Effective teaching depends significantly on the contexts within which teachers work—department and school organization and culture, professional associations and networks, community educational values and norms, secondary and higher educational policies" (McLaughlin and Talbert 1990, p. 2).

Among those exploring this notion of the context of teachers' work are McLaughlin and Talbert (1990), Lieberman (1992), Louis (1990), Johnson (1990), and Little (1992). Although their theoretical and methodological formulations differ, each scholar employs a mode of inquiry that construes teachers' work in the context of the professional community of the school, which in turn is affected by the social, political, physical, and economic factors that shape the school organization.

The School as Community

Bryk and Driscoll (1988) develop a concept of the school as a social unit that cuts across the levels of administrator, teacher, and student. They explore the antecedents and consequences of community in high schools and investigate the school community's role in perpetuating tradition and memory, the values it expresses implicitly and explicitly, the activities which bind its members to the school and to one another, and its participants' management of multiple tasks of both a social and academic nature. A fuller picture of the theoretical underpinnings of the construct may be found elsewhere (Driscoll 1989). For studies using this concept see Bryk and Driscoll 1988; Driscoll 1989, 1990; Bryk, Lee, and Holland 1993.

This construct of school community builds on an understanding of some classic social theory about places where individuals work and live. Clearly schools are places characterized by many associative relationships—links formed from the common bond of shared work, what the German sociologists Tonnies (1957) and Weber (1947) termed *gesellschaft* (of society). These associative relationships are based on rational assessments of common interests or purposes. But a concept of a school as a community must also embody the traditions, sentiments, and values which also bind the organization together in a web of communal relationships. These communal relationships (of the community, or *gemeinschaft*) are based on subjective feelings—sentiments and traditions which bind people together. Bryk and Driscoll's (1988) concept of school community contains elements of both these associative and communal relationships.

Similarly, another distinction which informs this particular vision of community is that put forth by Gusfield, who makes a distinction between what he terms the "territorial" view of community and the more "phenomenological" view (Gusfield 1975, pp. 33–35). The territorial concept of community is rooted in a concept of interdependence, frequently exemplified by shared space. Any viable concept of community must reflect this notion of a common set of needs or problems which may lead to a common cooperative effort to find the best solution for all. In its broadest sense, community becomes the means through which the group, faced with a common situation, achieves a kind of homeostasis.

But community is more than group problem solving. It has a phenomenological aspect as well, reflected most recently in work by MacIntyre (1981), Green (1985), and Bellah et al. (1985). In all of these formulations, community is what provides the context from which individuals derive meaning. It is characterized not so much by shared space as by shared meanings. Community in this view is more than a mere artifact of people living (or working or studying) in the same place; it is rather a rich source of "living tradition"—what MacIntyre defines as (1981, p. 207) "an historically extended, socially embodied argument, and an argument precisely in part about the goals which constitute that tradition." Thus this idea of tradition and of its cohort, the practices which embody and enact that tradition, are also central to any viable notion of community. As Bellah indicates, a community is most accurately a "community of memory, one that does not forget its past."

From these theoretical roots is derived a concept that comprises three essential dimensions. Together, they form a constellation of characteristics termed school community.

First, schools organized as communities exhibit a shared value system across the school. Thus some sense of common purpose should be evident in the administration, the faculty, and the students. Such shared value systems derive not only from the common expectations and preparation of participants but also from shared history.

Second, schools organized as communities exhibit a common agenda for participants which acts as a unifying factor. Two kinds of activities are present: those which bind the students to each other and to all those present, and those which link the participants to the institution and its traditions on a more abstract level—to its community of memory, to use Bellah et al.'s (1985) term. Such activities may be rituals which bring together large numbers of people at one time and which have symbolic value, or they may be construed as the common experiences in curriculum and socialization shared by all over time.

Finally, in a school organized as a community, there is a particular configuration of formal organizational characteristics. The most important of these include collegial relations among adults in the institution and a concept of the teacher's role which extends outside the academic arena of the classroom. That is, the teacher's role is diffuse rather than specific with respect to its responsibilities.

This concept of school community reflects the needs that are derived from shared activities and territory but also embodies the culture of sentiments, traditions, and practices that link its members and from which they take meaning. Community is neither spontaneous nor passive; it is derived from a living memory and is both created and nurtured by its members.

The role of parents as members of the school community is left unspecified in this earlier work by Bryk and Driscoll, in part because their theoretical framework was linked to secondary analyses of data that contained little information about parents. But it is consonant with the work to extend the notion of school community to include as members parents and families who may participate in the school's agenda in different ways but who form a critical support for its activities and purposes. As we shall see below, however, this implies that parents must be drawn into both the work of the school and the general sentiments surrounding it, and that they must join the common agenda of activities that bind members to the institution.

Implications of the Vision of School Community for Schools and Parents

What difference does it make if we construe the school as a community? A good deal. This particular vision does more than merely reclaim Dewey's legacy. Like any powerful image, it suggests new possibilities and relationships among actors in the school setting. It is a particularly valuable lens for examining traditional views of the relationship between home and school and the ways we think about parents becoming involved in their child's education.

At least three implications flow from a serious consideration of the school as a community. First, the image of community reorders the way educators think about parents as participants in their child's education. Second, accepting parents as members of the school community and incorporating them into the image of school community and its purposes encourages educators to think of creative ways in which parents can engage in the core work of the institution. And third, accepting parents as members of a school community has implications for the construction of a cultural narrative that both roots the school and orients its members toward the future. I discuss each of these below.

Parents: Cooptation or Engagement?

Many of the organizational theories that have been used to frame principals' perspectives of their schools in academic settings share a curious attribute: they present the school as an organization bounded by school walls and boundaries that are "permeable" at best. Parents are by definition organizational outsiders who fall outside these boundaries. Principals are trained to be "boundary spanners"; in fact, through techniques of limited engagement and cooptation, they learn strategies that help them, to use Thompson's (1967) terminology, buffer the technical core of teaching. In short, instruction is placed far away from these outsiders, and principals and their administrative staff function as the links between the "real" work of the organization—i.e., what happens in classroom—and what happens at home. (See, for example, Campbell et al. 1990.)

Such a vision may not represent the best in academic theory any more than it represents the best ideas of reflective practitioners or professors. But the notion of parents as outsiders who can be engaged only in limited fashion through appropriate channels is a theme that runs through much of our administrative literature. Many principals have been trained in strategies that presume such a state of affairs to be the norm. In few schools, for example, are parents free to walk directly into a classroom except during the normal morning and afternoon rituals of arrival and departure, or to deliver an occasional misplaced book or forgotten lunch. Parents are planned for as outsiders; their contacts are managed and awaited through report card nights, teacher conferences, and the occasional PTA meeting, much as a bride awaits her in-laws' infrequent visits. Their sanctioned roles within the organization are carefully prescribed: chaperones on trips; presenters on career days; supporters of the extracurriculum, a class play, a school festival, a book fair, or athletics (cf. Jackson 1968; Lortie 1975).

The idea of the school as a community challenges this conception of parents as organizational outsiders. While they may be infrequent participants in the full life of the organization, they must be seen as critical and vital participants in the overall purposes of the communal school organization: the growth in development and knowledge of the whole child. Because the child brings much from home to the school community, the school must reach out to include those parents and caretakers who help to shape and support the total well-being of the child. Only in this way can the school best help the child to learn.

Construing parents as members of the school community, albeit members who may be absent for much of the school day, is quite different from thinking of them as organizational outsiders. Strategies of cooptation in which they are "brought along" to agree with the school staff, techniques to minimize their effect on the technical core of the organization, and engagement strategies which seek to keep them as far away as possible from the real work of school, all seem out of place with a view that sees them as joint members of a common enterprise. What this view does imply is engagement rather than management of parent influence. In a communal view, parents are resources in more than an occasional sense. Contact with them is something that is not to be managed but rather welcomed and even relied upon. A communal assumption is that parents, like the adults who form the core of the school's staff, want to, and should be able to, support the school's mission and the overall welfare of the child. The child's success and learning are supported by all.

Indeed, parents are not kept at arm's length everywhere in American education. As Rust (1993) points out, parents are a natural constituency and are considered more genuine members of the school community in early childhood settings. Their participation is often welcomed and even expected in many schools for young children. The welfare of the child is believed to be served by frequent interaction between home and school. Yet somehow this notion of parents as members of the school community evaporates slowly but surely with each passing year.

In part, such gradual estrangement from the institution is encouraged by norms that foster parental participation solely on the school's terms and in the time frame of the school day alone. But relying on a traditional school calendar can mean that widespread parent participation becomes a reality only if a majority of parents are not employed outside the home. Thus a broad commitment to engagement with parents across a range of settings must take into account the economic realities parents face and may require the development of new venues that accommodate variable schedules in creative ways.

Engagement in What?

Suffice it to say that notions of substantive engagement with parents are not important in most teacher or principal preparation programs. When principals and teachers are exhorted to involve parents in the schools, they tend to be channeled toward the marginal or peripheral functions mentioned above.

The real challenge is to think of ways in which parents can become involved in the *key* element of the educational organization, its academic program. If the animus of the communitarian school is the support and sustenance of teaching and learning, then accepting parents as full members of the community means finding ways to enable their participation in this core mission of the organization.

Such a view has often been seen as a challenge to the expertise and insight of other academic professionals in the organization. Teachers believe, and rightfully so, that their experience and education make them uniquely qualified to guide and shape the educational experiences of students. Substantive parental involvement in the heart of the educational enterprise has often been seen as encroachment on this professional territory. Parental interest is often seen as parental interference.

However, parental involvement is hardly a supplanting of the teacher by the parent. Teachers do have a special purchase on the educational enterprise and bring professional skills honed through advanced study and extensive experience to their interactions with students. The challenge is not to *replace* the teacher but to think in creative ways about how the educational reach of the school can be *extended* to include parents and community members as resources. In some cases, this may mean that parents must themselves be educated and informed about how to become resources. But in meeting that challenge, schools can cement the relationships that form the support structure for the ongoing learning schools hope to foster.

How might such inclusion of parents be accomplished? Certainly, the traditional roles of parental interaction, marginal as they may be, are good places to start. Inviting parents to engage in the life of the community outside the classroom as well as inside it is a critical first step in jointly constructing a set of shared values and experiences that are the glue of communal relationships.

Other possibilities exist as well. Three models that connect parents with the core mission of the school are increasing parents' role in governance, rethinking the relationship between the school and the community around principles and values that support the academic mission. and paying attention to the ways in which teachers and parents communicate about the academic work of the child. This is by no means a comprehensive list, and each plan is quite different from the others in scope and purpose.

School-Site Governance

One reform that has gained popularity in the past decade is increased participation by parents in the governance of the school site. This strategy is designed to bring community involvement closer to the decisions that affect what happens in the classroom. In the past decade, school site councils have become the linchpin of several urban reform strategies.

School Based Management, for example, first instituted in Dade County, Florida, and later in New York City, is one such plan. Each school volunteering to participate develops a council which must by statute include parents and community members. The jurisdiction of the council varies from school to school, according to the plan, but typically each council has some discretionary funding (such as Chapter I monies) and authority over school improvement activities. A more radical version of site governance is found in Chicago, which underwent a major mandatory restructuring of all schools. Under this plan, parents and community members comprise eight of the eleven members of each school-site council. The powers given to the site council are substantial, including the negotiation of a principal's contract, the control of discretionary funds (excluding teachers' salaries, for example) and the development and implementation of a School Improvement Plan.

But it is still not clear that in school-site plans parents are truly involved in making the decisions that shape the core of the organization. Malen, Ogawa, and Kranze (1990), in a comprehensive review of the literature on site-based management, found that the measurable effects of these programs, especially with respect to changes in academic programs and achievement scores, are mixed. In part, this is because many variants on site-based management can be found. In some cases, parents have advisory power only, even when they believe themselves to have decision-making authority. In others, mandates for school councils in general and parents in particular were not clear and impeded efficient functioning of the councils. And third, even when parents possess real power and legislative responsibilities are clear, norms of civility may dictate that parents defer to the "professional" members of school councils (i.e., teachers and principal) and at least initially incorporate few new views into school governance (Malen, Ogawa, and Kranze 1990).

Amidst all this confusion, there is little evidence that such councils directly affect school performance. For example, there is little research to support the hortatory claims that parental governance authority will improve student performance such as those made at the time of the Chicago School Reform Act of 1988.

Does a paucity of solid research on the effects of parent governance mean that these programs are misguided? Not necessarily. While such programs may fall far short of rectifying, or even beginning to address, all of schools' serious problems, their failure to demonstrate that reform directly causes increased student achievement is not surprising. Governance, communication, empowerment, and participation—hallmarks of most school-site management councils—are amorphous concepts. An increasing parental voice may promote school conflict as well as school cooperation, depending on the culture of an individual school. Yet such programs, imperfect as they may be, challenge the school community to join administration, teachers, parents, and even students in a common enterprise that supports teaching and learning.

The Comer Model

James Comer's plan (described in his 1980 book *School Power* and now in place in nearly one hundred schools) rests on the assumption that schools will succeed only if the same values supporting child development are held by school and home. He starts with the premise that values supporting the health and development of children are difficult to maintain in conditions of poverty and urban turbulence. Thus his blueprint for school reform includes a substantial component for educating the community and supporting the parents.

In essence, the School Development Program restructures the school in ways that fundamentally alter our notion of the school as merely an academic agency. The theory of the program rests solidly in the province of child development and a broad notion of a child's social, emotional, cognitive, physical, and language development.

Four components are essential to the School Development Program. First, the governance and management team represents all adults in the school community. Typically it includes the principal, two teachers, three parents, and a mental health team member. The group meets weekly to establish policies for the school in curriculum, staff development, and school climate; to plan and carry out resource allocation and needs assessment; to coordinate the activities of all groups in the schools; and to work with a parent group planning a social activity calendar. A second component of the School Development Program is the mental health team, consisting of a classroom teacher, a special education teacher, a social worker, and the school psychologist. The team provides input to the governance council and additionally serves as a resource for teachers. The third component of the program is the implementation of the curriculum and staff development activities developed as part of the governance and management team's comprehensive school plan (Haynes, Comer, and Hamilton-Lee 1988b).

The fourth component of the program is the parent participation program. Far from being an add-on function, this component is seen as integral to the activities of the governance and management team.

> It consists of three sequential levels of parent participation. The first level is concerned with structuring broad-based activities for large numbers of parents. At the second level, approximately one parent per professional staff member works in the school as a classroom assistant, tutor or aide. At the third level, a few highly involved parents

participate in school governance. The project provides
consultation and material resources to make parent
participation operational at all three levels. (Haynes,
Comer, and Hamilton-Lee 1988b, pp. 13–14)

The School Development Program integrates parental
involvement into a radical restructuring of the school which
supports teachers, parents, and students. The program has a
coherent and all-encompassing philosophy devoted to the
improvement of mental health and the provision of resources
essential for teaching and learning. Parents' involvement in their
child's school can vary by degree, but the concept of
involvement is a central element in any success the program
achieves. Yet this serious commitment to a school reordering
requires a level of resources few schools can match without
additional funds. In the Comer schools, we see the possibilities
for a fundamental realignment of the traditional school, *if*
substantial extra resources such as time and money are allocated
to address a variety of pressing needs shared by the
community's children. The school takes on more than a narrowly
defined academic mission. Its daunting task, however, is nothing
less than the joint construction of a set of values shared by school
staff and parents that nurture and support the children and their
learning. Comer's model implies that this cannot be the task of
traditional educators alone and must involve an integration of
services from many professionals and community members.

Epstein's Work on Parental Involvement

Joyce Epstein and her colleagues at Johns Hopkins have
developed a research and implementation program that presents
some simpler strategies to connect parents and the child's
academic work. The focus of their program has been to assist
teachers and administrators in finding ways to involve parents
in their child's schoolwork. Studying the techniques used most
often by teachers, she found:

Teachers reported widespread use of three techniques that
stress reading and books: having parents read to the child
or listen to the child read; asking parents to take their child
to the library; and loaning books and teaching materials to
parents for use with children at home. Other practices

> (discussions, informal learning activities, contracts, and
> parent observations) were less frequently used by
> teachers, and were less often rated as effective and
> satisfying techniques. (Epstein 1987, p. 126)

Epstein also found that parents were willing to spend
more time helping their child with homework if they received
some direction on how to help. The parents and teachers who
worked together on assisting children rated each other more
positively than those who did not. Improved general parent-
teacher relations extended to more positive attitudes and
academic behaviors on the part of students as well. Epstein
reflects:

> A story builds from all of the sources in the survey:
> Principals actively support parent involvement, especially
> in reading activities; teachers request more parent
> involvement on reading activities at home; parents
> conduct more learning activities in reading than in other
> subjects; and the students' achievement in reading is
> improved. These results suggest the importance of subject-
> specific connections. If principals exercise leadership, if
> teachers request and parents give assistance to students in
> particular subjects, then students' mastery of those skills
> should improve. (Epstein 1987, p. 129)

This research, then, suggests that students do better in
school when parents are given specific directions by subject
teachers on how to help their children. Administrative support
and encouragement assists in maintaining these connections and
the overall climate between home and school may improve as
well.

Thus a good start at involving parents in the heart of the
school is to think of smaller yet challenging ways to develop the
organization. Few teachers routinely think of homework in terms
of what parents can do to support their child's work; yet if they
did, parents and other caretakers would at least have the
opportunity to engage the academic mission of the community.
Just as we have suggested that principal preparation must
change to take into account productive parental engagement, so
must teacher education reflect that parents are resources who

may be seeking simple but specific directions about how they can help their child.

The Joint Narrative That Roots the School Community

Finally, the third implication of school community for the way we think about parents and schools involves the creation of a joint narrative. A review of some of the work that has articulated how community is formed and sustained will clarify this concept.

Most discussions of community allocate a critical role to narrative in the formation of community. The common values, practices, and understandings that shape community and imbue it with meaning for its members are rooted in its tradition. The community's history and beliefs are reflected in its narrative, in the stories it tells about itself. Membership in a community means that one's own personal narrative or story is joined to that of others and to the tradition that shapes the common understandings which bind all together. One both contributes to the whole and is enlarged by it. Bellah et al. (1985, 1991) argue that individuals find meaning in their lives through the process by which they become committed to communal ideals.

The narrative or tradition is made real and celebrated through rituals, routines, and ceremonies that teach members new and old about the community. Because the stories and practices that comprise the joint narrative embody core values of the community, they can be rich and powerful, sometimes quasi-religious or inspirational in nature even in the most secular of settings. An example of this was seen in Greenwich Village on a cold Thursday in March at a full-scale commemorative ceremony which annually marks one of the seminal events in the birth of the American labor movement. It may be instructive to describe the ceremony that embodies this narrative in order to illustrate how recalling the past can point a community toward the future.

Like most ceremonies that tell the story of a community, this secular liturgy both remembers the past and inspires the members assembled. Held every year at the site of the 1911 Triangle Shirtwaist Fire, in which 146 workers died because sweatshop conditions and locked doors made it impossible for them to escape, the ceremony reflects every detail of the Triangle Shirtwaist tragedy. The modern-day counterpart of the Fire Ladder company that answered the alarm tolls a ceremonial fire bell beneath black bunting hung from windows where workers jumped to their death. Speeches by union personnel, politicians, and (on this day) survivors and survivors' children all recollect the lessons learned that day about the importance of protecting the health and safety of all workers. But at the same time, the narratives of the past are rooted in a contemporary awareness of the present-day challenges to these fundamental principles, reminding the members that it is these same conditions which animate the union's activity more than eight decades later.

Much work has been done that emphasizes the importance of such traditions and narratives in sustaining the school community. Several school studies detail the rituals which unite students and teachers. Wilkinson's (1964) work on British public schools, for instance, remarks on the distinctly unifying function of chapel ceremonies in these institutions. He notes, "The same magical device may serve both to direct emotions into communal expression and to symbolize certain values, especially the values of self restraint." Weinberg (1967) also notes the communicative function performed by these central ceremonies. Cookson and Persell (1985) and Lesko (1988) remark on the importance of manifestations of school traditions in imparting desired values to students. In addition, the unifying function of athletics in American schools is documented at length by Coleman (1961).

How can parents be joined to the narrative that embodies the community's traditions? First, parents must have some say in shaping the narrative. The rich and diverse experiences of parents and their children must be recognized and interwoven as strands of the communal story. This does not mean that the school should react in a "politically correct" fashion to current notions of multiculturalism which permit at best a shallow acknowledgment of the differing cultural contexts from which students come but leave the core understandings of the institution unchanged. In the best of all possible worlds, multiculturalism is not a specialized curriculum but a set of understandings that become part of the everyday fabric of the institution. This means that participants in the community must know one another and have some sense of who they are and the journeys that each member has taken to arrive at this common place.

Here the traditional roles of parental involvement can again be of assistance. Participation in school fairs and in career days is not a bad place to start. But understanding depends on *regular* opportunities for interaction and exchange, not once-a-year special fetes with limited participation.

The idea that parents should influence what the school teaches and that schools should respect the places from which students come has been seen as a fundamental challenge to democratic schooling. Indeed, does this mean that the school should merely mirror the values of the parents and families that comprise it, whatever they may be?

Hardly. Because the school as community has always been a Janus-like concept, from Dewey onward, comprising not only the values students bring to the institution but also the destinations to which they are headed. In an essay on moral education, William Proefriedt (1985) likens schools to the novelist Thomas Wolfe's image of a train. Just as Wolfe's train brings him from the small town to the big city, changing him forever, Proefriedt argues, so does a school transport its students from the context of their individual cultures and narratives toward participation in the greater societal community.

This "stand-between" function of the school was particularly central to Dewey's vision of community. He believed that although schools were strongly linked to the home environment, they were also part of the larger democratic society. Schools should reconstruct only the elements of society "such as make for a better future society," presenting a "purified medium of action" that eliminates unwanted, undesirable facets of the larger society. But as schools built curriculum around both familiar and unfamiliar experiences, each individual could "escape from the limitations of the social group in which he was born and come into living contact with a broader environment" (Dewey [1916] 1966, p. 20).

Schools have the obligation, then, to join the narratives of participants with some rendering of the narrative of a democratic society. They have an opportunity to model how differing interests and concerns can be blended and accommodated and to show how communities composed of individuals can learn to speak with a new and stronger voice than any one member can muster. That voice is richer for each member who helps to build the communal vision and who faces the challenges and struggles embodied in that process.

But it is perhaps this last implication of community—that is, the construction of a joint narrative, which includes the home experience of children even as it prepares them for the mosaic of values and cultures that comprise modern democratic society— which is most exciting. By facing this charge squarely, schools and parents together can begin to build a true "rainbow curriculum" that prepares students as citizens and scholars.

REFERENCES

Anderson, C.S. 1982. The Search for School Climate: A Review of the Research. *Review of Educational Research* 53: 368–420.

Bellah, R., R. Madsen, W. Sullivan, A. Swidler, and S. Tipton. 1991. *The Good Society*. New York: Knopf.

Bellah, R., S. Tipton, A. Swidler, and W. Sullivan. 1985. *Habits of the Heart*. New York: Basic Books.

Bossert, S. 1988. School Effects. In *Handbook of Research on Educational Administration*, ed. N. Boyan, 341–354. New York: Longman.

Brookover, T.W.B., C. Beady, P. Flood, J. Schweitzer, and J. Wisenbaker. 1979. *School Social Systems and Student Achievement: Schools Can Make a Difference*. New York: Praeger.

Bryk, A.S., and M.E. Driscoll. 1988. *The High School as Community: Contextual Influences and Consequences for Students and Teachers*. Madison, WI: National Center for Effective Secondary Schools.

Bryk, A.S., V. Lee, and P. Holland. 1993. *Catholic Schools and the Common Good*. Cambridge: Harvard University Press.

Campbell, R., L. Cunningham, R. Nystrand, and M. Usdan. 1990. *The Organization and Control of American Schools*. 6th ed. Columbus: Merrill.

Coleman, J.S. 1961. *The Adolescent Society*. New York: Free Press.

Coleman, J.S., E. Campbell, C. Hobson, J. McPartland, A. Mood, F. Weinfeld, and R. York. 1966. *Equality of Educational Opportunity Report*. Washington, DC: United States Government Printing Office.

Coleman, J., and T. Hoffer. 1987. *Public and Private Schools: The Impact of Communities*. New York: Basic Books.

Comer, J. 1980. *School Power: Implications for an Intervention Project*. New York: Free Press.

————. 1988. Educating Poor Minority Children. *Scientific American* 259(5): 42–48.

Cookson, P., and C. Persell. 1985. *Preparing for Power: America's Elite Boarding Schools*. New York: Basic Books.

Dewey, J. [1897] 1970. My Pedagogic Creed. *School Journal* 54: 77–80. Reprinted in *Foundations of Education in America*, ed. J. Noll and S. Kelly, 235–243. New York: Harper & Row.

————. [1900] 1956. *The School and Society*. Chicago: University of Chicago Press.

————. [1916] 1966. *Democracy and Education*. New York: Free Press.

Driscoll, M.E. 1989. The School as Community. Ph. D. Diss., University of Chicago.

————. 1990. The Formation of Community in Public Schools: Findings and Hypotheses. *The Administrator's Notebook* 34(4).

Epstein, J.L. 1987. Parent Involvement: What Research Says to Administrators. *Education and Urban Society* 19(2): 119–136.

Green, T. 1985. The Formation of Conscience in an Age of Technology. *American Journal of Education* 94: 1–32.

Gusfield, J. 1975. *Community: A Critical Response*. New York: Harper Colophon.

Haynes, N., J. Comer, and M. Hamilton-Lee. 1988a. The Effects of Parental Involvement on Student Performance. *Educational and Psychological Research* 8(4): 291–299.

————. 1988b. The School Development Program: A Model for School Improvement. *Journal of Negro Education* 57(1): 11–21.

Jackson, P. 1968. *Life in Classrooms*. New York: Teachers College Press.

Johnson, S.M. 1990. *Teachers at Work: Achieving Success in Our Schools*. New York: Basic Books.

Lesko, N. 1988. *Symbolizing Society: Stories, Rites, and Structure in a Catholic High School*. New York: Falmer.

Lieberman, A., ed. 1992. *The Changing Contexts of Teaching*. Chicago: National Society for the Study of Education.

Little, J. 1992. Opening the Black Box of Professional Community. In *The Changing Contexts of Teaching*, ed. A. Lieberman, 157–170. Chicago: National Society for the Study of Education.

Lortie, D.C. 1975. *Schoolteacher*. Chicago: University of Chicago Press.

Louis, K.S. 1990. Social and Community Values and the Quality of Teachers' Work Life. In *The Contexts of Teaching in Secondary Schools: Teachers' Realities*, ed. M. McLaughlin, J. Talbert, and N. Bascia, 17–39. New York: Teachers College Press.

MacIntyre, A. 1981. *After Virtue*. South Bend: University of Notre Dame Press.

Maclean, N. 1976. *A River Runs through It*. Chicago: University of Chicago Press.

Malen, B., R. Ogawa, and J. Kranze. 1990. What Do We Know about School-Based Management? A Case Study of the Literature and a Call for Research. In *Choice and Control in American Education*. Vol. 2. *The Practice of Choice, Decentralization, and School Restructuring*, ed. W. Clune and J. Witte, 289–342. New York: Falmer.

McLaughlin, M., and J. Talbert. 1990. The Contexts in Question: The Secondary School Workplace. In *The Contexts of Teaching in Secondary Schools: Teachers' Realities*, ed. M. McLaughlin, J. Talbert, and N. Bascia. New York: Teachers College Press.

McLaughlin, M., J. Talbert, and N. Bascia, eds. 1990. *The Contexts of Teaching in Secondary Schools: Teachers' Realities*. New York: Teachers College Press.

Miskel, C., R. Fevurly, and J. Stewart. 1979. Organizational Structures and Processes, Perceived School Effectiveness, Loyalty, and Job Satisfaction. *Educational Administration Quarterly* 15: 97–118.

Noddings, N. 1988. An Ethic of Caring and Its Implications for Instructional Arrangements. *American Journal of Education* 96: 215–230.

Proefriedt, William. 1985. Education and Moral Purpose: The Dream Recovered. *Teachers College Record* 86: 399–422.

Purkey, S.C., and M.S. Smith. 1983. Effective Schools: A Review. *Elementary School Journal* 83(4): 427–452.

Raywid, M.A. 1988. Community and Schools: A Prolegomenon. *Teachers College Record* 90: 198–210.

Rossman, G., H.D. Corbett, and W. Firestone. 1985. *Professional Cultures, Improvement Efforts, and Effectiveness*. Philadelphia: Research for Better Schools.

Rowan, B. 1990. Commitment and Control: Alternative Strategies for the Organizational Design of Schools. *Review of Research in Education* 16: 353–392.

Rust, F. 1993. *Changing Teaching, Changing Schools: Bringing Early Childhood Practice into the Elementary Schools*. New York: Teachers College Press.

Rutter, M., B. Maughan, P. Mortimore, J. Ouston, and S. Smith. 1979. *Fifteen Thousand Hours: Secondary Schools and Their Effects on Children*. Cambridge: Harvard University Press.

Schneider, B., and J. Coleman. 1993. *Parents, Their Children, and Schools*. Boulder, CO: Westview.

Sergiovanni, T., and R. Starratt. 1979. *Supervision: Human Perspectives*. 2d ed. New York: McGraw-Hill.

Thompson, James. 1967. *Organizations in Action*. New York: McGraw-Hill.

Tonnies, F. 1957. *Community and Society*. Charles Loomis, trans. East Lansing: Michigan State University Press.

Weber, M. 1947. *Theory of Social and Economic Organization*. A.M. Henderson and Talcott Parsons, trans. New York: Macmillan.

Weinberg, I. 1967. *The English Public Schools*. New York: Atherton Press.

Wilkinson, R. 1964. *Gentlemanly Power: British Leadership and the Public School Tradition*. London: Oxford University Press.

9

Education Reform and Policy Implications

Kathryn M. Borman
Louis Castenell
Karen Gallagher
Sally B. Kilgore
Debra A. Martinson

Although severe national fiscal difficulties and widespread cynicism threaten to cripple the national will to reshape educational policy at any level, public awareness and an accompanying desire to remedy the problems besetting schools through systemic reforms have never been stronger (Kozol 1991; Howe 1993; Smith and O'Day 1990). This combination of factors creates opportunities for private-sector groups and others to effect change. In this chapter we explore the ways in which such efforts, sometimes backed and partially funded by the government, can reshape the nature of schooling. In particular, we focus on the effects of two types of communities: neighborhoods (geographically and ethnoculturally defined) that pursue local interests, and the larger business community, intent on furthering its own agenda. We deal with both the barriers to and opportunities for positive change, concluding with a plan for reform that takes into account the sometimes antithetical objectives of these constituencies while maintaining a focus on both the social and pedagogical aspects of schools.

In the 1980s and early 1990s, educational policy moved toward a greater awareness of and sensitivity to local issues. During this time, school reformers created specific agendas that emphasized local strengths and needs while acknowledging large-scale national themes such as standards for particular subjects. National educational reform themes have also originated with organized business groups, such as the National Alliance of Business and the Business Roundtable (Borman, Castenell, and Gallagher 1993), state governors (who, in turn, may be influenced heavily by business interests), and teachers' unions. All of these have, to some degree, put their own desires before the interests of children and their parents. As we approach the mid-1990s, policymakers continue the trend toward a locally oriented national educational policy by targeting four specific areas for reform: (1) approaches to teaching and learning, (2) types of cultural understanding, (3) arrangements for local school funding, and (4) cognizance of the needs of families (Howe 1993).

At this writing, new federal legislation framed under the rubric of Goals 2000, encompasses what was in the past a disconnected set of policies. Under President Clinton, programs including the School-to-Work Opportunities Act and the reauthorization of the Elementary and Secondary Act will offer federal assistance in implementing education reform. According to the documentation accompanying the Goals 2000 Educate America Act,

> The bill encourages a bottom-up approach to reform. States and local communities will develop their own improvement plans, tailored to their special needs. Business and labor will work together to define the knowledge and skills needed to create secure economic futures for employees and employers alike. The federal government will use its resources to assist local reform efforts and help them implement their improvement plans and will support the development of model standards against which states, communities, schools, and individuals can measure their progress. (U.S. Department of Education, 1994: 4)

The intended goals of federal policy makers are both clear and encouraging. Not only are current policies toward schools becoming more closely coordinated and coherent than was previously true, but these policies are also calling for explicit assistance at the state and local levels in the formulation of specific strategies and actions. While such smaller and larger issues as providing better measures to assess student progress and guaranteeing that all receive a high skills education with access to high wage work remain, it is clear that systemic reforms are the order of the day.

The Importance of Local Community

Local communities and their constituencies can either hinder or promote educational change, yet they have been all but ignored by planners and administrators, who often design new programs without seeking input from the people they attempt to serve. In part, this may be due to vagueness about the concept of a local community.

"Community" is usually thought of geographically, but it can also be defined in terms of ethnicity, race, and social class. Recognition of this heterogeneity can be reflected by teachers, policymakers, curriculum specialists, and others who emphasize diverse local features—myths, folklore, and group political and social experience. It can also provide teachers with constructive ways of taking language differences into account instead of using them as a basis for labeling particular children "at risk" and consigning them to special education.

Social class serves as a route for bringing communities into educational discourse. In our society, neighborhoods are clearly delineated by social class; Boston, Chicago, Los Angeles, and New York, with their devastatingly poor and gloriously affluent neighborhoods, provide clear examples of this. What might be a given in one neighborhood may be an alien concept in an adjacent school district. Social class, especially class differences within districts, can be a factor in determining which children should be labeled "at risk."

What does it mean to be "at risk"? The definition of the term varies by community; by using the term generically, policymakers may in fact "obscure the needs of the persons they mean to help" (Ellwood 1988). No single, unified welfare (or any other) policy will work for all families—varying life circumstances (number of parents, number of employed adults in the household, number of children) result in enormously diverse needs among low-income families. Solutions that would be ideal for a single mother with a full-time minimum-wage job would not apply to a two-parent family in which both adults were unemployed. In addition, within particular family structures, needs vary by location and circumstance. The experiences and hence the needs of urban families are very different from those in rural areas. An awareness of these specific community needs is essential to effective reform.

Barriers to Reform

National Interests

Political concerns have inhibited the creation of truly sound instructional programs, particularly a coherent federal policy for economically and socially marginalized students. For example Chapter 1, the major federal entitlement for "disadvantaged" students, has been compromised by pork barrel interests. Although studies have consistently shown that compensatory education has little enduring impact on learning, Chapter 1 remains popular among school-based administrators and members of Congress alike for several reasons. First, school-based administrators, particularly principals, are reluctant to exclude children whose parents request participation even though their children may not meet the criteria for inclusion or derive any real benefit from the program. Second it is advantageous for administrators to keep the criteria loose in order to enlarge the program.

Compensatory education includes a wide variety of at-risk types, but enrollment decisions are made using statistical indicators such as family background or demographic trends. This reliance on national-level, generic definitions ignores the importance of local, unique situations. Should trends in youth problems and demographics determine which children are considered at risk? In either case, anticipated trends are being used to shape policy and resource distribution. Should generic programs, tied more tightly to pork barrel interests than instructional soundness, remain in place? Current reforms in the Elementary and Secondary Education Act (ESEA) and also present in the newly legislated America 2000: Educate America Act suggest that a new framework is being developed emphasizing local community ingenuity and creativity in creating improved teaching and learning strategies.

Service Delivery

Meeting the needs of at-risk children is further complicated by a lack of incentives for the creation of community-based agency alliances, particularly among social service agencies providing parallel assistance. Although interagency networks such as United Way have begun campaigns to coordinate service delivery, these efforts by themselves are not enough to guarantee effective client-agency interaction (Helton, Barnes, and Borman 1994). The splintered, incoherent nature of social-service delivery systems persists because national conceptions of individual and community strengths have generally been narrow and ethnocentric. As a consequence, shared goals and service delivery systems have been slow to develop. This problem is rooted in our society's myth of the rugged individual—the conception of the nation as sets of unconnected entities guided by self-interest. Castenell and Kilgore (1994) analyze this tendency, showing how coordinated and focused activity in response to a major national educational policy initiative (The New American Schools Design Corporation) became attenuated across Ohio and within its multiple demographic, educational, political, and economic centers. As a consequence, relatively weak sets of proposals to design "break-the-mold" schools emanated separately from these centers in competition with one another. Systemic reform under the rubric of state-wide educational plans addresses the problem of individual units competing with each other for scarce resources.

Local Interests

An additional complicating factor is the exclusion of certain groups from policy formation and implementation at all levels. Certain groups have been dogged by historical and systematic exclusion from political decision making, particularly the nation's Blacks. Other racial and ethnic minorities—notably American Indians and specific Hispanic groups—have been similarly disenfranchised, creating a major barrier to the strengthening of community schools. In addition, as several chapters in this volume document, local school boards are often divided among themselves; the diversity of local communities can result in group conflict and competing allegiances that are difficult to cast aside.

Opportunities for Change

Although formidable barriers impede the formation of broad educational coalitions, considerable opportunities are also present. Many possibilities exist for instigating individual-level change with an eye toward national trends—i.e., thinking globally and acting locally.

National and Regional Interests

How can targets for specific policy initiatives be identified? John Ralph and others urge educators to bear in mind *specific outcomes* for youth when formulating policy. For example, economists have illustrated that more years of schooling definitively enhance an individual's income and overall satisfaction with life. Years of schooling, then, emerges as a crucial criterion, and the reduction of dropout rates is a desirable and highly specific goal which can be pursued on the local and individual level.

Dropout rates in particular neighborhoods—especially those with large concentrations of very poor families—may be several times higher than the national average, even for members of the same ethnic group. While such statistics by themselves are depressing, they reinforce the persistent point made earlier in this chapter and throughout this volume: the urgent need for local reform agendas implemented through partnerships of social service agencies, businesses, schools, colleges, and universities. Some promising local reforms rely on this sort of cooperation while including national policy priorities. For example, the National Science Foundation currently funds thirteen centers in various locations throughout the United States, all focused on recruiting traditionally unrepresented minorities into careers in science and engineering and providing them with the appropriate skills to succeed.

In the classroom, incentives can reward and motivate teachers and counteract "teacher burnout." However, the most effective incentives seem to be those fashioned at the *district* level. School districts must develop incentives that run in tandem with their strategic direction (Dworkin and Townsend 1994) while taking into account differences among local schools. Administrators devising incentive plans must also consider their vision of teachers' work, issues related to recruitment and retention of teachers, the level of teachers' commitment to school and district, and at a more mundane level, the costs. Some of these concerns involve global conceptions of the education process; others relate directly to local interests. To arrive at a consensus requires that teachers' unions, district administrators, the community, and schools of education agree on a common purpose.

Consensus among these groups is necessary for agreement not only on teacher compensation systems but also on overall investment strategies for schools. These constituencies must cooperate to achieve a revenue pool that follows regional economic boundaries as opposed to traditional local school districts. Commercial and industrial properties that both draw labor from and contribute goods and services to a whole region, for example, should be taxed and the funds shared regionally, ensuring that boundaries for educational opportunity within regions will not be stronger than the boundaries across them.

At least one state, Ohio, has established regional resources zones that meld local and national interests. Regional teacher centers, although financed centrally by the state, provide a locally administered program of teacher-generated staff development initiatives. Moreover, universities in each of the state's six regions are expected to provide unobtrusive assistance in guiding these initiatives to address regional needs as defined, for example, by economic and employment trends.

Local Interests

Incentives for local-level reforms are almost as varied as the differing communities that implement them. To date, Philadelphia's Pew Charitable Trust has invested more than fifteen million dollars in local schools, focusing on three major objectives: (1) the organization of teachers' work, (2) the involvement of parents, and (3) the transformation of the curriculum—all areas which require local agreement about definitions and objectives. Through "charters" which function as both pacts and academic guidelines, Philadelphia's high schools are being transformed. Teaching methodology, parental involvement, and students' academic progress have all been renegotiated by these very constituencies of parents, teachers, and students.

The Philadelphia reform process differs from those in Kentucky and in Massachusetts as presented by Glenn (1994), but the common thread in such success stories is that each reform effort emphasizes local factors. "Local" may mean statewide, as illustrated by the Kentucky case, or metropolitan-centered, as in Massachusetts. In these areas, officials integrated local and national objectives to produce programs sensitive to such issues as race, ethnicity, and social class in each locale.

What, then, is the prognosis for investment strategies that create local community consensus upon which to build educational change in the United States? There are some favorable indicators. For example, despite the somewhat dysfunctional nature of the competitive process, most activity in response to federal educational initiatives has been at the local level. School districts, propelled by various forces, have undertaken widespread school reform efforts with or without federal monetary or legal incentives. Administrators are learning to consider unique local characteristics when devising programs to meet local needs and national reform imperatives.

Unfortunately, such sensitivity to neighborhood concerns is no guarantee of success, particularly when powerful interest groups attempt to shape the schooling process in self-serving ways.

The Influence of Business

The voice of business interests, such as the Business Roundtable (BRT), the National Alliance of Business (NAB), individual industries, and even presidential economic advisers, has dominated educational reform discussion. Although the social organization of schools has not been explicitly addressed by many of these spokespersons (with the notable exception of NAB), their concern with what is frequently termed "systemic change" has important implications for how schools and classrooms are organized. The current business focus constitutes a barrier to creative locally oriented investment strategies simply because actions based on the profit motive sometimes directly oppose fulfillment of individual and societal needs. For example, during the 1980s, business operations produced results counter to the national need for creation of meaningful jobs and a diverse labor-market economy. Instead, low-wage (under $10,000 per annum), direct service (retail sales, fast-food) jobs proliferated, while business exported manufacturing jobs to other countries and did little to develop high-tech jobs or job-related skills (Borman 1991; Ray and Mickelson 1993). Business involvement in school reform has tended to focus on the production of graduates who will fill industry's needs for reliable, trainable workers, although often the qualities corporate leaders claim to value most are not those fostered by their proposed reforms. In addition, since women and minorities are underrepresented at the policymaking levels of business, they are excluded from the planning of these reforms. Still, a few programs, like the Boston Compact, have managed to ease the school-to-work transition, reduce bureaucracy, and upgrade the curriculum.

Influences on Business Reform Efforts

The Global Web

According to current secretary of labor Robert Reich (1991), business arrangements today constitute a "global web." Satellites, low-cost shipping, worldwide availability of capital, global technological development, and low-cost, capable labor pools allow manufacturing firms and, increasingly, service-based companies to carry out labor-intensive activity in areas of the world where the ratio of labor costs to labor capability is most profitable. Reich argues that the United States workforce is unevenly advantaged in the global labor market. Symbolic analysts, who constitute 33 percent of all U.S. workers and are among the best-trained in the world, and in-person service workers (27 percent of the workforce) compete well. The 40 percent of the workforce engaged in routine production work are placed at a serious disadvantage by Reich's global web: they must compete with others on a worldwide basis for their jobs. For example, data-entry personnel in the United States earning $7.00 per hour cannot compete with English-speaking data-entry workers in India who work for $2.00 a day, receiving raw data in Delhi overnight and returning it via satellite the next day. While job creation in the service sector may partially compensate for jobs lost to foreign workers, salaries and benefits in service jobs are hardly comparable—the result is a decline in real wages. Exacerbating this pattern is the increase in part-time positions, a strategy aimed at reducing the investment of firms in workers. According to the U.S. Bureau of Labor Statistics, the number of involuntary part-time workers jumped 121 percent between 1970 and 1990, to 4.9 million (Kilborn 1991).

Because of their concerns for creating a globally competitive workforce, U.S. firms have focused on altering traditional arrangements in schools in order to "close the education gap" between inadequately skilled workers and jobs demanding high skills. Still, the entire corpus of the business reform rhetoric ignores the current profile of low-skill, low-wage service-sector jobs actually available to youth, hurries past any consideration of inclusion of citizens in formulating reforms, and focuses instead on upgrading "standards" and filling a "skills gap" without recognizing the role of business in the elimination and export of jobs and the creation of an involuntary part-time workforce. The rhetoric seems to focus instead on ascertaining how best to instill desirable qualities in future workers.

Corporate Demands on the Educational System

A major concern of business reformers has been the evaporation of *motivation* and *discipline* as opposed to lack of *academic knowledge* and *skills* displayed by individual workers (Ray and Mickelson 1993). The underlying ideology of such business reform efforts is most clearly displayed in such works as Kearns and Doyle's *Winning the Brain Race: A Bold Plan to Make Our Schools Competitive* (1988), Chubb and Moe's (1990) analysis of choice and the rationale for judging schools with respect to the educational marketplace, and Peters and Waterman's (1982) description of the corporate culture of the nation's most "effective" companies. In this reform rhetoric, qualities such as "democracy," "citizenship," and workplace-related traits (including "punctuality," "neatness," and "civility") frequently emerge as desiderata. While such traits as "problem-solving skills" and "organizational effectiveness and leadership" often appear on lists of the skills that employers currently profess to value in new employees, entry-level positions occupied by recent high school graduates rarely demand that young workers display traits such as organizational effectiveness or creative thinking. The National Center on Education and the Economy's Commission on the Skills of the American Workforce provides this dismal account:

> [O]nly an estimated 5 percent of employers organize work so as to require a high level of skill among workers . . . this country's declining productivity is more the result of how employers organize work than a shortage of skilled workers. Although in surveys employers initially report such a shortage, the great majority consistently cites the need for a low skill workforce that would tolerate an ethic of obedience and a hierarchical organization. (Roditi 1992, p. 340)

Minority Involvement in Business-led Reform

The BRT, with an agenda specifically targeting school governance and organization, has been extremely active in national reform efforts. Until recently, BRT's membership was exclusively White and male, raising a number of issues central to race and gender politics. The overall lack of participation by women and minorities in reform efforts has been attributed to lack of individual interest rather than exclusion by White male corporate leaders, a rationalization that ignores the important gatekeeping function of traditional power brokers. In reality, display of "interest" by itself is insufficient to gain most members of marginalized groups seats around the table.

Although it is difficult to prove a direct relationship between the exclusion of particular minority voices and subsequent policy emanating from the business community, particular state and local outcomes display a clear relationship to conservative business ideology. The exclusion of traditionally disenfranchised groups has helped to create a climate of indifference as businesses collectively and individually pursue educational change strategies; more effort should be made to include women and minorities in the policymaking process and to prevent a backlash against them.

For example, whenever women have gained ground in a profession, a backlash against them has occurred. Thus, although business-supported efforts to "upgrade" teaching and teacher education may be applauded for enhancing the status of the occupation and raising appallingly low salaries, policymakers must be aware of how this increase in prestige might operate to push women and minorities out of the profession. Also needed are more strategies to offset the exodus of talented women and minorities, programs such as the Ford Foundation's Teaching Leadership Consortiums in place in Alabama, California, Florida, Georgia, North and South Dakota, Louisiana, Ohio, and Mississippi, which expressly recruit ethnic and minority students. If, as Edelstein asserts (personal communication, 1992), business is still "trying to figure out its role" in teacher education, support of such initiatives with tangible resources in the form of scholarships is an appropriate business activity.

Business and State Educational Policy Reforms

Business involvement in U.S. schools has historically taken several forms. The near-universal participation of representatives from the business community on local school boards led, for one thing, to the development of school system management structures that resemble the hierarchical management of U.S. firms. Cooperative education is another long-established arrangement, by which there is frequent and systematic interaction between the schools and specific firms regularly serving as settings for youths pursuing vocational training. In fact, the majority of school-business alliances have been built around the issue of linking the school to the world of work. It is hardly surprising, then, that businesses show a preference for investment in programs and policies that strengthen the workplace competencies of high school students and are typically less enthusiastic about early childhood education programs (Berenbeim 1991).

During the 1980s, perceiving an erosion of the "competitive edge" in international markets of U.S. manufacturing interests and a demographic decline in the actual numbers of new young workers, business leaders joined state governors in applauding federal policy, as expressed in *A Nation at Risk*, to toughen up the nation's K–12 academic curriculum. The devotion of corporate leaders to school reform at the same time that many of these individuals exercised corporate strategies potentially destructive to long-term educational improvement is, to say the least, ironic. While they espouse a deep commitment to school reform, businesses practice a number of strategies which run counter to real structural change: investment in foreign capital; paternalistic approaches to teacher-education reform; and a strong, persistent emphasis on hierarchical organization and low-skill jobs. To date, business-backed, statewide educational reform efforts have been extremely effective in creating a reform agenda tailored to a given state's needs *as perceived by reform-minded business interests*. However, corporations do not always place a high value on the traditional educational goal of encouraging the full development of individual potential.

Local-level Corporate Involvement

Businesses have also taken up various issues confronting local schools, especially the school-to-work transition for so-called at-risk youth. These efforts, in fact, were among the earliest educational change concerns evoking the involvement of both individual firms and collectively organized business groups.

Among the best publicized of these efforts has been the Boston Compact. Amid much fanfare, the compact was announced in September 1982 by members of the compact's coalition of local chief executive officers and school administrators. The compact, a formal arrangement signed by local representatives from business, trade unions, universities and colleges, and the school department, centered on the desire of businesses to have a well-prepared local labor pool. The business community agreed to hire four hundred 1983 high-school graduates in permanent positions and to employ as many as one thousand graduates over a two-year period, if, in fact, these graduates met entry-level requirements (Farrar and Cipollone 1988). Working through the local Private Industry Council (PIC), the business signatories also agreed to recruit additional companies, increase the number of summer jobs for youths (from 750 to 1,000 by 1983), and strengthen summer employment opportunities for city youth.

In its organization and aims the Boston Compact is similar to many school-business arrangements that have developed elsewhere during the past ten to fifteen years. Initially these collaborations, as in Boston, targeted secondary school students and sought to provide tutoring services, job-skills training, and school-to-work transition experience through summer employment and placement following graduation. The emphasis has been on readiness for work for secondary school students, a focus that has been problematic in the Boston case and elsewhere because at least two issues tend to be overlooked: the low skill levels of students entering the ninth grade—due to neglected or overlooked academic problems from earlier grades—and a lack of attention to teaching and teachers. Teachers' needs and desires to improve their skills and to change outdated curriculum through staff development, training, and collaboration have been consistently ignored despite business interests in restructuring teaching as a career. In sum, the Boston Compact and similar programs are not without their flaws, although such business-school partnerships continue to be promoted by the Business Roundtable and the National Alliance of Business.

Lessons from the Boston Compact

In fairness, it must be emphasized that business groups at the local level have addressed the important and consequential issue of the school-to-work transition through programs such as the Boston Compact, tutoring arrangements, and a continuing commitment to cooperative education. Furthermore, lessons are being learned from the programs and used to improve them. California, Minnesota, and, most recently, South Carolina have carried out plans to eliminate badly outdated curricula, reorder school governance, and the like. Other states, notably Kentucky, have adopted comprehensive state-mandated school reform programs. These successes reflect the 1980s' trend toward a new federalism manifest in the creation at the state governors' level of a virtual mandate to beef up standards, create a climate of accountability in schools, and employ tough new chief state school officers to direct operations.

Still, the basic agenda of such programs remains the creation of a trainable and profitable workforce. The assumption appears to be that these school-based interventions can lead students to future workplace success. But are they sufficient? Disturbing trends of declining earning power for young workers show that success in the workplace is a broad, macroeconomic issue in at least two ways. First, both federal and business policies during the 1980s have resulted in the elimination of jobs in the manufacturing sector and an overall reordering of occupational structures and the skills required by a new, service-oriented job market (Borman 1991). Second, such corporate strategies as technological change and investment in foreign human capital have eroded opportunities for U.S. high school students, many of whom attend schools targeted for reform by business. Unfortunately, those most affected by this elimination of jobs or their transfer to foreign countries are the poor and minority youth which has traditionally held these same low-skill and semiskilled jobs. Business leaders have not yet directly addressed these overwhelmingly significant issues for the very school reforms they claim to desire.

Without maintaining that business interests have ignored or consciously exploited these trends, one can conclude that business reform strategies have been primarily motivated by self-interest, a rather mild criticism. However, when reform efforts are placed against a macroeconomic background, it becomes difficult to understand the contradictions between business investment in narrow-gauge educational change and such corporate strategies as foreign economic capital investment without making harsh judgments about business motivation to direct energy toward meaningful educational reform.

Future Outlook

Indeed, given the concerns of both formal groups such as the Roundtable and those of firms more generally, a cynical view of business-related interest in educational change is inevitable. While U.S. firms call for a better prepared workforce to withstand competition from abroad, they continue to invest in foreign capital. Further, it seems clear that workplace practices discourage anything more than routine, low-skill activities (Borman 1991). Indeed, ethnographic studies, including Borman's (1991) study of job settings in factories and service-sector businesses, show a persistent requirement of tolerance for dull, routine tasks in most workplaces employing recent high school graduates.

Until business can honestly examine its own motives and practices it is difficult to see how those most endangered by corporations' continued reliance upon hierarchically organized systems and low-skilled, dutiful workers can benefit from business interest in educational reform. It is likely that in cities and towns with a strong local presence of utilities and other companies with traditionally robust commitments to the public weal, educational change may truly be systematic (Berenbeim 1991). But the prognosis is bleak elsewhere unless we experience a change in the public will and a desire to include organizations representative of the interests of women, racial and ethnic minorities, and children.

Investment Strategies for Reforming Schools

As we have argued, many difficulties impede the formulation of blueprints for educational change. At least three tasks await reformers, especially with regard to the organization of both the academic and the social curriculum: challenging allegiance to national standards as opposed to teacher-initiated reform; integrating technology into classrooms; and the persistence of social and economic inequities.

Current school arrangements create major impediments to learning. The organization of time and space in most schools severely restricts teachers' options in creating learning experiences, since the prevalence of age-graded classes too often produces children who are judged inadequate at an early age and also limits students' opportunities to serve as mentors or tutors; and regulatory statutes create obstacles that drain teachers' enthusiasm and creativity from instructional tasks. Unless such problems are remedied, no amount of inspiration in the curriculum will allow our youth to reach higher standards. The flexibility of locally directed reform programs more easily allows the removal of these time-space constraints than does the rigid, hierarchical approach common to most business attempts at school change.

Another concern is the need to focus on an organizational structure that ensures that students will master core academic subjects. Diagnostic and tutorial technology addresses this need without compromising flexibility and should be available in every classroom for regular monitoring of student development. Curricular resources must be expanded to enrich instructional options. Peter Senge, an MIT organizational psychologist, argues that "poorly designed systems, not incompetent or unmotivated individuals . . . cause most organizational problems."

Major reversals of the gains of the Civil Rights movement and even the New Deal characterize the contemporary period and are intensified by racism. Any program of social reform, including educational reform, must make the struggle against racism central to its program. Given the importance of transnational corporations in our global web, such a program must indeed be global in its scope.

The Plan for Reform[1]

Districts must create planning councils that reallocate authority within the district and include representatives from the school board, the district administration, the teachers' association, individual schools, and families. Indeed, any community undertaking reform should be organized to provide information on alternative approaches now used in school districts, as well as in other organizations. These data will help participating districts make effective choices and encourage them to focus on problems inherent in the social organization of schools which curtail teachers' abilities to develop the capabilities of their students. Selecting from the strategies outlined below, each planning council would make a proposal to community members that would improve conditions and initiate changes in each successive year of the implementation phase.

Organizational practices must be designed to create a school setting that permits customized education for all children (customized to address individual interests, aptitudes, and ways of learning), thus enabling all children to achieve high standards. Using the work of W. Edwards Deming (1986), we can identify systemic needs that must be remedied before "total quality education" is feasible. Managers of education must create an environment in which (1) a customer orientation is desirable, (2) monitoring students' progress is possible, (3) customizing the education of each child is feasible, (4) the capacity to solve problems increases, and (5) the motivation to teach and to learn are high. The following strategies should be considered by communities in addressing these systemic needs:

- Allow students to participate in developing a plan for their own education.

Developing a commitment to learning involves participating in decisions about learning. Even preschool children can set goals—such as learning to button coats, identify colors, or sing a song. When children reflect about their own accomplishments and needs for learning, they become part of the monitoring system of the organization. Initially children's goals may not be exhaustive and are likely to be short-term. As children mature and planning becomes more routine, longer and more comprehensive plans can be considered.

- Encourage teachers to become advocates for and coaches of all children.

The incentives, responsibilities, and technological support given to teachers affect the degree to which teachers become coaches and advocates for all children. Inducements based on the proportion of students attaining certain standards have different consequences from those based on average test scores. In the first instance, every child counts; in the second, improvements can be achieved by focusing on only a portion of the student population.

The allocation of responsibilities affects the degree to which teachers become advocates for all children. When teachers are both advocate and judge of the same child, their role as advocate is compromised. Children and parents naturally tend to conceal information that may be essential to effective instructional strategies (Lareau 1989; Lightfoot 1978). A coaching model for teaching, as opposed to a judgmental one, requires the creation of external forms of skills appraisal—through computer-based evaluations, public performances, portfolio evaluations by other teachers, and state or national tests.

Other strategies to enhance coaching and advocacy for all students include structuring long-term relationships among teachers and students. Computer software, such as the Geometric Supposer, that fosters joint inquiry among teachers and students, should be made available at all levels.

- Create flexibility of time and space in schools.

If more flexibility in time is to be created, time constraints must be removed not only within a day or a year but also over several years. Children develop differently and unevenly: Albert Einstein didn't talk until he was four. Allowing latitude for different developmental patterns allows greater opportunity for more students to reach high standards. Multiage, multigrade systems appear to allow for the greatest flexibility, although alternatives exist. In Japan, for instance, students progress from one grade to the next at the elementary level without regard to performance (Leetsma and Walberg 1992). Customizing education within wide age and grade spans provides maximum advantage for both fast and slow learners.

School calendars should be reorganized to reduce substantially the loss of learning that occurs among low-income students during summer vacations. Although extending the school year is the only certain avenue to reducing such loss, districts initially could choose between six-week and one-month vacation periods that occur two or three times a year, respectively, to minimize some of the loss in momentum that occurs with long breaks. Family support centers would extend the time available for students to learn—both after school and during the summer.

Through the use of peer tutoring programs, community projects, large lectures or demonstrations, and computer technology, middle and secondary teachers should be able to free approximately ten hours each week for planning and review. A portion of that time should be allotted for planning within clusters at the elementary level and for interdisciplinary planning at the secondary level. Elementary-level schools will likely need more external support but could still acquire three to four hours of release time for faculty.

Management information systems can accommodate far more flexibly scheduled secondary-level course work. Most subjects should be taught in two-hour sessions once a week to allow for demonstration or thoughtful independent pursuit of assignments. Community projects that build on classroom experiences should be incorporated into the schedule. Reconfiguration of secondary-school instructional time and space would allow large lectures and demonstrations, small tutorials and labs, and community projects. Students' schedules would vary from day to day.

Spatial arrangements should be altered to accommodate computer workstations, multimedia demonstrations, small-group meeting areas, offices for teachers, and large lecture arenas. In some cases, these changes may be made in the first year of implementation.

- Foster flexible and challenging curriculum materials.

Curriculum materials must allow for diverse strategies in reaching national goals. With modern technology, textbooks have become expensive anachronisms that hinder rather than encourage learning, at best providing only learning guidelines. Such guidelines can be provided in other forms; at the same time, print materials should be reconfigured to help students learn. Making the transition from textbooks to other forms of print material requires the adjudication of competing interests in the publishing industry and increased access to historical texts, literature, and public data banks. Legal arrangements to allow schools to duplicate materials as needed and to provide copyright reimbursement or subscription fees to publishers should be encouraged and developed.

Support services should be created to help teachers develop or secure print, visual, and audio materials for their programs. Design team members can prepare directories of multimedia software, acquire and organize original source material, and secure access to public data banks (stock reports, news reports, and so on) for teachers or support staff to use.

- Institute ongoing diagnostic capabilities within each school.

Total quality education requires that diagnostic information be available continuously to allow students and teachers to adjust their strategies over time. As a result, teachers will need increased time for planning and review to use this information.

Existing technologies, such as those associated with IBM and Apple, can allow teachers to review students' work in the context of national goals for learning—building on existing inventories that gauge students' progress against current textbooks. Such systems should include computer-generated diagnostics that reflect the culmination of a student's work over a given period, and could largely replace classroom testing.

- Create learning organizations through professional development.

According to management analyst Peter Senge, a learning organization must have leaders who design, teach, and reward. That is, leaders must design governing principles which teach subordinates to make decisions consonant with the mission of the organization. Leaders also must make decisions and give rewards that support individual efforts to develop skills and knowledge that enhance the capacity of the organization. As part of their first-year activities, teachers and parents will establish governing principles to guide the development and design of the school organization.

By the very nature of such community projects, teachers will become learners of history, art, mathematics, science, and geography. Developing the capacity of the organization, however, requires the creation of additional opportunities for learning. There should be collaboration between teachers and community organizations to construct a professional development program that enhances capacity for self-governance, enriches knowledge of curricular strategies, and expands understanding of the mathematics and science embodied in the life of the community.

Professional development, however, cannot be limited to course- and project-based learning. To expand all teachers' understanding of the core academic subjects, community internships in local associations and businesses are crucial. Initially such internships should be short-term and should be financed by local businesses. After three years, schools could be expected to subsidize (at least partially) teachers' sabbaticals, allowing them travel and internships in other regions of the country. At a minimum, such sabbaticals should be granted once every five years for four months. Local internships could be offered in the offices of architects, city planners, manufacturers, lawyers, newspaper publishers, building contractors, historic preservationists, artists' groups, social service agencies, and even city hall politicians. Concurrently, seminars with other teachers and professionals will allow teachers to digest their experiences in relation to specific applications of geography, mathematics, science, English, and history.

- Move authority from the district office to schools.

Early efforts at quality circles did not work in industry because, according to Bill Sheeran, a technology vice-president at General Electric Company's appliance operation, companies "didn't empower employees to carry through." Similarly, observers of private schools in this country believe that many private schools are more effective than public schools because they are not encrusted with an inflexible district bureaucracy that undermines both customer and local-community orientation. This observation has led to experiments with site-based management in Miami (Dade County), Santa Fe, and a number of other districts.

The district level has three unique functions. First, it sets goals and standards for the whole system, including negotiation of objectives for specific schools, with the governing bodies of those schools reflecting districtwide goals in light of local conditions and staff and parental preferences. Second, district policy designs and implements a system of accountability for student outcomes to ensure that all schools meet their goals. Thus most of the work of developing alternative assessments will become a district function. Third, the district negotiates with the larger community and state and federal governments to achieve funding and a regulatory climate that will help schools teach children.

The primary function of the school is to create a context in which teachers can help students learn. The school and the district negotiate what constitutes effective productivity. Once broad goals have been established, the school needs to control its own budget, personnel allocations, and basic curriculum. In keeping with the effort to create communities of learning, decisions on these issues must be made jointly by the principal, teachers, parents, and (as appropriate) students.

Within this framework, a variety of tasks now handled by the district must be rethought, including purchasing, transportation, curriculum development, staff development, and certain ancillary services like counseling, which presently may become unwitting methods of control. For instance, after-school tutoring programs may be impossible because of a district-set busing schedule, or teachers may find it difficult to incorporate certain geographic concepts because the district restricts map purchases in their subject area. On the other hand, full responsibility for such tasks may be overwhelming for a given school. Principals are too busy to negotiate busing contracts, and elementary teachers lack the time to design alternative maps for their students.

These tasks can be handled in a number of ways to ensure that they support the educational activities of the schools. These include the following:

Delegation to schools. Some tasks can be delegated to the school. When combined with the use of task-based pay to create new positions in schools, delegation will give each school increased capacity to take on such responsibilities.

Creation of controlled markets. Some tasks may be more efficiently handled centrally. To ensure that such tasks are handled responsively, however, the funds earmarked for these services should be allocated to schools with the stipulation that the services must be purchased from public agencies, among them the central office. Schools would then negotiate with the office in question over the amount, nature, and cost of the services. Allowing for limited markets, this will create a consumer orientation in the district office.

Creation of open markets. Other tasks may be handled either inside or outside the district. Cities have such an arrangement for garbage collection, and many districts now contract out for busing and some staff training. These tasks could be handled much like those assigned to controlled markets, except that schools could purchase services externally or internally. The central unit could bid to offer the service, but it would have to compete with private service vendors. Alternatively, the central unit might be reconstituted as a clearinghouse to help schools purchase services appropriately.

The use of these approaches will depend on local circumstances. For instance, large or isolated districts may opt to use controlled markets, whereas those in areas in which there are a variety of vendors may choose to rely more upon open markets. Controlled markets may also be preferred where coordination among schools or comparability from school to school is prized.

- Create a system of parental choice among schools.

A number of policymakers advocate choice systems to create a customer orientation within schools and to enhance parental commitment. Not all school districts, however, have geographical or demographic configurations that are compatible with such a policy, and sometimes apprehension is great among the interested parties. Yet experts such as Charles Glenn (1993) note that choice systems are often most beneficial to minority students, who have the least opportunity to opt out of neighborhood schools. Because districts often differ along these lines, choice should be seen as only one of several ways to achieve a customer orientation.

- Create new incentives for teachers.

Edward Lawler (1990), who has studied private-sector salary systems for more than twenty years, concludes that American businesses tend to adopt current fads and procedures devised by others without thinking strategically about what their own incentive systems should accomplish. This situation leads to periodic crazes for outmoded procedures such as merit pay, which, according to W. Edwards Deming, "nourishes short-term performance, annihilates long-term planning, builds fear, demolishes teamwork, and nourishes rivalry and politics."

The strategic requirement for an incentive system is that it should build a community committed to supporting the learning of all its children. Thus, certain pitfalls must be avoided, including inappropriate competitiveness, limited or non-performance-linked indicators, token rewards, and a lack of fairness. Reforms should encourage school districts to consider schoolwide or team incentives and rewards for capacity building within the school or team.

- Create a system of public accountability that ensures quality and equity.

Providing a public accountability system requires a holistic view of the mission and accomplishments of schools and a system of school assignment or choice that reflects a strong commitment to equity. Such a commitment requires that evaluations and assessments be based on standards that reflect what is actually taught in schools. Such standards should reflect expectations of thoughtful analysis and strong expository skills. Consistent with the desire to address a child's full range of talents, a variety of subjects—beyond core academic areas—should be available for assessment. Initially, qualified individuals will need to work with the design staff to develop the means of assessing mastery and expertise beyond the core subjects.

Students' achievement should be assessed with criterion-referenced tests and through performance and portfolio evaluations. The evaluation of school effectiveness, however, should also reflect the quality of the school disciplinary climate; evidence of commitment to excellence; the development of the capacity of the organization; the students' commitment to citizenship; and parental support or satisfaction. School boards should have primary responsibility for providing annual accountability reports to the public.

Finally, any districtwide reform should be periodically (at least annually) assessed. By the end of the first year of the plan outlined here, the planning council would propose changes in governance, finance, and accountability that address systemic needs in the social organization of all district schools.

The Need for Coalition

As this chapter illustrates, both local neighborhoods and business alliances have met with moderate success in individual reform projects. Neither, however, is capable of implementing a comprehensive plan such as the one described here. Local groups lack the power and influence necessary for removal of some barriers; they also tend to have less experience with and knowledge of effective management techniques. Business alliances, on the other hand, do not possess the necessary microlevel knowledge of particular community needs and patterns or the sensitivity to local diversity that is crucial to the success of any reform effort.

In order for businesses and neighborhood groups to work together in creating a productive and effective education system, it will be necessary for each to admit its weaknesses and work with the other to fill in the gaps. Corporate leaders must acknowledge the value of ethnic and community diversity, while local leaders should recognize that systematic management techniques from business can be adapted to suit their purposes. When each side is willing to learn from and to teach the other, students will benefit.

NOTES

1. The principal author of the Plan for Reform presented here is Sally B. Kilgore. It is taken from Borman (1994).

REFERENCES

Berenbeim, R.E. 1991. *Corporate Support of National Education Goals*. Report no. 978, The Conference Board. New York: The Conference Board.

Borman, K.M. 1991. *The First Real Job: A Study of Young Workers*. Albany: State University of New York Press.

Borman, K.M., L. Castenell, and K. Gallagher. 1993. Business Involvement in School Reform. In *Politics of Education Yearbook*, ed. C. Marshall. Washington, DC: Falmer Press.

Castenell, L., and S.B. Kilgore. 1994. Creating Shared Visions: The Process of Community Deliberation. In *Investing in U.S. Schools: Directions in Educational Policy*, ed. B. Jones and K. Borman. Norwood, NJ: Ablex.

Chubb, J.E., and T.M. Moe. 1990. *Politics, Markets, and America's Schools*. Washington, DC: Brookings Institution.

Deming, W.E. 1986. *Out of Crisis.* Cambridge, MA: MIT Press.

Dworkin, G., and D. Townsend. 1994. Teacher Burnout in the Face of Reform: Some Caveats in Breaking the Mold. In *Investing in U.S. Schools: Directions for Educational Policy,* ed. B. Jones and K. Borman. Norwood, NJ: Ablex.

Ellwood, D. 1988. *Poor Support: Poverty in the American Family.* New York: Basic Books.

Farrar, E., and A. Cipollone. 1988. After the Signing: The Boston Compact 1982 to 1985. In *American Business and the Public School,* ed. M. Levine and R. Trachtman. New York: Teachers College Press.

Glenn, C. 1994. Choice and Urban School Reform. In *Investing in U.S. Schools: Directions for Educational Policy,* ed. B. Jones and K. Borman. Norwood, NJ: Ablex.

Helton, L., E. Barnes, and K. Borman. 1994. Urban Appalachians and Professional Intervention: A Model for Educators and Social Service Providers. In *From Mountain to Metropolis: Appalachian Migrants in American Cities,* ed. K. Borman and P. Obermiller. Westport, CT: Bergin and Garvey.

Howe, H. 1993. Advice to the New Administration: We Need Four More National Education Goals. *Education Week* 12:44.

Jones, B., and K. Borman, eds. 1994. *Investing in U.S. Schools: Directions for Educational Policy.* Norwood, NJ: Ablex.

Kearns, D., and D.P. Doyle. 1988. *Winning the Brain Race: A Bold Plan to Make Our Schools Competitive.* San Francisco: Institute for Contemporary Studies.

Kilborn, P. 1991. More People Forced into Part-Time Work. *Chicago Tribune* (September 1) sec. 8: 1.

Kozol, J. 1991. *Savage Inequalities: Children in America's Schools.* New York: Crown.

Lareau, A. 1989. *Home Advantage.* London: Falmer.

Lawler, E.E. 1990. *Strategic Pay: Aligning Organizational Strategies and Pay Systems.* San Francisco: Jossey-Bass.

Leetsma, R., and H.J. Walberg. 1992. *Japanese Educational Productivity.* Ann Arbor: University of Michigan Press.

Lightfoot, S. 1978. *Worlds Apart.* New York: Basic Books.

Lott, B. 1987. *Women's Lives.* Pacific Grove, CA: Brooks/Cole.

A Nation at Risk, National Commission on Excellence in Education, April 1984. Washington, DC: National Commission on Excellence in Education.

Peters, T., and R. Waterman. 1982. *In Search of Excellence.* New York: Harper & Row.

Ray, C., and R. Mickelson. 1993. Restructuring Students for Restructured Work: The Economy, School Reform, and Non-College-Bound Youths. *Sociology of Education* 66: 1–200.

Reich, R.B. 1991. *The Work of Nations.* New York: Alfred A. Knopf.

Roditi, H.F. 1992. High Schools for Docile Workers. *The Nation* (March 16): 340–343.

Senge, P.M. 1990. The Leader's New Work: Building Learning Organizations. *Sloan Management Review* (fall): 7–23.

Smith, M.S., and J. O'Day. 1991. Systemic School Reform. In *The Politics of Curriculum and Testing: The 1990 Yearbook of the Politics of Education Association,* ed. S. Fuhrman and B. Malen. New York: Falmer Press.

10

Schools Must Do More for Children— Child Advocacy as an Educational Responsibility

Judith H. Cohen

Introduction

As more child abuse and neglect cases come before the courts, school personnel are being asked to expand their services in response to the needs of children. The following case histories illustrate the disparity of response in how schools perceive their responsibilities as they move away from their traditional role as educator to a more encompassing role as child advocate. Schools can and must do more for our children, who may have no other advocate in their lives.

In twelve-year-old John's[1] appearance before a family court judge, he was accused of stealing assorted merchandise from at least two different department stores in a local shopping center. He admitted to having shoplifted a baseball cap valued by the store at $4.99 and pleaded guilty to a charge of petit larceny. Given the chronic nature of his behavior, the judge placed John in a detention center for the full psychosocial evaluation needed to make an appropriate disposition in this case. John was taken from the courtroom in handcuffs.

The shoplifting occurred at 1:40 in the afternoon on a school day. Why wasn't the child in school? Further inquiry into his school history demonstrated that the school knew the following about John:

268 Transforming Schools

- He was a chronic truant.
- He had an extremely troubled home life, living in a single room and sharing a bed with his elderly, handicapped mother in a rooming house located in the worst part of his poor community. His alcoholic father lived in the same rooming house, but was separated from John's mother because of a history of family violence. The family was on public assistance;
- He had low intellectual ability and was not making good progress in school, having been retained one time;
- His graduation from sixth grade was in doubt because of his truancy and poor academic performance.

No intervention had ever taken place to address John's psychosocial needs. His chaotic home life continued to deteriorate and he continued to fail most school subjects but he was never evaluated for special programs, although such an evaluation was clearly indicated given his low ability and high risk of continued failure. John's physical health was poor: he suffered from asthma and had broken and neglected teeth. He was poorly dressed, was often unsupervised, and spent much time on the streets engaging in minor criminal behavior.

Subsequently, through the family court's intervention, John was placed in a residential program where he remained over the summer months. The residential program's psycho-educational evaluation determined that John had an IQ in the mid 70s, a significant perceptual dysfunction, minimal literacy, and few resources to deal with either the demands of school or the stresses of his life. The program found John to be immature and impulsive, but well-behaved and cooperative in a highly structured environment that provided supervision and guidance and made appropriate demands on him. At the end of the summer, John was returned home to his mother, who continued to await assistance in finding better living arrangements and who still had not been scheduled for needed major orthopedic surgery. At his most recent court appearance, John promised to stay out of trouble and try to do well in the middle school in the same community. (The academic work he did in the summer residential program was used for credit so that he could be promoted from 6th grade.) He carried his schoolbooks to court with him and completed his homework assignments.

Given his poverty, the continuing lack of supervision at home, and a lack of access to a school program that could address the reality of his limited skills and ability, the prognosis for John is guarded at best. John has neither the ability nor any interventional assistance to guide him through the troubled times that surely lie ahead.

Eleven-year-old Jane was the subject of a neglect petition brought against her mother, and her history shows many similarities to John's. Jane and her mother also lived in a rooming house in the poorer section of a different community. They too shared a bed and were on public assistance. Jane's mother, an alcoholic and drug addict, also failed to supervise Jane adequately and frequently left the child alone at night while she engaged in prostitution. Jane's mother admitted to stealing money given to Jane by her biological father (who lived in the community and was married to another woman), using drugs in the child's presence, and beating her with a belt.

At this point the similarities between the two cases cease. Jane's school was actively involved in all aspects of her welfare. They reported her problems to child protective services and she was seen twice weekly by the school social worker, as well as daily by the school learning disability specialist (as the result of a psycho-educational evaluation that demonstrated her under-lying learning problems). Her daily well-being was monitored by both her classroom teacher and her school principal. School personnel taught her to view the school as a resource and to seek the assistance of any school personnel in dealing with problems. The school gave her sandwiches to take home, collected clothes for her, and bought her an alarm clock so that she could be at school on time. In addition, the school arranged for Jane to receive a scholarship for summer camp since they would be unable to monitor her over the summer months. The school argued that Jane should continue to live in their community instead of being placed in foster care as the child protective services and court personnel proposed. As the situation with Jane's mother continued to deteriorate, the school and child protective services worked cooperatively to have Jane begin living with her biological father and his family near the school.

Given the intervention provided by the school in coordination with the family court and child protective services, Jane's future looks more optimistic than John's. In fact the differing personalities of the two children are striking: John is sullen and uncommunicative; Jane is friendly and talkative, optimistic and out-going. Which child is more likely to succeed?

Why was one school district activated toward intervention whereas the other did nothing to aid a child with equally obvious needs? The differences between the two school districts are as dramatic as those between the children themselves. John lives in a community known to be the poorest and most crime-ridden in the area. His school district was cited for fiscal mismanagement and the state education department appointed a special supervisor to monitor its affairs. John is far from unique in a community where most children's needs are not addressed by either their families, the community, or the social service agencies. The district has a long waiting list for special education evaluations and inadequate special programs for handicapped children. There is constant turnover of both teachers and administrators, and the district's overall academic performance is poor. The presiding judge of the family court admitted his frustration in dealing with a school district that has both overwhelming numbers of needy children and inadequate resources to provide for their needs.

Jane resides in a poor section of a school district that has a very affluent population; it has both a large number of middle-class families and a sizable poverty component. The community values education highly and the schools have a well-paid and competent professional staff. The district possesses both the financial resources and the educational leadership needed to address the needs of its student population with appropriate energy and concern.

Educational Equity and Child Services

Why should John and Jane receive such markedly different treatment from their schools? Why do severe disparities exist that allow communities less than fifteen miles apart geographically to be worlds apart in terms of educational equity? The issue of school equity has been highlighted recently by the political rhetoric of the presidential campaign, by social activists, and most recently by judicial action. Educational equity is a purely theoretical construct for many children, and the quality of their education and general well-being may well depend solely on the political boundaries of the communities in which they live. Jonathan Kozol's (1991) study of the disparities between schools that educate white middle-class children and those that educate poor minority children paints dramatic pictures of these "savage inequalities." After visiting approximately thirty neighborhoods throughout the country, Kozol found that schools today are more socially and racially segregated than they were during the civil rights era. He concludes that "In public schooling, social policy has been turned back almost one hundred years," and that this nation "has turned its back upon the moral implications, if not yet the legal ramifications, of the *Brown* decision" (1991, p. 4).

Echoing these sentiments, social critic Anna Quindlen writes in the *New York Times* of a school without windows that was converted from either a movie theater or a bowling alley and is located in a commercial area of the Bronx. In school, she says, children should learn to respect themselves, but in this environment they learn "that they barely deserve oxygen" (1992). While recognizing the government's obvious limitations in righting social ills, Quindlen comments that there are areas in which government "can narrow the chasm between haves and have-nots," and that public education is one such area (1992).

This chasm is easily documented. Kozol (1991, p. 237) presents figures showing a difference between the highest spending per pupil ($11,372 for a suburban New York district) compared to that for a neighboring poverty community ($6,339) during 1986–1987, a gap which widened to almost $7,000 for the school year 1989–1990. A recent report on per-pupil spending by

Long Island school districts concludes that in Nassau County, a relatively homogeneous community, "with few exceptions the smaller the school districts, the whiter and wealthier they are and the more money they spend per student, with less tax effort" (Saslow 1993). The report characterizes Jane's school district as providing a "publicly-supported private school equivalent that spends more than $13,000 a year per student." John lives in a community whose district is described as "just working to survive" (Saslow 1993). These disparities have not gone unnoticed by New York State's highest leadership, but a recent proposal by the state education commissioner to merge many Long Island school districts in order to promote equity and reduce administrative overhead was withdrawn because of intense political debate and obvious local self-interest. New York Governor Mario Cuomo has proposed a plan to finance schools through income tax rather than through property taxes in order to address the marked differences between schools in rich and poor school districts (Lyall 1993). The conventional thinking that funding disparities are a result of the difference between urban and suburban housing patterns is clearly mistaken. It appears that schooling in minority areas is vastly different from schooling in predominantly White communities, regardless of urbanicity (Lyall 1993).

Proposals for mergers of school districts and revised school financing plans have been described as "epic battles that have bogged down reformers for decades" (Blueprint, 1992). The courts are the latest forum for overhauling school finances. In July 1993, Massachusetts's highest court became the twelfth in the nation to require the legislature to rethink school financing and close the gap between wealthy and poor school districts (Costly, 1993). Money for elementary and secondary schools is usually the largest allocation of funds approved by state legislators, but according to a Texas senator embroiled in school funding battles, "distribution of that money often bears only a distant connection to what policymakers say students need and what they expect schools to provide" (Harp 1993, p. 10).

The decisions in these state-court lawsuits have contained strongly worded admonitions and have detailed the inadequate funding of poverty schools while requiring that states create school finance formulas which provide for more equitable funding of public education. The focus for states is to balance reliance upon local property taxes for education funding with district boundaries that clearly reflect economic disparities in community resources, but will school finance reform occur during the years that John and Jane need it most? Educators do not have time to wait.

Who Are Our Schoolchildren?

John and Jane are not atypical. Children born in poverty and continuing to live in poverty make special demands on our school system; more often than not, they do not succeed academically. The numbers of such children in the system is increasing rapidly—an index of social well-being that tracks sixteen key social factors including poverty, child abuse, teen suicide, and school dropout rates concludes that "the nation's overall social well-being has fallen to its lowest point since 1970." Indicators of children's health and well-being declined for the fifth year in a row (Dimensions 1992b). From the time of "The Great War on Poverty" of the 1960s to the present day, there has been a growing number of students who have fewer of the essentials needed to benefit from public education. These students suffer from poverty, family instability, drug and alcohol abuse, and neglect. They are often members of minorities, have handicaps, or are immigrants who have just arrived in this country. Additionally, the children frequently are not well motivated, have poor reading and writing skills, and show little respect for authority. With such children in their classes, today's teachers need more than stimulating ways to help children develop skills and acquire knowledge. Children such as John and Jane cannot be taught effectively nor will they succeed unless their psychosocial problems are addressed.

The "typical" intact American family is no longer predominant in our student population. While the divorce rate peaked during the 1980s, a drop in the number of marriages has resulted in a continuing increase in single-parent families. In fact, the census bureau reports that "one of the most significant changes in the composition of the American family has been the phenomenal rise in the number of single parents." Between 1970 and 1992 the number of single-parent households increased from 3.8 million to 10.5 million. While White single parents outnumber those of other groups, the relative proportion of single-parent households among minority groups is significant: in 1992, 62 percent of Black families and 34 percent of Hispanic families were headed by single parents. The vast majority of single parents are mothers (Rawlings 1993, pp. xii–xiii), and children in families headed by females do not fare well. While approximately 20 percent of all children under age eighteen live in poverty, the percentage increases to 58 percent for households headed by females, with minority groups impacted most strongly: 47 percent for households headed by White women, 80 percent for households headed by Black women, and 48 percent for households headed by Hispanic women (U.S. Department of Education, National Center, 1992, p. 108). There has been a tremendous increase in the number of children born out of wedlock. Whereas thirty years ago only one in forty White children was born to an unmarried mother, today the number is one in five, according to recent federal data. The statistics for minority children are even more startling—two out of three Black children are born to unmarried mothers, according to recent data (Marriott 1992). This rise in single-parent families is reshaping the notion of the typical American family (Lewin 1992). This startling development has had the profound result that many children are being raised by single parents who struggle economically while simultaneously attempting to provide appropriate supervision and guidance for their children.

Many children leave for school in the morning without parental supervision and return to empty homes after school. The percentage of mothers who work has contributed to the reshaping of the family. In 1991, 67 percent of all mothers with children under eighteen worked, and the incidence of working mothers ranged from 55 percent for mothers with children under three to 76 percent for mothers of children aged fourteen through seventeen (Ways and Means, 1992, p. 937). One study found that 5.2 million school-age children under thirteen are latchkey children, and linked their behavioral problems and delinquency to lack of parental supervision (Duke 1984, p. 47).

Many of the special needs of today's families result from extreme poverty, particularly among minority children (Brazelton 1990, pp. 40, 42). Children seem to bear an inordinate share of our nation's poverty. According to recent demographic data, poverty rates were highest for individuals under age eighteen, more than 20 percent of whom lived in poverty in 1991. This represented an increase of over one million children from the previous year. The impact on minority children is even greater. While in 1990, 20 percent of all children lived in poverty, the poverty impacts 15 percent of White children, 44 percent of Black children, and 38 percent of Hispanic children (U.S. Department of Education, National Center, 1992, p. 108).

Children of poverty often have unmet health needs that in turn create significant barriers to success in school. The Children's Defense Fund estimates that twenty-five million children live in families that do not have employer-provided insurance; eighteen million children are not covered by any form of private insurance; and more than eight million children have no private or public insurance (e.g., Medicaid) at all (*Health of America's Children*, 1992). A prominent pediatrician in asking the poignant question, "Why Is America Failing Its Children?" (Brazelton 1990) summarized the problem: "I have begun to regard the growing neglect and poverty of the young as the biggest threat to the nation's future. I also see evidence that we could start preventing this terrible waste, with remedies available right now—but we seem to have lost the will even to think about it" (Brazelton 1990, p. 42). The report "The Health of America's Children 1992" documents a grim reality: lack of adequate health care for children and mothers in the United States has put our children at high risk for infectious disease and physical and mental disabilities (Dimensions, November 1992).

Impoverished children like John and Jane are frequently placed in foster homes for extended lengths of time during their childhoods. Experts agree that the abuse and neglect that are part of the lives of many foster children are at the root of the educational and social problems these children face in school

(Cohen 1991a). The growing numbers of children placed in foster care and the myriad of problems resulting from child abuse, neglect, and substance abuse pose challenges to schools that they are not ready to handle. This is in spite of the fact that most child-abuse cases first come to light in the schools. Data show that the school achievement of children in foster care is well below that of their peers and that the schools and the social service agencies which frequently have legal guardianship of foster children have not provided adequate services to assist these children to overcome their handicaps. Significantly, by age seventeen, 47 percent of foster-care children are at least a year below their appropriate grade placement, as compared with 17 percent of other children not in foster care. It has been documented that in addition to poor achievement in school, foster-care children are at significantly greater risk for dropping out. The disruption in their lives combined with their psychological and academic needs places them at high risk for failure in a school environment that often provides little help for their educational deficits (D. Cohen 1991).

Possibly the neediest children, and those who make the most demands on our schools, are those whose lives are affected by drug and substance abuse. A legal commentator brings this problem into focus by saying that "[i]f cocaine use during pregnancy were considered a disease, its impact on children would be considered a national health care crisis" (Fink 1990, p. 1). Many experts believe that the significant increase in the number of foster children is linked to the introduction of crack cocaine during the mid-1980s and the inability of drug-addicted mothers to care for their children (Ways and Means, 1992, p. 899). Jane's mother was a habitual user of crack cocaine and her desperate need for money led her to prostitution, to stealing from Jane's piggy bank, and to beating Jane with both hand and belt while she was out of control on drugs. Both of John's parents were substance abusers; their need to find relief from lives of despair and poverty is too often typical of members of their local community. Drug and alcohol abuse resulted in patterns of neglect and abandonment in the lives of both John and Jane. Additionally, as more children born to drug-addicted mothers enter our schools, the number of learning-disabled, emotionally handicapped, and behavior-disordered children needing special education services will increase.

John and Jane are both children who have such handicaps. In this way they represent a significant and growing number of students in our schools. According to the education department's annual report on special education, these programs have grown faster during 1990–1991 than at any time during the previous decade (Viadero 1992). In 1989–1990 more than 11 percent of all students enrolled in elementary and secondary schools received services in federally supported special education programs (U.S. Department of Education Research, 1992, p. 64). Schools face shortages of special education teachers, school psychologists and speech therapists, and in particular special educators who are bilingual. When we reflect upon the quality of interventional assistance provided for Jane in an affluent school district and the total absence of such assistance for John in his poor school district, the dramatic disparities in levels of service become apparent.

In summary, the picture of today's school population has changed markedly from former times, and there are new concerns and roles for today's educators. The implications of the shifting patterns of family life range from such simple problems as what to do about Father's Day and Mother's Day to the far more complex issues of how to educate children who lack stability, are full of anger, and have unmet physical needs. Today's schools were designed at a time when children lived in nuclear families and the primary purpose of schooling was to educate a fairly homogeneous group. Today, only 10 percent of all households reflect the idealized and traditional notion of a family composed of a married couple with two children (Rawlings 1993, p. vi). How well have schools accommodated the dynamic needs of foster children, children from divorced families, abandoned children, children of working mothers, children from single-parent households, children of poverty, immigrant children, handicapped children, and children who reside in shelters for the homeless?

It is clear from the lives of John and Jane that some schools and some communities are better equipped to provide for at-risk students than others. In fact, the contrast between their stories attests to the differences in schools.

The poverty and family disintegration described here have adversely affected the way children such as John and Jane fare in school. Children of poverty often begin school less prepared for learning and are more likely to drop out of school. In school and in their communities they are too often surrounded by a violent and crime-ridden environment and often become involved in substance abuse.

More than 50 percent of all public school teachers polled in 1992 said that at least 25 percent of their students were unprepared for work at their grade level (Harp 1992). As such children present themselves at the preschool level, the need for extra resources is made abundantly clear. A survey of prekindergarten and kindergarten teachers revealed that 42 percent felt that one-third of their pupils, approximately 1.8 million children, were unprepared because of health, emotional, or domestic problems (Celis 1992a). Teachers and students attributed a preponderance of these problems to social causes and not specifically to issues of learning (U.S. Department of Education Research, 1992, p. 31).

While truly reliable statistics about the dropout rate are both scarce and suspect, it has been estimated that almost one child in three never completes high school (Tabor 1992), representing a decline of more than 10 percent in the number of high school graduates in 1991–1992 compared with 1969–1970 (U.S. Department of Education Research, 1992, p. 108). Some view the problem as having reached crisis proportions, particularly when dropout rates are examined for minority students (especially Blacks and Hispanics), students from low-income households, pregnant teens and students involved in alcohol or drug abuse. The dropout rate for minority children is much higher than that for White students, and among Hispanic students the problem is at a crisis level. While it has been estimated that in 1991, 13 percent of all students dropped out by high school, the figure for White students was 9 percent; for Black students, 14 percent; and for Hispanic students, 35 percent (U.S. Department of Education Research, 1992, p. 109). In spite of various educational initiatives, the dropout problem for Hispanic students today is approximately the same as in 1972, whereas there has been some improvement in the rate for Blacks and Whites (Celis 1992b).

Another alarming indicator of educational failure is the increase in crimes committed by young people. The incidence of violent crimes committed by youth has increased more than 25 percent within the last ten years (Violent Crime, 1992). The increase is found not only among poor juveniles in urban areas but among all races, social classes, and ways of life, from the inner cities to suburban populations (Lawton 1993). Crime statistics for Black male youths are particularly dismal; the arrest rate for this population is five times that of other groups (Violent Crimes, 1992). For an increasing number of our children a probation officer has become a surrogate parent (Lee 1992).

Social ills have also resulted in street crime and drug abuse invading what was once the safe haven of the school. The incidence of crime in New York City schools rose nearly 29 percent in the last school year (McFadden 1992), with both students and teachers reporting concerns about violence in their schools. In a 1989 national survey, 16 percent of all students between the ages of twelve and nineteen reported the presence of street gangs in school; 16 percent reported that their teachers had been attacked or threatened with attack; and 12 percent reported a theft from them in school (U.S. Department of Education, National Center, 1992, p. 116). Analysts believe that schools are dangerous because of overcrowding and a national pattern of violence and antisocial behavior by youth. Metal detectors and a security force are commonly seen in secondary schools across the country.

Drug and alcohol use among school-age children is still a significant problem. While there has been a meaningful decline in the use of hard drugs (down from a reported 55 percent in 1975 to 44 percent in 1991), drinking persists at a high level (90 percent reported alcohol use in 1975 to 88 percent in 1991) (U.S. Department of Education, National Center, 1992, p. 118).

The lives of John and Jane and the different roles played by their respective schools attest to extreme differences in the ability of schools to address their students' problems. Allan Shedlin, Jr., executive director of the Elementary School Center in New York City, has said: "The U.S. elementary school was designed for a society that no longer exists. Although the size and design of buildings might change to reflect economic and demographic changes, the role of the school and what goes on inside it are not generally responsive to the social realities now affecting children and their families" (Shedlin 1990a, p. 12).

It is clear that today's schools are faced with educating children who have many unmet psychosocial needs that ultimately can prevent them from succeeding. Although some schools derive benefit from funding that enables them to provide more adequately for their students, unfortunately schools in urban and poverty communities face a preponderance of children who are unlikely to succeed and also have few educational resources.

Abuse, Neglect, and Child Protective Proceedings

Children such as John and Jane are too often victims of child abuse and neglect. Jane first became known to the family court as the subject of a proceeding alleging that her mother abused and neglected her. John became known to the court because of his acts of juvenile delinquency, but he was clearly a neglected child. The legal system deals with the prosecution of abuse and neglect cases through child protective proceedings. Because of the increased number of such cases, the family court has had to change dramatically in an attempt to provide for children after abuse and neglect have been identified. In child protective proceedings, efforts are made to address the underlying social factors that lead to the abuse and neglect and thereby keep the family intact or enable the reunification of the family in the future. Unfortunately, as the number of the abuse and neglect cases continues to increase each year and as budgetary constraints limit social service resources, the legal system is unable to remedy the many deep-rooted and complex needs of children like John and Jane. Certainly the prosecution of child abuse and neglect does not at all address the need for preventive services and early identification for children and families at risk. By the time these cases enter the legal system, the mental, emotional, and physical scars on the children are quite evident.

The legal disposition of abuse and neglect cases often removes children or maintains the family with supportive services, but there is no place in the proceedings for meeting the children's specific needs.

New York State employs a centralized system for the reporting of child abuse cases by the use of a statewide hot-line phone number. Because of the urgent need to identify abused and neglected children, those professionals who have ongoing contact with children (i.e., physicians, dentists, nurses, police officers, teachers, child-care workers, psychologists, etc.) are mandated reporters and therefore are legally required to report it whenever they have reasonable cause to suspect that a child they see in their professional capacity is abused or maltreated (New York State Social Service Law, Section 413). In 1991 mandated reporters accounted for 63 percent of child protection investigations. Reports made by school personnel continue to constitute the largest and most reliable source of information on abuse and neglect cases (*State Central Register*, 1993). For example, in 1991 action was taken in 41 percent of the school-reported cases, whereas less than 7 percent of anonymous reports and less than 6 percent of neighbors' reports were found reliable (Remarks, 1992). New York State requires that all mandated reporters receive training in detecting child abuse and neglect and in procedures for reporting suspected cases as part of their licensing requirements.

If there is credible evidence that a child has been abused or neglected, a petition is brought on behalf of the child by the Department of Social Services and filed in Family Court. The respondent (person allegedly committing the acts), who is usually a parent, a paramour or a close relative, is notified of the petition and is required to appear in court to answer the allegations. A denial results in a hearing of the matter, but often the respondent admits to some items in the petition when presented with specific and detailed allegations of abuse or neglect. At this initial stage a law guardian can be appointed by the judge to represent the interests of the children named in the petition. The law guardian is an attorney who has received specialized training, is independent of the interests of either the prosecution or the defense, and is compensated from state funds.

The law guardian's role is that of advocate for the child to ensure that his or her situation and welfare are known to the court and that the child's "voice" is heard in the court proceedings. By virtue of their complex responsibilities, law guardians take on many roles in their legal representation of children, certainly as an attorney but also as a friend, therapist, psychologist, and social worker. It is most unfortunate that children do not have the benefit of an advocate until after they have suffered the consequences of abuse and neglect.

During the child protective proceedings in family court, children may remain with their families if there is no apparent likelihood of further abuse or neglect. The Family Court Act does contain provisions for the emergency removal of children at any stage in the proceedings if the circumstances warrant immediate action. It is common for legal custody of the child to be given by consent of the parent to the Department of Social Services while physical custody of the child is provided by foster care, kinship foster care (foster care provided by a relative), or the extended family.

Many of the families involved in child protective proceedings suffer from poverty and dysfunctional home lives and are often known to the Department of Social Services well before neglect or abuse petitions are filed. The legal process that accompanies the proceedings is lengthy, cumbersome, and intrusive, and ultimately may fail to address the many recognized and complex psychosocial needs of the families in crisis. Many who are associated with family court proceedings feel frustrated and anguished over the sheer volume of abuse and neglect cases, their severity and recidivism, and the legal system's inability to cure the root causes of abuse and neglect. It is often apparent that the needs of the child are not addressed in a legal system with an adversarial relationship between prosecution and defense and where the remedies are perceived as punitive.

In 1962 the New York State Family Court was established with the intent of creating a better judicial structure with personnel especially trained for dealing with domestic problems. Today the very nature of the court's functioning has changed markedly to deal with the dramatically different kinds of cases it

hears on a routine basis. The number of child protective proceedings in New York State continues to grow at alarming rates;
in 1984 in New York City alone there were 5,180 cases filed, and
by 1989 the number had quadrupled to 24,430 (McDonald 1992,
p. 2). In 1992 there were 230,930 cases reported to the central
registry in Albany, with the following allegations cited in the
majority of cases (*State Central Register* 1993, table 22):

Type of allegation	No. of Cases Reported
• Lack of supervision	31,034
• Lacerations, bruises, welts	15,022
• Lack of food, clothing, and/or shelter	12,812
• Excessive corporal punishment	10,575
• Sex abuse	10,295
• Educational neglect	8,526
• Lack of medical care	6,628

The large number of cases reported in Nassau County, the
county of residence for John and Jane, mirrors the increase both
in reported cases on the state level (13 percent more cases in 1992
than in 1991) and in cases reported on the national level, where
the growth in child abuse reports has averaged about 6 percent
each year since 1985 (*Annual National Data* 1992, p. 3). Some
argue that these increases are a reflection of more vigilant action
in reporting cases by both mandated reporters and interested
parties. However they are arrived at, the numbers are staggering
and indicate that a significant number of children are clearly at
risk in our society. Who can ignore data that report that on a
national basis four children die each day as a result of
maltreatment and that each day 7,300 children are reported to be
suspected victims of abuse or neglect? (*Annual National Data*
1992, p. 2). The executive director of the National Committee for
Prevention of Child Abuse speaks for us all when she says: "This
level of violence toward children demands comprehensive and
immediate action" (*Annual National Data* 1992, p. 2).

Today's Family Court has had to change dramatically and
has attempted to assume responsibility for protecting children,
but how effectively can the courts handle this role? The

presiding judge of the New York City Family Court has major concerns: "As unemployment, poverty, homelessness, and drug abuse have increased in the past decade, Family Court dockets have skyrocketed with scores of cases each day involving extremely serious family problems. Given the relative dearth of community-based services available to address these problems, today's Family Court must be very concerned about its basic ability to respond effectively to the critical needs of the children and families before it" (McDonald 1992, p. 2).

Data collected by the Federation on Child Abuse and Neglect unfortunately reveal that funding for child welfare services is not keeping pace with societal needs. Their research reveals that of the forty-four states that reported on such funding for 1991, only thirteen received additional funding and seven states suffered cutbacks. Even states that maintained their prior level of funding reported that this level of support did not provide for increased effort or services in the area of child abuse prevention (*Annual National Data* 1992, p. 4). The hands of the Family Court are tied when it mandates services to a family and the services are either inadequate or nonexistent.

Clearly the Family Court dockets are full of testaments to the societal ills that plague children in today's society. While it is certainly necessary to prosecute those who abuse and neglect children, it seems apparent that more effort needs to be placed on prevention. Punishment of the respondent does not ameliorate the lasting effect of abuse and neglect on children. Unfortunately the mechanisms to prevent child abuse require the kinds of allocation of funds that have not been made available. The Family Court is not the solution to problems that need to be addressed by community-based services that speak to those complex factors that result in the increasing numbers of child abuse reports. More efforts need to be made to identify children and families at risk, and funding needs to be provided for support services to deal with the endemic problems. The judicial system was never designed for this role, and it struggles to provide for children when the evidence of abuse and neglect is finally disclosed. While resources are limited and the need for funding is extreme, it is the opinion of those best informed that society can no longer afford to ignore the problem. The

Honorable Kathryn McDonald eloquently summarizes the argument for funding:

> The Family Court can, if required, adjudicate thousands of babies neglected by virtue of their mother's crack use, and order the provision of services, after the fact, to address the physical and developmental effects of prenatal drug exposure. However, how much more efficient—not to mention humane—it would be to provide drug treatment and prenatal care in the community in the first instance, to obviate the need for these extraordinary measures once the child is born. (1992, p. 3)

In summary, the proceedings in the Family Court system serve to punish offenders, attempt with inadequate resources to address underlying psychosocial problems in families (but not specifically the children in these families), and can do little if anything to promote child welfare by early identification of children and families at risk. Clearly, community-based social service systems, such as those that could be located within schools, can do more for children with regard to early identification and prevention of abuse and neglect.

Programs and Initiatives

As the needs of society have changed, so too has the role of the school. While waiting for legislative reform, schools have begun providing services that were once the sole province of the family or community. From day-care centers to school breakfast programs, from school-based health clinics to after-school latchkey-child care, school services have taken on new roles to provide for children. Reforms and expansions have transformed our schools into "a vast social service agency" (Kirst 1984); schools today are expected not only to educate our children but also to "cure society's ills" (Ravitch 1983).

For many years educators had the commonsense attitude that home and family are key to children's success in school. Children who come to school hungry, tired, poorly dressed, and unsocialized to the world of education encounter barriers to success in school. Notable school-based initiatives have attempted to compensate for these kinds of deficiencies in children's lives. Head Start, begun in 1965 as part of the War on Poverty, won the support of both liberals and conservatives. Head Start's legacy is the concept that early intervention through enriched pre-school education can make a long-term difference in the educational success of children who clearly were at risk for failure because of poverty. Head Start attempted to provide the kind of support structures for children within the school environment that previously were provided by home, community, and family. Most commentators feel that Head Start has, while making a difference in the children's school success, had indirect financial benefits. According to President Clinton, investment in preschool education pays off: "For every dollar we invest today, we'll save three tomorrow" on expenditures for criminal justice, welfare, and special education (Friedman 1993).

Recent research, however, criticizes the Head Start concept, not for what it does, but for what it was never designed to do. A new longitudinal study of Head Start suggests that children of poverty need far more than a preschool interventional program if they are to succeed. An early childhood educator comments: "The best program in the world for a very short time at age four is not going to help children survive the onslaught of neighborhoods devastated by crime and drugs" (Kantrowitz and McCormick 1992). A Chicago researcher proposes that schools need to do more than provide the traditional two years of "head start" and continue with four to six years of extra services for girls and seven to nine years for boys, who seem to be more susceptible to peer pressure. In summary, the Head Start experience informs us that poor kids need continuing and focused help long after they have left a successful preschool experience if the head start results are to last.

In December 1990 a group of educators, child advocates, researchers, and other concerned individuals formed an independent commission to discuss the effectiveness of another poverty program ("Making," 1993). Chapter 1 of the Elementary and Secondary Education Act of 1965 was designed to provide financial assistance to schools to meet the needs of children of poverty. Much of this funding had been allocated for remediation in primary-skill areas such as reading and mathematics. The group felt that while Chapter 1–funded programs were well-intentioned, they did not realistically meet the needs of children from poverty communities in the 1990s. Of particular interest in the group's proposals for revamping these programs was the realization that if children of poverty are to succeed, Chapter 1 resources should be used to integrate health and social services into the school environment. Specifically, the group called for such services as screening and treatment of children for vision, hearing, and dental problems, as well as for an immunization program. According to the group, it is common knowledge that when children are physically unwell, hungry, or suffering from other kinds of social stress, they have more difficulty succeeding in school. If resources are to be allocated for compensatory education, then resources should also be used to alleviate the physical and psychosocial barriers to learning.

Another example of the realization that provision for children's health needs must become part of the schools' responsibility is the school health clinic movement. A school-based clinic is a primary health care facility that is located in, adjacent to, or linked with a school. Clinics vary in size and services, but all share a common goal of providing health care and social services to students, particularly those students with unmet health needs. The movement has grown considerably since its inception in the mid-1980s, and as of 1991 there were 327 school clinics identified by the Center for Population Options, which operates a national resource center for the support of these clinics. Today's school clinics serve both elementary and secondary students (although a large percentage of the clinics are affiliated with secondary schools), and most are located either in urban settings with high proportions of Black and Hispanic children or in rural settings where students also have poor access to medical care (Waszak 1991). Clinics are funded by a variety of sources including community health clinics, public health departments, and hospitals or medical schools. Only a very few are funded by school systems themselves.

The benefits of school-based or school-linked health facilities are many. Placing a clinic in or adjacent to a school

increases the likelihood that the clinic will reach those students
who would not otherwise seek medical treatment or counseling.
The clinics are easily accessible to the students, and in turn, the
students are accessible to clinic staff to allow for on-going
monitoring and follow-up. While some controversy exists about
offering reproductive services as part of the clinic model, the
clinics presently offer a full range of medical services. In schools
with clinic programs, approximately half the average school
enrollment utilizes this broad spectrum of services (Waszak
1992, p. 17). Research on their effectiveness clearly demonstrates
that school-based clinics are important deliverers of health care
to children and adolescents (Waszak 1992, p. 24).

Other school-based initiatives that address the social needs
of students are beginning to appear all across the country; they
use a variety of service models. What the programs have in
common is the recognition that if children come from poverty
backgrounds and lack stability and guidance, the schools must
take these factors into account in order to structure learning
environments where success is more likely. In New Jersey, one
high school has been dramatically redesigned to allow an
extensive array of social services to be delivered to teen mothers.
In this school toddlers are provided with day care while their
teen-aged mothers finish high school (Chira 1991). In San Diego,
social workers, child abuse workers, probation officers, and
welfare administrators are housed on the grounds of an
elementary school (Chira 1991). Programs like these, providing
health care, counseling, day care, after-school programs, and
adult education, have been labeled "one-stop shopping schools"
by educators who see a need to provide social services on site
where poverty, abuse, and neglect are endemic in the school-age
population (Chira 1991). Currently there are almost one
thousand schools that provide social services on site in
elementary, middle, and high schools. While the programs are
still new, some positive effects have already been noted: higher
grades, better attendance, and improved behavior (Chira 1991).

In Brattleboro, Vermont, under a federally funded
program, home visitors are employed to link troubled families
who have young children to needed support services. The
method of service delivery in this program is to use case

managers who have strong links with both social service agencies and the schools (Cohen 1992b). In another initiative the Pew Charitable Trusts foundation recently announced that it would select five states to participate in an eleven-year, fifty-six million dollar effort to improve social, educational, and health services for children. Recognizing that support services for children are often "fragmented, reactive and crisis-oriented," and that several agencies can be involved with children and their families without the essential coordination of services, this project calls for a new approach (Sommerfield 1992). Toward this end, the project is designed to create family centers located near schools which will serve as resources for social, psychological, and medical services, focusing on children from infancy through age six.

Another avenue of reform and change in the role of schools is reflected in the trend away from large, impersonal secondary school settings to smaller, more intimate arrangements. Districts in Philadelphia, Chicago, New York City, Denver, Boulder, Providence, and San Francisco have modified secondary-school organization to do away with schools in which two thousand to five thousand students are housed in one factorylike school building. In these cities, small schools now enroll only about four hundred students each. The primary purpose of these new patterns is to create a sense of identity between student and teacher, so that in times when students receive less support from their families, teachers and school staff can fill the gap and assist adolescents during the stressful years of their secondary school experience (Chira 1993).

In 1987, New York City, under the auspices of the Elementary School Center, developed a plan to restructure and reconceptualize three schools in East Harlem as part of a pilot project that grew out of a nonprofit resource center established to promote schools as centers for child advocacy. The concept here was not to transform the essential mission of schools but rather to locate and coordinate social services in a setting where children and their families were readily accessed—the schools. While this project to turn the schools into centers for child advocacy has met with mixed results, the need to rethink the essential role of schools has grown into a national debate that can ultimately lead to dramatic changes in the role and function of schools. Allan Shedlin, Director of the Elementary School Center, feels that schools must be made a locus for child advocacy and proposes a holistic view of children that will require a revised concept of the elementary school through new systematic and collaborative approaches to meeting children's needs (Klopf, Shedlin, and Zaret 1988).

The most extensive efforts to provide on-site support for children and their families can be found in the state of Kentucky. In 1990, after the State Supreme Court ruled that Kentucky's educational system was unconstitutional, the Kentucky Education Reform Act, which mandated that education throughout the state be reformed, was signed into law (From Risk, 1993). Funded by a $1.4 billion tax increase, this plan is an ambitious initiative to comprehensively reform education and change the traditional roles of schools. As part of the reform act, a funding formula was used to create equity in financial support for schools across the state. An essential aspect of the reform program was the creation of family-resource and youth service centers in poverty schools.

The underlying philosophy behind the creation of these centers is the belief that children learn best when their parents and families support them by providing for their physical and emotional well-being, and that many families in Kentucky were unable to do so (Roeder 1992b). This new form of social service delivery attempted to coordinate many different forms of service and locate them in schools, which were both familiar and convenient. The Kentucky model is based upon a realization that the needs of families are complex and interrelated, and if education reform is to be effective, coordination of services through a multifaceted, multidisciplinary approach must be undertaken. Essential to the establishment and effectiveness of such programs is not only good will but financial support commensurate with the task. The reform movement in Kentucky had backing not only from the state board of education but also from influential legislative leaders, who, with the Governor, ensured that the full amount of money requested was allocated for the program.

Have the debate and these different initiatives made a difference? While it may be too soon to judge these new programs in terms of hard data, the growing awareness of childhood needs has never been more newsworthy. While the Kentucky reform movement has only just completed its second year of implementation, a preliminary study has reported these positive results: the centers have been implemented quickly and effectively; administration has been flexible and appropriate; and, most importantly, teachers, parents, students, school administrators, and center operators have all been supportive (Roeder 1992a).

According to Shedlin, we as a society have become too accustomed to the dreadful lives of many of our school children:

> The latest lexicon of childhood descriptors in the United States, in fact, might prompt us to question whether we rightly merit the title of "civilized" nation: "crossfire children," "crack babies," "shelter kids," "throwaway children," "boarder babies." And added to this parlance of shameful childhood modifiers is the fact that we are no longer shocked when children are routinely referred to as "homeless," "abused," "abandoned," or "missing." (Shedlin 1990a)

Something must be done, and society has begun looking to the schools to do it. Clearly some attitudes about the role of the school have changed. Only a few years ago parents boycotted schools that planned to dispense contraceptives to teens in school-based health clinics, but in 1992 a Gallup poll revealed that 68 percent of people surveyed favored the distribution of condoms in schools (De Witt 1992). Thus an idea that was truly startling some years ago has grown in public acceptance. Recent surveys of public opinion reveal that taxpayers are even willing to support school-based initiatives by paying higher taxes if they can be assured that the money will be targeted for better services for children (Shedlin 1990).

School personnel are well-intended but have difficulty separating their traditional role of educating children from their intense desire to provide for children when others have not. Some have called today's teachers "parents by proxy," and certainly teachers' jobs have expanded into areas that they are both untrained for and unsure about (Cohen 1991b). The tension between role priorities in teaching and the function of the schools has to be clarified before more reforms are begun. However, it seems abundantly clear that the American school system must do more to engage families in becoming committed to education and that there are viable models for providing essential social services for families within the school setting.

Conclusion

There is an intense national dialogue about educational reform that raises fundamental questions about the purpose, structure, and effectiveness of schools. People often look to schools to solve the social ills that damage our children. According to Lawrence Cremin, there is a "longstanding . . . tendency to try to solve social, political, and economic problems through educational means, and in so doing, invest education with all kinds of millennial hopes and expectations" (1990, p. 92). Schools today are having increasing difficulty meeting even their traditional goals of educating children, in part because, as one superintendent aptly put it, hungry, sick and abused children cannot learn and "If you don't get into that you can't accomplish the educational mission" (Bradley 1993). Many schools are beginning to address the problem of providing for these noneducational needs and are struggling to find both the financial support and the structures needed for them to do so.

Many acknowledge that schools are the best structure for providing for child welfare. The systems of family, neighborhood, church, judiciary, and social services that have more traditionally addressed the social welfare needs of children are overburdened and fragmented. The proposals of Allan Shedlin and the work of the Elementary School Center clearly document the many reasons why schools are the appropriate structure for child advocacy:

- Schools are a natural, strategic, and available social agency.
- Schools are an accessible, existing resource within all communities.

- Schools are the only institutions that reach all children regardless of gender, ethnicity, race, and socioeconomic status.
- Schools have historically fulfilled a role as a central community resource.
- Schools have more opportunity to closely interact with children's families and communities than any other social service provider.
- Schools are keenly aware of the unique circumstances of communities that differ geographically, have varying degrees of resources, and are composed of markedly different groups of people.
- Schools have a long-standing and sincere moral commitment to children.
- Schools are most often composed of dedicated individuals who have committed themselves to work for the betterment of children (Klopf, Shedlin, and Zaret 1988, pp. 5–9).

Clearly there are obstacles to activating schools as centers for advocacy, and much needs to be done to educate teachers about their expanding roles as well as to create new jobs for a core of people trained in social services and child advocacy. We must strengthen preservice and in-service education of teachers to better equip them with the necessary skills to perform effectively. The recent example of school personnel being required to assume the responsibility of reporting child abuse and neglect speaks to the likely success of such forms of advocacy provided that appropriate training takes place and procedures are clearly specified and understood. We most certainly must create support systems in schools so that teachers have both referral networks and access to assistance when they discover children with unmet needs. Schools need to find ways to better collaborate with families and other community residents who are needed to make a difference in the lives of the children in their distinctive communities. Such issues as school size and organizational arrangements of children within the school need to be clearly examined so that each child is known individually to the professional staff and all children feel that they are important in the school community.

More needs to be done in terms of the broader systems and structures needed to support such initiatives. Schools are already burdened and too often overwhelmed with even the seemingly simple task of meeting the day-to-day learning needs of children. School personnel are often frustrated because of their inability to accomplish broader educative missions that will ensure that each child can reach appropriate educational goals. Schools do not know how to respond to the many social critics that label contemporary schooling a failure and often use catch phrases such as "school reform" and "restructuring" to identify the need for initiatives without truly recognizing the many complex reasons why change either doesn't take place or doesn't succeed. According to Linda Darling-Hammond, a nationally known commentator, school reform has not had a marked impact since "schools pretty much look today like they did thirty years ago," and "putting the reforms in place in 80,000 public schools represents a formidable barrier" (Rothman 1993). The scope and mission of schools need to be rethought and reconceptualized, and schools need the broad, systematic backing of both state and national policymakers. In an era when the federal budget crisis is keenly felt, more funding needs to be found to get initiatives off the ground. Until systems for promoting child welfare are conceptualized, actualized, supported, and funded, the critical needs of many of our children, the lives of every Jane and John, will continue to be subject to the vagaries of environment and chance, and too many of these children will suffer unfairly.

NOTES

1. All names and places have been changed to protect identities.

REFERENCES

Barringer, F. 1992. Rate of Marriage Continues Decline. *New York Times* (July 17): A20.

A Blueprint for Long Island Tax Cutters. 1992. *Newsday* (December 6): 36.

Bradley, A. 1993. Mission Impossible? *Education Week* (February 10): 6.

Brazelton, T.B. 1990. Why Is America Failing Its Children? *New York Times* (September 9): 40, 42.

Butterfield, F. 1992. Seeds of Murder Epidemic: Teen-Age Boys with Guns. *New York Times* (October 19): A8.

Caplan, N., M. Choy, and J. Whitmore. 1992. Indochinese Refugee Families and Academic Achievement. *Scientific American* (February).

Celis, W. 1992a. Teacher Defeats Odds to Get Preschool Pupils Ready for an Education. *New York Times* (June 17): B11.

———. 1992b. Hispanic Dropout Rate Stays High, Since Children Work in Hard Times. *New York Times* (October 14): B9.

Chira, S. 1991. Schools' New Role: Steering People to Services. *New York Times* (May 15): A25.

———. 1993. Is Small Better? Educators Now Say Yes for High School. *New York Times* (July 14): 1.

Cohen, D. 1991a. Foster Youths to Get Help with Educational Deficits. *Education Week* (June 12): 8, 9.

———. 1992a. Despite Widespread Income Growth, Study Finds Increase in Child Poverty. *Education Week* (August 5): 24.

———. 1992b. Case Managers Coaxing Families toward Change. *Education Week* (November 4): 1.

Cohen, J. 1991. What Is a Teacher's Job? An Examination of the Social and Legal Causes of Role Expansion and Its Consequences. *Harvard Journal of Law and Public Policy* 14: 427–445.

Costly School Overhaul for Massachusetts. 1993. *New York Times* (July 7): A13.

Cremin, L. 1990. *Popular Education and Its Discontents*. New York: Harper & Row.

DeParle, J. 1991. In New Social Era, Moynihan Sees "New" Social Ills. *New York Times* (December 9): A13.

De Witt, K. 1992. Poll Shows 68 Percent Support Distribution of Condoms at Schools. *New York Times* (August 28): A12.

Dimensions. 1992a. Children's Failing Health. *Education Week* (November 4): 3.

Dimensions. 1992b. Social Well-Being. *Education Week* (October 21): 3.

Duke, D.L. 1984. *Teaching: The Imperiled Profession.* Albany: State University of New York Press.

Federation on Child Abuse and Neglect, Prevention Information Resource Center. 1992. *Annual National Data on Child Abuse Reporting and Fatalities.* Albany, NY: Federation on Child Abuse and Neglect, Prevention Information Resource Center.

Fink, J. 1990. Effects of Crack and Cocaine Upon Infants: A Brief Review of the Literature. *Law Guardian Reporter*, no 2.

Friedman, T. 1993. Clinton Offers Tuition Aid Linked to National Service. *New York Times* (March 2): A18.

From Risk to Renewal. 1993. *Education Week* (April 21): part 3, 1.

Garfinkel, I., and S. McLanahan. 1986. *Single Mothers and Their Children: A New American Dilemma.* Washington, DC: Urban Institute Press.

Gross, J. 1992. Collapse of Inner-City Families Creates America's New Orphans. *New York Times* (March 29): 1.

Harp, L. 1992. Teacher Survey Cites Students' Lack of Readiness. *Education Week* (September 23): 11.

———. 1993. Dollars and Sense: Reformers Seek to Rethink School Financing to Make It a Powerful Lever of Change. *Education Week* (March 31): 9.

The Health of America's Children in 1992. 1992. Washington, DC: Children's Defense Fund.

Kantrowitz, B., and J. McCormick. 1992. A Head Start Does Not Last. *Newsweek* (January 27).

Kirby, D., C. Waszak, and J. Zieger. 1991. Six School-Based Clinics: Their Reproductive Health Service and Impact on Sexual Behavior. *Family Planning Perspectives* 23: 6–16.

Kirst, M. 1984. *Who Controls Our Schools?* New York: Freeman.

Klopf, G., A. Shedlin, and E. Zaret. 1988. *The School as Locus of Advocacy for All Children.* New York: Elementary School Center.

Kozol, J. 1991. *Savage Inequalities: Children in America's Schools.* New York: Crown.

Lee, F. 1992. Growing Up under the Eyes of a Probation Officer. *New York Times* (November 19): B1.

Lewin, T. 1992. Rise in Single Parenthood Is Reshaping U.S. *New York Times* (October 5): 1.

Lewton, M. 1993a. Anywhere, at Any Time Violence in Schools Spreads Past Cities. *Education Week* (May 5): 1

———. 1993b. Violence-Ridden District Weighing Burial Insurance for Students. *Education Week* (January 27): 8.

Lyall, S. 1993. Cuomo Proposes Tax on Incomes to Aid Schools. *New York Times* (January 7): 1.

Making Schools Work for Children in Poverty. 1993. *Education Week* (January 13): 46.

Marriott, M. 1992. Fathers Find That Child Support Means Owing More Than Money. *New York Times* (July 20): 1.

McDonald, K. 1992. Changes in Children's Issues through the Eyes of Family Court. *Law Guardian Reporter* 8: 1–3.

McFadden, R.D. 1992. Crime in Schools Is Said to Rise by 29 Percent. *New York Times* (September 4): B2.

Portner, J. 1992. Baltimore Plan to Offer Teenagers Norplant Raises Ethical, Medical, and Legal Questions. *Education Week* (December 16): 13.

Quindlen, A. 1992. Without Windows. *New York Times* (December 16): A31.

Ravitch, D. 1983. *The Troubled Crusade: American Education, 1945–1980.* New York: Basic Books.

Rawlings, S. 1993. *Household and Family Characteristics: March 1992.* Washington, DC: Bureau of the Census.

Remarks by Department of Social Services Commissioner D'Elia. 1992. *Power to Intervene: The Role of Education in Child Protection Proceedings.* Conference: Nassau County, NY, April 8, 1992.

Roeder, P. 1992a. *Assessment of Family Resource and Youth Services Centers.* First Year Reports to the Pritchard Committee. Lexington, KY: The Pritchard Committee for Academic Excellence.

————. 1992b. *Family Centers in Kentucky Schools: Politics and Policy in Education and Welfare Service Delivery*. Lexington, KY: The Pritchard Committee for Academic Excellence.

Rothman, R.D. 1992. Obstacle Course, Barriers to Change Thwart Reformers at Every Twist and Turn. *Education Week* (February 10): 9.

Saslow, L. 1993. Comparing School Spending and Taxes. *New York Times* (January 31): A8.

Shedlin, A. 1990a. Acting for Children in a "Crossfire" World. *Education Week* (November 14): 44.

————. 1990b. Shelter from the Storm. *American School Board Journal* (August).

Sommerfield, M. 1992. PEW Sets $56-Million Effort to Create Children's-Services Systems in 5 States. *Education Week* (August 5): 26.

Special Report: Children and Health Insurance. 1992. Washington, DC: Children's Defense Fund.

State Central Register, Reporting Highlights, 1974-1992. Albany, NY: Federation on Child Abuse and Neglect, Prevention Information Resource Center.

Strum, C. 1993. Helping Children Beat the Odds against Them. *New York Times* (June 18): B1.

Tabor, M.B.W. 1992. Living on the Edge. *New York Times Supplement* (August 2): 16.

Viadero, D. 1992. Report Finds Record Jump in Special-Ed. Enrollment. *Education Week* (August 5): 19.

Violent Crime by Youth Is Up 25 Percent in 10 Years. 1992. *New York Times* (August 30): A27.

U.S. Department of Education, National Center for Education Statistics. 1992. *The Condition of Education 1992*. Washington, DC: U.S. Government Printing Office.

U.S. Department of Education Office of Research and Improvement. 1992. *Digest of Education Statistics 1992*. Washington, DC: U.S. Government Printing Office.

Waszak, C., and S. Neidell. 1992. *School-Based and School-Linked Clinics, Update 1991*. Washington, DC: Center for Population Options.

Ways and Means, Committee on, U.S. House of Representatives. 1992. *Overview of Entitlement Programs: 1992 Green Book*. Washington, DC: U.S. Government Printing Office.

Ways and Means, Subcommittee on, U.S. House of Representatives. 1993. *Sources of the Increase in Poverty, Work, Effort and Income Distribution Data.* Washington, DC: U.S. Government Printing Office.

Learning and Assessment

A driving force behind recent school reform initiatives is the conviction that the academic performance of students in elementary and secondary school can be improved. One of the major strategies advocated to accomplish this goal is the establishment of national curriculum standards which require the rigorous teaching of content and as a consequence enable teachers to engage in more demanding and exciting work (Smith, O'Day, and Cohen 1990). Some claim that one outcome of a national curriculum would be the development of a national student assessment. While few researchers or policymakers have taken issue with the general concept of standards or assessments, there has been considerable controversy over recent proposals to nationalize assessment.

The chapters in this section are designed to look more closely at this issue, beginning with a discussion of what "curriculum" is and how it has developed within elementary and secondary schools in the United States. This discussion is followed by an in-depth analysis of the way the current proposal for national standards was created. The next chapter examines why national standards may be problematic from a political-social perspective. The last chapter in the section shows the positive effects of making coursework more demanding but discusses other policies, as well as standards that may alter student course-taking behaviors.

Nature of the Curriculum

In his chapter, Ivor Goodson asserts that what gets studied in school provides us with a microcosm of the history of the social struggle and, in part, class conflict. By scrutinizing the content and structure of school knowledge one can gain important insights into the social and political purposes of schooling. Looking at historical conceptions of curriculum in Western Europe and the United States, Goodson demonstrates how curriculum differentiation emerged as a powerful mechanism for determining what gets taught to whom. Goodson argues further that despite the many alternative ways of conceptualizing and organizing curriculum, the subject matter retains its supremacy. Even today we deal with the curriculum essentially as subject; the conflicts and compromises around the school curriculum and within school subjects represent a fragmentation and internalization of the struggles over schooling.

Using the example of vocational education in the United States, Goodson shows how vocational education was conceptualized to fit within democratic conventions of education. Rather than establishing separate vocational schools, the political compromise that emerged was the differentiation of internally vocational subjects within the overall high school curriculum. Goodson suggests that the development of the American high school curriculum established stable subject categories with unstable internal properties. The subject, the basic unit in the curriculum, has resisted change. This does not mean that there have been no changes—subjects have been restructured, integrated, and modernized. However, it is the configuration of these subjects and their internal fragmentation which provide a lens into broader societal issues.

A National Curriculum and Standards

One of the major reform strategies for elementary and secondary schooling in the United States has been the development of a national system of standards. The system currently being proposed by the Department of Education would require that students should know and be able to do certain things and that assessments should be made that are aligned with those standards. David Stevenson's chapter examines how this system came to be a fundamental part of the current reform movement by examining its political underpinnings, with particular attention to the shifting roles of state and federal education authorities. Stevenson offers several explanations for the fact that national standards have gained prominence in the last decade. Consistent findings from large-scale research indicate that several factors contributed to the poor performance of schools. These factors tended to focus on school organizational issues, such as giving school professionals greater autonomy in school-based decisions and allowing parents and students to choose their schools, rather than on issues of learning and instruction. Researchers examining learning and instruction continue to demonstrate that current classroom practices are ineffectual and the assessments used to measure learning are flawed. The National Council of Teachers of Mathematics, for instance, faced with poor mathematics performance by students and problematic instructional and assessment techniques, developed a series of standards that incorporated new understandings of how students learn and how instruction should be organized. The results of the National Council's efforts is widely recognized as likely to lead to improved mathematics learning and instruction. The climate of concern over performance, the research base that showed different schools offered different opportunities for learning, and the activities of The National Council seem to indicate that national standards offer a reasonable strategy for change.

Stevenson explains that the development of national standards require bipartisan support if it is to be successful. The stage for such bipartisan cooperation was in place when the nation's governors and the Bush administration agreed that the reform of elementary and secondary education was a national priority. To set the stage for reform, the governors established a set of national education goals and a panel to monitor the nation's progress toward those ends. It soon became apparent that once there are standards there have to be new forms of assessment; it is this movement toward a national system of assessment that has become the focus of debate. The Clinton administration has continued to press for the development of voluntary national content and performance standards. Such standards would be voluntary for states and local school districts and would not be tied to federal funding. In this way, the current administration hopes to forge a working relationship between local, state, and federal government.

In the next chapter, Michael Apple examines how curriculum is embedded in social, cultural, and economic conflict. What counts as knowledge, the ways in which knowledge is organized, who is empowered to teach it, what counts as an appropriate display of having learned it, and who is allowed to ask and answer these questions are part of how power structures are reproduced and altered in American society. Because the curriculum embodies these complex relationships of power, Apple believes that the educational justification for a national curriculum and national testing needs to be examined very seriously.

Apple claims that a national curriculum and testing are not inherently problematic but can become so, depending on the social forces that push for their implementation. Arguing that we have a de facto, somewhat covert, national curriculum through the textbook and test publishing markets, Apple questions whether a system of national goals and nationally standardized tests will result in holding schools more accountable for their students' achievement. Recognizing that individuals with both conservative and liberal political agendas support national standards and tests, Apple notes that the costly coordinated efforts to implement such a system are antithetical to conservative ideology. He sees the danger of educational consumerism becoming magnified through privatization and a national curriculum. Apple asserts that while proponents of a national curriculum believe it will promote social cohesion and improve schools by providing a mechanism to measure knowledge against an objective criterion, the result will be the opposite. He contends that it will ratify and exacerbate gender, race, and class differences. It will lead to more blame being put on students and poor parents and especially on the schools that they attend.

Effects of the Curriculum on Educational Aspirations and Employment Outcomes

In the last chapter in this section, Thomas Hoffer examines the effects high school course work has on college enrollment and employment. This discussion bears on national curriculum issues, because professional groups are working to establish national curricular standards. As we saw in Stevenson's chapter, the National Council of Teachers of Mathematics has strongly advocated that students spend more time studying mathematics from elementary through high school, yet supporters of higher graduation standards in the areas of mathematics and science are faced with increased costs for hiring new mathematics teachers. Moreover, students may lose interest in school if they have to work harder to graduate and are forced to take courses they do not see as interesting or useful. Using data from the study High School and Beyond and the Longitudinal Study of American Youth, Hoffer shows what learning gains can be achieved through increased course work in science and mathematics.

Hoffer begins his analyses by examining the paths that students follow after high school graduation. In the first year after high school, over half of the students are not enrolled in any type of postsecondary educational program, 15 percent are in public two-year institutions, and slightly over one-quarter are in public or private four-year institutions. Nearly all those students who concentrated in science and mathematics in high school were enrolled in a four-year college or university program during the first year after high school; many of the students who enrolled in four-year institutions, however, did not take much science or mathematics in high school. Although one-quarter of the High School and Beyond students went on to college, not all of them graduated. Interestingly, Hoffer finds that high school course work in science and mathematics is significantly related to persistence in a four-year college or university, even when controlling for social and academic background factors. Looking at the effects of science and mathematics course work on participation in scientific and technical fields, Hoffer finds that science and mathematics course work has a strong relation to students' intended major fields of study.

High school science and mathematics course work appears to have few effects on employment for noncollege students. Additional vocational courses, in contrast to more course work in science and mathematics, is significantly associated with longer periods of employment for noncollege students. Examining why students differ in their levels of participation in high school science and mathematics, Hoffer finds that socioeconomic background factors have the greatest effects. He posits three explanations for these background-related differences; different preferences, different opportunities, and different abilities. While it is difficult to disentangle these differences from one another, difference in ability appears to have the greatest effect on mediating the influence of socioeconomic factors.

Citing the significant effects of prior achievement on subsequent course taking, Hoffer maintains that if more students started high school with a solid preparation in science and mathematics, more would, or at least could, take further course work in these areas. He contends, however, that current proposals to increase course work through school choice, increased graduation requirements, and "employer linkages" will be ineffectual. School choice would affect only small numbers of students, and increasing graduation requirements in science and mathematics is problematic because those states which have raised requirements find that the greatest growth in course enrollments have occurred in the lower-level courses. The option which Hoffer thinks has some promise is altering the linkages between high schools, higher education, and employers. Given the value of the college diploma, higher requirements for science and mathematics in high school would probably lead more students to take more course work in these areas. Currently employers pay little attention to the high school records of prospective employees. If employers used high school grades as a major factor in hiring decisions, this might in fact be the best incentive for altering student behavior.

11

The Context of Cultural Inventions: Learning and Curriculum

Ivor F. Goodson

The school has always been a contested terrain where various social groups, forces, and influences battle for priority, and much research has been done on the policy implications and outcomes of this continuing struggle. One undeveloped area, however, has been the battle over the school curriculum. In scrutinizing this conflict we can examine in microcosm many of the social and political battles over priorities within schools. Far from being a technically rational product which dispassionately summarizes a society's most valued knowledge, the school curriculum can, in fact, be seen as a carrier and dispenser of social priorities.

Schooling, certainly in its particular state-system form, is a relatively recent invention. The emergence of national systems of schooling has been the subject of a number of recent studies (e.g., Ramirez and Boli 1987, pp. 2–17), which detail a number of features common to mass schooling systems as developed in the nation-states of Western Europe (Boli 1989).

The social and political construction of mass schooling derived a good deal from previous models operating in higher and religious education. For instance, from Mir's analysis of the construction of "classes" as organizational units, we learn that they were first described in the statutes of the College of Montaign in France: "It is in the 1509 programme of Montaign that one finds for the first time in Paris, a precise and clear division of students into *classes*. . . . That is, divisions graduated by stages or levels of increasing complexity according to the age and knowledge required by students" (Hamilton and Gibbons 1980, p. 7).

Mir argues that the College of Montaign in fact inaugurated the Renaissance class system in education—but the vital development to reconstruct is how organization into classes came to be associated with a curriculum prescribed and sequenced for stages or levels.

The Jesuits were one of the first religious groups to establish a tradition of highly centralized curriculum control within schools. The Ratio Studiorum was "arguably the most systematic course of study ever devised. This carefully graded curriculum organized into classes foreshadowed the 'standards' or grades that later became a basic organizing principle for all western systems of education" (Tomkins 1986, p. 13). The Jesuits carried their systems to many countries. In Canada, for instance, the Jesuit College in Quebec was founded in 1635 (a year before Harvard College was founded in Massachusetts). The curriculum, taught in French, comprised Latin, Greek, grammar, rhetoric, and philosophy, as well as history, geography, and mathematics.

Among the British, the *Oxford English Dictionary* cites the earliest occurrence of the word "curriculum" in a 1633 publication in Glasgow. Hamilton believes that Glasgow was a focal area for the development of graded educational structures because of the influence of the religious ideas of Calvin (1509–1564):

> As Calvin's followers gained political as well as theological ascendancy in late sixteenth-century Switzerland, Scotland and Holland, the idea of discipline—"the very essence of Calvinism"—began to denote the internal principles and external machinery of civil government and personal conduct. From this perspective there is a homologous relationship between curriculum and discipline: curriculum was to Calvinist educational practice as discipline was to Calvinist social practice. (Hamilton and Gibbons 1980, p. 14)

Hence, the evidence garnered from Paris and Glasgow in the sixteenth and seventeenth centuries can be summarized in this fairly stark statement of the juxtaposition of curriculum and patterns of social control and organization:

> The notion [was] that classes came into prominence with the rise of sequential programmes of study which in turn resonated with various Renaissance and Reformation sentiments of upward mobility. In Calvinist countries [such as Scotland] these views found their expression theologically in the doctrine of predestination [the belief that only a preordained minority could attain spiritual salvation] and, educationally, in the emergence of a national but bipartite education system where the "elect" [i.e. predominantly those with the ability to pay] were offered the prospect of advanced schooling, while the remainder [predominantly the rural poor] were fitted to a more conservative curriculum [like appreciation of religious knowledge and social virtue]. (Hamilton 1980, p. 286)

In this statement one can discern some of the unique characteristics of curriculum as it developed. Alongside the power to *designate* what went on in classrooms a new power emerged: the power to *differentiate*. This power was to prove of considerable significance in the construction of systems of mass schooling.

State involvement in and sponsorship, funding, and control of mass education developed first in western Europe; this model was later utilized in patterns of national development throughout the world. "Yet most comprehensive studies of education almost entirely overlook the historical origins of state systems of schooling . . . thereby ignoring the sociological significance of the successful institutionalization of this social innovation" (Ramirez and Boli 1987, p. 2). The state's involvement in schooling crucially intersects the economic history of western Europe. While some of the early models for state school systems predate the Industrial Revolution, it seems probable that the displacement of the domestic production system by the factory system was something of a watershed. The factory system, by breaking up existing family patterns, left the socialization of the young to penetration by state systems of schooling. Yet Ramirez and Boli (1987) stress the sheer

universality of mass state-sponsored education and hence argue
that the state's compelling interest in education

> was not solely a response to the needs of an industrialized
> economy, to class or status conflicts, or to unique historical
> conjunctures in particular countries, such as the character
> of the central bureaucracy in Prussia, the revolutions and
> reactions in France, the power of the peasantry in Sweden,
> or the extension of the franchise to the working classes in
> England. (Ramirez and Boli 1987, p. 2)

The common feature uniting the wide range of initiatives
by states to fund and manage mass schooling was, they argue,
the desire to construct a national polity; the power of the nation-
state, it was judged, would be unified through the participation
of the state's subjects in national projects. Central to this
socialization into national identity was the project of mass state
schooling. The sequences followed by those states promoting a
national project of mass schooling were strikingly similar.
Initially there was the promulgation of a national interest in
mass education; this was followed by legislation to make
schooling compulsory for all. To organize the system of mass
schools, state departments or ministries of education were
formed. State authority was then exercised over all schools—
both those "autonomous" schools already existing and newly
created schools specifically organized or opened by the state.

As we have seen, the link between schools and an
essentially "meritocratic" view of the social order was
discernible at the time of the Reformation. As the
industrialization of Europe and the embourgeoisement of society
progressed, this pattern was refined and promoted:

> [W]ith the embourgeoisement of much of European
> society during the nineteenth century, the significance of
> schooling as a general means of occupational success and
> social mobility became broadly institutionalized. In this
> way, there was an economic and social ideology that
> supported universal education and that complemented the
> political ideology of state-directed schooling for purposes
> of national progress. Though this "human capital" theory
> of progress, which facilitated linkages between the state
> and school, originated among the bourgeoisie, the

bourgeois classes fought against the expansion of schooling in the nineteenth century. However, the economic success of the bourgeoisie so greatly aided the organizational and extractive powers of the state that it was unable to contain the drive toward universal public education. (Ramirez and Boli 1987, pp. 13–14)

However, the achievement of universal public education, specifically where organized in "common schools," did not mark the final stage in the institutionalization of fair and equitable democratic schooling. As we have seen, the school curriculum may be employed not only to designate but also to differentiate. This power was to be substantially explored in the era of universal public education and of common schooling, as can be seen in the case of Britain, one of the first countries to industrialize. British demand for universal public education had developed considerably by the mid-nineteenth century forming an important plank in the populist agitations of the Chartists in the 1840s.

Reviewing formal school theory, Bernstein (1971, p. 47) argues for pedagogy, curriculum, and evaluation as the three message systems through which formal state education is realized in the contemporary period. The general connection between "class" pedagogies and a curriculum based on sequence and prescription had begun to emerge prior to the nineteenth century, and in the 1850s the third tier of Bernstein's trilogy of "message systems" began to develop with the inauguration of the first university examination boards. The centennial report of the University of Cambridge Local Examinations Syndicate (1958, p. 1) states that "the establishment of these examinations was the universities' response to petitions that they should help in the development of schools for the middle class."

By the mid-nineteenth century, the power of curriculum to differentiate was becoming institutionalized. The birth of secondary *examinations* and the institutionalization of curriculum *differentiation* were almost exactly contemporaneous. For instance, the Taunton Report (1868) classified secondary schooling into three grades on the basis of years to be spent in school. Taunton asserted:

> The difference in time assigned makes some difference in
> the very nature of education itself; if a boy cannot remain
> at school beyond the age of 14 it is useless to begin
> teaching him such subjects as require a longer time for
> their proper study; if he can continue until 18 or 19, it may
> be expedient to postpone some studies that would
> otherwise be commenced earlier. (Taunton Report, 1868, p.
> 587)

The Taunton Report noted that "these instructions
correspond roughly but by no means exactly to the gradations of
society." In 1868, secondary schooling until age eighteen or
nineteen was for the sons of men with considerable incomes
independent of their own exertions, or of professional men, or of
men in business whose profits put them on the same level. These
students received mainly a classical curriculum. The second
grade, composed of students who attended classes up to age
sixteen, was for the sons of the "mercantile classes." Their
curriculum was less classical and more practical in orientation.
The third level of secondary schooling, until the age of fourteen,
was for the sons of "the smaller tenant farmer, the small
tradesmen, (and) the superior artisans." Their curriculum, based
on the three R's, was similar to that of the lower classes but
demanded a higher level of performance. Meanwhile, most of
the working class attended daily elementary schools in which
they were taught rudimentary skills in the three R's. By this time
curriculum functioned as a major identifier of, and mechanism
for, social differentiation. The power to distinguish among
students established a lasting place for a differentiated curriculum in schooling.

This kind of link to earlier religious notions of education,
and indeed differentiation, can be discerned in other parts of the
world. The notion of intelligence subject to "discipline" was
consistent with early Calvinist dogma, in which the intellect was
disciplined by the moral sense and the will that it might carry
out Christian tasks; knowledge was not pursued for intrinsic
education but in order to carry out moral and religious missions.
This notion of disciplined intelligence drew on the philosophy
called "Scottish Common Sense" for its justification. Hence, from
their early Calvinist origins in Scotland, notions of discipline as

curriculum were carried to other parts of the world. Tomkins (1986, p. 35) has argued that Scottish Common Sense "dominated philosophical thought in the English-speaking world during most of the nineteenth century and strongly influenced American college curricula." He states, "its influence was even stronger and more long-lasting in Canada."

That the link between these notions of discipline and differentiation sprang from Calvinist origins can be clearly confirmed in the work of Egerton Ryerson, the most influential architect of the Canadian public education system. Ryerson fully embraced notions of disciplined intelligence but considered it crucially linked to two distinctly different types of curriculum. The first of these was an essentially preparatory level "requisite for the ordinary duties of life." This curriculum comprised the study of English language and literature, mathematics, natural science, and "the outlines of mental and moral philosophy, evidences of Christianity, geography, and history." The social curriculum was devised for those planning college followed by "professional pursuits": the clergy, law, politics, and business, in most cases. The main components of the social curriculum were classics, mathematics and the physical sciences, moral science, rhetoric and belles lettres, and theology (McKillop 1979).

In the United States, the theory of mental discipline had considerable influence during the mid-nineteenth century, but Kliebard (1987, p. 8) judges that by the 1890s it was "starting to unravel as a consequence of increased awareness of social transformation." At the same time the struggle for the American curriculum, particularly in relation to early Republican dreams of a common school, intensified (see Franklin 1986).

In 1892 the National Education Association appointed a so-called Committee of Ten to look into the issue of uniform college entrance requirements. Charles W. Eliot, president of Harvard and an advocate of mental discipline who was also a humanist with a concern for educational reform, chaired the committee. Its report laid down important ground rules for school curricula and was later seen as symptomatic of the "crass domination exercised by the college over the high school." In fact this domination served in time to facilitate curriculum differentiation:

> The academic subjects that the Committee saw as
> appropriate for the general education of all students were
> seen by many later reformers as appropriate only for that
> segment of the high school population that was destined
> to go on to college. In fact, subjects like French and algebra
> came to be called college-entrance subjects, a term
> practically unknown in the nineteenth century. Even
> subjects like English became differentiated with standard
> literary works prescribed for those destined for college,
> while popular works and "practical" English were
> provided for the majority. (Kliebard 1986, pp. 15–16)

The dreams of creating a common school were coming under
severe strain, because the Republican common core had
essentially come to be viewed as preparatory to university
education. The expanding universities were thereby seen as
sources of cultural property and of individual occupational
mobility.

In fact, by the end of the nineteenth century most Western
state systems of education had placed the universities at the apex
of accreditation. In Britain this was formalized into Type 1
schooling for students desiring university and professional
preparation and other types of schools for other types of people.
In Canada, Egerton Ryerson promoted a belief in one curriculum
for university preparation and one for "everyday life," and in the
United States the dream of the common school for all started
feeling pressure from groups who began to develop the case for
different curricula for different destinations.

But although differentiation was expanding as an aspect of
internal school curricula, the commonalities of mass schooling
were in evidence by the end of the nineteenth century. Assessing
these is significant because certain apparent "givens" such as
school subjects have by now entered the account. We have noted
that a sequencing of curriculum for "forms" or "classes" had
emerged in the late Middle Ages and was certainly a prominent
feature of much state schooling by the nineteenth century. A
system of "forms" or "classes" is not, however, a classroom
system. The distinction is a vital one to grasp. For instance,
English public schools in the nineteenth century were often
organized into forms and had a formal pattern of curriculum,
but there were *no* classrooms as such, or subjects as such—in

short a classroom system as such did not exist. Hence the public schools followed "no common pattern of education, though they agreed on the taking of Latin and Greek as the main component of the curriculum." Each public school "evolved its own unique form of organization with idiosyncratic vocabularies to describe them." The curriculum sometimes depended on the learning of common texts but such texts might not be taught in any collective manner—rather, pupils worked through them at an individual pace. Further, "where students were divided into 'forms' (a term referring originally to the benches on which they sat) this was done in rough and ready manner for the convenience of teaching and not with the idea of establishing a hierarchy of ability or a sequence of learning" (Reid 1985, p. 296).

In the state system of schooling inaugurated in Britain in the late nineteenth century, however, a classroom system was rapidly institutionalized. In a sense we can see the classroom system as a standardized invention which essentially drives out more idiosyncratic and individualized forms of schooling. The classroom system in this sense provides a system for mass schooling to be administered by local and national bureaucracies. Hamilton (1980) judges that by dawn of the twentieth century,

> the batch production rhetoric of the "classroom system"
> (for example, lessons, subjects, timetables, standardization,
> streaming) had become so pervasive that it successfully
> achieved a normative status—creating the standards
> against which all subsequent educational innovations
> came to be judged. (Hamilton 1980, p. 282)

In Britain the dominant political economy of state schooling by the beginning of the twentieth century incorporated the trilogy of pedagogy, curriculum, and evaluation. This last was effected through the establishment of university examination boards, which had pervasive and long-lasting effects on curriculum. The onset of the classroom system inaugurated a world of timetables and compartmentalized lessons, which was manifested in curriculum as the school subject. If "class and curriculum" entered educational discourse when schooling was transformed into a mass activity in Britain, "classroom system and school subject" emerged as that mass activity became a state-subsidized system. And in spite of many alternative ways of conceptualizing and organizing curriculum that have arisen since, the convention of the subject retains its supremacy. In the modern era we are essentially dealing with the *curriculum as subject*, and the university examination boards had a great deal of influence in determining the relative importance of subjects.

While inaugurated in the 1850s, the classroom system was established on its present footing in Britain with the definition of the Secondary Regulations, a listing of the main subjects in 1904, followed by the 1917 establishment of a subject-based "School Certificate." Subsequently, curriculum conflict began to resemble today's battle in its focus on the definition and evaluation of *examinable* knowledge. Hence the School Certificate subjects rapidly became the overriding concern of grammar schools and the academic subjects it examined soon established ascendancy on these schools' timetables. The Norwood Report (1943) stated that:

> a certain sameness in the curriculum of schools resulted from the double necessity of finding a place for the many subjects competing for time in the curriculum and the need to teach these subjects in such a way and to such a standard as will ensure success in the School Certificate examination. (Norwood Report, 1943)

The normative character of the system is clear, and as a result of these "necessities" the curriculum had "settled down into an uneasy equilibrium, the demands of specialists and subjects being widely adjusted and compensated" (Norwood Report 1943). The extent to which university examination boards thereby influenced the curriculum through examination subjects is evident, and the academic subject–centered curriculum was in fact strengthened in the period following the British 1944 Education Act. In 1951 the introduction of the General Certificate of Education allowed subject examinations to be taken separately at the Ordinary (O) level (whereas for the School Certificate blocks of "main" subjects had to be passed); and the introduction of an Advanced (A) level increased subject specialization and enhanced the link between academic examinations and university disciplines. The academic subjects which dominated

O- and especially A-level examinations were necessarily closely linked to university definitions; even more crucially, they were linked to patterns of resource allocation. Academic subjects claiming close connections to university disciplines were for the "able" students. From the beginning it was assumed that such students required "more staff, more highly paid staff and more money for equipment and books" (Byrne 1974, p. 29). This assumption helped establish the crucial and sustained connection between academic subjects and preferential resources and status.

This system, predominant with regard to staffing and resources of academic subjects in grammar schools, had important implications for other types of schools and styles of curriculum. Echoing Taunton, the Norwood Report asserted that schooling had created distinctive groups of pupils, each of which needed to be treated "in a way appropriate to itself." In these instances, the social and class basis of differentiation remained the same, but the rationale and mechanism behind it differed significantly. The argument, which had focused on time spent at school, now emphasized different "mentalities," each requiring a separate curriculum. First, "the pupil who is interested in learning for its own sake, who can grasp an argument or follow a piece of connected reasoning" should be "educated by the curriculum commonly associated with grammar schools [and enter] the learned professions or [take] up higher administrative or business posts" (Norwood Report 1943, p. 2). The second group, with interests in the areas of applied science or applied arts, were to attend technical schools (which never developed very far). Finally, pupils who deal "more easily with concrete things than with ideas" would follow a curriculum that made "direct appeal to interests, which it would awaken by practical touch with affairs" (Norwood Report 1943, p. 4). In other words, a practical curriculum would prepare them for a future of manual work.

We see then the emergence of a definite pattern of using curriculum to *prioritize* pupils, resulting in a "triple alliance between academic subjects, academic examinations and able pupils" (Goodson 1993, p. 33). Working through patterns of resource allocation, this alliance causes a process of pervasive "academic drift" afflicting subgroups promoting school subjects. Hence subjects as diverse as woodwork, metalwork, physical education, art, technical studies, bookkeeping, needlework, and domestic science have pursued status improvements by creating enhanced academic examinations and qualifications. Likewise, schools defined as different from grammar schools, namely, technical schools and secondary modern schools, also were drawn into the process of academic drift and ultimately ended up competing for success through academic subject–based styles of examination.

The conflict and compromises around the school curriculum and within school subjects represent at once a fragmentation and an internalization of the struggles over schooling: fragmentation in that conflicts now take place through a range of compartmentalized subjects and internalization as these conflicts now occur within school and subject boundaries. These struggles have been partially expressed through, and encapsulated in, more general traditions at work within schooling.

In Britain, then, the first half of the twentieth century saw the organization of a state system of mass schooling in which three different types of schools were built on the foundations of differentiated curriculum. In examining the system, one can readily discern the continuities since the Taunton Report of 1868. In the United States, which built on dissimilar origins and social structure, a different intersection of curriculum division and labor division emerged from the original common school plan.

In their 1893 report, the Committee of Ten specifically ruled out any preparation for life in general or future occupations as an underpinning rationale. They were concerned exclusively with academic training and academic disciplines of study. The brief of the committee was to define a school curriculum in line with university admissions policies. This close linking of school curriculum to university admissions gave vital ammunition to opponents of the hegemony of academic subjects, who often also opposed the common school. To present the common school as closely linked to universities was to implicitly leave it without vocational purpose beyond that of preparing the elite for professional careers. This central contradiction allowed a coalition of forces to lead an attack on both the hegemonic academic curriculum and also, therefore, on the common curriculum and the common school. Hence, by 1917, vocational education for occupations for which the majority were destined came to be seen "as such an urgent necessity as to require federal aid."

> The significance of the success of vocational education was not simply that a new subject had been added, nor that a major new curriculum option had been created, but that many existing subjects, particularly at the secondary level, were becoming infused with criteria drawn from vocational education. This became evident in the increasing popularity of such courses as business mathematics and business English as legitimate substitutes for traditional forms of these subjects. In very visible ways, the whole curriculum for all but the college-bound was becoming vocationalized. (Kliebard 1986, p. 129)

John Dewey immediately recognized the differentiating potential of vocational education and began a critique of the provocational arguments of Massachusetts education commissioner David Snedden, a leading advocate of vocationalizing. Dewey (1915) summarized Snedden's view as "the identification of education with acquisition of specialized skill in the management of machines at the expense of an industrial intelligence based on science and a knowledge of social problems and conditions" (Dewey 1915, p. 42). Dewey was clear on the effects of this and, echoing back to the Calvinist origins of curriculum disciplines and differentiations, argued that vocational education was likely to become "an instrument in accomplishing the feudal dogma of social predestination" (Dewey 1916, p. 148). Clearly it has come a long way from the common school of the republic—and is traveling fast in an entirely different direction of social and cultural production and reproduction.

> Hence in the "scant three decades" since the Committee of Ten recommendations: direct training for one's future occupational role had emerged as a major, if not the predominant element in the high school curriculum for

that segment of school population whose "probable destiny" did not include attendance in colleges. (Kliebard 1986, pp. 149–150)

In a sense vocational education was "the most successful innovation in the twentieth century" in the United States, since "none other approaches it in the range of support it received and the extent to which it became implemented into the curriculum of American schools."

On one level the success of vocational education can be attributed to the fact that it acted as a kind of magic mirror in which the powerful interest groups of the period could see their own reflected ways of reforming what was increasingly regarded as a curriculum out of tune with the times. (Kliebard 1986, p. 150)

Of course this judgment is in a sense circular. Powerful interest groups no doubt helped create "the climate of public opinion to which they then responded with their favored remedy, a remedy sanctioned by only *certain* powerful interest groups—the universities were plainly ambivalent about the change." Additional scholarly investigation of the views of the labor unions and immigrant and radical groups is needed. Powerful at the time, these groups had their own associations and media; some of the more influential groups pursued their objectives at this time with considerable vigor and success.

Interestingly, in America the remedy to this problem differed from solutions implemented in Britain and elsewhere. Vocational education was seldom pursued through separate vocational schools, perhaps because the rhetoric of the common school was as vital to democratic imagery as it clearly was to the historic intentions of the founders of the American republic. Hence the political compromise which emerged retained the common school structure while internalizing differentiation:

The comprehensive high school established itself as the typical, if not the quintessential, American educational institution, with curricular tracking, both formal and informal, attending to the differentiating function that social efficiency educators considered so critical. (Kliebard 1986, p. 151)

Not just social efficiency educators, it would seem, but also the powerful interest groups which Kliebard mentions but fails to identify desired this outcome. No doubt further research in this specific area would greatly elucidate the peculiar potency of social-efficiency curriculum reforms. Certainly Ross Finney had a clear vision of the social order as it was related to social efficiency goals. The pattern of curriculum differentiation was, for him, closely akin to a pattern of social differentiation based on leadership and followership which "leads us again to the notion of a graduated hierarchy of intelligence and enlightenment."

> At the apex of such a system must be the experts, who are pushing forward research in highly specialized sections of the front. Behind them are such men and women as the colleges should produce, who are familiar with the findings of the experts and are able to relate part with part. By these relatively independent leaders of thought, progressive change and constant readjustment will be provided for. Back of these are the high school graduates, who are somewhat familiar with the vocabulary of those above them, have some feeling of acquaintance with the various fields, and a respect for expert knowledge. Finally, there are the duller masses, who mouth the catchwords of those in front of them, imagine that they understand, and follow by imitation. (Apple 1990, p. 77)

Essentially the story of American schooling at this stage seems to be one of common purposes vitiated by internalized differentiation and subject fragmentation. This internalization of conflict is nowhere clearer than in the internal history of school subjects. For like the common school label the school subject label survived in both cases—the rhetoric, at least, remained the same. For the full story we have to open the covers and examine changing subject definitions. The story of the American high school curriculum therefore paradoxically combines stability of categories with unstable internal properties. Kliebard captures this complexity well in reviewing the struggle for the American curriculum in the years 1893–1958:

> The one fortress that proved virtually impregnable was the school subject. The subject as the basic unit in the

curriculum successfully resisted the more ambitious
efforts to replace it with anything like functional areas of
living or projects arising from student interest. . . . But
subject labels alone may be misleading. Some of the
reforms advanced by the various interest groups were
accomplished within the overall context of the subject
organization of the curriculum. To be sure, not all the
changes may be regarded as signs of progress, but modest
successes were achieved in restructuring, integrating and
modernizing the subjects that comprise the curriculum.
The subjects survived but in an altered form. (Kliebard
1986, p. 269)

In Britain the last twenty-five years of school reform
provide a different testimony to the fate of common school
movements. The common, comprehensive school came late to
Britain after centuries of aspiration and struggle. In 1965 the
Labour government began systematic reorganization of the
tripartite system (grammar, technical, and secondary modern
schools) into a unified system of comprehensive schools for all
(from age ten to eleven to age sixteen to eighteen). In this
historical moment the common school was established but still
struggling to achieve a common curriculum which alone could
accomplish its purposes. From the beginning of comprehensive
schools the influence of what Kliebard has called "powerful
interest groups" was apparent. For instance the House of
Commons motion which led to comprehensive reorganization
was worded this way:

This House, conscious of the need to raise educational
standards at all levels, and regretting that the realization
of this objective is impeded by the separation of children
into different types of schools, notes with approval the
efforts of local authorities to reorganize secondary
education on comprehensive lines which will preserve all
that is valuable in grammar school education for those
children who now receive it and make it available to more
children. (Inner London Education Authority, 1967, p. 1)

As we have noted, the grammar schools were seen essentially as
gateways to university and professional life. The examinations
for which they prepared students originated with universities,
whose response to the motion petitions that they should help in

developing "schools for the middle classes." The House of Commons motion pays homage to this particular tradition in British secondary schooling—that of training a privileged minority. In phrasing the motion for the birth of the common school in these terms, the House implied that this favoritism could be sustained in the common school era, although perhaps it would now be extended to more children. But plainly a grammar school curriculum designed to prepare pupils for university and professional life could *never* provide a basic curriculum for a common school, unless *all* pupils intended to pass through university to become professionals. The irony of the motion had then to be grasped as essentially a statement of obeisance to powerful interest groups in British society; and so it was to prove.

Thus, from the beginning, the British common school was built on grounds which favored the grammar school curriculum of the elite minority and opened the way for internal differentiation and subject fragmentation behind the doors of the common school. As early as 1969, just four years after the House of Commons motion, a British sociologist warned that inside the common school a "curriculum for inequality" was in action. Shipman (1971) spoke ironically of the possibility that the intended convergencies of curriculum development would come from the introduction of new courses into

> a school that is still clearly divided into two sections, one geared to a system of external examinations, the other less constrained. The former is closely tied to the universities and is within established academic traditions. The latter has a short history and is still in its formative stages. (Shipman 1971, pp. 101–2)

Shipman made it clear that the problem was not due to the intrinsic character of the two types of curriculum but in their division into two separate sections which "may be producing a new means of sustaining old divisions." Two different traditions produced then "two nations" of pupils:

> One is firmly planted in revered academic traditions, is adapted to teaching from a pool of factual knowledge and has clearly defined, if often irrelevant subject boundaries. The other is experimental, looking to America rather than

our own past for inspiration, focuses on contemporary
problems, groups subjects together and rejects formal
teaching methods. One emphasizes a schooling within a
framework of external examinations, the other attempts to
align school work to the environment of children.
(Shipman 1971, p. 104)

But in juxtaposing the academic and pedagogic traditions,
Shipman left out a third continuing element in the British
secondary school. There had always been a utilitarian tradition
concerned with preparing the child for the work environment.
This utilitarian strain, in the guise of vocational education,
helped shatter the notion of unified purpose in the American
common school. In Britain it became the focus of those
concerned with the results of the comprehensive school. It was in
fact the Labour prime minister James Callaghan who, in 1976,
masterminded a "great debate" on education. His priorities
became clear in a speech he gave at Ruskin College in Oxford in
October 1976. "No new policies were proposed but the
government had now established that educational standards,
and the relationship of education to the economy, were to be as
much of a priority as comprehensive reform in solution"
(Callaghan 1976). Hence, a decade after its inception the
comprehensive reform of schooling was forced to share its
preeminence with the need for education to serve the economy.

In the following decade any question of equal concern for
comprehensive school reform and education for the needs of the
economy vanished. With the election of Margaret Thatcher in
1979, comprehensive schools came under attack from a variety of
sources—but again, the need for more vocational education was
the main rationale offered for internal differentiation. The
government launched a Technical and Vocational Initiative
funded by the central government to restructure the internal
curriculum of the secondary schools. In addition, an Assisted
Places scheme was funded to sponsor private and direct-grant
schools, traditionally the preserve of the middle and upper
classes. In the latter schools the traditional academic curriculum
predominated, while the state schools rapidly pursued a more
vocational focus. The British experience with comprehensive
schooling reads in certain specific ways like a rapidly

compressed rerun of the history of the American common school. Powerful interest groups have sought to erode the ideal of a common school and to reestablish and enhance differentiation through the promotion of vocational initiatives. In Britain the history of secondary schooling may now be coming full circle, with moves to reintroduce grammar schools and technical schools (renamed city technology colleges) alongside "comprehensive" schools. Significantly, the new National Curriculum which has been legislated for the public sector schools has not been extended to the private "public schools." Again, as is happening in different ways in the United States, this is taking place alongside a reconstitution of the social configuration of schooling.

The nature of school subjects provides a microcosm wherein the history of the social forces which underpin patterns of curriculum and schooling might be scrutinized and analyzed. As we have seen, such scrutiny often poses major questions about the social and political purposes of schooling. Behind the rhetoric of "mass education" and "common schooling" a variety of more specific and differentiated social and political purposes operate this complexity and the associated policy implications cannot be captured without opening the black box that is school curriculum.

REFERENCES

Apple, M.W. 1990. *Ideology and Curriculum,* 2d. ed. NY: Routledge.

Bernstein, B. 1971. On the Classification and Framing of Educational Knowledge. In *Knowledge and Control,* ed. by M.F.D. Young. London: Macmillan.

Boli, J. 1989. *New Citizens for a New Society—The Institutional Origins of Mass Schooling in Sweden.* Oxford: Pergamon Press.

Byrne, E.M. 1974. *Planning and Educational Inequality: A Study of the Rationale of Resource-Allocation.* Slough: National Foundation for Education Research. NJ: Humanities Press.

Callaghan, J. 1976. Speech, Ruskin College, Oxford, 18 October 1976.

Dewey, J. 1915. Education vs. Trade Training—Dr. Dewey's Reply. *The New Republic* 3:42–43.

————. 1916. *Democracy and Education 1946: An Introduction to the Philosophy of Education*. New York: Macmillan.

Franklin, B. 1986. *Building the American Community*. New York and Philadelphia: Falmer.

Goodson, I.F. 1993. *School Subjects and Curriculum Change*. New York and Philadelphia: Falmer.

Hamilton, D. 1980. Adam Smith and the Moral Economy of the Classroom System. *Journal of Curriculum Studies* 12(4).

Hamilton, D., and M. Gibbons. 1980. Notes on "The Origins of the Educational Terms Class and Curriculum." Paper presented at American Educational Research Association, Boston, April.

Inner London Education Authority. 1975. *Organization of Secondary Education: Appendix to Report #1 of the Development Subcommittee Presented to the Education Committee on 6 May 1975*. London. The Authority.

Kliebard, H.M. 1986. *The Struggle for the American Curriculum 1893–1958*. Boston: Routledge and Kegan Paul.

McKillop, A.B. 1979. *A Disciplined Intelligence*. Montreal: McGill-Queens University Press.

Norwood Report. 1943. *Board of Education: Curriculum and Examinations in Secondary Schools*. Report of the Committee, Chairman Sir Cyril Norwood, of the Secondary School Examination Council. London: HMSO.

Ramirez, F.O., and J. Boli. 1987. The Political Construction of Mass Schooling: European Origins and Worldwide Institutionalism. *Sociology of Education* 60: 2–17.

Reid, W.A. 1985. Curriculum Change and the Evolution of Educational Constituencies: The English Sixth Form in the Nineteenth Century. In *Social Histories of the Secondary Curriculum: Subjects for Study*, ed. I.F. Goodson. Philadelphia: Falmer.

Shipman, M. 1971. Curriculum for Inequality. In *The Curriculum: Context, Design and Development*, ed. R. Hooper. Edinburgh: Oliver and Boyd.

Taunton Report. 1868. *Schools Inquiry Commission*.

Tomkins, G.O. 1986. *A Common Countenance: Stability and Change in the Canadian Curriculum*. Scarborough, ON: Prentice Hall.

University of Cambridge Local Examinations Syndicate. 1958.
Centennial Report, Cambridge.

12

The Role of Standards and Assessments in National Reform

David Lee Stevenson

A dominant national reform strategy for elementary and secondary schooling in the United States is the development of academic standards of what students should know and be able to do, and high quality assessments aligned with those standards. In this chapter, I examine how standards and assessments came to be key elements in the current model of national reform, the bipartisan adoption of a standards model of reform, and tensions between federal and state roles in the current reform efforts.

From Schools to Systems

For decades, the reform of American education primarily focused on schools as the unit of change. The seemingly endless literature on school effectiveness has been built, at least in part, on the notion that schools are units of reform and that there is a model for how effective schools work. This research effort dramatized differences among schools and searched for evidence that some schools mattered more than others in raising academic achievement. When equity was a concern, it was expressed as creating racially balanced schools, equalizing funding across schools, or narrowing the gap in academic performance among schools (Purkey and Smith 1983).

There certainly were schools that were more effective than others, but the problem for policymakers was in trying to replicate such effective schools. For example, one key component of school-based reform was the "charismatic principal." The charismatic principal proved to be difficult to reproduce despite repeated efforts to create them among principals or principals to be. And even in those schools that were deemed to be effective, the effectiveness was many times short-lived. Charismatic principals would move on to other positions, or with the routinization of school reform, the effectiveness would begin to fade.

This long American tradition of reforming education one school at a time continues today with the Coalition of Essential Schools, Accelerated Learning Schools, and the projects to reinvent schools of the New American Schools Development Corporation. The recent gifts of the Annenberg Foundation of fifty million dollars to the Coalition of Essential Schools and fifty million dollars to the New American Schools Development Corporation assures that school-by-school reform will continue for some time.

Most of the effective schools research was conducted on samples of public schools until James Coleman and his colleagues (Coleman, Hoffer, and Kilgore 1982; Coleman and Hoffer 1987) began comparisons of private and public schools using the U.S. Department of Education's High School and Beyond data set, a longitudinal study of a national sample of tenth grade students. The differences between the private and public sectors became sources for the explanations of school differences. The sources of such differences might be the social capital created by parents being able to choose their children's schools or the freedom of private schools from some forms of regulations. Regardless of the explanation for the school effects or the disputes about the significance of such differences (*Sociology of Education* 1982, 1983 and 1985), the debate had shifted from differences among schools to differences between sectors, from why public schools were different from each other to why public schools were different from private schools.

One outgrowth of this debate was a rationale for greater parental and student choice of schools. And providing choice, whether among the public schools or by allowing public school students to choose private schools, became a remedy and in some cases the remedy for reforming America's schools (Chubb and Moe 1990). As the temperature of the rhetoric began to lower, it was evident that most policymakers had embraced the concept of school choice within the public sector and the remaining fault line among reformers was the issue of whether the expansion of choice should include the use of public funds to support students' enrollment in private schools.

Most of the school effectiveness studies, whether on differences among public schools or between private and public schools, had been conducted by sociologists, anthropologists, or political scientists. The focus had been on explanations at the organizational level, and the measures of effectiveness had typically been standardized multiple choice tests that in most cases were not designed to be aligned with the content of classroom instruction. Neither the type of assessments nor the lack of alignment was viewed as a serious problem since standardized tests were widely used for purposes of school accountability, and they were seldom aligned with the content of instruction. And how could one study a sample of schools with a single achievement test aligned to instruction when instruction differs among schools and across classrooms?

Through the private-public school comparisons, the effective school literature opened the way for policy environment explanations of the poor performance of schools. However, such explanations tended to stop at the level of providing schools with regulatory relief, allowing school professionals greater autonomy in school-based decisions, and permitting parents and students to choose their schools. The technical core of schooling—learning and instruction—remained beyond the bounds of the organizational critique of schools. It was left to learning theorists to provide a systematic critique of learning and instruction.

Learning Theories and Reform

While the effective school literature was growing, cognitive science had been developing very different understandings of how students learn and how instruction needed to be redesigned. For many years these ideas were marginal to reform efforts, which were guided by policy analysts. The waves of reform to raise graduation requirements, implement minimum competency testing, and develop state accountability systems were guided less by new conceptions of student learning, and more by state departments and state legislatures looking for quick policy fixes to perceived declines in the productivity of schools.

The learning theory critique of current school practice was powerful because it in essence stated that the current methods of instruction and learning were seriously flawed (Association for Supervision and Curriculum Development 1989). Current practice went against research evidence about how students learn. Instruction needed to be radically overhauled from drill and practice instruction that focused on memorization and the recitation of facts, often outside of a meaningful context, to instruction for understanding that would help the students think critically and develop the capacity to solve complex problems.

While there had been similar critiques of instruction and learning before, theoretical developments and empirical evidence now began to resonate with policy concerns about the productivity of schooling. The results from the National Assessment of Educational Progress continued to show little progress in student performance (1992) and the international assessments in mathematics and science consistently showed that U.S. students were outperformed by students in other countries, particularly economic competitors such as Japan (Keeves 1992). The results of these assessments entered the highest level of political discourse about the state of American education, the need for educational reform, and America's economic competitiveness.

The learning critique of instructional practice was exemplified, to a significant degree, in the curriculum evaluation standards of the National Council for Teachers of Mathematics

(NCTM) (1989). Here was a prescription of how mathematics education needed to be radically overhauled in order to incorporate new understandings of how students learn and instruction should be organized. It highlighted the need for increased emphasis on students being able to communicate about mathematics and to generate solutions to complex problems. The emphasis on students showing their work and providing solutions to problems with multiple answers was beginning to change the dialogue about what kinds of student assessments were useful and appropriate. The development of the NCTM standards was a significant achievement, because it did not advocate change at the margins but rather called for a dramatic change in mathematics education based on new understandings of how students learn, good pedagogical practice, and the nature of the discipline.

The strength of the NCTM standards was also political. Fluency in mathematics has been seen as a critical skill for workers in a high-technology economy and as necessary to make the workforce internationally competitive. Results of the international assessments provided continuing evidence that U.S. students were not as competent in mathematics as were the students of America's economic competitors. Finally, a broad consensus had been created in the mathematics community from elementary school teachers through university mathematicians. The combination of a perceived national economic need, evidence of poor performance, and the strong unified vocal support of the mathematics community pushed the NCTM to the front of the reform stage. Before long, the NCTM standards had become the prototype for national content standards, definitions of what students should know and be able to do.

National Education Goals

While the debate about why schools were not effective had begun to include a discussion of the policy environment and to redefine how instruction and learning should take place within schools, there was still little national bipartisan political agreement on an acceptable paradigm for how to improve education. To develop such a framework required a bipartisan setting where there was a need for building consensus across party lines and for producing policy documents that would articulate this consensus. The National Governors' Association (NGA) became central to this function.

Governors have a significant stake in education since in many states almost half of their state budgets go to education. However, public comparisons of the performance of states in the area of education were uncommon until the U.S. Department of Education developed the "wall chart" in 1984. The wall chart was a tabular display of characteristics of a state's educational performance compared with other states. The characteristics included measures of the performance of students in different states on the SAT and ACT. The response of critics to the "wall chart" was to deride its inaccuracies and the lack of comparability (Ginsberg, Noell, and Plisko 1988). A response of the governors was to develop an NGA publication series, *Time for Results* (1986), that documented what states were doing to improve education and the academic performance of students in the state. *Time for Results* was followed by publications on restructuring American education that outlined the elements of elementary and secondary education that needed to be changed (National Governors' Association 1988, 1989).

At the same time, NGA was working with the White House to establish a set of national education goals. President Bush invited the nation's governors to an Education Summit at Charlottesville, Virginia, in the fall of 1989. This was the beginning of the process of establishing a set of national education goals that were formally agreed to in January 1990 (The White House 1990). The six national education goals were stated in terms of outcomes, and the preamble of the goals document stressed that there would be many ways that states and local districts could reach the goals. The political focus and rhetoric had shifted toward accountability for outcomes in exchange for flexibility and relief from regulations.

The agreement that created the goals also called for the creation of a National Education Goals Panel to monitor the progress of the nation and the states toward the goals. The Goals Panel, composed of six governors—three from each political party and four members of the administration, provided another forum for a bipartisan discussion of education reform on a national level. With a narrow charge of reporting on the nation's and states' progress toward the national education goals, the Goals Panel provided a forum for political discussion of educational reform without committing either political party or any political organizations to policy initiatives.

While the initial discussions of the Goals Panel were about what were valid indicators of the nation's progress toward the national goals, the dominant issue in the Goals Panel's discussion became how to measure and promote reaching the student achievement goal. To provide advice about the selection and development of indicators the Goals Panel created resource groups of national experts. The papers from the resource group for the student achievement goal described the need for national standards and a system of assessments (National Education Goals Panel 1991a; Smith and O'Day 1991). Issues of primary concern were how to develop a set of national standards and how to develop assessments aligned to them. This was the main message that the Goals Panel took to a series of regional hearings throughout the country during the spring and summer of 1991.

National Tests

Much of the public response to the conversation of the Goals Panel and the education goals focused on whether there should and would be national academic standards and a national test. As the Goals Panel began its discussions about academic standards, there was a consensus that national content standards, definitions of what students should know and be able to do, would have to be voluntary. On the issue of assessment, several groups suggested the value of having national tests. The President's Education Policy Advisory Committee, chaired by Paul O'Neil of Alcoa, suggested that a national test might be a key element of educational reform. At about the same time, former Governor Kean of New Jersey had created an advocacy group called Educate America, which endorsed the idea of a national test. National testing received a further push from the

Bush Administration's America 2000 proposal, which advocated the development of national standards and American Achievement Tests, although the specifics of what these tests would be and how they would work were not described in the initial policy proposal (U.S. Department of Education 1991).

Since the proposed American Achievement Tests in America 2000 were to be in grades 4, 8, and 12, and these were the same grades as were tested by the National Assessment of Educational Progress (NAEP), many observers assumed that the federal government might develop or encourage the development of a NAEP-like test for individual students. There was some discussion within the U.S. Department of Education of using the NAEP assessment frameworks and making sample items available to commercial test publishers and others to develop assessments.

Within the political policy forums, the main alternative to the idea of a single national test was a national system of assessments. This idea was promoted by Governor Romer, chairman of the National Education Goals Panel. He repeatedly talked about how a national test would not be a good idea but rather suggested the development of a national system of assessments. States or clusters of states would develop assessments that were aligned with the national standards. This would allow for states to have different examinations and yet provide for comparability of scores across states.

Comparability of test results had been a topic of interest, at least since the Alexander-James report on whether the National Assessment of Educational Progress (NAEP) should be conducted at the state level (National Academy of Education 1987). For many years, some had advocated that NAEP should be carried out at the state level as well as the national level in order to provide states with information about how their students were performing against a national sample of students as well as against students in other states.

It was argued that without comparability, there would be no public accountability for the outcomes of state education systems. States would not know how they were performing and there would not be an appropriate and adequate measure of progress toward the national goal on student achievement. The possibility of creating new assessments in which all states and districts would be "above average," similar to the results from the extensive use of standardized tests, led to increased pressure for comparability. While comparability was desired for institutional accountability, it also was desired so that results of the assessments could have meaning and consequences for students. Albert Shanker, president of the American Federation of Teachers, and others argued that the education system would change dramatically only if its incentives changed. Incentives were needed for students to take schooling seriously and to invest effort in their performance. Students needed to know that their performance on these public assessments would matter in the admission to postsecondary schooling or for their opportunities in the labor market. The assessment results would provide valuable information to students and parents about student performance against national academic standards.

The policy debate about assessments, therefore, hinged on two points, both of which were seen as "technical" but which had significant implications for the arguments for and against a national test. The first issue was whether it is possible to equate different assessments into a common scoring framework to yield comparable scores. Equating was seen as necessary given the push for institutional accountability for results, which was an underlying premise of the national education goals, and given the need for accountability against a common standard. Second, the need for valid and reliable individual scores that would be valued by postsecondary education institutions as well as employers required a greater degree of precision than would be required for purposes of institutional accountability. These possible uses of test scores raised questions about consequences of introducing assessments for individuals and institutions and the conditions that would have to be met before assessments could be appropriately used. This issue was referred to as "consequential validity." The answers to these two "technical" points were critical for the substantive arguments of those who argued for a national system of assessments rather than a single national test (National Education Goals Panel 1991b).

Both those who favored a national test and those who favored a national system of assessments were dissatisfied with the current use of tests and assessments. Both groups wanted assessments to perform functions for which the current assessments were not designed. They wanted assessments that were tied to instruction and the curriculum, not assessments that were disconnected. They wanted assessments that would inform and improve instruction. They wanted assessments that would examine those "higher-order skills" that were seen as a neglected but necessary part of learning and that were required to create a competitive workforce. To this extent they were willing to support the development of performance-based assessments.

National Council on Education Standards and Testing

Most of the discussion of national standards and assessments had occurred without congressional participation or legislative actions. The summit at Charlottesville was attended by the President and the Governors, the National Education Goals Panel was created by executive order of the President, and the national standard-setting groups were funded by federal executive agencies. The exception was the legislation that created the National Council on Education Standards and Testing. The Council was established to determine the feasibility and desirability of establishing voluntary national standards and a system of assessments. The Council was cochaired by Governor Roy Romer of Colorado and Governor Carroll Campbell of South Carolina, both of whom were members of the National Education Goals Panel.

Established in June of 1991, the Council issued its report to Congress, the Secretary of Education, and the National Education Goals Panel on January 24, 1992. The Council's report recommended that there be voluntary national standards and a national system of assessments tied to those standards. The Council continued to stress the need for comparability of results. "The Council finds it essential that different assessments produce comparable results in attainment of the standards" (National Council on Education Standards and Testing 1992, p. 30). It also stressed the need for assessments to address important technical issues of reliability, validity, and fairness, particularly when the results of the assessments were used for high-stakes purposes for students or educators.

During the deliberations of the Council, the U.S. Department of Education, in conjunction with other federal agencies, funded standard-setting projects in several subjects (history, geography, science), as well as providing states with funding to develop curriculum frameworks in mathematics, science, and other subjects.

Clinton Administration

In early 1993, the Clinton Administration introduced Goals 2000: Educate America Act. The legislation would set into law the national education goals, establish a national education goals panel, and a national education standards and assessment council. The Goals 2000 bill stressed two important features in the use of standards and assessments. First, it recommends the development of voluntary national content and performance standards and a process by which such standards could be certified as national standards. It also explicitly acknowledges that such standards would be voluntary for states and local school districts and that federal money would not be tied to whether states had adopted these national standards. Second, the bill provides money to states to develop state reform plans for education. States that participate in Title III of Goals 2000 will develop a state reform plan which will include plans for the development of state standards for what students should know and be able to do in the core academic subjects as well as assessments aligned to those standards.

National standards were to be models, or benchmarks, that states could use in developing their own state standards. In the proposal of the Clinton administration, there was no mandated connection between national and state standards. The legislation reaffirmed the primary role of the state in the development of academic standards and assessments. It also minimized the role of any federal body in certifying standards by making it voluntary for states to submit their standards or assessments for certification.

The primacy of state standards and state assessments also is evident in the Clinton administration's bill reauthorizing the Elementary Secondary Education Act. The proposed legislation for Title I (previously Chapter 1) links the program to state content and performance standards. Districts and schools are held accountable for their performance as measured by the state assessments which are aligned to the state content and performance standards.

Some federal programs, such as Title I, have permitted schools to have low expectations for the academic achievement of students and to offer limited opportunities for learning by teaching a "watered-down" curriculum. State standards provide an anchor for federal programs and the expenditure of federal funds. They provide a way to integrate federal dollars and programs into state and local reform efforts and create an avenue to assure that schools that receive federal dollars will be held to the same standards for Title I students as for other students.

These two legislative proposals clearly signal the fundamental role of the state in a model of national reform. There is no mention of national tests or even consortia of states developing assessments. The federal role has been redefined and limited to providing assistance to states in the development of state reform plans, including content and performance standards and aligned assessments, and to providing assistance to local communities for the implementation of local reforms.

These two pieces of legislation also provide a different perspective on the place of reforming individual schools. The legislation creates a framework of academic standards and legislative assessments in which school reform can take place, but the two proposals continue a federal effort to drive funds to local schools to encourage school-based reform efforts. They also encourage schools and local education agencies to incorporate the funds from the various categorical programs into schoolwide reform activities. For example, Title I of the Clinton administration's bill proposes changing from 75 to 50 the percentage of poor children in a school that is required before a school can provide a schoolwide program rather than a targeted assistance program. The funds for professional development also are directed for school use and require that teachers and school

building administrators play key roles in defining what types of
professional development are needed and should be acquired.

Conclusion

Despite the concerns of many educators that America was
headed toward a national curriculum and national testing, the
current resolution of the movement toward challenging
academic standards and assessments reinforces the state and
local role in educational reform and limits the federal role to
providing funding and encouraging states to develop standards
and aligned assessments. The debate, in policy circles, quickly
moved to voluntary national standards so that there would be no
fear of a prescribed set of national standards that might be the
basis of a national curriculum. If a national curriculum develops,
it will be through the independent choices of the states to use the
same or similar academic standards and curriculum. Without
mandatory national standards for all students, the argument of
national testing, even the creation of a national system of
assessments rather than a single national test, is difficult to
maintain. The technical issues, equating and consequential
validity, that had been at the core of the debate about national
standards and national testing could not frame a dialogue that
would maintain political support for a system of national
assessments. Comparability could not be maintained if states
were free to develop their own standards and aligned
assessments. If states develop their own assessments, the federal
government could not prescribe to states how they should use
the results of the assessments.[1]

In the Goals 2000 law, there was one remnant of the debate
about consequential validity. If a state decided to have its assessments certified by the National Council on Education Standards
and Improvement, it could not use the assessment for high-stake
purposes (i.e., selection, retention, graduation) for a period of
five years after the date of enactment of Goals 2000 Act.

After five years of public policy discussion, the concerns
about a national curriculum and national testing have faded.
There were very few advocates for a federally prescribed

national curriculum. And while the push for a national test and a
system of national assessments was strong, neither of these could
rhetorically overcome the political problems inherent in the
"technical issues." The Goals 2000 law resolved these issues by
reaffirming the state role in the development of standards and
assessments, thereby defining comparability and consequential
validity as local issues.

NOTES

This paper is intended to promote the exchange of ideas among
researchers and policymakers. The views expressed here are those of the
author, and no official support by the U.S. Department of Education is
intended or should be inferred.

REFERENCES

Association for Supervision and Curriculum Development. 1989. *Toward
the Thinking Curriculum: Current Cognitive Research*, ed. Resnick
and Cropfer. Alexandria, VA: Author.

Chubb, J.E., and T.M. Moe. 1990. *Politics, Markets, and America's Schools.*
Washington, DC: Brookings Institution.

Coleman, J.S., and T. Hoffer. 1987. *Public and Private High Schools: The
Impact of Communities.* New York: Basic Books.

Coleman, J.S., T. Hoffer, and S.B. Kilgore. 1982. *High School Achievement:
Public, Catholic, and Private Schools Compared.* New York: Basic
Books.

Ginsberg, A.L., J. Noell, and V.W. Plisko. 1988. Lessons from the Wall
Chart. *Education Evaluation and Policy Analysis* 10: 1–12.

Keeves, J.P., ed. 1992. *The IEA Study of Mathematics III: Analysis of
Mathematics Curricula.* Oxford, New York.

National Academy of Education. 1987. *The Nation's Report Card: Improving the Assessment of Student Achievement*. Washington, DC: Author.

National Assessment of Educational Progress. 1992. *NCEA Research and Development Report: International Mathematics and Science Assessments: What Have We Learned?* Washington, DC: U.S. Department of Education.

National Council on Education Standards and Testing. 1992. *Raising Standards for American Education: A Report to Congress, the Secretary of Education, the National Education Goals Panel, and the American People*. Washington, DC: Author.

National Council of Teachers of Mathematics. Commission on Standards for School Mathematics. 1989. *Curriculum and Evaluation Standards for School Mathematics*. Reston, VA: National Council of Teachers of Mathematics.

National Education Goals Panel. 1991a. *Measuring Progress toward the National Education Goals: The Potential Indicators and Measurement Strategies*. Washington, DC: Author.

————. 1991b. *Potential Strategies for Long Term Indicator Development*. Washington, DC: Author.

National Governors' Association. 1986. *Time for Results: The Governors' Report on Education*. Washington, DC: Author.

————. 1988. *Restructuring the Education System*. Washington, DC: Author.

————. 1989. *Restructuring in Progress*. Washington, DC: Author.

Purkey, S., and M.S. Smith. 1983. Effective Schools: A Review. *Elementary School Journal* 83: 427–452.

Smith, M.S., and J. O'Day. 1991. Systemic School Reform. In *The Politics of Curriculum and Testing: The 1990 Yearbook of the Politics of Education Association*, ed. S. Fuhrman and B. Malen. Philadelphia, PA: Falmer Press.

Sociology of Education. 1982. 55 (April/July). Special two-volume series on the debate surrounding public and private schools (1981).

————. 1983. 56 (October). Series of papers on the public and private school debate, see 170–234.

————. 1985. 58 (April). Third special issue devoted to public and private school debate.

U.S. Department of Education. 1991. *America 2000: An Education Strategy Sourcebook*: Author.

The White House. 1990. *National Education Goals,* January 31, 1990.
    Washington, DC: Author.

13

The Politics of a National Curriculum

Michael W. Apple

Introduction

Education is deeply implicated in the politics of culture. Its curriculum is never simply a neutral assemblage of knowledge, somehow appearing in the texts and classrooms of a nation. It is always part of a *selective tradition*, and is someone's selection, some group's vision of legitimate knowledge. It is produced out of the cultural, political, and economic conflicts, tensions, and compromises that organize and disorganize a society. As I argue in *Ideology and Curriculum* (Apple 1990) and *Official Knowledge* (Apple 1993), the decision to define some groups' knowledge as the most legitimate, as official, while other groups' knowledge hardly sees the light of day, says something extremely important about who has power in a society.

Consider social studies texts that continue to speak of the "Dark Ages" rather than using the historically more accurate and much less racist phrase "the age of African and Asian Ascendancy." Or consider books that treat Rosa Parks as merely a naive African-American woman who was simply too tired to go to the back of the bus rather than discussing her training in organized civil disobedience at the Highlander Folk School. The realization that teaching, especially at the elementary school level, has in large part been defined as women's work—with its accompanying struggles over autonomy, pay, respect, and deskilling—also documents the connections between curriculum and teaching and the history of gender politics (Apple 1988b).

Thus, whether we like it or not, differential power intrudes into the very heart of curriculum, teaching, and evaluation. What *counts* as knowledge, the ways in which knowledge is organized, who is empowered to teach it, what counts as an appropriate display of having learned it, and—just as critically—who is allowed to ask and answer all of these questions are part and parcel of how dominance and subordination are reproduced and altered in this society (Bernstein 1977; Apple 1988a). There is, then, always a *politics* of official knowledge, a politics that embodies conflict over what some regard as simply neutral descriptions of the world and what others regard as elite conceptions that empower some groups while disempowering others.

Speaking in general about how elite culture, habits, and tastes function, Pierre Bourdieu (1984, p. 7) puts it this way:

> The denial of lower, coarse, vulgar, venal, servile—in a word, natural—enjoyment, which constitutes the sacred sphere of culture, implies an affirmation of the superiority of those who can be satisfied with the sublimated, refined, disinterested, gratuitous, distinguished pleasures forever closed to the profane. That is why art and cultural consumption are predisposed, consciously and deliberatively or not, to fulfill a social function of legitimating social difference.

As he goes on to say, these cultural forms, "through the economic and social conditions which they presuppose . . . are bound up with the systems of dispositions (habitus) characteristic of different classes and class fractions" (Bourdieu 1984, pp. 5–6). Thus, cultural form and content function as markers of class (Bourdieu 1984, p. 2). The granting of sole legitimacy to such a system of culture through its incorporation within the official centralized curriculum, then, creates a situation in which the markers of taste become the markers of people. The school becomes a class school.

The contemporary tradition of scholarship and activism has been based on exactly these insights: the complex relationships between economic capital and cultural capital; the role of the school in reproducing and challenging the multitude of unequal relations of power (which go well beyond class, of course), and the roles that content and organization of the curriculum, pedagogy, and evaluation all play.

It is exactly now that these kinds of issues must be considered most seriously. This is a period—which we can call the *conservative restoration*—when conflict over the politics of official knowledge is severe. At stake is the very idea of public education and a curriculum that responds to the cultures and histories of large and growing segments of the American population. Even with a "moderate" Democratic administration now in Washington, many of this administration's own commitments embody the tendencies addressed below.

I intend to instantiate these arguments through an analysis of the proposals for a national curriculum and national testing. But in order to understand these issues, we must think *relationally*, and connect these proposals to the larger program of the conservative restoration. I intend to argue that behind the educational justification for a national curriculum and national testing is a dangerous ideological attack, the effects of which will be truly damaging to those who already have the most to lose. I shall first present a few interpretive cautions. Then I shall analyze the general project of the rightist agenda. Third, I shall show the connections between the national curriculum and national testing and the increasing focus on privatization and "choice" plans. And, finally, I want to discuss the pattern of differential benefits that will likely result.

The Question of a National Curriculum

Where should those of us who count ourselves a part of the long progressive tradition in education stand in relationship to the call for a national curriculum?

At the outset, I wish to make clear that I am not opposed in principle to a national curriculum. Nor am I opposed in principle to the idea or practice of testing. Rather, I wish to provide a more conjunctural set of arguments based on my claim that at this time—given the balance of social forces—there are very real dangers which are important to recognize. I shall confine myself largely to the negative case here, and my task is to raise serious questions about the implications of these developments in a time of conservative triumphalism.

We are not the only nation where a largely rightist coalition has put such proposals on the educational agenda. In England, a national curriculum, first introduced by the Thatcher government, is now mostly in place. It consists of "core and foundation subjects" such as mathematics, science, technology, history, art, music, physical education, and a modern foreign language. Working groups to determine the standard goals, "attainment targets," and content in each subject have already brought forth their results. This curriculum is accompanied by a national system of achievement testing—one that is both expensive and time-consuming—for all students in state-run schools at the ages of seven, eleven, fourteen, and sixteen (Whitty 1992, p. 24).

The assumption in many quarters in the United States is that we must follow nations such as Britain and especially Japan or we shall be left behind. Yet it is crucial that we understand that we *already* have a national curriculum, which is determined by the complicated nexus of state textbook adoption policies and the market in textbook publishing (Apple 1988b; Apple and Christian-Smith 1991). Thus, we have to ask whether a national curriculum—one that will undoubtedly be linked to a system of national goals and nationally standardized instruments of evaluation—is *better* than an equally widespread but somewhat more covert national curriculum established by textbook adoption states such as California and Texas, which control 20 to 30 percent of the market in textbooks (Apple 1993). Whether or not such a covert national curriculum already exists, however, there is a growing feeling that standardized national curricular goals and guidelines are essential to "raise standards" and to hold schools accountable for their students' achievement.

We can concede that many people representing an array of educational and political positions are involved in the call for higher standards, more rigorous curricula at a national level, and a system of national testing. Yet we must ask the question: which group is in the leadership of these "reform" efforts? This leads to another, broader question: who will benefit or lose as a result of all this? I contend that, unfortunately, rightist groups are setting the political agenda in education and that, in general, the same pattern of benefits that has characterized nearly all areas of social policy—in which the top 20 percent of the population reap 80 percent of the benefits (Apple 1989; Danziger and Weinberg 1986; Burtless 1990)—will be reproduced here.

We need to be very cautious of the genetic fallacy, the assumption that *because* a policy or a practice originates within a distasteful position it is fundamentally determined, in all its aspects, by its origination within that tradition. Take Edward Thorndike, one of the founders of educational psychology in the United States, for instance. The fact that his social beliefs were often repugnant—as evidenced by his participation in the popular eugenics movement and his notions of racial, gender, and class hierarchies—does not necessarily destroy every aspect of his research on learning. While I am not at all a supporter of this paradigm of research (its epistemological and social implications continue to demand major criticism),[1] this requires a different kind of argument than one based on origin. (Indeed, one can find some progressive educators turning to Thorndike for support for some of their claims about what needed to be transformed in our curriculum and pedagogy.)

It is not only those who are identified with the rightist project who argue for a national curriculum. Others who have historically been identified with a more liberal agenda have attempted to make a case for it (Smith, O'Day, and Cohen 1990).

Smith, O'Day, and Cohen suggest a positive, if cautionary, vision for a national curriculum. A national curriculum would involve the invention of new examinations, a technically, conceptually, and politically difficult task. It would require the teaching of more rigorous content and thus would require teachers to engage in more demanding and exciting work. Teachers and administrators, therefore, would have to "deepen their knowledge of academic subjects and change their conceptions of knowledge itself." Teaching and learning would have to be seen as "more active and inventive." Teachers, administrators, and students would need "to become more thoughtful, collaborative, and participatory" (Smith, O'Day, and Cohen 1990, p. 46).

In Smith, O'Day, and Cohen's (1990) words:

> Conversion to a national curriculum could only succeed if
> the work of conversion were conceived and undertaken as
> a grand, cooperative learning venture. Such an enterprise
> would fail miserably if it were conceived and organized
> chiefly as a technical process of developing new exams
> and materials and then "disseminating" or implementing
> them. (p. 46)

And they go on to say:

> A worthwhile, effective national curriculum would also
> require the creation of much new social and intellectual
> connective tissue. For instance, the content and pedagogy
> of teacher education would have to be closely related to
> the content of and pedagogy of the schools' curriculum.
> The content and pedagogy of examinations would have to
> be tied to those of the curriculum and teacher education.
> Such connections do not now exist. (p. 46)

The authors conclude that such a revitalized system, one in
which such coordination would be built, "will not be easy, quick,
or cheap," especially if it is to preserve variety and initiative. "If
Americans continue to want educational reform on the cheap, a
national curriculum would be a mistake" (Smith, O'Day, and
Cohen 1990, p. 46). I could not agree more with this last point.

Yet they do not sufficiently recognize that much of what
they fear is already taking place in the very linkage they call for.
Even more importantly, what they do not pay sufficient attention
to—the connections between a national curriculum and national
testing and the larger rightist agenda—constitutes an even
greater danger. It is this I wish to focus on.

Between Neoconservatism and Neoliberalism

Conservatism by its very name announces one interpretation of
its agenda: it conserves. Other interpretations are possible, of
course. One could say, somewhat more wryly, that conservatism
believes that nothing should be done for the first time
(Honderich 1990, p. 1). Yet in many ways, in the current
situation, this is inaccurate. For with the Right now in
ascendancy in many nations, we are witnessing a much more

activist project. Conservative politics now are very much the
politics of alteration—not always, but clearly the idea of "Do
nothing for the first time" is not a sufficient explanation of what
is happening either in education or elsewhere (Honderich 1990,
p. 4).

Conservatism has in fact meant different things at different
times and places. At times it involves defensive actions; at other
times it involves taking the initiative against the status quo
(Honderich 1990, p. 15). Today we are witnessing both.

Thus, it is important to set out the larger social context in
which the current politics of official knowledge operates. There
has been a breakdown in the accord that guided a good deal of
educational policy since World War II. Powerful groups within
government and the economy and within "authoritarian
populist" social movements have been able to redefine—often in
very retrogressive ways—the terms of debate in education, social
welfare, and other areas of social policy. What education is *for* is
being transformed (Apple 1993). No lcnger is education seen as
part of a social alliance which combines many "minority"[2]
groups, women, teachers, community activists, progressive
legislators and government officials, and others who act together
to propose (limited) social democratic policies for schools (e.g.,
expanding educational opportunities, limited attempts at
equalizing outcomes, developing special programs in bilingual
and multicultural education, and so on). A new alliance has been
formed, one that has increasing power in educational and social
policy. This new power bloc combines neoliberal elements of
business with the New Right and with neo-conservative
intellectuals. Its interests are less in increasing the life
opportunities of women, people of color, and labor than in
providing the educational conditions believed necessary both for
increasing international competitiveness, profit, and discipline
and for returning us to a romanticized past of the "ideal" home,
family, and school (Apple 1993).

The power of this alliance can be seen in a number of
educational policies and proposals: (1) programs for voucher
plans and tax credits to make schools operate like the thoroughly
idealized free-market economy; (2) the movement at national
and state levels to "raise standards" and mandate both teacher

and student "competencies" and basic curricular goals and knowledge, increasingly through the implementation of statewide and national testing; (3) the increasingly effective attacks on the school curriculum for its antifamily and anti–free enterprise "bias," its secular humanism, its lack of patriotism, and its supposed neglect of the knowledge and values of the "Western tradition" and of "real knowledge"; and (4) the growing pressure to make the perceived needs of business and industry into the primary goals of the school (Apple 1988b; Apple 1993).

In essence, the new alliance in favor of this conservative restoration has integrated education into a wider set of ideological commitments. The objectives in education are the same as those which serve as a guide to its economic and social welfare goals. These include the expansion of the "free market," the drastic reduction of government responsibility for social needs (though the Clinton Administration intends to mediate this in not very extensive—and not very expensive—ways), the reinforcement of intensely competitive structures of mobility, the lowering of people's expectations for economic security, and the popularization of what is clearly a form of Social Darwinist thinking (Bastian et al. 1986).

As I have argued at length elsewhere, the political Right in the United States has been very successful in mobilizing support *against* the educational system and its employees, often exporting the crisis in the economy onto the schools. Thus, one of its major achievements has been to shift the blame for unemployment and underemployment, for the loss of economic competitiveness, and for the supposed breakdown of traditional values and standards in the family, education, and paid and unpaid workplaces from the economic, cultural, and social policies and effects of dominant groups to the school and other public agencies. "Public" now is the center of all evil; "private" is the center of all that is good (Apple 1985).

In essence, then, four trends have characterized the conservative restoration in both the United States and Britain—privatization, centralization, vocationalization, and differentiation (Green 1991, p. 27). These trends are actually largely the results

of differences within the most powerful wings of this alliance—
neoliberalism and neoconservatism.

Neoliberalism has a vision of the weak state. A society that
lets the "invisible hand" of the free market guide all aspects of its
forms of social interaction is seen as both efficient and
democratic. On the other hand, neoconservatism is guided by a
vision of the strong state in certain areas, especially over the
politics of the body and gender and race relations, over
standards, values, and conduct, and over what kind of
knowledge should be passed on to future generations (Hunter
1988). [3] These two positions do not easily sit side by side in the
conservative coalition.

Thus, the rightist movement is contradictory. Is there not
something paradoxical about linking all of the feelings of loss
and nostalgia to the unpredictability of the market, "in replacing
loss by sheer flux"? (Johnson 1991a, p. 40).

The contradiction between neoconservative and neoliberal
elements in the rightist coalition are "solved" through a policy of
what Roger Dale has called *conservative modernization*. Such a
policy is engaged in

> simultaneously "freeing" individuals for economic
> purposes while controlling them for social purposes;
> indeed, in so far as economic "freedom" increases
> inequalities, it is likely to increase the need for social
> control. A "small, strong state" limits the range of its
> activities by transferring to the market, which it defends
> and legitimizes, as much welfare [and other activities] as
> possible. In education, the new reliance on competition
> and choice is not all pervasive; instead, "what is intended
> is a dual system, polarized between . . . market schools
> and minimum schools." (quoted in Edwards, Gewirtz, and
> Whitty forthcoming, p. 22)

That is, there will be a relatively less regulated and
increasingly privatized sector for the children of the better-off.
For the rest—whose economic status and racial composition will
be thoroughly predictable—the schools will be tightly controlled
and policed and will continue to be underfunded and unlinked
to decent paid employment.

One of the major effects of the combination of marketization and the strong state is "to remove educational policies from public debate." That is, the choice is left up to individual parents and "the hidden hand of unintended consequences does the rest." In the process, the very idea of education being part of a *public* political sphere in which its means and ends are publicly debated atrophies (Education Group II 1991, p. 268).

There are major differences between democratic attempts at enhancing people's rights over the policies and practices of schooling and the neoliberal emphasis on marketization and privatization. The goal of the former is to *extend politics*, to "revivify democratic practice by devising ways of enhancing public discussion, debate, and negotiation." It is based inherently on a vision of democracy as an educative practice. The latter, on the other hand, seeks to *contain politics*. It wants to *reduce all politics to economics*, to an ethic of "choice" and "consumption" (Johnson 1991a, p. 68). The world in essence becomes a vast supermarket.

Enlarging the private sector so that buying and selling—in a word, competition—is the dominant ethic of society involves a set of closely related propositions. This position assumes that more individuals are motivated to work harder under these conditions. After all, we "already know" that public servants are inefficient and slothful, while private enterprises are efficient and energetic. It assumes that self-interest and competitiveness are the engines of creativity. More knowledge and more experimentation are created and used to alter what we have now. In the process, less waste is created. Supply and demand remain in a kind of equilibrium. A more efficient machine is thus created, one which minimizes administrative costs and ultimately distributes resources more widely (Honderich 1990, p. 104).

This ethic is not meant to benefit simply the privileged few. However, it is the equivalent of saying that you have the right to climb the north face of the Eiger or scale Mount Everest, provided, of course, that you are very good at mountain climbing and have the necessary institutional and financial resources (Honderich 1990, pp. 99–100).

Thus, in a conservative society, access to a society's private resources (and remember, the attempt is to make nearly *all* of society's resources private) is largely dependent on one's ability to pay. And this is dependent on one's being a person of an *entrepreneurial or efficiently acquisitive class type*. On the other hand, society's public resources (that rapidly decreasing segment) are dependent on need (Honderich 1990, p. 89). In a conservative society, the former is to be maximized, the latter is to be minimized.

However, the conservatism of the New Right does not merely depend in large portion on a particular view of human nature—the view of human nature as primarily self-interested. It has gone further; it has set out to degrade human nature, to force all people to conform to what at first could only be claimed to be true. Unfortunately, in no small measure it has succeeded. Perhaps blinded by their own absolutist and reductive vision of what it means to be human, many of our political leaders do not seem to be capable of recognizing what they have done. They have set out, aggressively, to drag down the character of a people (Honderich 1990, p. 81), while at the same time attacking the poor and the disenfranchised for their supposed lack of values and character.

Curriculum, Testing, and a Common Culture

As Whitty reminds us, what is striking about the rightist coalition's policies is its capacity to connect the neoconservative emphasis on traditional knowledge and values, authority, standards, and national identity with the neoliberal emphasis on the extension of market-driven principles (also embraced by Clinton) into all areas of society (Whitty 1992, p. 25). Thus, a national curriculum—coupled with rigorous national standards and a system of testing that is performance driven—is able at one and the same time to be aimed at "modernization" of the curriculum and the efficient "production" of better "human capital" *and* represent a nostalgic yearning for a romanticized past (Whitty 1992, p. 25). When tied to a program of market-driven policies such as voucher and choice plans, such a national system of standards, testing, and curriculum—while perhaps internally inconsistent—is an ideal compromise within the rightist coalition.

But one could still ask, won't a national curriculum coupled with a system of national achievement testing contradict in practice the concomitant emphasis on privatization and school choice? Can it really simultaneously achieve both? I maintain that this apparent contradiction may not be as substantial as one might expect. One long-term aim of powerful elements within the conservative coalition is not necessarily to transfer power from the local level to the center, although for some neoconservatives who favor a strong state in the area of morality, values, and standards, this may indeed be the case. Rather, these elements would prefer to decentralize such power altogether and redistribute it according to market forces, thus tacitly disempowering those who already have less power while employing a rhetoric of empowering the consumer. In part, both a national curriculum and national testing can be seen as "necessary concessions in pursuit of this long term aim" (Green 1991, p. 29).

In a time of a loss of legitimacy in government and a crisis in educational authority, the government must be seen to be doing something about raising educational standards. After all, this is exactly what it promises to offer to "consumers" of education. This is why a national curriculum is crucial. Its major value does not lie in its supposed encouragement of standardized goals and content and of levels of achievement in what are considered the most important subject areas. This concern with achievement, of course, should not be totally dismissed. However, the major role of a national curriculum is rather in providing the framework within which national testing can function. It enables the establishment of a procedure that can supposedly give consumers "quality tags" on schools so that "free market forces" can operate to their fullest extent. If we are to have a free market in education in which the consumer is presented with an attractive range of choices, both a national curriculum and especially national testing then act as a "state watchdog committee" to control the "worst excesses" of the market (Green 1991, p. 29).[4]

However, let us be honest about our own educational history here. Even with the supposed emphasis of some people on student portfolios and other more flexible forms of evaluation, there is no evidence at all to support the idea that what will ultimately be installed—even if only because of time and expense—will be anything other than a system of mass standardized paper-and-pencil tests.

Yet we must also be clear about the social function of such a proposal. A national curriculum may be seen as a device for accountability that will help us establish benchmarks so that parents can evaluate schools. But it also puts into motion a system in which children themselves will be ranked and ordered as never before. One of its primary roles will be to act as "a mechanism for differentiating children more rigidly against fixed norms, *the social meanings and derivation of which are not available for scrutiny*" (Johnson 1991a, p. 79).

Thus, while the proponents of a national curriculum may see it as a means to create social cohesion and to give all of us the capacity to improve our schools by measuring them against objective criteria, the effects will be the reverse. The criteria may seem objective, but the results will not be, given existing differences in resources and class and race segregation. Rather than cultural and social cohesion, differences between "us" and the "others" will be generated even more strongly, and the attendant social antagonisms and cultural and economic destruction will worsen.

Richard Johnson helps us understand the social processes at work here.

This nostalgia for "cohesion" is interesting, but the great delusion is that all pupils—black and white, working class, poor, and middle class, boys and girls—will receive the curriculum in the same way. Actually, it will be read in different ways, according to how pupils are placed in social relationships and culture. A common curriculum, in a heterogeneous society, is not a recipe for "cohesion," but for resistance and the renewal of divisions. Since it always rests on cultural foundations of its own, it will put pupils in their places, not according to "ability," but according to how their cultural communities rank along the criteria taken as the "standard." A curriculum which does not

"explain itself," is not ironical or self-critical, will always
have this effect. (Johnson 1991a, pp. 79–80)

These are significant points, especially the call for all
curricula to *explain themselves*. In complex societies like ours,
which are riven with differential power, the only kind of
cohesion that is possible is one in which we overtly recognize
differences and inequalities. The curriculum then should not be
presented as "objective." Rather, it must constantly *subjectify*
itself. That is, it must "acknowledge its own roots" in the culture,
history, and social interests out of which it arose. It will
accordingly neither homogenize this culture, history, and social
interest, nor will it homogenize the students. The "same
treatment" by sex, race and ethnicity, or class is not the same at
all. A democratic curriculum and pedagogy must begin with a
recognition of "the different social positionings and cultural
repertoires in the classrooms, and the power relations between
them." Thus, if we are concerned with "really equal
treatment"—as I think we must be—we must base a curriculum
on a recognition of those differences that empower and
disempower our students in identifiable ways (Johnson 1991a, p.
80; Ellsworth 1989).

Foucault reminds us that if you wish to understand how
power works, you should examine the margins, look at the
knowledge, self-understandings, and struggles of those whom
powerful groups in this society have cast off as "the other" (Best
and Kellner 1991, pp. 34–75). The New Right and its allies have
created entire groups of "others"—people of color, women who
refuse to accept external control of their lives and bodies, gays
and lesbians, the poor (and the list could go on). It is in the
recognition of these differences that curriculum dialogue can
occur. Such a national dialogue should begin with the concrete
and public exploration of how we are differently positioned in
society and culture. What the New Right embargoes—the
knowledge of the margins, of how culture and power are
indissolubly linked—becomes a set of indispensable resources
for this task (Johnson 1991b, p. 320).

The proposed national curriculum of course would
recognize some of these differences. But, as Linda Christian-
Smith and I argue in *The Politics of the Textbook*, the national

curriculum serves both to partly acknowledge difference and at the same time to recuperate it within the supposed consensus that exists about what we should teach (Apple and Christian-Smith 1991; see also Apple 1993). It is part of an attempt to recreate hegemonic power that has been partly fractured by social movements.

The very idea of a common culture upon which a national curriculum—as defined by neoconservatives—is to be built is itself a form of cultural politics. In the immense linguistic, cultural, and religious diversity that makes up the constant creativity and flux in which we live, it is the cultural policy of the Right to override such diversity. Thinking it is reinstituting a common culture, it is instead *inventing* one, in much the same way as E. D. Hirsch (1987) has tried to do in his self-parody of what it means to be literate (Johnson 1991b, p. 319). A uniform culture never truly existed in the United States, only a selective version, an invented tradition that is reinstalled (though in different forms) in times of economic crisis and a crisis in authority relations, both of which threaten the hegemony of the culturally and economically dominant.

The expansion of voices in the curriculum and the vehement responses of the Right become crucial here. Multicultural and antiracist curricula present challenges to the program of the New Right, challenges that go to the core of their vision. In a largely monocultural national curriculum (which deals with diversity by centering the always ideological "we" and usually then simply mentioning "the contributions" of people of color, women, and "others"), the maintenance of existing hierarchies of what counts as official knowledge, the revivifying of traditional Western standards and values, the return to a "disciplined" (and one could say largely masculine) pedagogy, and so on, are paramount. A threat to any of these becomes a threat to the entire worldview of the Right (Johnson 1991a, p. 51; Rose 1988).

The idea of a common culture—in the guise of the romanticized Western tradition of the neoconservatives (or even as expressed in the longings of some socialists)—does not give enough thought, then, to the immense cultural heterogeneity of a society that draws its cultural traditions from all over the world.

The task of defending public education as *public*, as deserving of widespread support "across an extremely diverse and deeply divided people, involves a lot more than restoration" (Education Group II 1991, p. x).

The debate in England is similar. A national curriculum is seen by the Right as essential to prevent relativism. For most of its proponents, a common curriculum must transmit both the common culture and the high culture that has grown out of it. Anything else will result in incoherence, no culture, merely a "void." Thus, a national culture is "defined in exclusive, nostalgic, and frequently racist terms" (Johnson 1991a, p. 71).

Richard Johnson's (1991a) analysis documents its social logic.

> In formulations like these, culture is thought of as a homogeneous way of life or tradition, not as a sphere of difference, relationships, or power. No recognition is given to the real diversity of social orientations and cultures within a given nation-state or people. Yet a selective version of a national culture is installed as an absolute condition for any social identity at all. The borrowing, mixing and fusion of elements from different cultural systems, a commonplace everyday practice in societies like [ours], is unthinkable within this framework, or is seen as a kind of cultural misrule that will produce nothing more than a void. So the "choices" are between . . . a national culture or no culture at all. (p. 71)

The racial subtext here is perhaps below the surface but is still present in significant ways.[5]

The national curriculum is a mechanism for the political control of knowledge (Johnson 1991a, p. 82). Once it is established, there will be little chance of turning back. It may be modified by the conflicts that its content generates, but it is in its very establishment that its politics lies. Only by recognizing its ultimate logic of false consensus and, especially, its undoubted hardening in the future as it becomes linked to a massive system of national testing can we fully understand this. When this probable future is connected to the other parts of the rightist agenda—marketization and privatization—there is reason to make us pause, especially given the increasingly powerful conservative gains at local, regional, and state levels (Apple 1993).

Who Benefits?

Since leadership in such efforts to "reform" our educational system and its curriculum, teaching, and evaluative practices is largely exercised by the rightist coalition, we need always to ask, "Whose reforms are these?" and "Who benefits?"

A system of national curricula and national testing cannot help but ratify and exacerbate gender, race, and class differences in the absence of sufficient resources both human and material. Thus, when the fiscal crisis in most of our urban areas is so severe that classes are being held in gymnasiums and hallways, when many schools do not have enough funds to stay open for the full 180 days a year, when buildings are disintegrating before our very eyes (Apple 1993), when in some cities three classrooms must share one set of textbooks at the elementary level (Kozol 1991)—I could go on—it is simply a flight of fantasy to assume that more standardized testing and national curriculum guidelines are the answer. With the destruction of the economic infrastructure of these same cities through capital flight, with youth unemployment at nearly 75 percent in many of them, with almost nonexistent health care, with lives that are often devoid of hope for meaningful mobility because of what might simply be called the pornography of poverty, to assume that establishing curricular benchmarks based on problematic cultural visions and more rigorous testing will do more than affix labels to poor students in a way that is seemingly more neutral is to totally misunderstand the situation. It will lead to more blame being placed on students and poor parents and especially to the schools that they attend. It will also be very expensive. Enter voucher plans with even wider public approval.

Basil Bernstein's analysis of the complexities of this situation and of its ultimate results is more than a little useful here. He says, "the pedagogic practices of the new vocationalism [neoliberalism] and those of the old autonomy of knowledge [neoconservatism] represent a conflict between different elitist ideologies, one based on the class hierarchy of the market and the other based on the hierarchy of knowledge and its class supports" (Bernstein 1990, p. 63). Whatever the oppositions between market- and knowledge-oriented pedagogic and curricular practices, present racial, gender, and class-based inequalities are likely to be reproduced (Bernstein 1990, p. 64)

What he calls an "autonomous visible pedagogy"—one that relies on overt standards and highly structured models of teaching and evaluation—is justified by referring to its intrinsic worthiness. The value of the acquisition of say, the Western tradition, lies in its foundational status for "all we hold dear" and by the norms and dispositions that it instills in the students. "Its arrogance lies in its claim to moral high ground and to the superiority of its culture, its indifference to its own stratification consequences, its conceit in its lack of relation to anything other than itself, its self-referential abstracted autonomy" (Bernstein 1990, p. 87).

Its supposed opposite—one based on the knowledge, skills, and dispositions "required" by business and industry and one that seeks to transform schooling around market principles—is actually a much more complex ideological construction:

> It incorporates some of the criticism of the autonomous visible pedagogy . . . criticism of the failure of the urban school, of the passivity and inferior status [given to] parents, of the boredom of . . . pupils and their consequent disruptions of and resistance to irrelevant curricula, of assessment procedures which itemize relative failure rather than the positive strength of the acquirer. But it assimilates these criticisms into a new discourse: a new pedagogic Janus. . . . The explicit commitment to greater choice by parents . . . is not a celebration of participatory democracy, but a thin cover for the old stratification of schools and curricula. (Bernstein 1990, p. 87)

Are Bernstein's conclusions correct? Will the combination of national curricula, testing, and privatization actually lead away from democratic processes and outcomes? Here we must look not to Japan (where many people unfortunately have urged us to look) but to Britain, where this combination of proposals is much more advanced.

In Britain, there is now considerable evidence that the overall effects of the various market-oriented policies introduced by the rightist government are *not* genuine pluralism or the "interrupting [of] traditional modes of social reproduction." Far from this. They may instead largely provide "a legitimating gloss for the perpetuation of long-standing forms of structured inequality" (Whitty 1991, pp. 20–21). The fact that one of its major effects has been the disempowering and deskilling of large numbers of teachers is not inconsequential either (Apple 1993).

Going further, Edwards, Gewirtz, and Whitty have come to similar conclusions. In essence, the rightist preoccupation with "escape routes" diverts attention from the effects of such policies on those (probably the majority) who will be left behind (Edwards, Gewirtz, and Whitty forthcoming, p. 23).

Thus, it is indeed possible—actually probable—that market-oriented approaches in education (even when coupled with a strong state over a system of national curriculum and testing) will exacerbate already existing and widespread class and race divisions. Freedom and choice in the new educational market will be for those who can afford them. "Diversity" in schooling will simply be a more polite word for the condition of educational apartheid (Green 1991, p. 30; see also Karp 1992 and Lowe 1992).

Afterthoughts by Way of Conclusion

I have been more than a little negative in my appraisal here. I have argued that the politics of official knowledge—in this case surrounding proposals for a national curriculum and for national testing—cannot be fully understood in an isolated way. A national curriculum and national testing needs to be situated within larger ideological dynamics in which we are seeing an attempt by a new hegemonic bloc to transform our very ideas of what education is. This transformation involves a major shift— one that Dewey would have shuddered at—in which democracy becomes an economic, not a political, concept and where the idea of the public good withers at its very roots.

But perhaps I have been too negative. Perhaps there are good reasons to support national curricula and national testing even as currently constituted precisely *because* of the power of the rightist coalition.

It is possible, for example, to argue that only by establishing a national curriculum and national testing can we stop the fragmentation that will accompany the neoliberal portion of the rightist project. Only such a system would protect the very idea of a public school, would protect teachers' unions which in a privatized and marketized system would lose much of their power, would protect poor children and children of color from the vicissitudes of the market. After all, it is the free market that created the poverty and destruction of community that they are experiencing in the first place.

It is also possible to argue, as Geoff Whitty has in the British case, that the very fact of a national curriculum encourages both the formation of intense public debate about what knowledge should be declared official and the creation of progressive coalitions against such state-sponsored definitions of legitimate knowledge.[6] It could be the vehicle for the return of the political which the Right so wishes to evacuate from our public discourse and which the efficiency experts wish to make into merely a technical concern.

Thus, it is quite possible that the establishment of a national curriculum could have the effect of unifying oppositional and oppressed groups. Given the fragmented nature of progressive educational movements today, and given a system of school financing and governance that forces groups to focus largely on the local or state level, one function of a national curriculum could be the coalescence of groups around a common agenda. A national movement for a more democratic vision of school reform could be the result.

In many ways—and I am quite serious here—we owe principled conservatives (and there are many) a debt of gratitude. It is their realization that curriculum issues are not only about techniques that has helped to stimulate the current debate. When many women, people of color, and labor organizations fought for decades to have society recognize the selective tradition in official knowledge, these movements were often (though not always) silenced, ignored, or recuperated into dominant discourses (Apple 1993; Apple and Christian-Smith 1991). The power of the Right—in its contradictory attempt to establish a national common culture, to challenge what is now taught, and to make that culture part of a vast supermarket of choices and thus to purge cultural politics from our sensibilities—has now made it impossible for the politics of official knowledge to be ignored.

Should we then support a national curriculum and national testing to keep total privatization and marketization at bay? Under current conditions, I do not think it is worth the risk—not only because of its extensive destructive potential in the long and short run but also because I think it misconstrues and reifies the issues of a common curriculum and a common culture.

Here I must repeat the arguments I made in the second edition of *Ideology and Curriculum* (Apple 1990). The current call to return to a common culture in which all students are to be given the values of a specific group—usually the dominant group—does not in my mind concern a common culture at all. Such an approach hardly scratches the surface of the political and educational issues involved. A common culture can never be the general extension to everyone of what a minority means and believes. Rather, and crucially, it requires not the stipulation of the facts, concepts, skills, and values that make us all "culturally literate," but the creation of the conditions necessary for all people to participate in the creation and recreation of meanings and values. It requires a democratic process in which all people—not simply those who are the intellectual guardians of the Western tradition—can be involved in the deliberation over what is important. This necessitates the removal of the very real material obstacles—unequal power, wealth, time for reflection—that stand in the way of such participation (Williams 1989, pp. 35–36). As Raymond Williams (1989) so perceptively puts it:

> The idea of a common culture is in no sense the idea of a
> simply consenting, and certainly not of a merely conform-
> ing society. [It involves] a common determination of

> meanings by all the people, acting sometimes as individu-
> als, sometimes as groups, in a process which has no par-
> ticular end, and which can never be supposed at any time
> to have finally realized itself, to have become complete. In
> this common process, the only absolute will be the keep-
> ing of the channels and institutions of communication
> clear so that all may contribute, and be helped to con-
> tribute. (pp. 37–38)

In speaking of a common culture, then, we should not be
talking of something uniform, something to which we all
conform. Instead what we should be asking is precisely, for that
free, contributive and common *process* of participation in the
creation of meanings and values. It is the very blockage of that
process in our institutions that must concern all of us.

Our current language speaks to how this process is being
defined during the conservative restoration. Instead of people
who participate in the struggle to build and rebuild our
educational, cultural, political, and economic relations, we are
defined as consumers (of that "particularly acquisitive class
type"). This is truly an extraordinary concept, for it sees people
as either stomachs or furnaces. We use and use up. We don't
create—someone else does that. This is disturbing enough in
general, but in education it is truly disabling. Leave it to the
guardians of tradition, the efficiency and accountability experts,
the holders of "real knowledge," or to the Christopher Whittles
of this world who have given us commercial television in the
classroom and intend to franchise "schools of choice" for the
generation of profit (Apple 1993). Yet we leave it to these people
at great risk, especially to those students who are already
economically and culturally disenfranchised by our dominant
institutions.

As I noted at the outset, we live in a society with identifiable winners and losers. In the future we may say that the losers
made poor "consumer choices" and that's the way markets operate. But is this society really only one vast market?

As Whitty reminds us, in a time when so many people
have found out from their daily experiences that the supposed
"grand narratives" of progress are deeply flawed, is it
appropriate to return to yet another grand narrative, the market?

(Whitty 1992). The results of this narrative are visible every day in the destruction of our communities and environment, in the increasing racism of society, in the faces and bodies of our children, who see the future and turn away.

Many people are able to disassociate themselves from these realities. There is almost a pathological distancing among the affluent (Kozol 1991). Yet how can one not be morally outraged at the growing gap between rich and poor, the persistence of hunger and homelessness, the deadly absence of medical care, the degradations of poverty. If this were the (always self-critical and constantly subjectifying) centerpiece of a national curriculum (but then how could it be tested cheaply and efficiently, and how could the Right control its ends and means?), perhaps such a curriculum would be worthwhile. But until such a time, we can take a rightist slogan made popular in another context and apply it to their educational agenda—"Just say no."

NOTES

A draft of this chapter was presented as the John Dewey Lecture, jointly sponsored by the John Dewey Society and the American Educational Research Association, San Francisco, April 1992. I would like to thank Geoff Whitty, Roger Dale, James Beane, and the Friday Seminar at the University of Wisconsin, Madison, for their important suggestions and criticism. An extended version will appear in *Teachers College Record*.

1. See, e.g., Gould (1981). Feminist criticisms and reconstructions of science are essential to this task. See, for example, Haraway (1989), Harding and Barr (1987), Tuana (1981), and Harding (1991).

2. I put the word "minority" in quotation marks here to remind us that the vast majority of the world's population is composed of persons of color. It would be wholly salutary for our ideas about culture and education to bear this fact in mind.

3. Neoliberalism doesn't ignore the idea of a strong state, but it wants to limit it to specific areas (e.g., defense of markets).

368 *Transforming Schools*

4. I am making a "functional," not necessarily an "intentional," claim here. See Liston (1988). For an interesting discussion of how such testing programs might actually work against more democratic efforts at school reform, see Darling-Hammond (1992).

5. For a more complete analysis of racial subtexts in our policies and practices, see Omi and Winant (1986).

6. Geoff Whitty, personal communication. Andy Green, in the English context, argues as well that there are merits in having a broadly defined national curriculum but goes on to say that this makes it even more essential that individual schools have a serious degree of control over its implementation, "not least so that it provides a check against the use of education by the state as a means of promoting a particular ideology" (Green 1991, p. 22).

REFERENCES

Apple, M.W. 1985. *Education and Power*. New York: Routledge.

———. 1988a. Social Crisis and Curriculum Accords. *Educational Theory* 38: 191–201.

———. 1988b. *Teachers and Texts: A Political Economy of Class and Gender Relations in Education*. New York: Routledge.

———. 1989. American Realities: Poverty, Economy, and Education. In *Dropouts from School*, ed. Lois Weis, Eleanor Farrar, and Hugh Petrie, 205–223. Albany: State University of New York Press.

———. 1990. *Ideology and Curriculum*. 2d. ed. New York: Routledge.

———. 1993. *Official Knowledge: Democratic Education in a Conservative Age*. New York: Routledge.

Apple, M.W., and L. Christian-Smith, eds. 1991. *The Politics of the Textbook*. New York: Routledge.

Bastian, A., N. Fruchter, M. Gittell, C. Greer, and K. Haskins. 1986. *Choosing Inequality*. Philadelphia: Temple University Press.

Bernstein, B. 1977. *Class, Codes and Control*. Vol. 3. New York: Routledge.

———. 1990. *The Structuring of Pedagogic Discourse*. New York: Routledge.

Best, S., and D. Kellner. 1991. *Postmodern Theory: Critical Interrogations*. London: Macmillan.

Bourdieu, P. 1984. *Distinction*. Cambridge: Harvard University Press.

Burtless, G., ed. 1990. *A Future of Lousy Jobs?* Washington, DC: Brookings Institution.

Danziger, S., and D. Weinberg, eds. 1986. *Fighting Poverty*. Cambridge: Harvard University Press.

Darling-Hammond, L. 1992. Bush's Testing Plan Undercuts School Reforms. *Rethinking Schools* 6 (March/April): 18.

Education Group II, eds. 1991. *Education Limited*. London: Unwin Hyman.

Edwards, T., S. Gewirtz, and G. Whitty. Forthcoming. Whose Choice of Schools? In *Sociological Perspectives on Contemporary Educational Reforms*, ed. Madeleine Arnot and Len Barton. London: Triangle Books.

Ellsworth, E. 1989. Why Doesn't This Feel Empowering? *Harvard Educational Review* 59: 297–324.

Gould, S.J. 1981. *The Mismeasure of Man*. New York: Norton.

Green, A. 1991. The Peculiarities of English Education. In *Education Limited*, ed. Education Group II, 6–30. London: Unwin Hyman.

Haraway, D. 1989. *Primate Visions*. New York: Routledge.

Harding, S. 1991. *Whose Science, Whose Knowledge?* Ithaca: Cornell University Press.

Harding, S., and J. Barr, eds. 1987. *Sex and Scientific Inquiry*. Chicago: University of Chicago Press.

Hirsch, E.O. Jr. 1987. *Cultural Literacy*. New York: Vintage.

Honderich, T. 1990. *Conservatism*. Boulder, CO: Westview Press.

Hunter, A. 1988. *Children in the Service of Conservatism*. Madison: University of Wisconsin Law School, Institute for Legal Studies.

Johnson, R. 1991a. A New Road to Serfdom. In *Education Limited*, ed. Education Group II, 31–86. London: Unwin Hyman.

———. 1991b. Ten Theses on a Monday Morning. In *Education Limited*, ed. Education Group II, 306–321. London: Unwin Hyman.

Karp, S. 1992. Massachusetts "Choice" Plan Undercuts Poor Districts. *Rethinking Schools* 6 (March/April): 4.

Kozol, J. 1991. *Savage Inequalities*. New York: Crown.

Liston, D. 1988. *Capitalist Schools*. New York: Routledge.

Lowe, R. 1992. The Illusion of "Choice." *Rethinking Schools* 6 (March/April): 1, 21–23.

Omi, M., and H. Winant. 1986. *Racial Formation in the United States*. New York: Routledge.

Rose, S. 1988. *Keeping Them Out of the Hands of Satan*. New York: Routledge.

Smith, M., J. O'Day, and D. Cohen. 1990. National Curriculum, American Style: What Might It Look Like. *American Educator* 14: 10–17, 40–47.

Tuana, N., ed. 1989. *Feminism and Science*. Bloomington: Indiana University Press.

Whitty, G. 1991. Recent Education Reform: Is It a Postmodern Phenomenon? Paper presented at the conference on Reproduction, Social Inequality, and Resistance, University of Bielefeld, Germany.

———. 1992. *Education, Economy, and National Culture*. Milton Keynes, England: Open University Press.

Williams, R. 1989. *Resources of Hope*. New York: Verso.

14

High School Curriculum Differentiation and Postsecondary Outcomes

Thomas B. Hoffer

Introduction

At the forefront of current efforts to improve American secondary education are deep concerns over the quality and quantity of science and mathematics education. International comparisons have shown that American students lag well behind their European and Asian counterparts in their command of these subjects. This situation has proved alarming to political leaders, who believe that prospects for future economic growth are closely tied to the level of technical expertise in the population at large. The Bush administration's education reform manifesto, America 2000, set the goal that U.S. students should be first in the world in science and mathematics achievement by the year 2000. The recent recommendations of the U.S. Department of Labor (1991) report *What Work Requires of Schools* argues strongly that scientific and technical training need to be increased and improved for all Americans, not just the relatively small number of specialists. The Clinton administration has largely concurred with these prescriptions in the initial formulations of its own reform agenda, Goals 2000.

Reform efforts have been led largely by the professional associations of science and mathematics teachers, the National Science Teachers Association (NSTA) and the National Council of Teachers of Mathematics (NCTM), the American Association for the Advancement of Science (AAAS), and the National Academy of Sciences. These groups have directed most of their attention to the articulation of curriculum goals and contents. All have come out strongly in favor of increasing the time that students devote to science and mathematics, advocating that all students study both subjects every year from the early elementary grades through the end of high school.

The proposed expansion of participation in science and mathematics would represent a massive change over current practice. Three national studies of high school transcripts have been conducted over the past twelve years, and they show that current practice falls far short of these ideals. In 1990, only 19 percent of high school graduates completed biology, chemistry, and physics. While this represents a large and rapid increase from 1982, when only 11 percent completed all three, it is still very far from complete enrollment (National Center for Education Statistics 1993, table 47). Similarly, only about 18 percent of the 1990 graduates completed a course in trigonometry, which typically has two years of algebra and one of geometry as prerequisites (National Center for Education Statistics 1993, table 35).

Advocates of higher graduation standards in the areas of mathematics and science have few public critics, but grassroots support for tougher standards is likely to be far from unanimous. Two reasons for this relate to the means of achieving the goals; another refers to the end itself. With respect to the means, the new standards would be fairly expensive, since new science and mathematics teachers would have to be hired. The standards would also require students to work harder for a high school diploma, and it is not clear how far schools can go before students withdraw effort, rebel, or quit.

These practical concerns are likely to be seriously addressed, however, only when the affected groups— policymakers, school officials, parents, and students—are themselves convinced of the value of higher standards. One criterion of value is the difference taking more course work makes in earning a college degree and finding a job. I address this issue by drawing on some of the data collected in recent years on high school course work and postsecondary outcomes. I will focus on the effects of students' high school course work in science and mathematics on three postsecondary outcomes: (1) the likelihood that students will go to college, and stay enrolled once they have started; (2) the likelihood they will enroll and stay enrolled in a scientific or technical major field of study in college; and (3) the likelihood they will find full-time employment after high school.

Why Might High School Coursework Make a Difference?

Why might a more rigorous program of high school studies be helpful once students graduate? One possible benefit is that these students simply have a better knowledge base in science and mathematics. For students going on to college, this could either make new mathematics or science courses easier or allow them to move through the college mathematics and science curricula at a higher level. The former may reduce the probability of dropping out of college, for some students may quit after failing or struggling with a mathematics or laboratory science course. The latter benefit may result in greater odds of graduating in a major which requires more mathematics and science—which typically leads to higher-paying jobs after college or graduate school.

High school course work in science and mathematics may also promote the development of general skills, such as how to solve problems or how to keep up with the daily workload that more demanding courses entail. These skills are obviously important to success in college, and many believe they are becoming increasingly important for entry-level employment (SCANS 1992).

While these are plausible hypotheses, it is important to bear in mind that students who complete more rigorous high school programs are a select group and are likely to differ from other students in terms of social background, pre-high-school academic achievement, and future orientations. Since these variables are associated with most postsecondary outcomes of interest, research which ignores these factors is almost certain to overestimate the effects of completing more demanding high school programs. It is possible, in fact, that once these background variables are controlled for, no effects of high school coursework on later outcomes will be found.

Prior Research

Effects on College Enrollments

Virtually all of the research done on the effects of high school course work on college enrollment has classified students according to their overall programs of study, or tracks. The effects of track placement on college plans and college enrollments have generally been found to be substantively large and statistically significant (for reviews of the effects of high school tracking, see Gamoran and Berends 1987; and Oakes, Gamoran, and Page 1992).

An important shortcoming of most prior research on curriculum effects on postsecondary education outcomes is that different types of high school courses are not distinguished. The student curriculum program enrollments (whether self-reported or coded from transcripts) which are normally used cannot be translated back into specific courses, and the estimated effects are thus difficult to interpret. The self-reported programs are particularly ambiguous, since they may well reflect students' postsecondary aspirations, as well as whatever courses they completed.

A second shortcoming is that the effects of self-selection on the part of students are difficult to rule out as a potential source of bias. Students who take higher levels of science and mathematics may differ from those who take lower levels in ways which surveys do not measure very well. While this cannot be ruled out conclusively in any nonexperimental study, it is worth seeing if the general pattern of results holds within select subpopulations, as well. In the analyses presented here, I use the longitudinal data to restrict the sample to students who actually enrolled in college in the year after high school. The question then becomes one of whether differences in these students' high school experiences are related to different chances of success in college over the next four years.

A final problem concerns the assumed causal order of variables in the estimated models. While prior research has been careful to avoid confusing track or course-work effects with background effects, the variables included under the rubric of background have differed from study to study, with important consequences for the research results. The conceptual model on which most research, including the present study, has relied is schematically represented in Figure 14.1. The most rigorous studies of track effects on high school outcomes have controlled for an extensive set of prior characteristics, usually including measures of academic achievement from some point around the beginning of high school. Some studies also control for academic achievement at the end of high school (Jencks and Brown 1975), but this changes the meaning of estimated course-work or track effects on postsecondary outcomes, since one would expect that most of the course-taking effects derive from the higher levels of achievement the courses generate.

Effects on College Majors

Some research supports the notion that entering college with higher levels of mathematical and scientific competence increases one's chances of succeeding in a scientific or technical major field of study. Lee's (1988) analysis of the 1984 High School and Beyond (HS&B) data examined the effects of high school course work on selection of major plans among high school seniors. Lee found that the number of science courses completed and academic achievement in mathematics were the strongest predictors of senior-year intentions to pursue a science, mathematics, or engineering (SME) major among students who planned to go to college. Using the same database and similar methods, these findings have been essentially corroborated by Ware and Lee (1988) and Maple and Stage (1991) in analyses which stratified by gender and ethnicity.

Just as the research on higher-education enrollments is subject to selection biases, research on SME major selection may

FIGURE 14.1. Conceptual model of high school curriculum effects on post-secondary outcomes, with measures listed below.

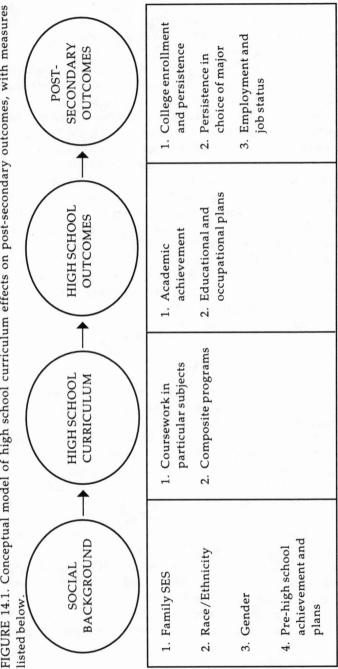

also overestimate the effects of science and mathematics course work. Again, the chance of selection bias may be reduced by restricting the analysis to individuals who started in a four-year college or university and who also had the same initial plans for (or against) an SME major. If high school course work differences then are found to be associated with different rates of maintaining or rejecting SME as a major, the claims of prior research would be strengthened.

Effects on Employment

For students not going to college, it is reasonable to expect that a better grasp of the basic quantitative skills taught in high school would make them more attractive to potential employers. In a recent analysis of the 1985 National Assessment of Educational Progress (NAEP) Young Adult Literacy Survey, Rivera-Batiz (1992) found that individuals with higher levels of quantitative skills were more likely to have full-time employment. It is not clear exactly how employers find out about the quantitative skills of applicants and new hires. Bishop (1989) points out that U.S. employers very rarely request any record of applicants' course work or test scores from high schools. Presumably employers find out from informal cues or on-the-job performance. In any case, the NAEP findings lend credence to the claims of business leaders about the importance they attach to quantitative and analytic skills.

Studies of the effects of high school experiences on early-career employment outcomes have found significant effects of high school course work (Hotchkiss and Dorsten 1987; Kang and Bishop 1989). The Hotchkiss and Dorsten study went beyond the ambiguous self-reported programs to analyze the effects of specific vocational course sequences identified from transcript data. Kang and Bishop extended that analysis by disaggregating academic course work into the main subject areas and including those indicators alongside the vocational course-work measures. While both of these studies used data from the High School and Beyond study which I use here, they looked at outcomes only in the first two years after high school. Their analyses can be usefully updated with the later data now available.

It is thus worthwhile to reopen the issue of the effects of secondary school curriculum differentiation, and to do so with measures of the specific patterns of course work the students have completed. The courses of particular interest in current policy debates are in science and mathematics. These are also the courses which are most amenable to survey analysis, for they are generally organized in relatively standard sequences, and course titles and contents are more standardized than in language arts and social studies.

Data

The data used here are drawn from two sources. The main analyses use the first four cycles (1980 base year through the 1986 third follow-up) of the High School and Beyond 1980 sophomore cohort study (Sebring et al. 1987). HS&B began in 1980 with a national sample of 1,015 high schools. Random samples of about thirty students were drawn from the sophomore and senior cohorts in each school and were administered questionnaires and achievement tests. After the students finished high school, systematic subsets of the original samples were retained for follow-ups every two years. The present analysis uses only the data collected on the sophomore cohort. Of the 29,000 sophomores surveyed and tested in 1980 and 1982, about 14,000 were retained for subsequent follow-up data collections. Of these, some 12,000 participated in the base year and first three follow-ups. My working sample, however, consists of the 9,000 students for whom high school transcript data were also collected. I use these data because they more accurately measure the mathematics and science courses the students completed than self-reports. The measures used in the analyses are described in the Appendix.

The HS&B data are complemented at various points with data from another panel study, the Longitudinal Study of American Youth (LSAY). The LSAY is a much smaller panel, but it collected a great deal of information about high school science and mathematics course taking which HS&B did not. The LSAY started in fall 1987 with a sample of 2,829 tenth-graders and

3,116 seventh-graders from fifty pairs of public high school and middle schools (see Miller et al. 1993 for a full description of the LSAY study design and database).

High School Course Work in Science and Mathematics

While the current reform efforts may soon result in major changes in the content of the secondary science and mathematics curricula, the courses and sequences which schools have offered have changed little over the past several decades. The high school mathematics curriculum actually begins in the eighth grade for the top 20 percent or so, when they take first-year algebra. The standard sequence beyond that consists of geometry, second-year algebra, trigonometry, analytic geometry, and calculus. Many students never start this sequence, taking only arithmetic courses of one stripe or another through the middle and upper secondary grades. Data from the LSAY's 1987 national sample of public school seventh-graders showed that, six years later (1993—when most of the students were in their final year of high school), only 82 percent had completed a first course in algebra; 64 percent, algebra and geometry; 51 percent, geometry and algebra 2; 31 percent, trigonometry, geometry, and two years of algebra; and only 9 percent had completed the full sequence culminating in a calculus course (Hoffer and Nelson 1993).

The high school science curriculum is less standardized than the mathematics curriculum but is still fairly easy to characterize. The most common sequence starts with laboratory biology, moves on to laboratory chemistry, laboratory physics, and advanced courses in biology, chemistry, or physics. Data from the LSAY show that 80 percent of public school students completed at least one lab course, 51 percent completed at least two, 31 percent completed three or more, but only about 6 percent completed an advanced course in biology, chemistry, or physics (Hoffer and Nelson 1993).

While the LSAY survey has the most current data on course taking, the survey has followed the older cohort for only two years beyond high school at this point and is thus not as well suited as the older High School and Beyond survey for current purposes.

The HS&B data indicate that relatively few students in the early 1980s completed advanced sequences of mathematics or science courses. Drawing on the high school students' transcripts, HS&B constructed summary course-work variables for both subjects, counting only those courses which the student passed and thus earned graduation credit for (a course that runs for a full academic year typically earns one credit). The HS&B science course-work typology is defined as follows (the percentage of students at each level is in parentheses):

> *Concentrator*: earned one or more credits in each of the following: biology, chemistry, and physics in addition to any credits earned in general science courses (11 percent).

> *Four-Year College Bound*: earned one or more credits in an advanced physical science or an advanced life science in addition to any credits earned in general life or physical sciences (31 percent).

> *General Science*: earned one or more credits in general life science or general physical science and less than one credit in advanced science offerings (44 percent).

> *Limited or Nonparticipant*: earned less than one credit in science (13 percent).

The mathematics course-work variable is similarly described in the HS&B codebook:

> *Concentrator*: earned four or more credits in mathematics, at least one of which is from such advanced courses as analytic geometry, pure mathematics, solid geometry, analysis, calculus, mathematics 3, or statistics and probability (12 percent).

> *Four-Year College Bound*: earned four or more credits in mathematics, one of which was earned in algebra 1, 2, or 3; geometry; plane or solid geometry; trigonometry; or mathematics 1 or 2 (41 percent).

General Math: earned one to two credits in math with less than two in the college preparatory courses (43 percent).

Limited or Nonparticipant: earned less than one credit in math (4 percent).

Course work in the two subjects is strongly correlated. The gamma statistic, which measures the association between two ordinal variables and ranges from –1.0 to 1.0, is .76. Since high correlations among explanatory variables makes it difficult to identify unique contributions, I decided not to use the science and mathematics coursework variables separately and instead combined them to produce a typology of course work. To begin with, I simply cross-classified the two variables to construct sixteen different categories of science and mathematics course work. As Table 14.1 shows, four of the categories proved to have less than 0.5 percent of the cases in them, and another four had 2 percent or less of the 9,000 students in them. These small categories are best collapsed into substantively similar larger groups in order to simplify the analysis and exposition of coursework effects. To decide how to collapse the categories, I defined dummy variables for each cell and then regressed the postsecondary outcome measures on these. I then collapsed the smaller cells into the larger categories, which had regression coefficients which were the closest on average to those for the small cells. While this procedure simplifies the exposition, it is also useful because it identifies some interactions between science and mathematics course work which would be lost if the subjects were treated separately.

For present purposes, I reduced the sixteen cells to the following five clusters (the percentage of the sampled students in each cell is shown in parentheses):

1. Science and Mathematics Concentration (5 percent).

2. Science or Mathematics Concentration (11 percent).

3. Science and Mathematics College Preparatory (18 percent).

4. Science or Mathematics College Preparatory (23 percent).

5. Science and Mathematics General or Limited (43 percent).

TABLE 14.1. Percentage Distribution of Students by Patterns of Science and Math Course Work Completed during High School: 1980 HS&B Sophomore Cohort.

Science Course Work Pattern	Math Course Work Pattern				
	Concen-tration	College Prep	General	Limited	Total
Concentration	5	6	0	0	12
College prep	4	18	7	0	29
General	1	14	29	2	45
Limited	0	2	10	2	14
Total	11	40	46	4	100

Note: The science and math course-work variables are taken directly from the HS&B public-use files. See text for definitions of categories.

Transitions from High School to College and Work

Once individuals leave high school, the standards against which behavior can be usefully compared become much less clear-cut. Few would disagree that all students should learn certain skills and types of knowledge before finishing high school, but no similar consensus is likely to be found around what should be learned or done once they finish their compulsory schooling. For this reason, it is helpful to distinguish at the outset between the paths individuals follow and to then consider their success within the paths they choose (see Coleman and Hoffer 1987, chaps. 6 and 7, for further discussion of these points).

The principal paths are higher education and work. The HS&B data show that, in the first year after high school, over half of the cohort was not enrolled in any type of postsecondary educational program, about 15 percent were in public two-year institutions, and about a quarter (27 percent) were in public or private four-year institutions. As one would expect, two-year college enrollments declined sharply after two years, while four-year college enrollments were relatively stable (total percentages may not add to 100 because of rounding).

	Feb. 1983 (%)	Feb. 1984 (%)	Feb. 1985 (%)	Feb. 1986 (%)
Public or private 4-year	27	26	26	24
Public 2-year institution	15	13	6	4
Not enrolled	55	58	65	70
Other enrollment	4	3	3	2
	100	100	100	100

At the same time point, about one-third were working full-time, one-quarter were working part-time, 6 percent were unemployed and not full-time students, and another one-third were not in the labor force (most of these were full-time students). The percentage working full-time increased steadily after that point, but had only risen to 45 percent by 1986.

	Feb. 1983 (%)	Feb. 1984 (%)	Feb. 1985 (%)	Feb. 1986 (%)
Working full-time	32	39	43	45
Working part-time	28	29	24	27
Unemployed, not enrolled full-time	6	5	5	5
Not in labor force	34	28	29	24
	100	100	100	100

These are the main paths followed after high school. The first analytic question concerns the relationship of high school course work with choice of path. In most of the analyses, I begin by estimating the effects of high school course work on the odds of remaining in one or another of these statuses over the four years after high school. However, the educational and employment paths of HS&B respondents were far from fixed at this early juncture, for there was a great deal of movement in and out of work and college during the first four years after high school. Methodologically, if one analyzes data from only one or a small number of time points within a period of interest, one runs the risk of obtaining biased results. To guard against that problem, I also calculated the lengths of time that individuals occupied a particular state of interest, and then estimated the effects of the same factors on the durations. For present purposes, I consider two duration variables: (1) length of time enrolled full-time in a four-year college or university, from October 1982 to February 1986; and (2) length of time employed full-time, from October 1982 to February 1986.

Effects of High School Course Work on Later Outcomes

Effects on College Enrollments

Since high school course work in higher levels of the science and mathematics curricula is a standard part of the college preparatory track, it is not surprising to find a close association between course work and college enrollments. The HS&B data show the association is indeed strong: 81 percent of the students who concentrated in science and mathematics in high school were enrolled in a four-year college or university program during the first year after high school, compared with only 10 percent of the students who did not exceed the "general" level of course work in either subject.

Nonetheless, many students who started in four-year institutions did not take much science or mathematics in high school. The question, then, is whether this lack proved to be a handicap to success in college. To answer this, it is necessary first to define what is meant by "success," and then to control for factors other than high school coursework which also may affect success.

One measure of success in college is simple persistence. Many students leave college before graduation, and some of them probably leave because they find the work too difficult.

Others leave for very different reasons: they lacked the money to meet the expenses (or they had to work too many hours for money to keep up with their studies), their interests shifted to pursuits which did not require a baccalaureate, or perhaps the psychological adjustment proved too difficult. Of these, the economic reasons are the most straightforward and thus easiest to assess with survey data. The more personal reasons are not well measured in the available surveys, and may be associated with high school course work, and thus cannot be ruled out as alternative explanations of whatever course-work effects are found.

With this caveat, the HS&B data show that high school course work in science and mathematics is significantly related to persistence in a four-year college or university. I assessed this relationship by first estimating a logistic regression of a dichotomous indicator of college enrollment in spring, 1986, on measures of the students' social and economic backgrounds, initial high school (grade 10) achievement levels, and high school course-work variables. This equation was estimated only for students who enrolled in a four-year institution in the spring semester of the first year after high school (February of 1983). The results thus indicate the extent to which high school course work affects the likelihood of still being enrolled in college three years later, when most of the students would have been college seniors. To illustrate the effects of course work, I used the regression coefficients to calculate predicted probabilities of persistence for students who were at the sample average on all variables except the composite measure of high school science and math course work. As Figure 14.2 shows, students who concentrated in either science or mathematics or both during high school were about 8 percent more likely than non-concentrators to still be enrolled, controlling for social and academic background variables.

Among students who enrolled in a two-year college in the first year after high school, the effects of high school course work in science and mathematics are generally comparable to those for the four-year students.[1] The advantage of students who concentrated in science and mathematics is very large (see Figure 14.3), but these students represented only about 3 percent of the group

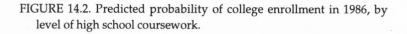

FIGURE 14.2. Predicted probability of college enrollment in 1986, by level of high school coursework.

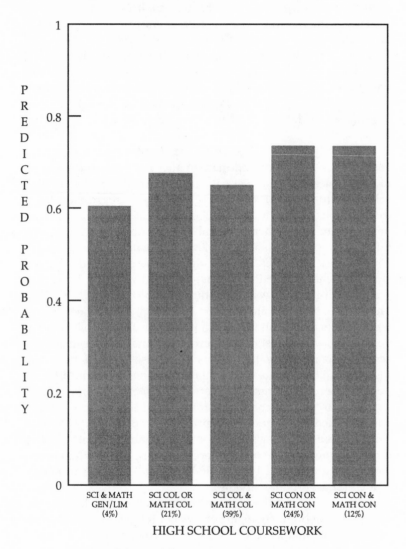

FIGURE 14.3. Predicted probability of community college enrollment or graduation in 1986, by level of high school coursework.

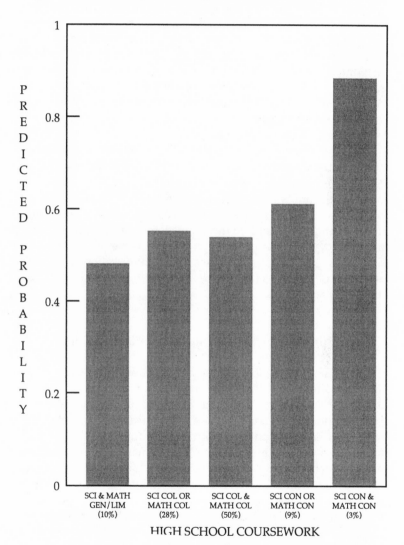

which went to community college. For the rest, more course work conferred a modest advantage.

Another angle on this question is afforded by use of the HS&B event-history data. Since the students reported the specific months they were enrolled in their respective higher-education institutions, it is possible to calculate the length of time each respondent was enrolled from the end of high school to the spring of 1986, when the third follow-up was completed. One can then use the duration of enrollment as the dependent variable and estimate the effects of high school course work on it while controlling for other variables.

The duration analysis essentially corroborates the previous analysis. Using ordinary least squares regression techniques, the results show that high school concentrators were enrolled about two more months than nonconcentrators who nonetheless had completed college-preparatory levels of both science and mathematics. Students who completed less than college-preparatory levels in both subjects were at a marked disadvantage, showing average enrollment durations that were about 4.5 months less than those at the college-preparatory level in both subjects.[2]

Effects on Scientific and Technical Majors

College students' choices of majors and persistence within them are two additional outcomes of interest. Of particular interest are decisions about participation in scientific and technical fields. Despite the substantially higher starting salaries and stronger long-term employment prospects for graduates in these fields, the number of students majoring in them has not expanded and has even declined in some specialties over the past decade (Dietz 1993). One factor which may affect decisions about whether to embark on a scientific or technical major and, once started, to remain in one, is the adequacy of one's high school preparation.

The HS&B data show that, among students enrolled in a four-year college during the first year after high school, the science and mathematics course-work variables have a large but, again, not surprising association with the students' intended major fields of study (see the Appendix for a description of the HS&B data on college majors and the coding procedures). The proportion of students in each major field in 1984, for example, who concentrated in either science or mathematics or both in high school ranges from a low of 17 percent in education to 50 percent in the science, mathematics, and engineering (SME) fields.

It is clear that SME fields attract students with a much higher average level of high school preparation in science and mathematics, but it is also clear that many of the SME aspirants do not have especially strong high school course-taking records. It is thus not trivial to ask whether differences in the students' high school preparations are associated with different levels of success within their college programs. In order to estimate the effects of high school course work on individuals' decisions about SME studies, I again restricted the analysis to those who were enrolled in a four-year college program during the first year after high school. I then applied a further restriction to include only those who indicated an intention to major in an SME field during their final year of high school. A logistic regression was used to estimate the effects of high school course work on the likelihood of maintaining the intention to major in an SME field by spring of 1986.

Only about 42 percent of the students with SME plans as high school seniors who also started at a four-year college after high school were still planning on an SME major in 1986. While many students moved into SME majors from other fields, the main trend is one of attrition. The results of the logistic regression analysis show that more advanced high school course work is also beneficial to students planning to major in scientific and technical fields.[3] The two factors with the strongest effects on persistence were gender (females were much less likely to maintain plans for an SME major), and concentrating in science and mathematics during high school. The predicted probabilities of still having an SME major in 1986 for students with different levels of high school course work are shown in Figure 14.4.

FIGURE 14.4. Predicted probability of persisting in SME major in 1986, by level of high school coursework.

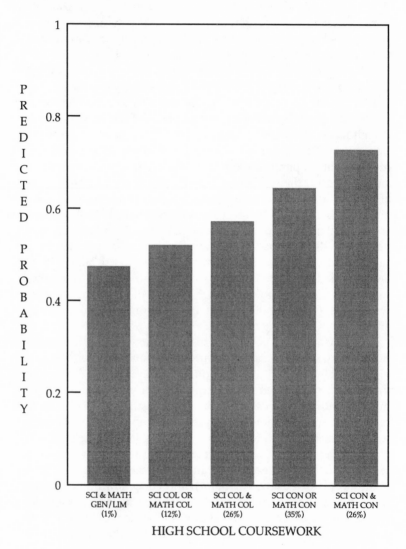

Effects on Employment

Each of the outcomes examined for college-going students shows clear advantages for students who completed more advanced science and mathematics course work during high school. Does a similar pattern hold for non-college-goers? To answer this question, I looked at two outcomes: duration of full-time employment among nonstudents and the occupational status of the jobs which the respondents landed. The control variables used in these analyses were the same as in the college-outcome models but also included indicators of the respondents' vocational course-work patterns during high school. As it turns out, the science and mathematics course-work indicators show no significant effects on the duration of full-time employment, controlling for the background and vocational course variables. Additional vocational courses, in contrast, are significantly associated with longer employment durations.

Are there effects of high school course work on the quality of the jobs held? Most of the jobs landed by non-college-goers are relatively low-status occupations which typically do not make high demands for scientific or mathematical knowledge. The three most common jobs in the first four years after high school among the HS&B cohort were retail clerk or cashier, waiter or waitress, and office clerical work. Even at this early stage of career development, though, some differentiation is found. The most widely used measure of occupational status, the Duncan SEI scale, has a standard deviation within the HS&B sample of the non-college-going subpopulation equal to 12.5, which is about half that found in the whole adult population (Stevens and Featherman 1981, table 2). Regressing the SEI scores of the HS&B respondents on measures of social background, high school achievement, and high school course work shows that high levels of course work in science and mathematics do lead to jobs with higher SEI ratings. However, the effects are substantively small and statistically weak and thus should not be given much weight. The most important predictors of higher-SEI jobs are gender (females have higher SEI at this stage in this subgroup), parental SES, and verbal achievement.[4]

Who Takes High School Courses in Science and Mathematics?

The preceding analyses have shown that high school course work in science and mathematics has positive effects on educational outcomes beyond high school, but that the effects on early occupational attainments among non-college-goers are not significant. The question then arises as to why students differ in their levels of participation in high school science and math. One factor is the students' social backgrounds. When the five-level composite measure is regressed on the measures of parental SES, gender, race, and Hispanic ethnicity, the results show that SES has by far the strongest effect, and that the background variables together account for 14 percent of the variance.[5]

At least three possible explanations of these background-related differences can be identified: (1) different preferences, (2) different opportunities, and (3) different competencies. While these factors are difficult to disentangle from one another, the HS&B data do contain sophomore-year achievement test data and measures of whether the students planned to go to college when they were sophomores. When these test scores and plans are controlled for, the SES difference reduces to about one-fifth of its original size, and the elaborated model accounts for 48 percent of the variance in coursework. The reduced effect of SES does not exclude class-related differences in preferences and opportunities, since those factors may have led to the competency differences.

At face value, the large effect of prior achievement on subsequent course taking suggests that if more students started high school with a solid preparation in these subjects, more would persist in the curricula. The mechanisms producing this effect are not clear, though. The main ambiguity concerns the extent to which prior achievement scores affect access (via the formal or informal rules of the school) versus motivation to study the courses. Both factors probably operate, and about the most one can say in light of the available evidence is that secondary schools need to reconsider their assignment rules and curriculum structure at the same time as efforts are made to improve the preparation of students coming into their programs.

How much do policies on science and mathematics course work vary from school to school? Analysis of the LSAY public school data show that about 20 percent of the overall variability among students in how far they progress in the science and mathematics curricula is associated with their particular school enrollments. Once the effects of student social background variables are factored out, the percentage of variance between schools falls to around 10 percent (Hoffer and Nelson 1993).

Discussion and Conclusions

If completing a rigorous program of high school science and mathematics has these benefits, why don't more students follow this path? Some of the proximate reasons have already been mentioned: students who achieve at lower levels, whose parents hold lower expectations, and who do not plan to go to college, are less likely to take science and mathematics courses. All of these can be considered "background factors," in the sense that they are largely in place by the beginning of high school.

Another set of factors are school policy variables. One school policy is the availability and content of counseling, which affects the information available to students. Many students do not see science or mathematics course work as useful to their futures; perhaps if counseled that the courses would be useful, more would take these courses.[6] A second, related, policy is the curriculum of the school and the requirements for graduation. Some have argued that the opportunities for advanced course work are less than the demand for the courses. One version of this claim holds that opportunities are restricted by virtue of "institutionalized beliefs" which maintain that only a select minority of students are able to comprehend such subjects as trigonometry, chemistry, and physics. A second version is that restrictions are imposed because of the lack of staff and resources available to teach additional sections of eleventh- and twelfth-grade mathematics and science. If students were encouraged or required to take more mathematics and science, the increases would most likely come at the expense of other subjects. This would thus involve replacing faculty in some areas with additional science and mathematics teachers. Science courses, particularly those with laboratory components, are also relatively expensive, and many districts may be reluctant to require more courses because of the lack of financial resources.

Currently, the main state- and district-level policy alternatives for increasing enrollments in more demanding courses are (1) to reduce barriers on enrollments through expansion of choice, and (2) to impose higher standards on schools. Considerable action has been taken on both fronts in recent years; the current debates focus on how much further to go in each direction. Advocates of greater choice believe that many families would like their children to take more demanding courses than they currently take but are unable to realize their preferences because of an inability to affect school policy. If choice were expanded, the argument goes, the competition among schools would lead to higher standards in the effort to attract and hold dissatisfied families.

The main evidence in support of this claim comes from comparisons of public and private high schools in the United States. Private schools, and particularly Catholic schools, are much more likely to place students in advanced science and mathematics sequences, controlling for student background variables (Coleman and Hoffer 1987; Bryk, Lee, and Holland 1993). Where the actual exercise of choice has grown the most, however, is within the public sector, and mainly in the form of magnet schools within urban districts. Are students in these districts completing more demanding programs than they would have without the expansion of choice? At this point, there is no evidence available one way or the other, but relevant data are being collected in the NELS:88 survey, and these will be available very soon. Until then, there are reasons to be skeptical. One is that choice is often exercised on behalf of programs which are oriented toward interests other than science and mathematics. A magnet program organized around the humanities, for example, is not likely to increase participation in science and mathematics. Another reason is that choice may increase the segregation of higher and lower achievers and thereby diminish the standards to which the latter are held.

If an expanded market is not politically feasible or practically efficient, the main alternative policy lever is to impose higher standards through bureaucratic means. In practice, this option is available mainly to the state-level authorities, since schools and local authorities often lack the power to set them in the face of financial constraints or local opposition. Almost all fifty states have in fact increased high school graduation requirements in science and mathematics during the last decades. The content of the requirements varies considerably, and some believe that they are so easily fulfilled as to be practically useless. This claim would be supported if evidence showed that higher course-work requirements are being fulfilled by expanding enrollments in only the simplest courses. Recent surveys of state policies show that most states have increased high school graduation requirements in these subjects over the last decade (Blank and Engler 1992). While enrollments have increased in most subjects (and dramatically in some cases—see National Center for Education Statistics 1993), the growth has been greatest in the lower-level courses. The claim would also be supported if evidence showed that students are not learning any more than they did before requirements were increased. The NAEP data for seventeen-year-olds, in fact, showed only very slight improvements through the 1980s (Mullis et al. 1991).

A third general policy option—one which has received much less attention—is to change the structure of short-term incentives for students to learn what is taught in advanced mathematics and science courses. This would involve, first and foremost, altering the linkages between high schools, higher education, and employers. Only the most selective colleges require more than one high school laboratory science class and more than algebra and geometry for admission. Given the value of a college degree, higher requirements would probably lead more students to fulfill the higher standards and would probably not depress college enrollments. The main problem with this proposal is that individually, colleges have little to gain from it. If one school raised its standards, then it would run the risk of reducing enrollments, since students could go elsewhere. There thus needs to be some collective leadership in higher education in order to exercise leverage on high school students.

The results of the analysis presented here show no clear indication of benefits of high school science and mathematics course work for non-college-goers. That finding, of course, does not mean that employers would not find ways to exploit greater skill levels if those skill levels were available. This is in fact the claim often made by business leaders. If business is serious about its claims that it needs greater skill levels in these domains, then it too might critically examine its linkages with the high schools. Employers currently pay little or no attention to the high school records of prospective employees, and there is thus little incentive for non-college-goers to work hard in high school (Bishop 1989). This lack of linkage stands in sharp contrast to Japan, where employers use high school grades as a main factor in hiring decisions (Rosenbaum and Kariya 1989 and 1991). Some limited experiments along these lines have been tried in recent years in some American cities, but a longer time frame may be necessary before the linkages become widely recognized, and can thus begin to affect student behavior.

Appendix

Student Social Background

Five variables are used here to represent student social background: family socioeconomic status (SES), respondent's gender, and respondent's race (African-American and Asian versus Caucasian) or Hispanic ethnicity. The SES variable is an equally weighted composite of mother's and father's education, father's occupation, family income, and a set of indicators of household possessions. HS&B developed composite measures of each of the background variables, drawing on new information as it was collected through the successive data collection cycles. The codebook variables I use are FUSES, SEXCOMP, and RACE2.

High School Achievement

All of the regressions include controls for four sophomore tests: mathematics, science, reading comprehension, and vocabulary recognition. As a way of controlling for the effects of high school course work in areas other than science and mathematics, I also included senior test scores in reading comprehension and vocabulary recognition in all of the models. The tests were administered to all HS&B respondents in spring 1980 and spring 1982. The test scores used were all simple raw scores (number of items answered correctly).

High School Course Work

Composite measures of high school course-work patterns in *science and mathematics*, developed by the HS&B staff with information collected from students' high school transcripts (SCIPATN and MATHPATN), are described in the text.

A composite measure of *vocational* course work, also from the transcripts and also in the main HS&B public-use file, was used in the analyses of employment outcomes. This variable has four levels defined as "Concentrator"= earned four or more credits in a single vocational education program, or earned four or more credits each in multiple instructional programs (e.g., business, marketing, etc.); "Limited Concentrator" = earned four or more credits in vocational education but less than four in a single instructional program; "Sampler" = earned from a fraction of a credit to four credits in vocational education; and "Nonparticipant"= earned no credits in vocational education. This variable was converted into three dummy variables for the regression analysis.

College Enrollments

The analyses of enrollment *status* used the HS&B biannual status variables for October 1982 through February 1984 (PSESOC82, PSESFE83, PSESOC83, and PSESFE84). Using the coding instructions included in the HS&B codebook, we calculated the October 1984 through February 1986 status variables. The *duration* variables for four-year college enrollment and two-year college enrollment were calculated from the HS&B event-history information; these tell what type of institution the respondent was enrolled in at each month since June 1982.

College Major Field of Study

HS&B collected information on fields of study by having the respondents write the name of their "actual or intended field of study or training" for each institution attended since high school. The answers were then coded into the U.S. Department of Education's *Classification of Instructional Programs* (CIP) categories. From these categories I classified the following fields as Science, Mathematics, or Engineering (SME) fields (CIP code ranges are in parentheses):

> Architecture and Environmental Design (04.0–04.9999)
>
> Computer and Information Sciences (11.0–11.9999)
>
> Engineering (14.0–14.9999)
>
> Engineering and Engineering-Related Technologies (15.0–15.9999)
>
> Life Sciences (26.0–26.9999)
>
> Mathematics (27.0–27.9999)
>
> Physical Sciences (40.0–40.9999)
>
> Science Technologies (41.0–41.9999)

Postsecondary Employment

Employment *status* (full-time, part-time) information for October, 1982, through February, 1984, were taken from the HS&B biannual variables JOBSOC82, JOBSFE83, JOBSOC83, and JOBSFE84. Using the coding instructions in the HS&B codebook, we constructed comparable measures for October, 1984, through February, 1986. The *duration* of full-time employment variable (coded in months) was constructed from the event-history information, which gave the months and average hours per week employed in each job held since June, 1982. The *SEI* (socioeconomic status) of the respondents' jobs was defined by using Stevens and Featherman's (1981) updated Duncan SEI scores for the 1970 U.S. Census Occupational Classification System codes. For respondents who held two or more jobs, the SEI of the most recent full-time employment was used in the analysis.

NOTES

This work is supported by National Science Foundation grant MDR-8550085. Ideas presented in this paper are attributable to the author and do not necessarily reflect the views of the National Science Foundation. Cynthia Nelson provided expert assistance on the file construction tasks. Address correspondence to Thomas B. Hoffer, NORC, 1155 E. 60th St., Chicago, IL 60637.

1. Estimates were obtained from a logistic regression of community college enrollment, graduation, or transfer to four-year college (= 1) versus no enrollment or degree in 1986 (= 0) on the same variables used in the analysis of four-year-college enrollments. The case base included students who were enrolled full- or part-time in a community college during February, 1983 (n = 1,462 with listwise deletion).

2. These results are from regressions of four-year-college duration on parental SES; student gender; race and ethnicity indicators; sophomore year test scores in mathematics, science, reading comprehension, and vocabulary skills; senior year test scores in reading comprehension and vocabulary skills; and four dummy variables for high school course work in science and mathematics. The omitted reference for the course-work dummies was "college-preparatory in both subjects," as described in the text. The sample was restricted to include only full-time students in four-year colleges and universities during February of 1983 (listwise n = 2,851). The model explained 12 percent of the total variance in enrollment durations.

3. The HS&B subsample used in this analysis included 671 respondents who had indicated plans for an SME major during their senior year of high school and who were enrolled in a four-year college in the first year after high school. The dependent variable for the logistic regression was a dichotomous indicator of whether the respondent was

still enrolled in college and planning on an SME major in spring of 1986. Independent variables included in the regression were identical to those used in the college enrollment and duration regressions.

4. These results are from an OLS regression of the SEI ratings for the respondents' most recently held jobs on the background, achievement, and course-work variables used in the employment duration analysis. The sample used here, however, excludes military personnel and thus includes only 2,417 cases. The regression model accounted for 14 percent of the variance in the SEI scores.

5. I also estimated the effects of the background variables with a multinominal logit equation, a method which is better suited for the categorical course-work outcome variable but more complicated to summarize. The results were qualitatively the same as the OLS results, with one important exception. The OLS model showed a very small and marginally significant effect of gender on course work, but the logit model clearly shows that males were much more likely to take the highest levels of science and mathematics. Moreover, this gender effect increases when achievement and college plans are controlled.

6. Parents, in contrast, seem to attach more importance to high school science and mathematics. Although many may not succeed in having their own children take more courses, they overwhelmingly support higher graduation requirements. The LSAY interviewed parents of eleventh graders in 1989 and found that 52 percent believed all students should take four years of science, and 75 percent believed all should take four years of mathematics. Unfortunately, only 25 percent of the parents answered "a lot" when asked how much influence they have on the number of high school science and mathematics courses their own children will complete; 50 percent answered "some," and the remaining 25 percent said "not much."

REFERENCES

Bishop, J. 1989. Why the Apathy in American High Schools? *Educational Researcher* 18(1): 6–10.

Blank, R.K., and P. Engler. 1992. Has Science and Mathematics Education Improved since *A Nation at Risk*? Washington, DC: Council of Chief State School Officers.

Bryk, A.S., V.E. Lee, and P. Holland. 1993. *Catholic Schools and the Common Good.* Cambridge: Harvard University Press.

Coleman, J.S., and T.B. Hoffer. 1987. *Public and Private High Schools: The Impact of Communities.* New York: Basic.

Dietz, J.S. 1993. Higher Education. In *Indicators of Science and Mathematics Education 1992,* ed. L.E. Suter. Washington, DC: National Science Foundation.

Gamoran, A., and M. Berends. 1987. The Effects of Stratification in Secondary Schools: Synthesis of Survey and Ethnographic Research. *Review of Educational Research* 57: 415–436.

Hoffer, T.B., and C.C. Nelson. 1993. High School Effects on Coursework in Science and Mathematics. Paper presented at the annual meeting of the American Educational Research Association, Atlanta, GA.

Hotchkiss, L., and L.E. Dorsten. 1987. Curriculum Effects on Early Post–High School Outcomes. *Research in the Sociology of Education and Socialization* 7: 191–219.

Jencks, C.S., and M.D. Brown. 1975. Effects of High Schools on Their Students. *Harvard Educational Review* 45: 273–324.

Kang, S., and J. Bishop. 1989. Vocational and Academic Education in High School: Complements or Substitutes? *Economics of Education Review* 8: 133–148.

Lee, V.E. 1988. *Identifying Potential Scientists and Engineers: An Analysis of the High School-College Transition.* Washington, DC: Report to the U.S. Office of Technology Assessment.

Maple, S.A., and F.K. Stage. 1991. Influences on the Choice of Math/Science Major by Gender and Ethnicity. *American Educational Research Journal* 28: 37–60.

Miller, J.D., T.B. Hoffer, R.W. Stucher, K.G. Brown, and C.C. Nelson. 1993. *LSAY Codebook: Student, Parent, and Teacher Data for Longitudinal Years One through Six (1987–1993).* DeKalb, IL: Social Science Research Institute, Northern Illinois University.

Mullis, I.V.S., J.A. Dossey, M.A. Foertsch, L.R. Jones, and C.A. Gentile. 1991. *Trends in Academic Progress: Achievement of U.S. Students in Science, Mathematics, Reading, and Writing.* Washington, DC: U.S. Government Printing Office.

National Center for Education Statistics. 1993. *The 1990 High School Transcript Study Tabulations: Comparative Data on Credits Earned and Demographics for 1990, 1987, and 1982 High School Graduates.*

Washington, DC: U.S. Department of Education, Office of Educational Research and Improvement.

Oakes, J., A. Gamoran, and R.N. Page. 1992. Curriculum Differentiation: Opportunities, Outcomes, and Meanings. In *Handbook of Research on Curriculum*, ed. P.W. Jackson, 570–608. New York: Macmillan.

Rivera-Batiz, F.L. 1992. Quantitative Literacy and the Likelihood of Employment among Young Adults in the United States. *The Journal of Human Resources* 27: 313–328.

Rosenbaum, J.E., and T. Kariya. 1989. From High School to Work: Market and Institutional Mechanisms in Japan. *American Journal of Sociology* 94: 1334–1365.

———. 1991. Do School Achievements Affect the Early Jobs of High School Graduates in the United States and Japan? *Sociology of Education* 64: 78–95.

Sebring, P.A. 1987. Consequences of Differential Amounts of High School Coursework: Will the New Graduation Requirements Help? *Educational Evaluation and Policy Analysis* 9.

Sebring, P.A., B. Campbell, M. Glusberg, B. Spencer, and M. Singleton. 1987. *High School and Beyond 1980*. Vol. 1. Washington, DC: National Center for Educational Statistics.

Stevens, G., and D.L. Featherman. 1981. A Revised Socioeconomic Index of Occupational Status. *Social Science Research* 10: 364–395.

U.S. Department of Labor, Secretary's Commission on Achieving Necessary Skills. 1991. *What Work Requires of Schools*. Washington, DC: U.S. Government Printing Office.

Vanfossen, B.E., J.D. Jones, and J.Z. Spade. 1987. Curriculum Tracking and Status Maintenance. *Sociology of Education* 60: 104–212.

Ware, N.C., and V.E. Lee. 1988. Sex Differences in Choice of College Science Majors. *American Educational Research Journal* 25: 593–614.

SECTION FOUR

New Strategies for Solving Educational Problems

The current educational reform movement has generated many new suggestions about how schools can be improved. Two in particular have gained a great deal of public and scholarly attention: professionalism and privatization.

Professionalism, the training and retraining of school professionals, is often seen as one of the major mechanisms for improving schools. Better-trained teachers and administrators would not only enhance the technical core of education but also raise the American public's confidence in school professionals. Developing increased teacher and administrator expertise would help to restore the status of school professionals and ultimately strengthen the bonds between families, communities, and schools. Breakthroughs in cognitive psychology and curriculum development have also placed pressure on educators to become more intellectually sophisticated and innovative.

The socialization process by which teachers and administrators attain their professional roles is of particular interest to the sociological community. The knowledge and beliefs teachers acquire through training and other socializing experiences can profoundly influence their decisions regarding school and classroom policy and curricular issues. How teachers see their role with their students, the type of information they emphasize in class, and the messages they use to create norms and values of behavior are thought to be deeply affected by preservice and in-service training. As transmitters of knowledge and evaluators of student academic performance, teachers are formidable gatekeepers and significant role models for students.

The extent to which teachers can exercise their influence depends greatly on the social context in which they work. Privatization is seen as one way to change the social milieu of schools so that teachers can be more effective in their roles, students can be more interested and cooperative, and parents can be more supportive of school activities. Proponents of privatization hypothesize that if schools were organized around markets and choice, the quality of education would improve.

It is important to underscore the intensity and commitment that both advocates and opponents have brought to discussions of market-oriented solutions to educational problems. Unlike curricular reforms or even mainstreaming students with special needs, plans to allow parents to choose schools, including private schools, for their children have produced a watershed of political activity unparalleled in the educational community (Cookson 1994). Public debates have focused on the effects choice would have on the very definition of education. But the societal conditions which moved privatization and choice into the center stage of educational discourse have received relatively little attention. Innovation has to some extent proceeded without a firm grounding in the sociological realities that shape the educational landscape.

Professionalism, Knowledge, and Power

One of the widely publicized reforms of teacher education programs is Teach for America, an independent, privately funded organization that seeks to recruit recent liberal arts graduates into teaching positions in economically deprived and socially disadvantaged schools. Teach for America's program is considerably shorter than traditional teacher education programs; participants assume roles as full-time teachers within a two-month period. Operating on a set of ideological principles which guide classroom beliefs, understandings, and practices, Teach for America is dramatically different in content and approach from the new professional school collaborative model being developed by the Holmes Group (1990).

Framing the analysis from a political sociology of
knowledge perspective, Thomas Popkewitz discusses how some
of the central ideas associated with modern school reform are
used as guiding principles in Teach for America. By selecting
certain words to convey ideas, Teach for America is framing the
way educational reform can be achieved. "Professionalism,"
"empowerment," and "teacher efficiency" are not merely terms
but terms that invoke socially constructed sets of relations
between teacher education and schooling. Such words are not
value neutral in their purpose or emotionality—they become
powerful in that they regulate styles of reasoning, action, and
self-reflection. Popkewitz contends that the sort of talk about
education that is considered legitimate, the people who are taken
as serious authorities, and what instructional practices are
judged as good provide the cognitive structure that defines
teacher and teaching. Thus, those who speak with authority are
those who speak in certain "codes" that are embedded in social
authority relations.

One of the terms Popkewitz uses to talk about these points
is the expression "at risk," which among Teach for America
participants refers to students who are having behavioral and
academic difficulties in school. Tracing the historical conception
of risk, Popkewitz shows how risk was used by insurance
companies as a social technology for organizing and
reclassifying individuals and events to determine probability of
loss. Over time, the term has developed into a form of reasoning
about schooling and learning, which evokes moral, juridical, and
political technologies. Exploring how "at-riskness" became
defined among educators, Popkewitz argues that by studying
language patterns one can distinguish the specialized language
that teachers use to normalize their occupational activities.
Furthermore, this specialized language helps to establish
teachers' occupational identity, which legitimizes speech and
thoughts about schooling.

Although teachers may have this specialized language, to
policymakers it does not constitute a sacred knowledge which
must be accessed in order to determine future strategies. Public
debate rarely relies exclusively on any one language or body of
scientific evidence. Popkewitz claims that "the history of

schooling is one in which theories are never realized as intended; as theories are put into social practice, there are always unintended, unanticipated, and unwilled consequences."

One of the unanticipated consequences of the continuous growth of big city school systems has been the demise of their strong central bureaucracies, which in the past were thought to exercise considerable authority and nearly undisputable control over school staff, students, and parents. Today, urban school superintendents often find themselves and their boards lack control over crucial policy matters, while court rulings, state laws, and federal mandates play a more significant role in defining the lives of students and teachers in schools. Fragmentary politics with multiple centers of power, both within and outside the public school system, now attempt to determine the functions of public education. In his chapter, Kenneth Wong describes the structure of fragmentary politics in big-city school districts.

Thirty years ago, big-city school superintendents and their boards were able to function relatively autonomously. Wong argues that isolated centralized decision making occurred less frequently than commonly believed and now is practically nonexistent. Urban school policy is often dominated by the powerful influences of major corporate actors (e.g., unions and state agencies), organized interests (e.g., racial and ethnic groups, and business, political, and public interest groups), and individual clients, who have become very effective in fostering institutional change through mechanisms of "choice and voice" (Hirschman 1971).

Using a historical database of the nation's largest central city school systems from the 1950s to the late 1980s, Wong shows how school politics have become increasingly fragmented through choice and because of loss of control to other corporate actors and multiple centers of power located in and out of the system. Confronted with the politics of voice and choice, the big-city school district's central office has seen both its quasi-monopoly over public education and its bureaucratic control eroded. Looking at the future, Wong maintains that big-city schools are not likely to return to bureaucratic dominance.

In discussing competitors to big city school systems, Wong examines both competition from suburban public school districts and families choosing nonpublic and public schools in central cities. While others cite concerns over school quality as a primary explanation for middle-class outmigration, Wong suggests that other factors may also be contributing to declines in White populations in big city systems. Those White populations who live in central cities have increasingly relied on nonpublic schools. Choice of public schools in urban areas has become an increasingly contested issue, with differences between chosen schools and neighborhood schools contributing to the politics of fragmentation. Although school choice has been controversial in some areas, Wong maintains that it has been quite effective in alleviating problems that confront central city schools.

Wong maintains that the administrative staffs of current school systems are ill-equipped to meet the demands of politically fragmented school systems where multiple actors make constant demands on the system. If school systems are to remain at all viable, administrators will have to exercise a new form of leadership that can move the system toward school improvement without fighting to recentralize control.

In their chapter, James Cibulka, Hanne Mawhinney, and Jerald Paquette address the issue of the knowledge and skills school leaders need to successfully manage the politically fragmented school systems in which they work. Focusing on the administrative theories used to define conceptions of leadership and implementation of change, Cibulka et al. argue that the field of educational administration is in intellectual disarray. Much of the training for educational administrators tends to ignore recent discoveries: new research on the role which interests and values play in educational policy, a greater understanding of teaching and learning, and a more developed sense of the constraints on making real changes in schooling.

What has changed most in educational administrator training is that there are more extensive opportunities for field-based experiences. Properly framed, more exposure to the problems of changing schools could potentially provide rich experiences, but without components that require critical reflection and problem-based methods, such field-based training is unlikely to improve matters. If educational administrative programs are going to be more effective, they must present more comprehensive models of organizational theory and leadership that are grounded in specific technologies of teaching and learning, must address how to achieve greater equality of achievement outcomes, and must learn how configurations of power can be rearranged so that there is greater parity of power for those who are currently least influential in the schooling system.

Cibulka, Mawhinney, and Paquette's chapter is a critique of the rational conceptions of school administration which have formed the intellectual core of administrative training for the last three decades. To examine the limits of "rational administration," the authors organize their discussion around several topics: educational goals and decision-making processes, social forces, the technical core of instruction, and administrative leadership. Using recent research, the authors review problems of rational educational leadership.

One basic assumption about reforming schools through rational management techniques has been that educational systems are goal-attaining organizations. It is apparent to sociologists, however, that decision making in education is rarely predictable; current research confirms that policymakers generally pursue a multitude of conflicting goals. These goals are often ambiguous and change with changing conditions. Research has led some to think of education policy as being determined through pluralist forms of political decision making. This does not offer much practical guidance to school officials about how to make education more productive. Yet models which take a more unitary approach end up offering no more than a legitimization of the status quo. The challenge is to develop a paradigm that incorporates a pluralist perspective which still makes large diverse school systems manageable.

In his essay, Wong suggests that most administrators and teachers are ill-equipped to deal with the demands of their work environment. From the perspective of both Popkewitz and Cibulka et al., the solution to the problem of preparation will not come from changing the basic organizational structure of training programs but rather from enhancing the scope and substance of what teachers and administrators need to know to be effective in a dynamic complex social system. As Wong points out, however, both choice and issues of privatization are likely to remain at the forefront of the educational reform movement. This position is underscored in Ellen Goldring and Anna Shaw Sullivan's chapter, which examines the growing privatization of services in public schools, and in Peter Cookson and Barbara Schneider's discussion of the reasons why public support for private schools has remained a central topic of public debate.

Why Privatization of Public Schooling?

The widening range of services available through private sources has become increasingly intriguing to politicians, business leaders, and policy analysts. Nearly every educational service is being scrutinized as a profitable venue for private for-profit entities. Goldring and Sullivan argue that the increased interest in privatization is grounded in public distrust of government-run enterprises—school systems are a prime example of poor performance, waste, and inefficiency. Making schools more like businesses would likely improve student test scores and reduce personnel and administrative costs. Casting a wider net than addressing privatization in traditional terms of vouchers or tuition tax credits, the authors also examine other school-related services being run by for-profit businesses and explain why this type of delivery may become the preference of many more school systems.

Beginning their analysis historically, Goldring and Sullivan contend that the type of educational services allocated to the private sector has dealt in the past with mainly "intermediate goods," such as food service, transportation, and supplies. Now privatization is being advocated for "final goods," such as private practice teachers and school management. They give special attention to the formation of private for-profit schools and new cooperative partnerships being forged between public schools and businesses. This trend, the authors note, has the support of private foundations which have made substantial contributions to fund many school-business partnerships.

Goldring and Sullivan maintain that the privatization movement is based on both philosophical and economic factors. Citing the work of Gormley (1991), they point out that not all citizens have equal access to services; privatization is seen as a mechanism to ensure superior service in education regardless of the individual's economic circumstances. Advocates of privatization assume that market incentives will lead to better-quality programs and thus to higher student academic performance. Reviewing the disadvantages as well as the benefits of privatization of services, the authors discuss some of the problems created by corporate funding, primarily in the health care industry. The pulls of a market economy can potentially create situations with undesirable social consequences. Schools that receive gifts from businesses may find themselves obligated to those businesses, perhaps at the expense of the children.

Although pointing out possible disadvantages of privatization, Goldring and Sullivan envision a better future where school systems will rely more upon private services. To prepare for such a future, the authors identify some cautions for schools to consider before moving into privatization, including establishing realistic criteria for short- and long-term success, gaining the support of those individuals likely to be affected by the change in services, and examining the legal and ethical implications of such social experiments. The authors conclude by emphasizing that the most important question about privatization is whether or not it will lead to higher student performance. In the last chapter, Cookson and Schneider take up many of the same issues but in the context of school choice.

Never before has an educational reform evoked the kind of antagonism, acrimonious debate, and unassailable commitment that school choice has. Cookson and Schneider examine the elements in American society and culture that give credibility to the belief that increased competition is likely to improve education. Placing the debate about school choice in a political and educational context, Cookson and Schneider argue that behind the rhetoric concerning school improvement the "choice movement" is a struggle about values, identity, rights, and freedom. School choice is more than a question of privatization;

it is about school and society and the balance of rights among individuals, families, and communities.

Cookson and Schneider speculate that the school choice movement began in the 1980s as a consequence of several interrelated social issues. During the 1980s the middle class continued to withdraw its support from public institutions. Having abandoned big cities, the middle class had no legitimate voice in influencing public policy as it related to urban education. The clients of urban schools—many recent immigrants from South America, Eastern Europe, and the Caribbean—pressured local and state governments to improve their schools. Religious groups were repelled by the lack of basic values and the "radical humanism" that was often said to characterize public schools. In general, there was a distrust of government and a feeling that the marketplace was a better provider of human services than the state.

Because the movement for school choice developed from the individual interests of many, it is not surprising that choice prototypes cover a multitude of student assignment plans that vary significantly in their underlying assumptions and operational procedures. In their chapter, Cookson and Schneider describe some of the major organizational features of various school choice plans including intra- and interdistrict choice, intra- and intersectional choice, controlled choice, charter schools, and vouchers. They also examine the effectiveness of school choice, drawing on the evidence from two types of studies: those that compare the cultures of choice and nonchoice schools, and those studies that look at more proximate outcomes such as student achievement, aspirations, and high school graduation rates. Although there has been considerable controversy over the magnitude of the differences between the test scores of public and private schools using large-scale national longitudinal data bases, the differences between public and private school educational aspirations and high school graduation rates show more robust positive effects from private schools. The authors conclude that these effects can be traced to organizational differences between different types of private and public schools.

In their summary, Cookson and Schneider hypothesize that it is unlikely that the structure of public education will become so radically transformed that privatization becomes the dominant form of schooling. They believe, however, that the issue of school choice will remain an integral part of school policy debates. The manner in which school leaders and other concerned groups engage in productive dialogue around issues of choice will become a major challenge to forging consensus. As Popkewitz argues, the language of school reform is not value free—terms such as "school choice" have embedded meanings. The implementation of any school reform, whether it is school choice or national standards, depends on sustaining a constructive dialogue among multiple actors and interested groups. These parties can develop the social trust needed for the improvement and transformation of public education only if there is an honest recognition of differences and a willingness to put the welfare of children first.

15

Policy, Knowledge, and Power: Some Issues for the Study of Educational Reform

Thomas S. Popkewitz

> The tale of Teach For America, an idea hatched in a senior thesis and brought to life in a single year by a young woman just out of college, captivated many Americans with its overtones of idealism, pluck and entrepreneurship. (*New York Times*, July 6, 1992, p. 1)

During the last decade, there has been a resurgence of interest in the problem of educational change. One of the more publicized of these reform programs is Teach For America.[1] Conceived in an honor's thesis at Princeton University, its founder sought to create an alternative teacher education program that brought liberal arts graduates into those areas of teaching where there is the shortest supply—within the poverty of America's central cities and rural areas. The program drew its first five hundred recruits from the finest private and public universities in the nation. After an eight-week training period at the University of Southern California, the students were placed as full-time teachers in rural Georgia and North Carolina, Baton Rouge and New Orleans, Louisiana, New York City, and the metropolitan areas of Los Angeles.

Teach For America had a great fascination for the American media, business and philanthropic communities and government. Teach For America (TFA) claimed legitimacy within the wider American discourse about privatization and choice as a practice of policy. Multiple articles and editorials in the *New York Times*, reports on the network news programs, a PBS special about the first year, as well as reports in *Newsweek, US News and World Report*, and *Forbes* magazine provided a somewhat romanticized gloss to the efforts of TFA as its program formed and the first summer institute began.

The media attention captured multiple streams of a general American social and political ideology of the 1980s— individual initiative and private enterprise can find solutions to the grave social issues of our time. Teach For America represented the utilitarian spirit of American enterprise: it was a "can do" attitude toward social problems. The program captured a general belief that social progress would occur through greater business and individual initiatives for finding solutions to social and economic problems. The program was to change how teachers were recruited and trained by circumventing established universities and the feeling of the entrenched ineptness of governmental bureaucracy, a legacy of the Reagan Era rhetoric about pulling government back from involvement in social affairs.

The program also epitomized an idealism of youth that the country had not witnessed since the early days of the Kennedy era and the creation of the Peace Corps. Five hundred youths who had grown up with privilege committed themselves to two years working with those who were often denied any privilege.

In this essay, the program of Teach For America provides a vehicle to explore more substantive issues of school reform. I focus on Teach For America as an emergent element in the structuring of power within the school arena.[2] As a primary institution for establishing purpose and will in society, schooling ties polity, culture, economy, and the modern state to the cognitive and motivating patterns of the individual.[3] The practices of Teach For America, from this perspective, are defined as part of the social relations of schooling, and its teacher education practices can be considered to be a strategic site in which social regulation and power relations are realized.

In this chapter, then, I explore three themes.

First, educational reform embraces issues of social production and of state regulation. While seemingly outside of state policy initiatives, Teach For America needs to be understood in the context of a state strategy to produce social amelioration. I use the concept of state to refer to more than governmental policy or legislation. It is used as a theoretical category to explore how the governmental strategies applied to construct reform, the categories and distinctions used to describe the phenomena of schooling, and the social contexts of teacher education and schooling interact as governing practices that produce social values and power relations.

Second, the distinctions, categories, and differences embodied in educational practices are not neutral descriptive terms; the amalgamation of performances and discursive practices are viewed as a particular, historically formed knowledge that inscribes certain ways of acting, feeling, talking, and seeing the world. We can understand the modes of presentation and styles of reasoning that relate Teach For America to schooling as constructing its subject—what is a teacher, a student, learning—and tie discourse to issues of power. To study school reform is to interpret how the agendas and categories discipline and construct our senses of choice and possibility.

The third theme involves a central issue about the purpose of school research and evaluation. I argue that when research and evaluation are related to policy questions they can help to illuminate the tensions, contradictions, and ambiguities that underlie the realization of educational reform, rather than be restricted simply to explorations about what policy is most efficient or useful. Although it may seem obvious, reforms respond to perceived issues and problems that, at face value, are not clearly defined and do not have linear outcomes. Evaluation, in its most productive sense, considers the tensions, struggles, and ambiguities that emerge in the formation and development of social practices and social goals.

State Policy, Policing, and Research and Evaluation

Since evaluations are typically commissioned by those with
power—albeit in the name of a common good—it is important to
consider the power relations which are embedded in social
research. Recent scholarship in social theory and methodology
highlights the ways in which the categories, distinctions, and
differences produced in social research are related to state
classification systems (see, e.g., Bourdieu 1990; Clifford 1988).
When the state is treated as a central actor, evaluation is typically
constructed within a particular kind of social field where
disciplinary interests of research are related to moral-political
issues.

Historically, there is a convergence of the formation of the
modern welfare state, with reform as its main project, and the
development of social and educational sciences (Popkewitz
1991). The great historical projects of twentieth century Western
capitalist societies were the constructions of the national welfare
state, technical material progress, and egalitarian individualism
(Kauppi and Sulkunen 1992). The belief in the human design and
correction of institutions took its form as the modern welfare
state emerged to ensure the workings of social, cultural, and
economic practices. The modern state constructed tactics by
which to plan and organize institutions in order to give direction
to social, political, and economic arenas. While previous eras
maintained beliefs in progress, notions that scientific reasoning
can identify the roots of social problems and produce strategies
for social betterment became firmly entrenched by the late
nineteenth century.

The nascent social sciences capitalized on the reform
tendencies of the welfare state, claiming that they could provide
the needed state expertise in a secular knowledge that described
the working of social institutions (Silva and Slaughter 1984;
Haskell 1984). What was previously seen as the work of divine
provenance became problems of human rationality.

Reform as a rational policy of intervention, then, is an
integral part of state regulation, monitoring, and steering. In this
sense, policy and policing are epistemologically related. Policing,
in its French and German origin, refers to the specific techniques

by which government, in the framework of the state, enables
individuals to be useful to society (Foucault 1988, p. 154). Older
forms of state planning involved political arithmetic or statistics,
in which the state collected demographic and other data to steer
reform policies during the formation of the modern state.

Research on policy and the evaluation of it have particular
characteristics as the state, schooling, and educational research
are related in the United States. School research and evaluation
emerged forcefully as a professional field in response to
increased U.S. governmental involvement in the educational
sector following World War II.[4] The particular forms that
evaluation took in the United States involved particular social
constellations.[5] The "accepted" forms in which questions were
asked about research, the conceptual schemes offered, and the
methods of data interpretation were part of the processes of
governance as the concepts of policing and policy interact. For
example, American research and evaluation maintained a tacit
assumption that expert knowledge can be put into the service of
the democratic ideal, an assumption that historically emerges at
the turn of the century as the American social sciences offered
their services to the broadening welfare state institutions of the
Progressive Era (see, e.g., Ross 1991; Silva and Slaughter 1984;
Popkewitz 1984).

A partial cataloging of research and evaluation questions
about school reform illustrates how certain groupings within
disciplinary fields interact with state categories of change and
reform.[6] One can examine the shifts in research problems during
the 1970s and 1980s as related to shifts in how the government
organized reform efforts. Research and development models of
the 1970s were replaced by more subtle, variegated models of
school change, including the acceptance of qualitative research
approaches to understand the local variations and
"impediments" to change. The use of qualitative models
provided ways to symbolically resolve the perceived breakdown
of certain American liberal values of social solidarity and
political democracy (Popkewitz 1981). The style of thought
associated with qualitative studies emphasized particular
notions of community, pluralism, and the efficiency of the
individual in social relations. At the same time, the portrayals of

social relations provided more intrusive strategies for social management. The relation between state and research communities, however, is not necessarily direct, but interactive. At a different and more fundamental layer, disciplinary knowledge entails responses to, and anticipations of, historical shifts to newly emergent visions of public interest. The use of budget programming and systems analysis in 1960–1970 in educational research was related to changes in social and political sensitivities as business accounting methods and military organizational approaches became appropriate for assessing and directing social institutions (Popkewitz et al. 1982, chap. 2). Constructivist psychologies in contemporary American education can be viewed as responses to changes in the work and sociocultural environments (see Popkewitz 1991; Noble 1989).

The spiraling of social scientific knowledge in and out of social affairs, what Giddens (1990) calls a "double hermeneutics," can be illustrated in recent reform practices. Economic theories of market have been introduced as a core value in social policy since the 1980s and have been inscribed in the entrepreneurial appeal of Teach For America. The making of markets as a policy goal is embodied in the University of Chicago school of economics articulation of a "Rational Choice" theory (see, e.g., Wolfe 1989). Put simply, it is assumed that people act rationally to maximize their self-interest. The role of government is to provide a mechanism that enables this self-interest to be maximized. If social policy can create pure markets, then the mechanism of individual choice can act as a regulating force that produces the greatest good. Notions of markets and choice in this conception of social policy replace the state and civil society in structuring moral obligations. Social scientific knowledge, in this context, is an integral part of the universe of social life: rational choice theory is built on state discourses while reentering the universe of state actions that it was to describe or account for.[7]

But the movement between systems of ideas and social and political movements maintains tensions and contradictions. Levi-Strauss's structuralism in the 1960s, for example, linked European notions of history with non-European notions of myths in a manner that made possible the construction of more democratic traditions (Robbins 1993). The structural discourse critiqued Eurocentrism by considering myths central to the organization of culture and society. The combination was to level the playing field of scholarly discourse at a time of decolonialization. The focusing on myths and history was to enable the self-representation of newly independent people. Yet by the 1980s, structuralism was seen as a conservative posture and was under attack among leftist intellectuals. Without celebrating the current discourses of postmodernism and neopragmatism in the United States, they can also be read as providing sentiments and dispositions that respond to and anticipate the changing historical patterns in which representations are produced.

My reason for starting with the relation of state practices and social science is neither to demean the effort of state actions nor to pose an anarchistic view of the social processes of schooling. Rather, my intention is to remind the reader that educational reforms, research, and evaluation are not merely a strategy that objectively describes the outcomes of educational practices. Politically sanctioned discourses organize perception and experience, producing governing systems of order; appropriations and exclusion are inscribed into the ongoing practices of schooling (for a general discussion of this issue, see Foucault 1979). The formation of school research and evaluation are historically state policy strategies to police social arenas; the notion of policing can be seen as a nineteenth-century conception of regulating and directing through the categories and distinctions that are applied to determine competence and salvation. Further, the policing functions of social science are most crucial with regard to the United States, where there is a pervasive historical amnesia concerning the school as a state institution. Sociopolitical values are hidden in research paradigms of education (see Popkewitz 1984, 1991). The problematic of reform must be understood as positioned within educational fields and their processes of social production, regulation, and the creation of human capabilities.

A premise of this chapter, therefore, is that neither the discursive practices of science nor the institutional patterns of school reform can be taken for granted. Reform policies, research, and evaluation entail scrutinizing the way the knowledge of schooling inscribes particular and historically formed patterns of governing of which the state is a part. My specific concern in this chapter is how reform practices organize and give value to certain types of social relations and, at the same time, produce regulation through the styles of reasoning and the classification schemes that are applied. By making the categories of research and evaluation part of the questioning involved in inquiry, I seek to introduce a self-reflexivity about the relation of knowledge, research communities, and power (see Bourdieu 1989 for a discussion of the problems posed by the social field of intellectuals).

Cognitive Structures and Constructing the Subject: Discourse and Power

I begin this section with what might seem a straightforward and unproblematic statement: schooling is an imposition of particular patterns of knowledge that are to be valued, and as such, schooling is a form of social regulation. My concern with regulation, however, is not meant to impute evil or to suggest some transcendent good through overcoming control. Rather, from the vast array of possibilities about what and how to learn, there is a selection of certain styles of reasoning to guide, organize, and evaluate the ongoing events of schooling. What is learned in school is not only about what to do and information to know. Learning about spelling, science, mathematics, or geography is also a learning of dispositions, awarenesses, and sensitivities toward the world which is being described. Much of the "hidden curriculum" literature and the sociology of school knowledge of the past two decades in the United States have indicated this dimension of schooling, although here I wish to extend and revise that understanding through a discussion of the relation of knowledge and power.

My emphasis on the knowledge of schooling, teaching, and teacher education is to link our ways of talking and reasoning—the forms by which we "tell the truth" about ourselves and others—with issues of regulation. First, we can consider schooling as having no objects to decipher or people to understand until languages are constructed to make those objects distinguishable and able to be scrutinized. Schooling is possible through the emergence of systems of ideas and institutional forms which enable its objects to be understood, thought about, and acted upon. Our ways of reasoning are systems of inclusion and exclusion as particular categories, differentiations, and distinctions are applied to the routines and performances of schooling. To think about and look at the child and the teacher entails applying systems of ideas that locate the child and teacher in a time-space continuum in which categories construct what is a learner, an achiever, and how persons are to be understood in the organized institutional spaces of classes and grades.

Second, systems of ideas become systems of regulation, as a result of the manner in which the systems of ideas construct objects through the rules and standards for thinking, speaking, talking, and feeling about those objects. This relation of knowledge and regulation becomes centrally important as schooling entails the selection, organization, and evaluation of knowledge.[8]

The idea of regulation may produce a strong reaction as it hits an American sensitivity—derived from the Enlightenment— which places a high value on individual initiative and on human purpose giving direction to social affairs. My concern with regulation, however, should not be read as disregarding these Enlightenment sensitivities. Reason and rationality are central to social efforts to improve our human conditions. But at the same time, my strategy of inquiry is to make reason and rationality the problem to be understood; that is, it is to explore the particular systems of ideas and rules of reasoning that are embedded in the practices of schools. We cannot assume reason and rationality are a unified and universal system by which we can talk about what is true and false; we must rather see them as historically contingent within systems of relations whose effects produce power.

Power as Sovereignty and Power as Effects

The problem of regulation can be pursued by considering the concept of power which underlies it. Two traditions can be considered within school studies. One is the sovereignty notion of power which emphasizes the role of unequal relations among actors. The second is a productive notion of power, that is, the deployment of power to produce the will to know. In one sense, the two notions of power are complementary: the former considers larger historical structures through which daily life is constructed; the latter focuses on the micropolitics in which subjectivities are constructed. But in certain important senses, the different views of power entail different epistemologies for constructing the objects of inquiry, the subject and agent of social change, and of the role of expert knowledge in the politics of everyday life.

In the sociology of school knowledge, the issue of power has generally been approached as a structural issue. A central premise is that society entails certain groups, social interests, and forces that have formed historically and whose practices dominate and repress other groups. A central political problem of research is to identify (and alter) the unequal relations between the rulers and the ruled. Power is something that people can own, and that ownership can be redistributed among groups in social arenas; hence the use of the term "sovereignty." If we can identify the origins of power—the sovereign groups that own power—it is reasoned that inequities can be challenged and the relation between the rulers and the ruled can be reformed.

The sovereignty notion of power makes the concern of inquiry to be identifying what groups are favored through decision-making processes and how the decisions distribute values to produce a context of domination and subordination. For example, a sovereignty notion of power is embodied in current educational literature that sees social interests inscribed in reform reports and government policies that argue for a "back to basics" curriculum. The consequence of the reforms, it is argued, is to re-produce gender, racial, and class distinctions in society (Carlson 1992a). My earlier use of state as an actor who contracts research reflects a structural view, although, as I discuss it later, my concern is to historicize the meaning of the state through examining the arena in which patterns of governing change (see Popkewitz and Pereyra 1993).

The sovereignty notion of power produces certain strategies for understanding the politics of schooling. Class is a central concept for describing the production of social inequities. Theorists have drawn their major insights from a cultural Marxism that emerged in Europe and the United States. Scholarship in the last decade has related concepts of gender and race to class to describe the complex nexus in which sovereignty is exercised. Structural concepts of agency, resistance, and contestation have been used to posit ways in which the hegemony of the rulers are challenged and change can be sought (see Weis and Fine 1993).

The sovereignty notion of power is paramount in the arguments about the "conservative restoration" in American politics during the 1980s. It is asserted that particular conservative groups of people assert their interests in schools through a variety of mechanisms, including defining cultural values and organizing the terrain in which political debate occurs (Shor 1986). The conservative restoration entailed the exercise of power by teaching a particular moral-religious view about gender through sex education or through advancing particular economic interests through the science and technology curriculum.

Postmodern and feminist literatures in the United States have challenged the sovereignty notion of power. This literature maintains the general political commitments for social change found in earlier critical studies of education but challenges the epistemological and political assumptions in the sovereignty model of power. (For distinctions within this literature concerning its political and nonpolitical foci, see Rosenau 1992.) It is argued that the sovereignty notion of power fails on a number of counts. Where the sovereignty notion of power posits unified historical processes and structures, change entails "an amalgamation of institutional and discursive practices that function as a collective assembly of disparate parts on a single surface" (Crary 1990, p. 6). If one examines the conservative restoration thesis, for example, one finds that the changes reported in economy, culture, and politics began well before the election of Reagan in the United States and entailed a reorganization of knowledge and practices that occurred in an uneven pattern, within multiple institutions, and over a period that was longer than the Reagan-Bush era (see Kuttner 1991; Lekachman 1982). What is reported as structural historical change in the conservative restoration is nonhistorical and nonrelational.

At a different level, the sovereignty notion of power fails to recognize theoretically the significance of the productive elements of power. While one can posit a generalized condition of capitalism as a background to the organization of power, for example, this does not provide an adequate theoretical grounding for understanding how the capillaries of power work in modern societies. For one thing, there is no one model of capitalism, nor is its history one of a single, unified development. At a different level, the historical contingencies and multiple boundaries in which race, class, and gender are constructed have no single origin or universal characteristics but are constructed in relational fields that are fluid and multidimensional. The rules, standards, and styles of reasoning by which we define the subjects—race, class, and gender—are not essential categories of logic but historically constructed categories that are part of and expressive in a weaving of systems of discursive, social, technological, and institutional relations.

Similarly, we can understand the state as a contingent notion about how power is deployed rather than as a structural category about how power represses. The former provides a strategy to understand the shifting terrains in which power is produced through changing constellations of actors and knowledge (see Popkewitz 1993). As Bourdieu (1984, 1989) argues, power involves a complex relation between positions in a social field and the dispositions and sensitivities (habitus) that construct and constitute those relations. Notions of resistance that stand in opposition to some unified structural patterns are repositioned through a focus on the changing patterns of relationship in which power is produced.[9]

As we shift our attention to power as a productive element, our attention moves from the controlling actors to the systems of ideas that normalize particular patterns. Inscribed in social relations are ordering principles that give coherence to the ways the individual and the community are to be made healthy and productive. The categories, distinctions, and differentiations employed define the important, the real, and the actor.

Postmodern theorizing entails a "linguistic turn," directing attention to the ways in which patterns of thought and reason are practices that construct the objects of the world and do not merely represent those objects. Michel Foucault's concern with how the modern subject is supervised and disciplined through social science discourses and feminist theories about how gender relations construct our perceptions, dispositions, and awarenesses are two such examples.[10] In each instance, the foci of power are to be found in the ways subjectivity is formed through disciplining practices. The rules, standards, and styles of reasoning by which individuals speak, think, and act in producing their everyday world are the subject of research (see Foucault 1988; also Dreyfus and Rabinow 1983; Noujain 1987; Rajchman 1985).[11]

But the concern is not only with reason but with how reason is constructed in the organization of institutions for self-discipline and to regularize the perceptions and experiences which determine individual action. The governing systems of order, appropriation, and exclusion that shape, fashion, and construct subjectivities are historicized through examining multiple layers of daily life.

Strategically, this approach to the study of power enables us to focus on the effects of power as the ways that individuals construct boundaries for themselves, define categories of good and bad, and envision possibilities. The concern of Marx with the productive characteristics of labor is inverted into the productive characteristics of knowledge itself (Dumm 1987). The effects of power are to be found in the production of desire and in the dispositions and sensitivities of individuals.

The focus on the effects of power provides a way, for example, to examine the effects of a teacher education program, focusing on how the teacher is constructed as a subject, that is, how the student teachers are "made" into thinking, acting persons within particular social relations and historically defined power relations. The regulation of schooling can be understood as an effect of the performances and discourses in schooling. Thought and reason are ordered through the discursive practices applied. Alongside and embedded in the cognitive styles associated with teaching and learning are sets of emotions, attitudes as well as expectations and demands.[12] Here, we can relate issues of knowledge and power. While never total, the effects of institutional practices (performances and discourses) can discipline the hopes, desires, and expectations that are inscribed in teacher education programs and classroom practices.

The shift to the effects of power does not disregard structural elements of power, such as macro changes in economy and culture. My earlier discussions of the state and privatization provide instances where it is important to be sensitive to historical structural relations when interpreting current practices. The styles of thought and perception exist in and are productive of particular institutions and institutional processes.[13] The focus on knowledge, however, is a strategy to recognize a shifting terrain of modernity in which power circulates, in which structural origins become less central (and defensible as a unified concept) for understanding how power is deployed. Later in the chapter I will consider critiques of the concept of power as effects which range from charges of relativism to a determinism because of the "loss of structural actors" who bear power. I will say here only that most of these critiques are more a social strategy of intellectuals to authorize their speech than a sustained analysis of the relation of epistemology and political practices.

Schooling and the Deployment of Power

We can think of the changes in the conditions of what we call the modern school as involving changes that were not merely changes in physical arrangements and institutional patterns. Changes occurred in the cognitive styles and patterns of reasoning by which individuals made sense of and acted in their social worlds (see, e.g., Berger et al. 1973; Foucault 1980).[14] Since at least the Protestant Reformation, schools have been institutions that relate the state, civil, and religious authorities, and moral discipline (Durkheim 1977; Luke 1989; St. Maurice 1993). Mass schooling was an invention of modernity in which there is a central public institution for bringing up children (the moral and cognitive development of children). Schooling redefined upbringing and socialization by forming new patterns of institutional relations that are outside the home and work (see, e.g., Lundgren 1983; Hamilton 1989; Englund 1991).

By the beginning of the twentieth century, the U.S. schools provided an institutional form to resolve the problems of social administration and upbringing produced through multiple transformations: industrialization, urbanization, immigration, and new political organizations associated with democracies. Mass schooling encapsulated moral tenets that joined the emerging tasks associated with the modern welfare state and a universalized civil religion associated with Protestantism.[15] The new patterns of schooling were to discipline and regulate individuals as productive members of a society.

Curriculum was (and is) an imposition of knowledge of the self and the world that would give order and individual discipline. The struggles for American curriculum changes that Kliebard (1987) so artfully explores were part of a visioning/re-visioning of social commitment and of individual service and faith. Pedagogy was a practice to discipline, manage, and create social capabilities for the individual, whether that management is called a pedagogy of child development, learning, social engineering, or social reconstruction. The knowledge of the world and its forms for understanding are sophisticated methodologies by which individuals are supposed to locate themselves within their world and to affect that world. The imposition was not of brute force but in the symbolic systems by which people are supposed to interpret, organize, and act in the world.

Pedagogy, within this context, can be understood as the deployment of power. The linguistic distinctions in school discourses are not merely categories for interpretation.

Pedagogical practices normalize social relations through their strategies for constructing and organizing the distinctions of schooling. Further, the particular forms given to social and educational theory entail visions and re-visions that are implicated in larger patterns of social change, such as those expressed through the modern state's tactics of reform.

In light of this, we can think of pedagogical practices as inscribing particular styles of reasoning that normalize social relations. Within current reform are words drawn from generalized discourses about educational reform—among them, "professionalism," "the reflective teacher," "multiculturalism," site-based management, and "empowerment." The terms, however, are not free-floating words that have fixed meanings over time; instead, they are located in a particular nexus of hierarchy and value expressing and aiming for a particular set of relations between teacher education and schooling.

In this sense, we can view reform efforts as incorporating modes of presentation and styles of reasoning that not only tell stories about schooling, teachers, and teacher education but which construct its subject through the distinctions that order and define the objects of schooling itself. The words are part of a system of rules of schooling that govern what sort of talk about education is possible, who are to be taken as serious talkers, and how desire, want, and cognition are to be constructed. (I again draw on Foucault 1980; Martin, Gutman, and Hutton 1988; and Foucault's Afterword in Dreyfus and Rabinow 1983.) Further, the words of reform are positioned within strategies that organize what questions are appropriate to ask: defining what the phenomena of practice are, and shaping how experience is to be managed and ordered as objects of inquiry—what is to be looked at and how that looking is to conceive of the things of the world.

Normalization and the Technologies of the School Gaze

The question that must occupy us, then, is what are the modes of presentation and styles of reasoning that underlie reforms? How does the ensemble of methods and strategies in a reform program construct systems of regulation that relate different social groupings and, importantly in the United States, people of color and poverty to schooling? I will pursue these questions through exploring the processes of normalization and the technologies that produce a school *gaze*. The norms that I am concerned with are more than those which give value and legitimacy to school processes. "Normalization" refers to how the objects of teaching are constructed so as to define and order the world of schooling and its subjects—that is, the norms that answer the questions about what is a teacher, a child, and learning. The production of the gaze enables us to consider the historical combination of methods and strategies that establish the world of objects to be known and organized. The processes of normalization and the production of a gaze involve issues of power as they constitute differential boundaries by which thought, action, and self-reflection are constructed in schooling.

At one level, norms are an integral part of the organization for teaching and teacher education. There are norms about children's development and achievement which have become part of the common sense of measuring school success. Norms also permeate the interactions of teachers and students, as indicated by ethnographic studies of classrooms (Page 1991; McNeil 1986).

We can also think of the normalizations in schooling as related to the ways in which the subject and subjectivities are constructed. By this I mean that certain ways of watching, seeing, and constructing images and visions are historically inscribed in the patterns of schooling. The importance of the normalization is that the images and visions are not neutral but inscribe sociopolitical distinctions. For example, the images of children in progressive pedagogical thought at the turn of the century drew on particular urban, middle-class and Protestant notions of childhood and society (Franklin 1987; Feinberg 1993; Kliebard 1987; St. Maurice 1993).

The process of normalization entails a reformulation of social distinctions and images into pedagogical theories about the child or school subjects. The particular social characterizations are made to seem universal and applicable to all—for example, the rhetorical forms and performances of schooling make it seem that all children go to a common school, that all children are given the same goals, and all are treated equally. At the same time, particular but seemingly universal characteristics and attributes are reinscribed into principles for judging the competence, achievement, and salvation of the person. A consequence is to obscure the sociopolitical distinctions.

The significance of the school gaze is it inscribes particular images and visions of the world as the legitimate "eye" of cognition. The norms imposed on the objects of the world are seen as natural and as part of an internal logic of what is looked at, not as historical inventions linked to processes of production and consumption. Bourdieu's (1984) study of the social constructions of taste, for example, focused on the "explicit and implicit schemas of perception and appreciation" that favored a particular gaze toward certain cultural objects as art, excluding others, while also providing norms for legitimating those "not yet consecrated—such as, at one time, primitive art, or nowadays, popular photographs or kitsch—and natural objects"[16] (p. 3). Bourdieu considers postimpressionist painting an example of the production of a gaze. It "asserts the primary modes of representation over the object of representation." The "seeing" demands that attention be paid to the modes of representation over the object that is represented, a categorical demand to "see" form which previous art had demanded only conditionally.

The production of a gaze occurs as a weaving of different discursive practices rather than through neat, linear processes. I speak of the intersection or scaffolding of ideas as forming a reasoning or logic to teaching. I use the word *logic* not to describe any formal system of linguistic relations but to direct attention to the ways we reason about and give coherence to the world and our self and as part of socially formed and historically bound practices. The production of a gaze is the production of a logic of practice by which one is to "see," feel, talk, and act toward the world.

The production of a gaze can be explored empirically through the practices of teacher preparation in Teach For

America.[17] The teacher preparation embodied a particular scaffolding of different systems of ideas whose effect was to normalize what is healthy, productive, and abnormal about the person in schooling. The child who sat at a desk in a certain way, who spoke in a certain manner, and who moved and acted in certain ways became the unspoken norm from which principles of personal competence and future achievement as a teacher were drawn.

The normality, however, was constructed through certain binary relations. Distinctions were inscribed about the normal child who succeeded in schooling and the child of color who was in opposition to the normalities. The child of color became the "other": one who lacked the motivational attributes, behavioral characteristics, and self-esteem to achieve.

The constructions of the binary oppositions did not occur through explicit discussions of criteria of success but through the particular categories and distinctions that posit oppositions between the normal child and children of color. The norms of inclusion and exclusion positioned children of color through talk about learning, classroom management, multiculturalism, and teaching particular disciplinary content, such as mathematics and science. The teachers, for example, described the pupils in their schools as children who had no discipline at home, whose parents did not read to their children, whose behavioral proclivities lacked the proper norms for them to learn properly—each contributing to a child who could not succeed in school.

The principles of order and disorder—the signification of what is normal and not within the normal—acted positively to organize what was the permissible and nonpermissible in schooling. The negatives of the child were recast as positives, such as children who learn through different "learning styles" or the child who has "potential." The notions of "learning styles" and "potential" formed a *doublet*. The doublet took negative social and cultural characteristics and remade them into positive elements from which to construct teaching.

The negative characteristics of a child were drawn from perceived universal principles about socioeconomic conditions but were brought back into the teaching context through an individualization that explained personal success and failure.

The principles of ordering stood in relation to other discourses of didactics and psychology. The child of color was an oppositional category—the "other"—who is spoken about in a psychological discourse about the lack of motivation and self-esteem.

The scaffolding of different norms that come together in schooling are not logical formulations of practices but a collective assemblage of disparate parts on a single social surface. Learning to teach in Teach For America, for example, embodied a multiple of "common senses" and "lived experiences" through which the American school is constructed. Further, the processes of normalization were an ensemble of technologies through which the objects of the world of schooling—children of various social, ethnic, and racial backgrounds—were differentiated and were to be known. The styles of reasoning were strategies of how to grasp and classify the possibilities of the things of the world—what is a child, a teacher, learning, progress, and so on.

My example from the study of Teach For America helps us understand how an overlapping and collective ensemble of practices inscribe a gaze that is disciplining and regulatory. That is, while there are physical objects in schooling, there are particular technologies to identify, classify, watch, and assess the phenomena and subjects of schooling. Biological and physical objects are reconstructed into cultural objects whose descriptions envision, image and revision the identities of children and teaching. The systems of ordering and classifying made the child into the other—a category that silently stood in opposition to what was deemed normal, healthy, and good. The practices of teaching, of learning, and of assessing progress become a way of thinking, seeing, feeling, and talking about the world and one's self.

The Historical Embeddedness of Teachers' Speech

The scaffolding on which normality and the school gaze are constructed can be elaborated through interpreting an interview of a Teach For America first-year teacher of Spanish. The teacher came from private, elite American universities and viewed the teaching experience as an opportunity to "give something back" to society for the privileges that she enjoyed. The teacher established a distinction between the school curriculum designed around textbooks, testing, and school standards, and the social background of the children who came to school. The teacher thought that the school enforced educational requirements—such as learning a foreign language such as Spanish—that do not meet the most pressing needs of the children.

> Students need English. . . . Students . . . need to be able to
> write simple sentences in English. . . . Students . . . need to
> be able to carry on a conversation without saying "ain't,"
> or "got none," or any of that. . . . Not every one of my
> students needs to know Spanish, but every one of my
> students needs better English skills. Desperately.

The discourse established certain canons of teaching—"to write simple sentences," the "need" of better English skills. These skills stood as logical and universal foundations that needed to be learned. The canons stood as monuments to an unchanging culture rather than as historically contingent and cultural arbitraries.

We can view the statement about the problem of teaching as a way in which the teacher resolves multiple demands and pressures of teaching. There is a recognition of a distinction between the expectations of the school and the experiences of the home. There is a recognition of the importance of schooling in redressing the cycles of poverty and discrimination through the manner in which instruction is organized. Yet there is also a recognition of the institutional dysfunctionality of schooling itself.

The conversation about "better English skills" encompasses structural relations in which the linguistic distinctions of appropriate language are constrained by the power relations. The linguistic distinctions sustain and give "the imposition of middle class, white English its air of naturalness" (Bourdieu and Wacquant 1992, p. 143). The bracketing of power through the efforts to reach down to those who are dominated by the constrained use of language is a strategy of power that Bourdieu calls "condescension."

The teacher placed a tension between school requirements and student "needs" in the context of the urban African-American community:

> I didn't realize the background my kids came from. . . . I didn't realize that my background was where I had a safe place where I could go home and study as much as I wanted. Whereas these kids, they're lucky if they can sleep at home, let alone do anything else. Even watch TV. All they do when they're home is have their parents yell at them and have their parents blow smoke in their face from their cigarettes and things like that. They can't study. And the school is just so disruptive. . . . There's so much pressure not to learn; there's so much pressure not to do what's expected of you that the best that most of these kids can hope for is to get through here without being permanently scarred.

We can read the first-year teacher's sentiments historically as not only those of a corps member but also as part of a historically embedded discourse that constructs the object of schooling through a particular gaze. Certain norms of the good student stand as an unarticulated but essentially ordered totality from which to understand diversity in schooling as the other of urban and rural children of color. Collectively, these others are the children of the school who "can't study," are "just so disruptive," and who are "pressured not to learn."

Populational Reasoning and Social Regulations

The construction of the gaze also embodied a populational reasoning. Along with the distinctions of the normal and abnormal there was a particular grouping of children through probability statistics that focused on particular discrete attributes as defining the person. The child was visioned as a uniform member of a population whose particular characteristics were defined as deviant: children from broken homes, crack babies, children with low self-esteem. The child embodied fragments of populations whose characteristics resulted in failure in school. Inscribed in "can't study," "just so disruptive," and "pressured not to learn" are probability statements that classify specific groupings of people through a doublet of pathology and the potential of remediation.

Populational reasoning also becomes a way of managing through the construction of doublets: a double relationship in which the negative of the other is cast as a positive that reason and rationality can guide. The negative moral characteristics of the other are the absence of reason and normality, but they also reconstitute the child of color as a logical domain to be studied and managed through pedagogical practices.

The populational reasoning no longer correlates "individuality" with some abstract norms or a responsible subject. Instead, individuality is related to other members of a population. The notion of population fixes on particular attributes of social groupings by decentering the totalities of relations among people, things, and events.

The populational reasoning dominated the construction of the child in schools. It inscribed certain doublets of thought which made the negative norms into positive characteristics of intelligence, potential, and high self-esteem. Teachers talked about children's "potential" in the Teach For America schools as a way to see children who should receive more positive instructional efforts. "Potential," however, reclassified the negatives of the home and community into signals of what the child missed but innately had and which proper instruction would bring to the surface. The pathology of the community became a positivity in which the behaviors, proper characteristics, and language of the child as other were to be rationally ordered and revisioned in the child through "relevant" teaching.

The reasoning about instruction carries the negative-positive doublet into the organization of teaching. Proper instruction and the meanings given to "discipline" and classroom reforms embodied a series of assumptions and presuppositions about the child, the teacher, and differential criteria about knowledge. Teacher in-service and teacher education, for example, were concerned with the learning of hands-on activities for children. Children were to be differentiated as having different learning styles. The instructional practices, however, took the negative-positive

norms as guiding how teaching was to be looked upon—hands-
on teaching made sense because the children learn differently
and need "practical," nonabstract experiences. The children of
color were classified as optimally taught by using prescribed
procedures and strategies, who learn best when psychologically
managed, and who are positioned as deviant and pathological in
relation to the norms that are privileged in schooling.

The populational reasoning and the child as "Other"
framed the curriculum practices of multiculturalism.
Multiculturalism was a central theme in American reform and
teacher education.[18] Multiculturalism is an educational phrase to
direct attention to unequal representations in the school
curriculum. Its major focus relates to the sovereignty notion of
power, seeking to redefine the relation among sets of actors who
ruled and were ruled. In the context of Teach For America, the
consequence of multiculturalism was less in the fact that people
of color became present and recognized within the school
curriculum. The multiculturalism existed within particular forms
of reasoning and value in which the logic to its practice was
constructed. Instruction about difference and diversity was
positioned within the doublet of the negative-positive. The silent
norms of practice continually located the child of color as the
"Other" to be remediated and regulated.

Thus we can see how a scaffolding of different practices
ascribe normality and abnormality. A certain binary reasoning is
coupled with a population ordering of children and statistical
reasoning which assigns group attributes as discrete but
essential elements of the child. The doublets of "potential,"
intelligence, and didactics revision the negativities as norms of
reasoning by which to organize teaching and supervise children.

The visioning-revisioning of people as populations is an
important element of the reasoning through which teachers and
children are constructed. Historically, populational reasoning
has been important for government programs that directed
attention to those who have suffered economically, socially, and
educationally. But to speak of populations is part of the double
hermeneutic mentioned earlier. It is a way of reasoning that
emerged with the state reform tactics concerned with
administering social welfare (Castel 1991; Hacking 1991; Smith

1990). Individuals and events are organized and reclassified in a manner that separates a particular event from its immediate historical situation. Applying the calculus of probability, the state can define social groupings and interests by reference to statistical aggregates of populations. It is part of the disciplinary talk about how children learn, about school achievement, as well as about the sociopsychological attributes believed to cause failures in school.

The notion of population produces a new form of individuality, one in which the person is defined normatively in relation to statistical aggregates from which specific techniques can be ascribed to the person and the growth or development monitored and supervised. The normalization is more than that of the consumption that is argued in Marxist theories:

> But normalization proceeds through techniques of governing the allowance and disallowance of activities beyond consumption as well. Francois Ewald, among others, has noted some of the elements by which populations are constituted in relation to risk and insurance. These are categories of norms which allow and disallow not only consumption, but activities that permit withdrawal from the special interventions of discipline by directly manipulating populations at large. Through the establishment of norms, people become parts of systems of equivalence that substitute, for an equality based upon particularity, an inequality based upon comparison to a standard which is based upon an average. No single person is ever average, and hence no one is ever completely normal. One's place in such a system is determined by the attributes one shares with others. Each attribute places a dimension of one's life on a specific continuum. Personhood itself is fragmented, and elements of it become signs of one's place in reference to a norm. (Dumm 1993, p. 189)

Again, my exploration of the learning of teaching in Teach For America is to understand the larger issues of the deployment of power. The various discursive practices that I describe are a part of the commonplace and doxa of American schools and its reforms. While paying attention to sovereign notions of power that include representations of peoples who have been historically excluded in American curriculum, the scaffolding of rules and standards that construct those reforms have remained to a large extent unscrutinized. A result, if this analysis is correct, is that the effects of power remain through the strategies of reform that are applied.

"At Risk": A Political Technology of Populational Reasoning

Particular systems of ideas appear in the construction of schooling that can help us understand how words are historically implicated in wider sets of practices that deploy power. If we take a commonsense term of schooling, "at risk," it is typically used to symbolize the failure of certain types of children to succeed academically or emotionally in school. The term is part of the double hermeneutics of schooling: it is part of the language of the state that gives focus to school reforms. It is also a professional term associated with programmatic attempts and research about instruction and children thought of as in special need.

Here we need to consider the term "at risk" as part of a system of ideas by which intention and purpose is formed. Rather than asking about the intent of agents—the state, school administrators, or teachers—we can place the terms of schooling as a problem of historical sensitivity which inquires into the sets of social circumstances and sociopolitical assumptions that are inscribed in the manner of usage. In focusing on risk for example, recent scholarship has located the changing meaning of the concept of risk as it is formed through the financing of insurance for commerce and as it is reinscribed into social welfare policies as a state tactic to organize for the welfare of citizens (see, e.g., Ewald 1991; Defert 1991; Castel 1991).

Risk helps to historicize the relation of language, institutions, and the deployment of power. Risk is a schema of rationality, embedded in a set of rules of language and classification that developed historically in the nineteenth century as commerce expanded. Risk is a way to institute a calculus of probabilities into social affairs. The invented schema is a way to organize and reclassify individuals and events so that they can be insured. Particular events are to be treated as part of a population and thereby managed for insurance purposes. Risk is to discipline commercial events.

It is best to speak of risk as a social technology that involves moral, juridical, and political dimensions. Risk is a moral technology as it is used to master time and discipline the future. Risk is a technique to administer justice through its conceptions of reparation and indemnification of damages, conceptions very different from the legal system itself, which is tied to particular people and events. Risk is also a political technology through its mechanisms that define social groupings and interests by reference to statistical aggregates of populations.

Risk becomes a technology of power as its classification schema moves from commerce into the social welfare tasks of the state. The use of the classificatory schema as a technology of power is particularly acute in schooling. "At risk" is a now common term about children who do not succeed in school or who are seen as potentially not succeeding—it is used to act in the present on the basis of future projections. When applied to people, the technologies of risk are totalizing. That is, it is an organizing schema of management and rationality that can be applied in any kind of institution. It refers to no specific reality and can be applied to anyone. This totalizing quality is continually found in pedagogical discussions: all children are potentially seen as "at risk" readers or dropouts.

With social policies and practices developing around populations at risk, there is a relocation of a system of thought and technologies from one classification system (insurance and commerce) into another social field (schooling). When introduced into professional practices, the technologies of risk introduce issues of government as populations are identified and placed under scrutiny through scientific practices associated with the calculus of probabilities. Risk produces strategies by which the particular attributes of populations can be more efficiently observed and supervised. At the same time, the practices (discursive and nondiscursive) associated with risk become available as part of the legally sanctioned system of relevance by which identity is to be constructed.

The illustration of risk as a multifaceted technology enables us to consider issues of the deployment of power more closely. First, it helps us to understand how the past becomes inscribed in the present. Second, it directs attention to the multiple effects of power in social institutions. Third, the inscribing of the technologies of risk into the social fabric did not occur in a sequential ordering of time—risk is not a developmental concept that evolved in a natural way. It is a concept that occurs through the intersection of multiple institutions in which the outcome could not be foretold. It is for this reason that I have spoken about the construction of the teacher as a scaffolding, to give attention to the amalgamations of practices that order schooling which are not tied to a serial notion of events.

The Alchemy of School Subjects

Previously I posed some questions: What are the modes of presentation and styles of reasoning that underlie reforms? How does this ensemble of methods and strategies in a reform program construct systems of regulation that relate urban and rural schools to people of color? The previous sections focused on the constructions of the child and teacher through a scaffolding that included binary reasoning about the other, the negative-positive doublets, and the probability treatment of children as members of populations. The representation of school subjects introduces a different set of ordering principles into the construction of the regulatory patterns.

We can view the forming of school subjects as entailing an "alchemy." The alchemy is a passage from the social spaces of disciplines (such as the sciences of physics) into the social space of schooling—that is, there is a movement from the production of knowledge in the culture of physics to a school curriculum knowledge called physics (see, e.g., Bourdieu 1990). This movement presupposes a change in mental ordering of knowledge as physics becomes a problem of school learning, but that change is not acknowledged.

In effect, school subjects are "imaginary subjects" and "imaginary practices" (Bernstein 1992). The forms given to school subjects have no basis in the world outside of the school. What is brought into school is not what scientists, mathematicians, writers, or artists do; rather the formal knowledge of schooling reformulates disciplinary knowledge to conform to expectations related to the school timetable, to conceptions of childhood, as well as to conventions of teaching which cast such knowledge into a school curriculum.

The social space of school is occupied as a world of social psychology, psychology, and group management. Science is teaching "cooperative small groups," or "whole-group instruction," or being "caring," "developing self-esteem," "being able to apply the concepts in real-life situations." If we take the conversations within Teach For America, learning mathematics is not how mathematicians see or work in the world; it is a children's world and a teaching world that is expressed as conversations about "helping others learn," "identifying a concept," "evaluating students' assignments," or "assessing students' progress," and "managing the classroom."

The distinctions within science or mathematics conform to rules of schooling that have little to do with the original disciplinary fields. The net result is something different from what is borrowed. School ceremonies, ritual performances, and discourses accepted school distinctions through the labels and assignment of categories of knowledge. Sitting in a science laboratory with all its paraphernalia, writing mathematical formulas on a blackboard, or reading textbooks labeled as physics assigned rhetorically a relation between disciplinary knowledge and school knowledge. The school textbooks make symbolic links between what is done in schools and disciplinary fields outside of schooling—textbooks tell about the concepts and information of science, mathematics, and social studies. In a high school mathematics classroom, the teacher told the children that they should act as "mathematicians," talked to them about the importance of learning, and then had them prepare for an examination by doing textbook exercises.

The example of learning mathematics cannot be considered merely a bad example or a misconstrual of mathematics in schools. Particular sets of rules are applied which function to reformulate and reconceptualize the knowledge of mathematics. These rules make knowledge into logic. By this I mean that the concepts, generalizations, and principles of school subjects are treated as logical and analytical things to be learned. These rules are not only of mathematics instruction but of the theories of school subjects that are historically inscribed in the organization of curriculum (see, e.g., Popkewitz 1987). The precoding of the world is important because the complexities and contingencies of daily life are revisioned as logical, hierarchical, and nontemporal.

Privileging school subjects as "things of logic" introduces a particular style of reasoning into teaching. A view of school knowledge is related to the medieval rules of God in which there is an assumption that school subjects embody a universe of well-ordered concepts waiting for proper investigation and expression. History, physics, mathematics, literature, and even the arts are taken as having logical disciplinary structures which function as foundations from which learning is to occur. Concepts divide, order, and represent phenomena which are to be instilled in the person who wishes to examine phenomena.

Knowledge as things of logic is sanctified by the common senses of schooling. Achievement is measured by how well subject content is learned. Such learning is sanctified through psychologies that differentiate cognitive learning from affective learning. The problem of didactics is the internalization of the appropriate definitions (learning of concepts) or making the given knowledge "relevant." Problem-solving is learning logical strategies and procedures for acquiring knowledge, such as having different hands-on manipulative materials to learn a mathematical principle or practicing interview techniques to learn social science methods. The formulated skills of problem solving are analytically described rather than viewed as socially constructed.

The rules of school subjects can be contrasted to practices of science, where disciplinary knowledge is directly related to the methods of inquiry—knowledge emerges from methods and is not independent. Further, the invention and innovation on the cutting edges of science entail strategies to make the known unknown and to raise questions about what is taken for granted;

just the opposite of school curriculum which privileges the logical and stable properties of knowledge.

Why is the making of school subjects into things of logic significant? The significance is more than in Friere's discussion of banking education, where students are conceived as empty vessels to be filled with the things of knowledge. The logical, analytical formulation of the world removes the social moorings from curriculum knowledge. Embedded in school subjects are unarticulated principles about the world as rational, change as harmonious and linear, and the individual as an ahistorical agent of progress (see, e.g., Popkewitz 1984). These assumptions in the form of school knowledge shape and fashion the questions constructed about social betterment and personal competence in the world. The socio-ethical and political implications of the way the organization of knowledge relates to the organization of the self in the world are lost.

The significance of the alchemy is also at a second layer. The ordering principles of curriculum teach teachers as well as students about who they are and what they are in their worlds— we might call this learning part of identity formation. The selection of knowledge entails not only information but rules and standards that guide individuals in effecting their knowledge of the world. Not only are grades achieved and certification given but schooling posits strategies and technologies for the ways teachers and students should reason about the world at large and themselves in that world. As well as learning concepts and information about science, social studies, and mathematics, there are problem-solving methods to inquire, organize, and understand what the world and the self are like. Learning information in schooling is also learning a manner and the manners of knowing, understanding, and interpreting. Learning mathematics or science is a dual strategy of not only learning content but normalizing a conception of the knower. Curriculum selection inscribes certain truths that secure and enhance the well-being of social life through what are accepted as problems, questions, and responses in classroom practices.

In this sense, we can view the imaginary subjects as positing a moral order through the rules of order, relations, and identity. The moral order is both prior to and a condition for the transmission of competence in the practices of teaching.

It is here that we can link the alchemy of school subjects to the normalizing technologies of the school gaze. The inscribing of populational reasoning and the binary relations which construct the child as the "Other" maintain epistemological forms that are homologous to those of the alchemy. The school subjects construct a moral order in which there is no social mooring. At the same time, the separation of content from method—of cognition from affect—enables the production of a gaze whose problem of schooling is the internalization of dispositions and sensitivities. The world of the child is seen as being guided only by the internal logics of learning, individual motivation, and personal learning styles. A world of hands-on experience reformulates and normalizes the objects of schooling into experience that exists as natural and as ahistorical.

The different forms of reasoning are woven together to become a logic of practice. When the different reasonings are placed in relation to each other within a field of social production, the resulting rules construct what is legitimate, plausible, and relevant in schooling. But the reasonableness is productive; it is deployed as the rules for constructing alternatives. Educational reform is the construction of systems of regulation and discipline but at the same time is a search for alternative modes of production.

Tensions in the Relation of the State and Teacher Education: A Problematic for Evaluation

This chapter began with an assertion that the study of policy involves more than studying the instrumental effects of school practices. I argued that the realization of policy involves multiple considerations of the effects of power, that is, the deployment of power through the constructions of distinctions, differentiations, and categories by which the object and subjects of schooling are constructed. Teach For America was an exemplar in this analysis, focusing on how particular systems of ideas position the child of color as the "Other" who is in need of remediation and supervision. I examined the deployment of power as a scaffolding entailing an amalgamation of different systems of ideas. The effect was to make children of color different from what is normal and acceptable.

In focusing on the processes of normalization and the gaze, I realize that it is a "nervous" theory; that is, there are intertextual networks, tensions, and slippages that disrupt the laws and discrepancies of the ways in which the world is constructed (see, e.g., Saper 1991). The gaze is not totalizing. My focus on the scaffolding that produces the gaze, however, was in order to understand dominating images and visions in U.S. practices. I wanted to examine how seemingly disparate systems of rules form homologous relations in the production of power. To see the various practices of schooling as existing within a relational field of power is intellectual and political—to make visible the forms by which truth is told is a strategy to disrupt them.

My discussion in this chapter can be read at a different methodological level, one that concerns a self-reflexivity about how the object of research is constructed.[19] The focus on power as how reason and rationality are socially constructed entails a shift in focus from the intent of people to the structuring of reason and knowledge itself. Intent and purpose are seen as embedded in the forms by which language structures what it is possible to say and feel, and, at the same time, makes it difficult to seriously consider other possibilities. The structuring of reason and truth becomes a focus to understand how purpose and intent are inscribed into social practices.[20]

The historicizing of structural categories (and notions of agency and resistance) is sometimes referred to as the "decentering" of the subject. I earlier signaled this shift as the relation between power as sovereignty and power as effects. The movement from the subject in historical practices to discursive practices is to understand how, at different historical times, people are made into subjects; that is, what are the social and institutional relations of power, for example, that authorize gendered concepts and make the body into a sexual object (Riley 1988). In a significant sense, the subject (the teacher, the child, school knowledge) are seen as both historical products and the site of certain practices, technologies, and institutional procedures of subjectification.

This movement to reasoning as inscribing power and regulation has drawn certain criticisms. In part, the decentering of the subject is perceived as posing a nonhumanistic world without politics and power (see, e.g., Clarke 1991; Carlson 1992b). The lack of humanism is seen through the evidence that there are no actors, no voice, and no one who can produce change in the organization of power and regulation. The lack of politics is discerned in the refusal to specify the actors who are good and bad; those who are ruled and rule.

My response to these criticisms has been told, in part, earlier. There are times when structural analyses are appropriate, although I think that a search for the final cause—the ruler of the ruled—is a chimera. Repression, domination, and power are historically contingent and emergent from multiple trajectories that have no single origin. As for the lack of politics, most of the criticism fails to recognize how issues of politics and power have been refocused through making the problem of the deployment of power and the construction of regulation central to the politics of social change. One needs only to examine feminist postmodern literature to understand how this shift in the politics of intellectual work relates to the formation of a specific social movement.

Other critics—those who complain of the loss of humanity—fail to recognize how their particular construction of humanism is itself historically constructed and part of the power relations that the critics leave unquestioned and unexamined. The search for the voice of the individual, "resistances," and contradictions are themselves inscriptions that presuppose a subject that needs to be historically reconstructed rather than assumed (I discuss this in Popkewitz 1991, chap. 8). The subject (and the issues of voice and resistance) are made into what is questionable and of "understanding the continual contestation as the categories of the subject embody the conditions in which power operates" (Butler 1992, p. 7). Further, the criticisms fail to recognize that defining what is lacking is itself a rhetorical style that establishes the criteria of the "lookers" as what is lacking rather than systematically examining the rules that are privileged in the complaints. I do not mean to imply that this privileging is avoidable, but rather that the critics tend not to recognize the different epistemological distinctions and rules or to recognize the historically shifting terrain of the political.

The irony of the "linguistic turn" and its decentering of social theory and philosophy is that its strategy reasserts a humanism. Its concern is with the "myriad ways the productive, cognitive and desiring capacities of the human subject" (Crary 1990, p. 3) are constructed. This strategy reinserts the human subject into history. Power is seen at any historical moment as "not some deep structure, economic base, or world view but rather the functioning of a collective assembly of disparate parts" that provides potential space for alternative acts and alternative intentions to be articulated (Crary 1990, p. 6).

The decentering of the subject is placing the subject back into history through understanding how reason and truth about the self has been constructed and disciplined. It enables a way of interpreting how forms of reasoning and rationality are deployments of power.

Finally, this chapter can be read as a challenge to certain modernist notions in research and evaluation about policy. This modernism is the assumption that rationality can identify the paths to salvation—the efficient school, the effective teacher, the authentic teaching. Each of these phrases assumes a world of certainty and of logically organized practices. Yet when we look at the practices of policymaking and research, we see that both are built on the dilemmas, tensions, and historically contingent efforts to improve our world. Research about schooling, at its best, can help to inform the debates about school practices by recognizing the multiple forms and contingent boundaries in which practice occurs. It can contribute to policymaking not by looking for moral, political, and cultural certitude, not by saying what should be done to help "others," but by understanding how the subjects of reform are formed, the politics of those relations, and how the standards for "telling the truth" misrecognize, in Bourdieu's sense, the power relations that underlie current efforts to transform schools.

NOTES

1. The book is tentatively entitled, The School Gaze and the Construction of Teaching: Teach For America in Urban and Rural Education. This discussion is drawn primarily from the first chapter. Prior to the first summer institute of Teach For America, I was asked to do an outside evaluation of the program. In this chapter I focus on the conceptual issues entailed in that program evaluation, described in a subsequent book. In the evaluation I sought to understand the practices and processes of the program as socialization. The notion of socialization in the evaluation, however, was different from the conventional one. Rather than considering how students adopt or adapt to existing practices or how they negotiate meanings, we took a view of socialization as related to a political sociology of knowledge (see Popkewitz 1991).

2. The project involved different people at different times. Their collective interaction with the data and the problematic of the evaluation helped me as I thought about this chapter. They are Sigurjon Mydral, Wesley Martin, Julia Craddle, Monica Kirchweger, and Sheewa Cho.

3. This is contrary to the argument of Berger (1967), who separates primary and secondary institutions of socialization, defining school as the latter.

4. I recognize that assessment procedures tied to science, particularly those of psychometry, were created with the development of mass schooling in the United States. But the use of reform and evaluation as a state strategy was institutionalized after World War II. There was a mobilization of educational research communities in European countries as well during the period after the 1960s. This mobilization currently involves relating school reform to teacher education and universities in many countries. See, e.g., Popkewitz 1993.

5. The relation of changing education theory to changes in the German education system and social changes in the nineteenth and twentieth century has been argued persuasively by Drewek (1993); also see Schreiwer and Keiner 1992.

6. The impulse for reform is so powerful in the educational field that it is practically impossible to distinguish research from evaluation. The name of the current research "game" is to privilege what is thought to lead to improved school practice. Over twenty nationally funded research centers exist as part of the current effort toward school reform. A task of many of these centers is to search for exemplary schools and

teacher education programs, and to explicate their characteristics. The questionable assumption is that qualities of good schooling can be identified and exported to other schools as one moves physical goods.

7. It is the interaction of "policy," theories of science, and reform practices that is inscribed in Teach For America. The idea that social institutions can be organized around markets and choice is part of the political horizon in which Teach For America was realized. Its premise of individual and private enterprise intervening in educational processes was previously reserved for state practices. One of the senior Teach For America staff members said of the staff and corps members, "We are all Reagan's children." We can understand that comment as recognizing a particular historical embedding of TFA: how social and political discourses about personal commitments and the realization of social goals are inscribed in the organization and practices of those who joined TFA.

8. Knowledge and regulation were doubly important in Teach For America, whose focus is on constructing the teacher of the poor and of children of color.

9. The concept of resistance entails more of a political hope of opposition to some unified structure of oppression than of a sustained analysis of the nuances and historical contingencies of power (see, e.g., Hargraves 1982; Butler 1992).

10. One can also read Kuhn's (1970) history of scientific revolution as arguing the ways in which cognition implicates feelings, wants, and desires. See his discussion of change in science and resistance to cognitive challenges. Kuhn, however, maintains a philosophical idealist interpretation of science.

11. These theoretical concerns can be found in feminist theory, although here they are focused upon a particular social arena. See Nicholson 1986; Weedon 1987; Barrett and Phillips 1992.

12. While discussions of learning and socialization in the United States tend to structure out considerations of upbringing, philosophically, at least, Marxist pedagogical discussions understood the relation of cognition and affect with political moral responsibility (see, e.g., Mikhailov 1990; Ilyenkov 1977).

13. Berger et al. (1973) discuss the formation of modern consciousness as related to the formation of bureaucracy and industrial work. If we had to take issue with Berger et al., it would be with the underdeveloped notion of power contained in their analysis.

14. This modern "self" has been described as fragmented, taxonomical, and without history except that which celebrates the present as

progress (see, e.g., Berger, Berger, and Kellner 1973.) Identity became multifaceted but related to abstract attributes from which specific elements can be nurtured through proper administration of present environments. Time was redefined into universal, rational segments that were no longer embedded in particular places. A train timetable embodies the new consciousness: emptying of time and space in which people were to locate themselves. The dimensions of consciousness can be understood as embedded in the sequencing and hierarchy of a school lesson plan which imposes a unidimensional space emptied of time except that of sequence. Space was neutralized as it was separated from the place where a person lived (also see Giddens 1990).

15. For a discussion of the secularization of religion into civics, see Bellah 1968.

16. I use Bourdieu here to emphasize the sociological dimensions of the gaze rather than its psychological and psychoanalytical funtions.

17. The construction of the "constructions" emerges from the analysis of interviews and observations of classrooms.

18. For efforts to challenge these doublets, see Sleeter and Grant 1994; Ladson-Billings and Tate 1993; and McCarthy 1992.

19. To foresee the obvious, I do not see the discursive practices of this chapter as free from issues of power. I take Bourdieu's and Foucault's admonishment that an epistemological vigilance is necessary (Foucault's manner of saying this is that all discourses are potentially dangerous).

20. See Koselleck 1991; Tally 1990.

REFERENCES

Barrett, M., and A. Phillips. 1992. *Destablizing Theory. Contemporary Feminist Debates*. Stanford: Stanford University Press.

Bellah, R. 1968. Civil Religion in America. In *Religion in America*, ed. W. McLoughlin and R. Bellah, 3–23. Boston: Houghton Mifflin.

Berger, P.L., and T. Luchmann. 1967. *The Social Construction of Reality: A Treatise in the Sociology of Knowledge*. Garden City, NY: Doubleday.

Berger, P., B. Berger, and H. Kellner. 1973. *The Homeless Mind: Modernization and Consciousness*. New York: Vintage.

Bernstein, B. 1992. *The Structuring of Pedagogical Discourse: Class, Codes, and Control*. Vol. 4. New York: Routledge.

Bourdieu, P. 1984. *Distinction: A Social Critique of the Judgment of Taste*, R. Nice, trans. Cambridge: Harvard University Press.

———. 1989. *Homo Academicus*. Stanford: Stanford University Press.

———. 1990. *The Logic of Practice*. Stanford: Stanford University Press.

———. 1991. *Language and Symbolic Power*, ed. J. Thompson. Cambridge: Harvard University Press.

Bourdieu, P., and L. Wacquant. 1992. *An Invitation to Reflexive Sociology*. Chicago: University of Chicago Press.

Butler, J. 1992. Contingent Foundations: Feminism and the Question of "Postmodernism." In *Feminists Theorize the Political*, ed. J. Butler and J. Scott, 3–21. New York: Routledge.

Carlson, D. 1992a. *Teachers and Crisis: Urban School Reform and Teachers' Work Culture*. New York: Routledge.

———. 1992b. Review Essay: Postmodernism and Educational Reform. *Educational Policy* 6(4): 444–456.

Castel, R. 1991. From Dangerousness to Risk. In *The Foucault Effect, Studies in Governmentality*, ed. G. Burchell, C. Gordon, and P. Miller, 281–298. Chicago: University of Chicago Press.

Clarke, J. 1991. *New Times and Old Enemies: Essays on Cultural Studies and America*. London: Harper Collins.

Clifford, J. 1988. *The Predicament of Culture: Twentieth-Century Ethnography, Literature, and Art*. Cambridge: Harvard University Press.

Crary, J. 1990. *Techniques of the Observer: On Vision and Modernity in the Nineteenth Century*. Cambridge: MIT Press.

Defert, D. 1991. "Popular Life" and Insurance Technology. In *The Foucault Effect: Studies in Governmentality*, ed. G. Burchell, C. Gordon, and P. Miller, 211–234. Chicago: University of Chicago Press.

Drewek, P. 1993. Social History of the German Educational System, Nineteenth-Twentieth Century. Paper given at the International Conference, The State, Civil Society and Education, Madison, WI.

Dreyfus, H., and P. Rabinow. 1983. *Michel Foucault: Beyond Structuralism and Hermeneutics*. Chicago: University of Chicago Press.

Dumm, R. 1993. The New Enclosures: Racism in the Normalized Community. In *Reading Rodney King: Reading Urban Uprising*, ed. R. Gooding-Williams, 178–195. New York: Routledge.

Dumm, T.L. 1987. *Democracy and Punishment: Disciplinary Origins of the United States*. Madison: University of Wisconsin Press.

Durkheim, E. [1938] 1977. *The Evolution of Educational Thought: Lectures on the Formation and Development of Secondary Education in France*. P. Collins, trans. London: Routledge and Kegan Paul.

Englund, T. 1991. Rethinking Curriculum History—Towards a Theoretical Reorientation. Paper presented at the annual meeting of the American Education Research Association, Symposium on Curriculum History. Chicago, April 1991.

Ewald, F. 1991. Insurance and Risk. In *The Foucault Effect: Studies in Governmentality*, ed. G. Burchell, C. Gordon, and P. Miller, 197–210. Chicago: University of Chicago Press.

Feinberg, W. 1988. The Political Technology of Individuals. In *Technologies of the Self: A Seminar with Michel Foucault*, ed. L. Martin, H. Gutman, and P. Huttan, 16–49. Amherst: University of Massachusetts Press.

———. 1993. Dewey and Democracy at the Dawn of the Twenty-first Century. *Educational Theory* 43(2): 195–216.

Foucault, M. 1979. Governmentality. *Ideology and Consciousness* 6: 5–22.

———. 1980. *Power/Knowledge: Selected Interviews and Other Writings by Michel Foucault, 1972–1977*, ed. C. Gordon. New York: Pantheon.

Franklin, B. 1987. The First Crusade for Learning Disabilities: The Movement for the Education of Backward Children. In *The Formation of School Subjects: The Struggle for Creating an American Institution*, ed. T.S. Popkewitz, 190–209. New York: Falmer.

Giddens, A. 1990. *The Consequences of Modernity*. Stanford: Stanford University Press.

Hacking, I. 1991. How Should We Do the History of Statistics? In *The Foucault Effect: Studies in Governmentality*, ed. G. Burchell, C. Gordon, and P. Miller, 181–196. Chicago: University of Chicago Press.

Hamilton, D. 1989. *Towards a Theory of Schooling*. London: Falmer.

Hargreaves, A. 1982. Resistance and Relative Autonomy Theories: Problems of Distortion and Incoherence in Recent Marxist Analyses of Education. *British Journal of Sociology of Education* 3(2): 107–125.

Haskell, T. 1984. Professionalism versus Capitalism: R.H. Tawney, Emile Durkheim, and C.S. Pierce on the Disinterestedness of Professional Communities. In *The Authority of Experts: Studies in History and Theory*, ed. T. Haskell, 180–225. Bloomington: Indiana University Press.

Ilyenkov, E. 1977. *Dialectical Logic: Essays on Its History and Theory*. H. Creghton, trans. Moscow: Progress.

Kauppi, N., and P. Sulkunen. 1992. *Vanguards of Modernity: Society, Intellectuals, and the University*. Juvaskyla, Finland: University of Juvaskyla, Research Unit for Contemporary Culture.

Kliebard, Herbert M. 1987. *Struggle for the American Curriculum*. New York: Routledge and Kegan Paul.

Koselleck, R. 1991. *Futures Past: On the Semantics of Historical Time*. K. Tribe, trans. Cambridge: MIT Press.

Kuhn, T. 1970. *The Structure of Scientific Revolutions*. 2nd ed. Chicago: University of Chicago Press.

Kuttner, R. 1991. *The End of Laissez-faire: National Purpose and the Global Economy after the Cold War*. New York: Alfred A. Knopf.

Ladson-Billings, G., and W. Tate. 1993. *Toward a Critical Race Theory of Education*. Madison: Department of Curriculum and Instruction, University of Wisconsin-Madison.

Lekachman, R. 1982. *Greed Is Not Enough: Reaganomics*. New York: Pantheon Books.

Luke, C. 1989. *Pedagogy, Printing, and Protestantism: The Discourse as Childhood*. Albany: State University of New York Press.

Lundgren, U. 1983. *Between Hope and Happening: Text and Context in Curriculum*. Geelong, Australia: Deakin University Press.

McCarthy, C. 1992. *Race and Curriculum*. London: Falmer.

McNeil, L. 1986. *Contradictions of Control: School Structure and School Knowledge*. New York: Routledge and Kegan Paul.

Martin, L., H. Gutman, and P. Hutton. 1988. *Technologies of the Self: A Seminar with Michel Foucault*. Amherst: University of Massachusetts Press.

Mikhailov, F. [1976] 1990. *The Riddle of the Self*. R. Daglish, trans. Moscow: Progress.

Nicholson, L. 1986. *Gender and History: The Limits of Social Theory in the Age of the Family*. New York: Columbia University Press.

Noble, D. 1989. Cockpit Cognition: Education, the Military, and Cognitive Engineering. *Artificial Intelligence and Society* 3: 271–296.

Noujain, E. 1987. History as Genealogy: An Exploration of Foucault's Approach. In *Contemporary French Philosophy*, ed. A. Griffiths, 157–174. New York: Cambridge University Press.

O'Donnell, J. 1985. *The Origins of Behaviorism: American Psychology, 1876–1920*. New York: New York University Press.

Page, R. 1991. *Lower-Track Classrooms: A Curricular and Cultural Perspective*. New York: Teachers College Press.

Popkewitz, T. 1981. Qualitative Research: Some Thoughts about the Relation of Methodology and Social History. In *The Study of Schooling: Field Methodology in Educational Research*, ed. T. Popkewitz and B. Tabachnick, 155–180. New York: Praeger.

———. 1984. *Paradigm and Ideology in Educational Research: Social Functions of the Intellectual*. New York: Falmer.

———. 1991. *A Political Sociology of Educational Reform: Power/Knowledge in Teaching, Teacher Education, and Research*. New York: Teachers College Press.

———, ed. 1987. *The Formation of School Subjects: The Struggle for Creating an American Institution*. New York: Falmer.

———, ed. 1993. *Changing Patterns of Power: Social Regulation and Teacher Education Reform*. Albany: State University of New York Press.

Popkewitz, T., and M. Pereyra. 1993. An Eight Country Study of Reform: An Outline of the Problematic. In *Changing Patterns of Power: Social Regulation and Teacher Education Reform*, ed. T. Popkewitz, 1–52. Albany: State University of New York Press.

Popkewitz, T., and A. Pitman. 1986. The Idea of Progress and the Legitimation of State Agendas: American Proposals for School Reform. *Curriculum and Teaching* 1(1–2): 11–24.

Popkewitz, T., B. Tabachnick, and G. Wehlage. 1982. *The Myth of Educational Reform: A Study of School Responses to a Program of Change*. Madison: University of Wisconsin Press.

Rajchman, J. 1985. *Michel Foucault: The Freedom of Philosophy*. New York: Columbia University Press.

Riley, Denise. 1988. *And that Name? Feminism and the Category of Women in History*. Minneapolis: University of Minnesota Press.

Robbins, B. 1993. *Secular Vocations: Intellectuals, Professionalism, Culture*. New York: Verso.

Rosenau, P. 1992. *Post-Modernism and the Social Sciences: Insights, Inroads, and Intrusions*. Princeton: Princeton University Press.

Ross, D. 1991. *The Origins of American Social Science.* New York: Cambridge University Press.

Saper, C. 1991. A Nervous Theory: The Troubling Gaze of Psychoanalysis in Media Studies. *Diacritics* 21:4: 33–52.

St. Maurice, H. 1993. Two Rhetorics of Cynicism in Curriculum Deliberation, or Two Riders in a Barren Land. *Educational Theory* 43(2): 147–160.

Schriewer, J., and E. Keiner. 1992. Communication Patterns and Intellectual Traditions in Educational Sciences: France and Germany. *Comparative Education Review* 36(1): 25–51.

Shor, I. 1986. *Culture Wars, School and Society in the Conservative Restoration, 1969–1984.* Boston: Routledge and Kegan Paul.

Silva, E., and S. Slaughter. 1984. *Serving Power: The Making of the Academic Social Science Expert.* Westport, CT: Greenwood.

Sleeter, C., and C. Grant. 1994. *Making Choices for Multicultural Education: Five Approaches to Race, Class, and Gender.* 2d ed. New York: Merrill.

Smith, D. 1990. *Conceptual Practices of Power: A Feminist Sociology of Knowledge.* Boston: Northeastern University Press.

Tally, C. 1990. Future History. In *Interpreting the Past, Understanding the Present*, ed. S. Kendrick, P. Straw, and D. McCrone, 9–19. New York: St. Martin's Press.

Weedon, C. 1987. *Feminist Practice and Poststructural Theory.* London: Basil Blackwell.

Weis, L., and M. Fine, eds. 1993. *Beyond Silenced Voices: Class, Race, and Gender in United States Schools.* Albany: State University of New York Press.

Wolfe, A. 1989. *Whose Keeper? Social Science and Moral Obligation.* Berkeley: University of California Press.

16

Can the Big-City School System Be Governed?

Kenneth K. Wong

Big-city school systems in the 1990s differ substantially from those of the early 1960s. Three decades ago, schools in central cities were governed by a strong central bureaucracy that functioned primarily to provide basic instructional services to the city's growing school-age population, which comprised predominantly White children from two-parent families. Public schools were supported by a sound local tax base. Today, the central-city school system is no longer governed by a strong central authority and its leadership lacks control over crucial policy matters. Court rulings, state laws, and federal mandates have played a significant role in defining the organizational life of students and teachers. Yielding to political demands, many districts have adopted shared decision making between the central office and the school site. In addition to basic instruction, urban schools now offer a wide range of social services to their clients, many of whom come from low-income, minority, single-parent family backgrounds. Urban schools now rely heavily on intergovernmental revenues.

Taken together, these changes have transformed the politics of education in the nation's big cities. In this chapter I examine the political and socioeconomic changes that have reshaped big-city school systems over the past thirty years; I argue that the top leadership of the central-city school system has lost much of its autonomy in making educational policy. Urban districts are dominated by fragmentary politics in which multiple centers of power, from both within and outside the public school system, have come to define the functions of public education. As this political fragmentation prevails, the big-city school system of the 1990s must confront the problems of producing a coherent system of governance.

To examine the thirty-year transformation in big-city schools, we constructed a database on the nation's largest central-city school systems from the 1950s to the late 1980s and gathered district-level information from a variety of sources, including Census reports, National Education Association publications, U.S. Department of Education statistics, U.S. Office for Civil Rights documents, and Council of Great City Schools publications. Furthermore, the database includes detailed information on institutional changes collected from the field in two of the districts—Chicago and Boston. The two-district field survey was directed at areas that are not readily documented in other sources, namely school governance and political changes. It gathered information from the school board, departments at the central office, teachers' unions, city agencies, civic organizations, interest groups, newspaper accounts, state reports, and other documentary sources. These data should allow examination of major changes in the institutional characteristics of central-city schools over time, thereby placing current events in their proper context. As data collection efforts are ongoing, the findings reported here should be considered preliminary.

I will first offer an analytical scheme that classifies the four major components of the politics of fragmentation in the central-city district. For each of the four types of politics, I review the current literature and present the relevant information from the database—both in aggregate trends and (where appropriate) in detailed two-district comparison—to substantiate the thesis that school governance has become so fragmentary that distinct substructures can be identified.

From Centralized Authority to Fragmentation

Big-city school politics in the early 1960s clearly fit the "bureaucratic insulation" model (Bidwell 1965; Peterson 1976; Weick 1976; Weber 1947). The school system resembled a complex hierarchical structure with centralized authority. The organization's insiders enjoyed autonomy from the influence of outsiders because insiders possessed expertise and information on how the system operated. External pressures from state and federal government were largely absent. Within districts, teachers' unions were still in their formative years and parent and community groups were generally not well organized. Strong professional identification and standard operating procedures connected activities performed at each level of this multilayered, loosely coupled organization. According to this model, professional administrators determined the use of most resources, exercised control over curricular and instructional matters, designed the administrative organization, and recruited the staff. School politics, in short, were largely embedded in the organizational milieu of the district.

The power of this bureaucracy is indicated by the growth in administrative staff during the 1960s and the 1970s. Between 1956 and 1978, the bureaucratic staff increased in size faster than the faculty did in major urban districts. As Table 16.1 shows, among sixteen central-city districts in 1956, on the average there was one professional administrative position for every eighteen teachers. By 1978, the proportion was one administrator to twelve teachers. As Table 16.1 suggests, the average administrator-teacher ratio narrowed by over 30 percent during this twenty-year period. Administrative growth was most pronounced in Boston, Dallas, Detroit, Milwaukee, and Portland during this period. The growing bureaucracy increasingly became organized by specialized functions with program administrators insulated from one another.

In retrospect, the top school leadership and its sizable bureaucracy of the 1960s and the 1970s were more fragile than their supporters and critics believed; the district organization proved to be permeable to influences from broader political and economic forces. Since the 1960s, the functions of public

education have been redefined by numerous mandates on equal
educational opportunities from state and federal agencies and
court rulings. Teachers' unions and other interest groups have
become centers of contending powers. In recent years the public

TABLE 16.1. Bureaucratic Power as Indicated by the Ratio of
Administrators to Teachers in Sixteen Central Cities, 1956 and 1978.

Ratio of Administrators to Teachers	1956	1978
Atlanta	1:24	1:16
Boston	1:19	1:7
Chicago	1:24	1:15
Cincinnati	1:12	1:12
Dallas	1:21	1:8
Denver	1:12	1:12
Detroit	1:15	1:7
Houston	1:19	1:16
Indianapolis	1:15	1:15
Los Angeles	1:18	1:14
Milwaukee	1:16	1:8
New York	1:20	1:14
Portland	1:19	1:6
St. Louis	1:24	1:15
Seattle	1:16	1:12
Washington, DC	1:14	1:13
Overall Average	1:18	1:12

Sources: U.S. Biennial Survey of Education, 1954–56, *Statistics of Local
School Systems, 1955–56* (Department of Health, Education, and
Welfare, 1956), pp. 44–130. National School Boards Association,
Survey of Public Education in the Nation's Urban School Districts
(Evanston, IL: NSBA, 1979), pp. 10–11.

has seemed increasingly skeptical that the urban school
bureaucracy can effectively address the persistent decline in
student performance and has begun looking for market solutions

to educational problems. Today, the district leadership and its bureaucracy have clearly lost control over most important policy matters—school finance, leadership succession, racial desegregation, and services for the disadvantaged.

Indeed, political demands and the seemingly intractable task of educating the special-needs population have destabilized leadership succession in big-city schools. Turnover among school superintendents has become fairly rapid since the mid 1970s, a departure from the historically stable trend in central-city systems. In Boston, for example, the average tenure for the twenty superintendents between 1856 and 1987 was six and one-half years. In Chicago, the twenty superintendents between 1871 and 1989 held their office for an average of six years. However, superintendents in the two systems since the mid 1970s have held shorter tenure. In Boston, in the fifteen-year period between 1972 and 1987, there were a total of eight superintendents, with an average tenure of less than two years each. Boston experienced a particularly unstable period in 1980 and 1981, when three superintendents left the job, including one who was fired before the contract had expired. In a less dramatic manner, Chicago's superintendency changed hands four times during 1975 and 1989, each tenure averaging three and one-half years. Most recently, Superintendent Ted Kimbrough stepped down after only three years at the system's helm. His short tenure is clearly not unique in the big-city context.

Outside recruitment of superintendents does not seem to contribute to rapid turnover. Since 1970, none of the school superintendents in Chicago has stayed in the job for more than five years; the high turnover coincides with a period during which most superintendents came from "inside" the system. The board-superintendent relationship became acrimonious during the 1980s—one superintendent resigned amid financial crisis and the other two did not get their contracts renewed. In contrast, prior to 1970, most superintendents were recruited from outside and virtually all retired following a fairly long tenure.

The rapid turnover of superintendency in these schools is just one more recent development calling into question the notion that the district's central authority enjoys a free hand in making school policy. Big-city school governance is readily shaped by the broader political and economic environment. In other words, an understanding of school politics must go beyond the bureaucratic structure of the central office. Certainly, when looking at metropolitan school systems now, one is hard pressed to make the case that these are schools controlled by an autonomous bureaucratic central office. Rather, the governance of today's big-city school systems is highly fragmented.

At the risk of oversimplifying, I present an analytical framework that captures the key elements of fragmentary politics in Figure 16.1. More specifically, the top leadership of the school system is no longer autonomous from powerful sources of policy influence. Major corporate actors (e.g., unions and state agencies), organized interests (e.g., racial and ethnic groups), and individual clients shape urban school policy through two different mechanisms—"voice" and "choice" (Hirschman 1971). "Voice" refers to the political process through which parents, other clients, and corporate actors select candidates, lobby government officials, influence legislation, and gain representation; "choice" designates the marketlike decisions made by parent-consumers to choose schooling services for their children.

FIGURE 16.1. The Structure of Fragmentary Politics in Big-City School Systems.

MECHANISMS OF INSTITUTIONAL CHANGE	UNIT OF ANALYSIS	
	District as a Unitary Actor	Multilevel within District
Choice (marketlike)	Competition from suburban and nonpublic schools	Choice within public schools
	(A)	(B)
Voice (political)	Mandates from higher-level governments	Shared decisionmaking
	(C)	(D)

Furthermore, voice and choice can be differentiated by shifting our unit of analysis of the school system. From the "unitary" perspective, the school system can be seen as a unitary actor making policy choices in a constrained environment. In this regard, competition from other educational providers (e.g., nonpublic schools) poses a challenge to the public school system as a whole. Likewise, from this perspective, state and federal government mandates can be seen as external constraints imposed on local school authority. Viewing the school system as a single entity yields valuable insight, but equally important is to take into consideration various components and multiple layers within the school system. Using this "organizational" perspective, school politics becomes a function of competition among organized interests within the system. Division of responsibilities among various layers of the district policymaking organization is also relevant in understanding the weakening of central authority.

As Figure 16.1 suggests, the interplay of the two policy mechanisms, choice and voice, and the two modes of analysis, unitary and organizational, is likely to produce four sets of fragmentary politics. These can be distinguished as: (1) politics of market competition, resulting when the nonpublic sector and suburban public schools compete with central-city districts for middle-class families (cell A in Figure 16.1); (2) politics of choice within the public sector, which occurs when parents can choose among district magnet schools, neighborhood schools, and other innovative programs (cell B); (3) politics of intergovernmental regulation, a result of higher-level-government imposition of regulatory constraints on local school policy (cell C); and (4) politics of shared decision making, which happens when teachers unions, parents, principals, and minority groups gain greater voice within the system (cell D).

Taken as a whole, the politics of fragmentation displays four characteristics: (1) the bureaucratic mode of school organization is increasingly challenged by the concept of consumer choice; (2) the district's central authority (i.e., the central school board, superintendent, and the central office managers) is losing its policy control to other corporate actors; (3) multiple centers of power are located both inside and outside the district; and (4) a system is developing with seemingly incoherent substructures, each shaped by a distinct set of fragmentary political forces, which in turn compete for scarce resources. I will discuss each of these four types of politics.

Politics of Market Competition

Market and Efficiency

Public schools in central cities clearly operate in a competitive environment. Public school districts and nonpublic schools can be seen as educational providers in a marketlike setting, competing for students. Indeed, as consumers, some parents register their dissatisfaction with central-city schools by sending their children to nonpublic schools or by moving to suburban public school districts.

Although the public sector continues to dominate educational services, a growing number of empirical studies identify bureaucratic power as a direct barrier to improving student performance in public schools. With the availability of the High School and Beyond (HS&B) surveys since 1980, researchers have been able to compare student performance between public and private sectors. In analyzing the first HS&B survey, Coleman, Hoffer, and Kilgore (1982) found that students in Catholic and independent private schools outperformed students with similar socioeconomic backgrounds in public schools by one grade level on standardized tests in basic skills. These differential outcomes, according to the study, are linked to different modes of organization. While the public schools are predominantly geographically based and are governed by exceedingly cumbersome mandates, parochial schools are organized around religious identity and are relatively free from external regulatory constraints. In response to critics, Coleman and Hoffer (1987) further compared students' academic growth in public, private, and Catholic sectors. The second study found virtually no difference in student outcomes between public and independent private schools. Catholic high schools, however, continued to show the highest rates of student academic progress in verbal and mathematical skills. Catholic schools also maintained the lowest dropout rates and their students were more likely to attend four-year colleges. In explaining the successes among students in Catholic schools, Coleman and Hoffer (1987) suggested the benefits of "social capital" in the religious community. In contrast, public schools are constructed largely by rules and mandates and generally lack the social and normative basis for frequent interaction among youths, families, and teachers. Consistent with Coleman's earlier findings, Chubb and Moe (1990) argue that the more market-oriented nonpublic schools are far more likely to produce what they call effective organizations. Consequently, Chubb and Moe proposed to eliminate the public-private boundary and grant full choice of schooling to all parents as the solution to urban school problems (see Wong, forthcoming, for a summary of criticisms of Chubb and Moe).

Suburban Districts as Competitors

One sign that central-city schools have changed over the past three decades is their vulnerability to competition from suburban public school districts. Within the metropolitan area, middle-class parents, particularly among Whites, have steadily moved to suburban districts. Although it remains unclear whether the middle-class outmigration is entirely motivated by concerns over school quality in the central city, "White flight" is largely responsible for a noticeable decline in White enrollment in big-city districts since the early 1970s.

The sociodemographic contrast is widening between the central city district and its surrounding suburban communities. In 1990, minority groups made up over 60 percent of the central-city school enrollment; Whites accounted for almost 80 percent of the suburban school population in major metropolitan areas. In the metropolitan Chicago area, typical Chicago public schools have 73 percent of their students classified as low income compared to only 12 percent in suburban schools (Scheirer 1989). As a 1985 report on metropolitan Milwaukee concluded, "[Our] study revealed two very different worlds of educational achievement; worlds separated by but a few miles, yet by much greater distances in terms of acquired skills, institutional success, and future prospects" (Witte and Walsh 1985). Similarly, Orfield and Reardon (1992) observe "a structure of educational opportunity that is highly stratified at every level by both race and class" and by residential choices. They find that students in central-city districts "have a narrower range of course offerings and fewer opportunities for advanced and college-preparatory coursework than their suburban counterparts." Given the pervasiveness of metropolitan inequality, policy analysts argue for a major restructuring of local school finance that would move toward a regional funding system (Orfield and Reardon 1992; also see Kozol 1991).

Middle-class outmigration has damaged central-city districts. Parents who move to the suburbs leave behind a district with a higher concentration of poor children, a weaker tax base, and declining political influence in the state legislature. Decisions of middle-class families to leave these districts tend to fuel the city-suburban conflict over state aid to disadvantaged students (Cronin 1973; Berke et al. 1984). In Illinois, for example, the 1978 state legislature reduced the weights assigned to poor students in finding formulas which, in effect, decreased state aid to inner-city schools. Of the eighty-six lawmakers who voted for the bill, eighty-five represented districts outside the city of Chicago. In contrast, forty-seven of the sixty-four legislators who voted against the measure came from both major political parties in Chicago. Regional cleavages within a metropolitan area tend to undermine funding support for central-city schools (Wong 1989).

Nonpublic Schools as Competitors

Consumer parents who choose to continue residing in the central city may choose nonpublic schools. One indication that central-city public schools may be gradually losing to their private-sector competitors is that parents who have choices seem to be less inclined to use the public services. Although nonpublic schools account for only about 11 percent of the total school enrollment nationwide, they enroll about 20 percent of the student population in nineteen central cities (see Table 16.2). Among central-city residents, the White population group has increasingly relied on

TABLE 16.2. Racial Differences in Public School Attendance in Nineteen
Large Cities, 1970–1980.

	White	Black	Hispanic	Overall
1970				
Enrollment in public school (in millions)	2.02	1.98	0.56	4.65
School-age population (in millions)	3.75	2.15	0.61	6.03
Percentage attending public school	53.90	92.40	92.20	77.10
1980				
Enrollment in public school (in millions)	.94	1.74	.71	3.54
School-age population (in millions)	2.08	1.94	0.81	4.37
Percentage attending public school	45.20	89.60	87.80	81.00

Sources: U.S. Census Bureau, *Census of Population*, 1970, vol. 1
(Washington: GPO, 1973), part 1, table 52, p. 1–271; part 2, tables 23
and 24; *ibid.*, 1980, vol. 1 (Washington: GPO, 1981), chap. B, table 43,
p. 1–29; chap. C, tables 25 and 26. U.S. Office for Civil Rights,
*Directory of Public Elementary and Secondary Schools in Selected School
Districts, Enrollment and Staff by Ethnic Group*, Fall 1970 (Washington:
GPO, 1972). Council of Great City Schools, *The Condition of Education
in the Great City Schools: A Statistical Profile, 1980–1986.*

Note: We have used the age cohort of 5–17 as an estimate of the city's
school-age population.

The nineteen cities are New York, Los Angeles, Chicago, Philadelphia,
Detroit, Dallas, Baltimore, San Francisco, Indianapolis, Memphis,
Washington, D.C., Milwaukee, Boston, Columbus, New Orleans,
Cleveland, Denver, Seattle, and Nashville.

nonpublic schools. As Table 16.2 shows, enrollment in public
schools as a percentage of the White school-age population fell
from 54 percent to 45 percent between 1970 and 1980 in nineteen
large districts. In contrast, an overwhelming majority of Blacks

and Hispanics remained in public schools in the nineteen
districts.

TABLE 16.3. Racial Differences in Percentage of School-Age Population
Attending Public Schools in Chicago and Boston, 1970–1980.

	White	Black	Hispanic	Overall
Chicago				
1970	45.7	90.6	72.6	72.4
1980	37.2	84.2	72.5	71.7
Boston				
1970	63.7	90.3	83.0	73.3
1980	49.4	93.7	89.8	73.6

Note and Sources: See Table 16.2.

Chicago and Boston generally follow this pattern of
differential choice between White and minority groups (Table
16.3). In Chicago, the percentage of White school-age children
who enrolled in the city's public schools fell from 46 percent to
37 percent between 1970 and 1980. While the city's Blacks
predominantly attended public schools, over one-fourth of the
Hispanic population went to parochial and other private schools.
In Boston, the percentage of White school-age students that
enrolled in public schools declined from 64 percent to 49 percent
between 1970 and 1980. However, nine out of ten Blacks and
Hispanics in Boston remained in the city's school system.

This shift to the nonpublic sector and suburban districts
complicates the search for causes of the persistent decline in
student performance in big-city schools since the early 1970s. On
the one hand, one may argue that middle-class outmigration has
contributed to a lowering in student performance in the city. On
the other hand, one may make a case that the declining test
scores have discouraged consumer parents, who would
otherwise remain in the urban district. In any event, clearly
today's big-city districts are performing poorly. Of the forty
member-districts in the Council of Great City Schools, only

seventeen produced an SAT score at or above the national average in 1988. On the average the urban districts were forty points below the national mean score of 904. In Boston, the mean composite SAT scores dropped rapidly from 858 to 752 between 1972 and 1982, but were more stable during the 1980s. The district's 1988 average score was 787, which was 117 points below the national average.

Combined Effects of Marketlike Competition

The ongoing outmigration of Whites to suburban districts and nonpublic schools tends to produce three major sociodemographic changes in the central-city district. First, central-city districts have experienced a decline in enrollment since the late 1960s and the early 1970s. Most major urban districts went through a cycle of enrollment decline—growth in the 1950s and through most of the 1960s, stability around the late 1960s and early 1970s, and decline since the 1970s. As a result, 1990 enrollment figures tend to correspond to those of the 1950s. For example, in Chicago, growth in elementary enrollment spanned a twenty-year period, climbing from 267,600 in 1950 to 434,400 in 1970. This increase was followed by gradual decline, ranging from 1 to 3 percent annually. Chicago elementary enrollment stood at 300,500 in 1990 (returning to the level of the 1950s). Chicago also suffered losses in secondary school enrollment, although the decrease was not as drastic as the elementary school decline. The district's attendance at the secondary level climbed from 100,600 in 1950 to 148,300 in 1975. Since the mid-1970s, enrollment in Chicago high schools has dropped considerably. In 1990, Chicago enrolled 100,800 secondary school students (again, a return to roughly the level of the 1950s).

Second, racial secession seems complete in urban districts. The clientele of the central-city school has changed significantly in recent decades. In the twenty-five largest U.S. cities the White population declined from 86 to 60 percent between 1950 and 1980. The change in the racial composition of their public-school student population was even more dramatic. Table 16.4 presents the change between 1971 and 1986 in the racial composition of the

TABLE 16.4. Racial Composition of Nineteen Large Central-City Schools, 1979–1986.

Racial Group	1971	1977	1981	1986
White	43.5	32.9	26.6	21.9
Black	42.7	47.8	49.2	48.2
Hispanic	12.1	16.3	20.1	24.4
Asian	1.6	2.6	3.8	5.1
Other	0.1	0.3	0.2	0.4
Total	100.0	99.9	99.9	100.0

Sources: U.S. Office for Civil Rights, *Elementary and Secondary Schools in Selected School Districts, Enrollment and Staff by Ethnic Group*, Fall 1970 (Washington, DC: GPO, 1972); U.S. Office for Civil Rights, *Directory of Elementary and Secondary School Districts, and Schools in Selected School Districts: School Year 1976–77* (Washington, DC: GPO, 1979); Council of the Great City Schools, *The Condition of Education in the Great City Schools: A Statistical Profile, 1980–1986*, table 4, pp. 8–14.

nineteen large central-city school systems that make up the Council of Great City Schools. Over this fifteen-year period the White, non-Hispanic percentage of the student body fell from 44 to 22 percent. Hispanic enrollment doubled from 12 to 24 percent, and the proportion of Black students increased from 43 to 48 percent.

Racial and ethnic minorities have made up the majority of public school students in most central cities since the early 1970s. In Chicago, for example, the number of White students has declined persistently since the late 1960s. By 1990, only 12 percent of elementary school students were White; African Americans and Latinos made up 59 percent and 27 percent of the elementary student population respectively. The secondary school student population was 12 percent White, 24 percent Latino, and 60 percent Black in 1990. Similarly, in Boston, Whites represented only 26 percent of both the elementary and the secondary student populations in 1987. In that same year, Blacks represented 47 percent and 49 percent of the enrollment at the elementary and secondary levels, respectively. The number of

Latino students increased from 12 percent to 19 percent in the elementary schools between 1977 and 1987. During the same period, Latino enrollment jumped from 8 percent to 16 percent of the total student population in Boston's high schools.

The third sociodemographic change attributable to White outmigration is a high concentration of poor children in the central-city school system. The change in the racial composition of the school population has been accompanied by a shift in the economic position of central-city residents. Between 1960 and 1970 the proportion of people with incomes below the poverty line declined nationwide, but the decrease among the central-city poor was only from 14 to 10 percent, falling short of the downward trend in suburban and nonmetropolitan areas. After 1970 the poverty trend within central cities worsened—the percentage of poor climbed from 10 percent in 1970 to over 15 percent in 1987. By 1990, one-third of the children in the nation's big cities fell below the poverty line. Poverty figures varied from 47 percent in Detroit, 43 percent in Atlanta, 38 percent in Milwaukee, 34 percent in Chicago, to 31 percent in Minneapolis.

Public schools clearly serve predominantly low-income children. In Chicago, 69 percent of students eligible for free school lunches were in schools whose student bodies were over 50 percent free-lunch eligible in 1990. Thirty-one percent of these children went to schools whose student bodies were over 90 percent free-lunch eligible. Further, an examination of Chicago's 368 elementary neighborhood schools also suggests that 71 percent of these schools had at least 80 percent low-income students (i.e., free/reduced lunch eligible) in 1988 (Wong 1992). In only 7 percent of the neighborhood schools was the majority of the student body not poor.

Politics of Choice within the Public Sector

During the 1970s, big-city school systems began to institute "mediated choice" programs. Public school choice programs, such as magnet schools, serve important institutional functions for the urban district: They promote racial desegregation in a voluntary manner, retain middle-class families in the city's public schools, and encourage localized reform and experimentation. Public school choice creates significant differences in the schooling opportunities among children *within* the central-city public school system, and schooling differences between choice and neighborhood schools contribute to the politics of fragmentation.

Significantly, public school choice programs depart from the tradition of "common schooling." Distinguished by academic specialties, such as the fine arts, mathematics and science, and foreign languages, their enrollment is not restricted by regular attendance boundaries. Students can choose among a designated number of curricular specialty programs in different schools regardless of family residence. While magnet schools enjoy discretion in pupil admission, they are often subject to broad district guidelines on the racial mix of the student body.

An indication that choice within the public sector is gaining support is the increase in the number of magnet schools in recent years. In 1983, there were 1,100 magnet schools in 130 urban districts of more than 20,000 students. By 1989, there were over 2,500 magnet schools, of which 60 percent operated at the elementary level. The centralized structure in school governance has become less pervasive as a result of magnet programs. Since 1970, the Chicago school system has adopted an open enrollment plan. The number of secondary magnet schools expanded from 2 in 1975 to 17 (i.e., about 20 percent of all secondary schools in 1990). Likewise, the number of elementary magnet schools has increased from 2 in 1970 to 69 in 1990 (i.e., about 15 percent of all elementary schools). In Boston, a major component in the Phase Two citywide desegregation plan was the setting up of 25 magnet schools (out of a total of 162 city schools in the fall of 1975). To facilitate desegregation, each school was required to meet the following racial criteria: 40–60 percent White, 30–50 percent Black, and 5–25 percent other minorities. According to an analysis of the enrollment in fall 1976, the 25 magnet schools seemed to have made progress toward desegregation (see Case 1977, p. 166).

Choice within the public sector has been controversial. Magnet programs tend to "cream off" better students and other resources from their neighborhood schools. The implementation of a systemwide choice plan has raised questions concerning distribution of school information to all parents, transportation costs, and compliance with civil rights provisions. Equally important are the income-class differences between magnet and regular neighborhood schools. In Chicago, for example, when compared to neighborhood schools, fewer magnet school programs enroll students who come from low-income families. Of the full-site magnet elementary schools, just 37 percent have an enrollment of 40 percent or less low-income students. In contrast, over 70 percent of the neighborhood schools have at least 80 percent low-income students (Wong 1992a).

Limited availability and other shortcomings notwithstanding, choice within the public sector has become quite effective in addressing problems that confront central-city schools. Magnet schools have brought about racial integration without aggravating racial conflict (Rossell 1990). Choice programs have also served to retain a middle-class presence in the central city (Wong 1992a). Finally, choice programs are innovative efforts to improve educational quality in inner-city neighborhoods. Clearly, the real challenge is to sustain student gains when small-scale choice programs become systemwide policy.

Politics of Intergovernmental Regulation

Constraints Imposed by Higher-level Governments

As a unitary actor, the urban district has to comply with external regulations. Urban schools are legislated by state and federal law, court decisions, and administrative codes. Clearly, regulations and mandates from external governmental sources tend to weaken the district's autonomy in setting school policy.

Chubb and Moe (1990) argue that local democratic politics have produced a bloated bureaucracy, which in turn undermines school effectiveness. Although regulations from the top of the system do threaten autonomy at the school building, two points should be considered. First, not all regulations are district initiated. Union contracts, staff development, budgetary planning, and textbook selection are clearly the kinds of decisions the central school board makes. Yet the central bureaucracy has almost no autonomy over a large number of regulations from state and federal agencies in the area of ensuring equal educational opportunities—racially balanced student and teacher assignment, safeguards for pupils in special education and other categorical programs, assessment and evaluation to meet state funding requirements, and detailed accounting of the use of state and federal funds. Second, Chubb and Moe do not differentiate layers of the "school bureaucracy." Clearly, federal and state agencies have grown in their influence over local school policy matters, and as students of intergovernmental relations learn, the district's bureaucracy is to a considerable extent the creation of federal and state categorical programs and their concomitant regulations (see Peterson, Rabe, and Wong 1986). In other words, much of the district's central bureaucracy and its functions may have very little to do with the local democratic process, a point that Chubb and Moe assert but fail to empirically link to their theories. The "problem of the school bureaucracy" is more than simply the intrusion of the district's regulatory power in the schoolhouse; equally important, it is the loss of district autonomy to higher-level governments. Two issues illuminate this loss: (1) urban schools' increasing dependence on federal and state aid, and (2) federal demands for school desegregation in the urban system.

Dependence on Intergovernmental Revenues

Since the Great Society reforms of the 1960s, the federal government has focused on educational-equity issues by promoting racial integration, protecting the rights of the handicapped, funding compensatory education, and assisting those with limited English proficiency (Peterson, Rabe, and Wong 1986). In 1991, the federal government allocated $6.2 billion to compensatory education, $2.4 billion to special education, and $200 million to bilingual projects. Chapter 1 (compensatory) programs, for example, provide services to more than five million disadvantaged pupils in prekindergarten through grade twelve. Between 1965 and 1992, the federal government disbursed more than $80 billion for compensatory education. Thirty-five percent of these monies go to districts with twenty-five thousand or more pupils. To be sure, federal grants for educational equity dropped during the Reagan and Bush years. In constant dollars, federal aid in 1990 fell short of the 1980 level (Wong 1994). Although the level of federal aid has fluctuated over time, the federal regulatory apparatus remains largely intact.

An equally important factor is state aid to public education. In recent years, the state has become the primary funder of public schools, increasing its share of total school revenues from 41 percent in 1968 to over 50 percent in the mid 1980s. Although the state is particularly keen on allotting resources to address interdistrict disparity in taxable wealth, an increasing number of states are also providing services for special-needs students. Every state now provides services to handicapped students, twenty states fund their own compensatory education programs and twenty-one states provide bilingual educational services (Wong 1991). Many of these state-funded programs involve the state's own (in addition to the federal) regulations on local service delivery. For example, the Chicago school board's budget is subject to approval by the Chicago Finance Authority, whose members are jointly appointed by the governor and the mayor.

Consequently, the combined fiscal effect of federal and state aid has reduced the relative importance of local sources in funding public schools. Indeed, central-city school systems are less dependent on local revenue sources than they once were. Between 1977 and 1987 the share of school system revenue coming from local sources declined from 51 percent to 46 percent in the Rustbelt and from 56 to 35 percent in the Sunbelt (Table 16.5). The level of state support increased in both regions but especially in the Sunbelt, where average state share of expenditures went up from 33 to 57 percent. And despite federal cutbacks in education, central-city schools continued to receive almost as high a percentage of their revenue from the federal government in 1987 as they had a decade earlier. The drop was only from 11 to 9 percent, considerably less than the overall decline in the federal role in education (from 10 to 6 percent of current expenditures).

TABLE 16.5. Sources of School Revenue of the Twenty-Five Largest
Central Cities, Rustbelt and Sunbelt, 1977–1987.

Year	Rustbelt			Sunbelt		
	Local (%)	State (%)	Federal (%)	Local (%)	State (%)	Federal (%)
1977	51.4	37.7	11.0	56.1	33.0	10.9
1982	39.9	47.2	12.9	37.2	52.7	10.1
1987	45.7	45.0	9.2	34.5	56.9	8.6

Note: In addition to the 19 cities mentioned in Table 16.2, this analysis
   includes data from Houston, San Diego, Phoenix, San Antonio, San
   Jose, and El Paso.

Sources: U.S. Bureau of the Census, *Census of Governments*, 1977, vol. 4,
   no. 1 (Washington, DC: GPO, 1979), table 10, pp. 80–137; *ibid.*, 1982
   (Washington, DC: GPO, 1984), Table 8, pp. 11–40; *ibid.*, 1987
   (Washington, DC: GPO, 1990), table 16, pp. 26–121.

Difficulties in Implementing Racial Desegregation

Another area where external regulation has been pervasive is
racial desegregation and civil rights. Judicial decisions and
federal administrative decrees since *Brown* have culminated in a
legal framework that offers legitimacy for national government
involvement in racial desegregation. Even in the presence of
occasional opposition from the White House, the Supreme Court
actively pursued desegregation in the South during the late
1960s and early 1970s. Consequently, between 1968 and 1972, the
degree of racial segregation in southern schools declined
sharply—the percentage of schools that were more than 90
percent minority decreased from 78 to 25 percent (Orfield 1988).

Federal desegregation policy clearly has shaped big-city
districts. In a sample of twenty-seven member-districts of the
Council of Great City Schools, sixteen reported having been
ordered by the federal judiciary to desegregate during the 1970s
and the 1980s. While four districts carried out desegregation
plans imposed from nonjudicial sources, only seven (or 25

percent of the sampled districts) did not formally implement a desegregation program.

An example of federal regulatory intervention is the decade-long process of desegregating schools in Boston. Boston's school desegregation case, *Morgan v. Kerrigan*, was filed in February 1972 and decided in June 1974. The district court ruled that the district's decade-long policies in school construction, pupil placement, and the assignment of Blacks to vocational programs and Whites to "examination schools" (Case 1977) had resulted in a segregated system. The ruling was subsequently upheld by the U.S. Supreme Court in May 1975. District Judge Arthur Garrity ordered the district to adopt a partial desegregation plan to transfer teachers and students in two predominantly low-income communities, Irish South Boston and Black Roxbury. This plan, or Phase One, required the city to bus between six and twenty thousand students to desegregate the schools beginning in September 1974. Antibusing sentiments escalated almost overnight and were followed by three months of violence during which the governor had to send in the National Guard. During the first school term of Phase One, only 75 percent of the students attended classes. In late October of 1974, Judge Garrity initiated steps toward Phase Two, which was aimed at systemwide desegregation in the fall of 1975. During Phase Two, 1975–76, twenty thousand of the district's seventy-six thousand students were bused and minority representation increased from 5 percent to 11 percent of the school staff. Fortunately, the level of violence decreased and incidents occurred in only 4 of the 162 desegregated schools during the school year. Still, even with this effort, 1 out of every 6 schools in the system remained racially identifiable (see Case 1977: 175). By 1977, 27 percent of the city's student population were included in the busing program. The court order stood until 1985, when the desegregation program bused 55 percent of the district's students out of their neighborhood schools.

Federal mandates notwithstanding, there has been no detectable change in the degree of racial desegregation in either the South or the United States as a whole since the early 1970s. The percentage of Blacks in predominantly minority schools was 63.6 percent in 1972 and 63.3 percent in 1986; the percentage in schools that were 90 percent or more minority fell only from 38.7 to 32.5 percent (Orfield 1988).

In Chicago and Boston, the degree of racial isolation is worse than the national average. Although the two districts have responded to federal pressure by implementing magnet schools and by reassigning students and teachers, racial isolation remains severe. In part because of declining White enrollment in the two districts, an overwhelming majority of minority students attend predominantly minority schools. In 1990 in Chicago, 98 percent of minority (Black/Hispanic) students enrolled in schools whose student bodies were more than 50 percent minority. This figure suggests a regression from the 1980s. In 1980, 93 percent of the minority students were in 50 percent minority schools. In 1985, it was 94 percent. Similarly, 73 percent of minority students enrolled in schools whose student bodies were more than 90 percent minority in 1990. The 1980 and the 1985 figures were 79 percent and 74 percent, respectively. Thus, Chicago schools remained highly segregated overall.

At the time of the 1974 ruling, Boston schools were 40 percent Black, and most Black students were confined to schools that were at least 85 percent Black. Patterns of racial segregation have become more severe. In 1977, 77 percent of minority students attended schools that were 50 percent minority, and only 2 percent of the minority students were in schools with more than 90 percent minority students in 1977. A decade later, school segregation remains prevalent in Boston—in 1987, 96 percent of minority students attended schools that were at least 50 percent minority and 13 percent of minority students enrolled in schools that had 90 percent minority students.

At the classroom-track level, segregation also remains severe. In Chicago, for example, Blacks were overrepresented in the vocational track, and Hispanics and Blacks were concentrated in the general education track. In the vocational track, Black enrollment increased from 59 percent to 89 percent between 1965 and 1990. In the general education track, Black enrollment jumped from 35 percent to 55 percent between 1965 and 1990. In 1990, 25 percent of the general education student population was Hispanic. Concentration of minority students in general and vocational tracks may be due to two factors. The first is demographic—after all, Chicago high schools in 1990 were 60 percent Black, 12 percent White, 24 percent Hispanic, and 4 percent others. The second factor relates to the general decline in educational performance by high school students over the past two decades.

Politics of Shared Decision Making

Within the school system, the top leadership no longer exercises complete control over policy decisions. In recent years, urban districts have decentralized decision making to the extent that various corporate actors (e.g., unions) and interest groups (e.g., Hispanic organizations that support bilingual education) at both the community level and citywide can substantially influence policy decisions. The top-down management model of the early 1960s has been undermined by at least three developments that facilitate a more dispersed power structure. These include: (1) minority representation has increased; (2) teachers unions have become autonomous power centers; and (3) parent and teacher councils have gained more power at the school site.

Minority Representation and Policy Consequences

In 1990, 51 percent of the member districts of the Council of Great City Schools had a Black school superintendent and several others had filled the job with Hispanics. Significant progress has also been made in the racial makeup of the big city school boards (Jackson and Cibulka 1992). Since the early 1980s, Blacks have held the superintendency in Chicago.

Increase in minority representation tends to bring about a more equitable distribution of school resources in the large cities. Minority influence can be seen in two ways. First, minority groups can put pressure on the district leadership to revise allocative practices. In 1986, a coalition of Black and Hispanic groups filed suit against the Los Angeles school district for failing to provide equal resources and experienced teachers to predominantly minority schools in the inner-city neighborhoods

(*Rodriguez* v. *Los Angeles Unified School District*). Five years later, the litigation was brought to an end when the state superior court approved a consent decree which required the district to equalize the distribution of experienced teachers among schools and to allocate basic resources and supplies on an equal, per-pupil basis (*Education Week*, 9 September 1992). Similarly, organized actions have been found in other cities where the school population has undergone major demographic changes.

Further, minority representation affects personnel policy, which in turn may have instructional consequences for disadvantaged minority pupils. Using data from the Office of Civil Rights, Meier, Stewart, and England (1989) examined second-generation discrimination in the classroom following the implementation of school desegregation plans in districts with at least fifteen thousand students and 1 percent Black. They found that Black representation on the school board has contributed to the recruitment of Black administrators, who in turn have hired more Black teachers. Black teachers, according to this study, are crucial in reducing the assignment of Black students to classes for the educable mentally retarded. Black representation on the instructional staff also reduces the number of disciplinary actions against Black students and increases their participation in classes for the gifted.

Given the unique classroom impact of minority teachers, it is important to document the minority gains in the teaching staff in the big-city districts. In Chicago, for example, among secondary school teachers, the Black-to-White ratio declined from 1:3.4 in 1965 to 1:1.8 in 1975, and further to 1:1.2 in 1990. Among elementary school teachers, the Black-to-White ratio clearly narrowed—from 1:1.8 in 1965 to 1:1.30 in 1975. By the 1980s, Blacks outrepresented Whites in the elementary teaching force—the ratio was 1:0.9 in 1985 and 1:0.8 in 1990.

Hispanic representation on the instructional staff in Chicago schools remains limited, even though the racial disparity ratio has been declining over time. In the secondary teaching force, the Hispanic-White ratio declined from 1:39.8 in 1975 to 1:15.8 in 1990. In the elementary sector, the ratio plunged from 1:22.5 in 1975 to 1:5.9 in 1990. Just as important is the increase in minority representation in Chicago's principalships.

Between 1970 and 1990, White representation in principalship has declined from 93 percent to 56 percent. During the same period, Blacks went from holding 7 percent to holding 37 percent of all the CPS principalships. In 1990, Latinos held almost 8 percent of the principalships. Based on the findings of Meier, Stewart, and England (1989), one would expect this increase in numbers of minority teachers and principals to reduce discriminatory practices in the classroom.

Teachers Unions as Autonomous Powers

The teachers unions have become autonomous power centers which threaten the unitary interests of districts. Grimshaw's (1979) study of Chicago's teachers union suggests that the organization has gone through two phases in its relationship with the city and school administration. During its formative years, the union largely cooperated with the administration (and the mayor) in return for a legitimate role in the policymaking process. Cole (1969) also finds that union recognition was a key objective in the 1960 teachers' strike in New York City. In the second phase, which Grimshaw characterizes as "union rule," the union became independent of both the local political machine and the reform factions. Instead, it looked to the national union leadership for guidance and engaged in tough bargaining with the administration for better compensation and working conditions. Consequently, Grimshaw argues that policymakers "no longer are able to set policy unless the policy is consistent with the union's objectives" (1979, p. 150).

The Chicago teachers union has become assertive since the late 1960s, when it obtained the right to collective bargaining. While Chicago teachers have organized several strikes since 1960, few school days were lost prior to 1970 (i.e., when collective bargaining was fully in place). Since 1970, strikes have often resulted in school closings. For example, eleven school days were lost in 1970, ten days in 1980, two days in 1985, and nineteen days in 1990. Using both the threat of strike and strike itself, the teachers union in Chicago has been able to obtain multiyear contracts in recent years. The union successfully negotiated for a two-year and a three-year contract in 1980 and in 1990, respectively.

In retrospect, union power seems to have greater impact on job retention than on wage increases. The uneven effect of union power is found in the Chicago data. In Chicago, the number of teachers has not been cut in direct proportion to the enrollment decline over the past twenty years. A good example of this is the 1988 Chicago school reform law, which granted job security to supernumeraries, i.e., teachers who lose their jobs because of declines in enrollment. Consequently, a stable teaching force has contributed to a significant reduction in class size in the two school systems. Indeed, today's class sizes are significantly smaller than those in the 1950s. In Chicago, the pupil-teacher ratio in elementary classes has been reduced from twenty-six to one to fifteen to one between 1950 and 1990. The average class size for secondary grades decreased from thirty-two to eighteen students during the forty-year period. Job retention also produces an aging, and perhaps more experienced, teaching force. Teachers in Chicago, on the average, had seventeen years of teaching experience in 1990, a gain of four years over the past decade.

While preventing the system from laying off its members, the Chicago Teachers Union has achieved limited success in raising teacher salaries in any dramatic manner. The gap between the top and the bottom schedules in the unified salary scale has remained virtually unchanged over time, and wages have barely kept pace with inflation. In current dollars, the average teacher's salary in Chicago grew by over 100 percent (i.e., from $16,000 to $34,000) between 1975 and 1990. When converted into 1982 constant dollars, however, these figures actually failed to keep pace with inflation—a decline from $29,700 to $26,000.

Toward Site-Based Decisionmaking

Finally, the central bureaucracy has shifted decision making on a variety of school issues to the site level. In the 1990s, urban districts have had some form of shared governance through which parents, community representatives, and school professionals participate in policymaking at schools. Examples of decentralized governance include the New York style of community control, site-based professional management in Dade County, Rochester, and Salt Lake City, and the Chicago experiment of establishing a locally elected parent council at each school. Currently we know a great deal about the varieties of site-level governance in terms of the distribution of power between the principal and parent representatives (Brown 1990; Clune and White 1988; Wong 1992b). We also know that governance reform can bring about social and organizational changes in the school community. Indeed, researchers have found that new governing structures can improve social relations among low-income minority parents, teachers, and pupils by creating a climate of trust and understanding that fosters staff morale and student aspirations and enhances parental support for teachers' work (Comer 1980, 1990; Rogers and Chung 1983; Edmonds 1979). Although there is a dearth of empirical research that links governance reform to classroom organization, the current literature offers a rich empirical base that suggests connections between governance reform and social relations in the school community.

Consistent with the nationwide trend toward decentralization, Chicago has institutionalized significant changes in the ways parents are involved in school policymaking. Field surveys from 1950, 1955, 1960, and 1965 find no structure for parental input. Beginning in 1970 and 1975, advisory councils on principal recruitment at the school level and board recruitment at the district level appeared. The 1980 and 1985 surveys found limited formal authority for parental participation in all Chicago schools. By 1990, as a result of the 1988 Chicago reform legislation, all Chicago schools have put in place extensive formal structures for parental empowerment. Today, elected parents dominate the eleven-member local school councils, which can hire and fire principals. Consistent with decentralized reform, the district's central office staff has been reduced from 5,867 to 3,666 positions between 1980 and 1990. However, the teacher contract is a major policy area that has been excluded from parental authority at both the district and the school levels (see Consortium on Chicago School Research 1992).

Conclusion

The politics of fragmentation has confronted the big-city district with the problem of maintaining a coherent system of governance. Institutional fragmentation has clearly weakened the district's central leadership in formulating and implementing a coherent set of policies to address pressing educational problems. Instead, diverse (and often competing) governing structures prevail. Regulations from higher-level governments require the district to maintain a complex administrative apparatus to fulfill legislative objectives; at the same time, the central school board also has been forced to yield more power to parents, teachers, and other corporate actors. In addition to coping with these political demands, the big-city system has been reshaped by consumer choices. While an increasing number of parents exercise school choice within the district, a great number of them have exited to suburban districts and the nonpublic sector. Confronted with the politics of both voice and choice, the big-city school district's central office has seen both its quasi-monopoly over public education and its bureaucratic autonomy eroded. That these changes have made life increasingly difficult for those who head central-city districts can be seen in the marked decrease in the tenure of superintendents.

In short, the bureaucratic control model of the pre-1960s is gone. Fragmentation in governing structures will remain for some time and will continue to shape our understanding of urban school politics. Indeed, institutional fragmentation and the creeping influence of choice challenge policymakers to address two questions—what major functions does the big-city school system serve and what kinds of institutional and political arrangements would best serve those functions? Given the politics of fragmentation and the lack of consensus on governance, it seems very unlikely that the big-city system will return to bureaucratic dominance. Yet decentralization alone has raised as many questions as it seems to answer. At the school and community level, the principal and parent council may not be able to coordinate the competing influences of the teachers unions and other organized interest groups. Local parent councils cannot reverse the structural tendency toward higher concentration of poor children in inner-city neighborhoods. Schools are not likely to come up with ways to improve the quality of teacher applicants. At the same time, a centralized authority with a strong administrative staff has proven a hindrance to creative solutions to urban education problems. Clearly, solutions to the policy dilemma of reaching for an optimal mix of centralization and decentralization (not only between the central administration and schools but also between state and federal agencies and the district as a whole) will be critical to the future of public education in central cities. Until then, the question "Can the big-city school system be governed?" will remain relevant.

NOTE

This is a revised version of a paper delivered at the 1992 annual meeting of the American Political Science Association. The research project was codirected by Paul E. Peterson and was supported by a grant from the Social Research Council. Research assistance was provided by Robert C. Lieberman, Tami Buhr, Melissa Bianchi, Jonathan Hanson, Gail Sunderman, Cindy Coltman, Tina Fontes, and Bruce Friedland.

REFERENCES

Berke, J., M. Goertz, and R. Coley. 1984. *Politicians, Judges, and City Schools: Reforming School Finance in New York*. New York: Russell Sage Foundation.

Bidwell, C. 1965. The School as a Formal Organization. In *Handbook of Organizations*, ed. J. March, 972–1022. Skokie: Rand McNally.

Brown, D. 1990. *Decentralization and School-Based Management*. London: Falmer.

Case, C. 1977. History of the Desegregation Plan in Boston. In *The Future of Big-City Schools*, ed. D. Levine and R. Havighurst, chap. 10. Berkeley: McCutchan.

Chubb, J., and T. Moe. 1990. *Politics, Markets, and America's Schools*. Washington, DC: Brookings Institution.

Clune, W., and P. White. 1988. *School-Based Management: Institutional Variation, Implementation, and Issues for Further Research*. New Brunswick, NJ: Center for Policy Research in Education.

Cole, S. 1969. *The Unionization of Teachers: A Case Study of the United Federation of Teachers*. New York: Praeger.

Coleman, J.S., and T. Hoffer. 1987. *Public and Private High Schools*. New York: Basic Books.

Coleman, J.S., T. Hoffer, and S. Kilgore. 1982. *High School Achievement*. New York: Basic Books.

Comer, J.P. 1980. *School Power*. New York: Free Press.

———. 1990. Home, School, and Academic Learning. In *Access to Knowledge: An Agenda for Our Nation's Schools*, ed. J. Goodlad and P. Keating. New York: College Entrance Examination Board.

Consortium on Chicago School Research. 1992. *Charting Reform: The Principals' Perspective*. Chicago, IL: The Consortium on Chicago School Research.

Cronin, J. 1973. *The Control of Urban Schools*. New York: Free Press.

Edmonds, R. 1979. Effective Schools for the Urban Poor. *Educational Leadership* 37: 15–24.

Grimshaw, W. 1979. *Union Rule in the Schools*. Lexington: D.C. Heath.

Hirschman, A. 1971. *Exit, Voice, and Loyalty*. Cambridge: Harvard University Press.

Jackson, B., and J. Cibulka. 1992. Leadership Turnover and Business Mobilization: The Changing Political Ecology of Urban School Systems. In *The Politics of Urban Education in the United States*, ed. J. Cibulka, R. Reed, and K. Wong, chap. 5. London: Falmer.

Kozol, J. 1991. *Savage Inequalities*. New York: Crown.

Meier, K., J. Stewart, and R. England. 1989. *Race, Class, and Education*. Madison: University of Wisconsin Press.

Orfield, G. 1988. Race, Income, and Educational Inequality: Students and Schools at Risk in the 1980s. In Council of Chief State School

Officers, *School Success for Students at Risk.* Orlando: Harcourt Brace Jovanovich.

Orfield, G., and S. Reardon. 1992. Separate and Unequal Schools: Political Change and the Shrinking Agenda of Urban School Reform. Paper delivered at the American Political Science Association annual meeting, Chicago. September 1992.

Peterson, P.E. 1976. *School Politics Chicago Style.* Chicago: University of Chicago Press.

Peterson, P.E., B. Rabe, and K. Wong. 1986. *When Federalism Works.* Washington, DC: Brookings Institution.

Rogers, D., and N. Chung. 1983. *110 Livingston Street Revisited: Decentralization in Action.* New York: New York University Press.

Rossell, C. 1990. *The Carrot or the Stick for School Desegregation Policy.* Philadelphia: Temple University Press.

Scheirer, P. 1989. Metropolitan Chicago Public Schools: Concerto for Grades, Schools, and Students in F Major. Draft Paper, Metropolitan Opportunity Project. Chicago: Metropolitan Opportunity Project, University of Chicago.

Weber, M. 1947. *The Theory of Social and Economic Organization,* T. Parsons and A.M. Henderson, trans. Glencoe: Free Press.

Weick, K. 1976. Educational Organization as Loosely Coupled Systems. *Administrative Science Quarterly* 21: 1–9.

Witte, J., and D. Walsh. 1985. Metropolitan Milwaukee District Performance Assessment Report. Staff report to the Study Commission on the Quality of Education in the Metropolitan Milwaukee Public Schools, Report 4.

Wong, K. 1989. Fiscal Support for Education in American States: The "Parity-to-Dominance" View Examined. *American Journal of Education* 97 (4): 339–357.

———. 1991. State Reform in Education Finance: Territorial and Social Strategies. *Publius: The Journal of Federalism* 21 (Summer) 125–142.

———. 1992a. Choice in Public Schools: Their Institutional Functions and Distributive Consequences. In *Politics of Policy Innovation in Chicago,* ed. K. Wong, chap. 9. Greenwich: JAI.

———. 1992b. The Politics of Urban Education as a Field of Study: An Interpretive Analysis. In *The Politics of Urban Education in the United States,* ed. J. Cibulka, R. Reed, and K. Wong, chap. 1. London: Falmer.

————. 1994. Resource Allocation and Educational Equity. Washington, DC: AERA.

————. Forthcoming. Bureaucracy and School Effectiveness. Vol. 6, "Educational Administration," ed. W. Boyd. *International Encyclopedia of Education.* 2d ed. London: Pergamon Press.

17

Administrative Leadership and the Crisis in the Study of Educational Administration: Technical Rationality and Its Aftermath

James G. Cibulka
Hanne B. Mawhinney
With the assistance of Jerald Paquette

Introduction

Americans and Canadians alike have been busy trying to reform their schools for the better part of the last decade. This is not the first of these reform episodes nor is it likely to be the last. That schools are remarkably impervious to reform efforts comes as no surprise to anyone today; the painful experience of failed reforms dating from the 1960s has brought home recognition of this reality. That decade's unbridled faith in the potential of science and technology to transform schooling has proven unfounded. Reform failures have tempered reformers' optimistic belief that professionals are capable of using the tools of technical rationality to overcome the problems of North American life, and confidence in the power of scientific approaches to administration and governance to guide and direct reforms in education has gradually eroded during the past twenty-five years.

Educational professionals, relying on the theories and tools of technical rationality, have been unable to solve the newly emergent complex problems of education. During this time, a demographic revolution, in addition to radically changing the ethnic, racial, and linguistic character and the value and belief heritage of North American society has exposed profound disagreement about fundamental issues of educational purpose. Demands for educational reforms resulting from these changes in the North American sociopolitical context became part of the nearly continuous wave of rising expectations which has buffeted our schools during the past quarter-century.

The reforms that educational experts have offered in response to these demands have for the most part proven ineffective, and the rational administrative theories from which they were derived have been shown to be fragile and incomplete. Although the literature on social policy implementation, organizational theory, and related areas now offers some explanation of why reform has failed, translation of this new knowledge into directions for real change in schooling has not been forthcoming. Already critics such as Sarason (1990), Chubb and Moe (1990), and others warn that current reform efforts will fail again. If they are correct, this pessimism raises an important question: how much have we really learned about the requirements for change in schools?

Educational administration as a field of study, given its important place in preparing and credentialing career administrators for our schools, provides a vantage point for addressing this problem. A focus on the field's core conception of leadership, with its close relationship to a dominant tradition of technical rationality in decision making, enables the argument that despite severe challenges to the rational paradigm and the emergence of a number of alternative conceptions of leadership, the rationalist legacy lives on in many reform proposals and much scholarship in the field of educational administration.

In April 1967, Luvern L. Cunningham, then director of the Midwest Administration Center at the University of Chicago, delivered a lecture entitled "The Administrator and Teacher" as part of the Seventy-fifth Anniversary Lecture Series "Teaching and Learning 1991." His speculation as to the nature of schools in 1991 is a helpful reconstruction of how the future appeared a quarter-century ago and can assist us in describing the perceived role of the school administrator as an agent of change.

Schools in 1991: Cunningham's 1967 View Forward

In a rich and provocative lecture, Cunningham argued that rationality, working with other forces, would reshape schooling as he then knew it. The driving force animating this reconstruction would be public dissatisfaction with the status quo. National assessment was a central component of this new rationality, since it would help the nation get a better reading on the effectiveness of its schools. In 1967 the National Assessment of Educational Progress (NAEP) was already in its initial phase; its expected outcome was a refined mechanism for measuring the "national educational product in much the same fashion as the Gross National Product" (p. 3).

Although this sounds remarkably prescient, other examples of this budding rationality had a shorter life. Cunningham espoused Planning-Programming-Budgeting systems and PERT (Program Evaluation and Review Technique), which did not survive President Johnson's adoption of them at the federal level and were not widely adopted by educational governing bodies. In 1967, however, Cunningham viewed these new decision technologies as part of what he called an "emerging family of themes" which would help educational administrators decide what they were about and what resources they needed, and, above all, would enable them to "get on with the task."

Central to this rational conception of school administration were planning and input-output approaches to measuring educational productivity. Computers were expected to bring greater rationality to management in much the same way that then-popular models of computer-assisted programs would improve instruction. It was thought that because of their capacity to store and manipulate information, computers would improve decision making throughout the educational enterprise.

For the most part, increased specialization was welcomed during this time as a rationalizing force, although Cunningham and others argued for balancing it with team approaches to teaching and administration. Specialization was part of a new openness in educational institutions brought about by federal investments in education, investments that led to specialized lines of research and development and opened educational institutions to greater public scrutiny. The objective of these programs was to train and place research and development (R & D) personnel, and Cunningham predicted that this new R & D capacity would lead to "the improved feedback of current performance of the larger school enterprise. The reporting of definitive results will in turn lead to new specializations at the instructional as well as the administrative levels" (p. 9).

Cunningham foresaw greater rationality leading to a human development perspective in education. Social problems of the time such as adolescent delinquency and dropping out required the restructuring of schools. Cunningham lamented the powerful hold the traditional "stereotyped view of the school" held on ways of thinking and acting during the process. Among these stereotypes was a narrow focus on cognitive rather than an emphasis on emotional and physical development. Cunningham called for greater attention to the medical and nutritional needs of children and for an educational approach which took responsibility for the individual from age three through the entire life span. In the last quarter-century, only bits and pieces of this vision have found their way into schools, and in a manner far short of the "invention of a new institution" Cunningham predicted, despite arguments by Kirst (1989) and others for more attention to coordinated services for children.

By 1991 schools would, Cunningham believed, be responsible for developing a diagnostic growth record and plan for each child. Borrowing from Herbert Blum, he envisioned the school becoming an "information processing factory" with the goal of maximizing human development. This would require new roles, and teaching and administration as they were known then would undergo tremendous changes brought on by the information processing aspect of this task and the inherent specialization which flowed from it.

Administrators were no longer to be "leaders" or "educational statesmen," as in the old terminology, but "data managers." They would become systems specialists, responsible for allocating inputs and intensifying outputs. Surmised Cunningham: "You can almost visualize him seated in a swivel chair focusing upon dials and rotating tapes that are organizing information, packaging it, storing it and reporting it on an assortment of screens and print outs" (p. 14). Handbooks (with such labels as "The Rational Education Manager") would help an administrator take immediate and appropriate action to deal with specific learning problems in ways dependent upon the particular characteristics of the pupil in question. In this vision, the central office would still be only a phone call away, ready to make helpful recommendations to the building manager. Here Cunningham cites his intellectual debt to Herbert Simon, who believed that the manager of the future would be a thinker and decision maker as well as an information processor.

Given the turmoil surrounding educational governance in the late 1960s, Cunningham's inclusion of this domain in his call for greater rationality comes as no surprise. He saw a need for appropriate metropolitan solutions, improved funding, and greater citizen access to schools, particularly for inner-city residents; he argued for a redesign of school systems that would balance the advantages of bigness (namely, "the maximization of values inherent in large-scale organization") with those of smallness. Counteracting bureaucratic dysfunction would require redistribution of power, authority, and wealth throughout the metropolitan community (and by implication, throughout state and provincial communities as well), and at the same time, would inevitably be accompanied by demands of teachers and other professionals for greater participation. Even students would take part in the new management system. While Cunningham worried about resistance to change from within these organizations, he accepted the demand for participation in policy matters as a natural, predictable occurrence.

Overall, then, Cunningham expected substantial modifications in the structure of educational institutions by 1991 because consumers were "fed up" with the nation's school system. His predictions assumed that societal dissatisfaction with education would prompt reform, and moreover that the direction of such reform was susceptible to largely technical solutions, upon which there would be underlying consensus. Cunningham did not approve of all the trends he described, but he did see rationalization of education, intensification of specialization, revision of educational government, and pressure for increased participation in decision making as central themes which would reshape schools by 1991 (p. 16).

Challenges to the Rational Paradigm in Educational Administration

A difficult question remains: Why are such rationalizing trends and the concomitant changes which Cunningham expected to accompany rationalization still in such short supply in schools? Also unanswered is the underlying question of why this model of rationality has proven to be a defective model of progress. Rationality as a model consists of two segments: (1) rationality as a problem of knowledge, and (2) rationality as a problem of interests and values. Not isomorphic by any means, these categories serve as useful organizing devices to illustrate the central point that faith in rationality has been severely eroded in the last quarter-century without being replaced by adequate theories or metaphors to help us reconstruct the schools for the future.

Rational Progress as a Knowledge Problem

The trends toward rationalizing education combine curiously with the pressure for new participation in decision making identified by Cunningham, since they represent contradictory paradigms of decision making and leadership. Technocratic rationality emphasizes centralized decision making by specialists using techniques of calculated rationalism. In contrast, the pluralism implied in demands for participatory decision making supports democracy and decentralization and adopts disjointed incrementalism as a rationale for policymaking. The coexistence of these trends in the North American political culture of the 1960s has been noted by a number of scholars. Some of them argue that the era of technical rationality and interest group pluralism epitomized in Cunningham's lecture had its debut in John F. Kennedy's commencement address at Yale University in 1962 (Bell 1973; Lowi 1979; Schön 1982; Straussman 1978; Sternberg 1989). In Kennedy's words:

> Old sweeping issues have largely disappeared. The central problems of our times are more subtle and less simple. They relate not to basic clashes of philosophy or ideology, but to ways and means of reaching common goals—to research for sophisticated solutions to complex and obstinate problems. (Lowi 1979, p. 275)

Although Lowi argues that this speech represents a milestone in interest-group politics, others suggest that it indicates the debut of technocratic politics (Bell 1973; Straussman 1978). Straussman views the speech as exemplifying the beginnings of a "politics of rationalism, science, and technology" (p. 135). Scholars generally agree, however, that both technocratic rationality and interest-group liberalism came to full flower in the 1960s, the era in which Cunningham noted their impact on educational trends.

Education during this time was guided by a positivistic science of administration and technical rationality, its "epistemology of practice" (Schön 1982, p. 31). Since then the promise of knowledge to be gained by technical rationality has increasingly been questioned, and people have become aware of the limits of the knowledge provided by technical rationality models. A discussion of emerging knowledge divides naturally into several subsections: knowledge of educational goals and decision-making processes, social forces, the educational production function, the technical core of education (i.e., the teaching and learning process), and administrative leadership.

Knowledge of Educational Goals and Decision-Making Processes

Cunningham's predictions of reformed schooling through rational management techniques depend upon the assumption that educational systems exist to attain goals. Evidence of goal-driven rationality, already present in 1967, could be seen in public demands for accountability through mechanisms such as the "specification of performance criteria for individuals, classrooms, buildings, and subdistricts within the metropolitan area" (p. 2). Thus Cunningham's argument was in line with the prevailing organizational perspective that considered goal orientation as the cornerstone of rationality in organizations. Pfeffer (1982, p. 7) noted, "the critical distinguishing feature of organizational theories taking the rational perspective is the element of conscious, foresightful action reasonably autonomously constructed to achieve some goal or value." Christened the "rational-actor model" by Allison (1971), this idealization characterizes the decision maker as a goal-oriented seeker after knowledge that will enhance decision making. This orientation supports a logical process of establishing goals, designing strategies for their implementation, and evaluating whether they have been achieved—a process that emphasizes accountability, efficiency, and outcomes.

In its ideal form the rational perspective adopted by Cunningham and others takes a determinate view of organizational events. Decision makers have knowledge of goals and can achieve them through orderly processes. From this perspective it is believed that decision makers can articulate a single set of specific and uniform goals using logical problem-solving procedures. This rational paradigm further assumes that organizational efficiency can be ensured because goals remain stable over a sustained period of time (Patterson, Purkey, and Parker 1986). In the rational-bureaucratic model, organizational behavior is purposive, intentional, and goal-directed; outcome predictability is "bounded only by the limits of current knowledge and technology" (Clark 1985, p. 69).

It has become clear, however, that decision making in education rarely addresses predictable and unambiguous issues with clear outcomes. Instead, it is often characterized by multiple goals and inconsistent preferences, unclear technologies for producing outcomes, and fluid participation of actors in the decision-making process (March and Olsen 1976). During the past quarter-century organizational theorists have criticized the rational-bureaucratic model's assumption of certain knowledge about organizational goals. These theorists have characterized educational organizations as loosely coupled systems (Weick 1976), garbage cans (Cohen, March, and Olsen 1972), or organized anarchies (March and Olsen 1976) rather than rationally coordinated organizations pursuing identifiable goals. Rejecting the rational-bureaucratic model's assumption that organizations can pursue a consistent set of predictable goals with certainty, these "postrational" perspectives point to the uncertainty produced in organizations with multiple, ambiguous goals. Some theorists go so far as to challenge the entire notion of organizational goals. Perrow (1982), for example, argues that organizations have constraints rather than goals. He suggests that "all sorts of people inside and outside of organizations use them for their own purposes, and each of these uses is a constraint upon other uses" (p. 687). Rational models of organization fail to explain non-goal-driven elements of decision making behavior; current theorists suggest that many other factors shape organizational behavior (Wilson 1989), including "situational imperatives, peer expectations, prior experiences, and professional norms" (Sykes 1990, p. 349).

Further, research on educational decision making confirms that policymakers generally pursue a multitude of competing and conflicting organizational goals (Firestone and Herriott 1982). School systems often face tensions created by trying to balance goals related to administrative efficiency with goals related to equity. Goals tend to be ambiguous, and they change as conditions change (Patterson, Purkey, and Parker 1986); indeed, state/provincial and district-level goals quite often have no connection to what occurs in the classroom (Lortie 1975; Patterson, Purkey, and Parker 1986; Weick 1976). Research confirms that, rather than being set by decision makers at the top of the educational hierarchy, goals emerge through a process of bargaining and compromise between forces both inside and outside the organization (Bacharach and Mitchell 1987).

Specifying performance criteria, as Cunningham (1967) suggested was required to ensure public accountability, becomes problematic in cases involving ambiguous or conflicting goals and lack of consensus among policy makers. The failure of the dominant rational perspective to provide policy makers with usable knowledge about the conflictual nature of agenda setting in school districts has led to the development of a number of political approaches to the study of educational organizations (Bacharach and Lawler 1980; Bacharach and Mitchell 1987; Wirt and Kirst 1989) that attempt to overcome the limitations of the rational model by generating knowledge about the goal conflicts pervasive in educational policy and implementation. Unfortunately, pluralist models of political decision making do not offer much practical guidance to school officials on how to make education more productive, efficient, and equitable. On the contrary, the full blooming of interest-group liberalism in education, as in other realms of public policy, has become a recipe for stalemate and a legitimation of the status quo (Lowi 1979; Sternberg 1989).

Knowledge of Social Forces

The prevailing rational model applied to educational organizations views social forces operating in the environment as external to the actual functioning of the organization (Patterson, Purkey, and Parker 1986). The model is based on the assumption of a relatively stable and certain external environment that will impinge on organizations only in rational and predictable ways. According to the rational perspective, decision makers can gain adequate knowledge of the world beyond the school system to ensure that the goals pursued are consistent with the needs of the community. Conceptually this model views educational organizations as closed systems (Griffiths 1988); however, during the past two decades research findings have confirmed that the environment of an organization critically influences the organization itself (Lawrence and Lorsch 1967; Meyer and Rowan 1977; Perrow 1982). Public schools, like business organizations, respond to changing social forces in the environment (Griffiths 1988), and the quarter-century since Cunningham presented his predictions has been marked by major changes in North American society. These changes have significantly increased the uncertainty faced by educational decision makers: minorities no longer accept automatically the American ideal of assimilation; an increasing number of interest groups create their own agendas; social movements such as the civil rights movement, the women's movement, and fundamentalism realign the political landscape. The result has been a collapse of consensus in the United States (Griffiths 1988).

The unpredictability of external social forces becomes problematic for decision makers choosing to adopt a rational perspective. Lack of knowledge about what to expect from the external environment undermines rational approaches to decision making in educational organizations. The problem is that the rational model's dependence on predictability as well as a high degree of consensus in the environment leaves decision makers without adequate knowledge of the changing social forces which have created an increasingly politicized context for education in North America (Bacharach and Mitchell 1987; Wirt and Kirst 1989).

Knowledge of the Educational Production Function

In 1967, when Cunningham made his predictions of rationality in education, efforts were already being made to apply economic concepts such as the production function to educational problems (Thomas 1968). One of the foci of these emerging studies in the economics of education was the efficiency of the internal allocation of resources in educational systems. The studies concerned themselves with "how to accomplish more for the benefit of students within the constraints of a more-or-less fixed budget" (Benson 1988, p. 365). Commonly the technique employed to address this concern was the educational production function, also called input-output or cost-quality analysis (Hanushek 1989).

To Cunningham (1967), these input-output analyses were promising additions to the tool kit of rational bureaucratic management. They could, he believed, assist educational decision makers in identifying "better input combinations, in terms of the desired outputs" and could also help appraise "the utility of new procedures and approaches to education" (p. 7). Ultimately these analyses would enable educational decision makers to measure directly the productivity of schools (Thomas 1968). Cunningham's targeting of input-output analyses was in line with the focus on the outcomes of schooling just emerging.

Although concerns for efficiency in educational systems were not new, until the late 1960s public educators had emphasized "securing adequate resources and facilities to provide access to schooling for all" (Boyd and Hartman 1988, p. 274). Then the findings of the Coleman Report (Coleman et al. 1966) suggested that schools were not an important determinant in student achievement and provided the original impetus for the large number of analyses of input-output relationships in schools that have followed (Hanushek 1989).

A production function "describes the maximum level of outcome possible from alternative combinations of inputs" (Monk 1989, p. 31). As Cunningham (1967) recognized, if the production function exists and is known, it holds tremendous possibilities for the efficient administration of schools and for improving their productivity. Recognition of this potential has fueled economic research addressing the production function in education during the past quarter-century.

Yet it is uncertain whether this new area of knowledge has really fulfilled its promise of providing knowledge useful for making educational practice more efficient. A number of assessments of production function studies argue that they have rarely produced knowledge useful in guiding educational policymaking (Benson 1988; Monk 1989). Production function studies have produced inconsistent results; where one study identifies several resources as significant, another study finds them insignificant (Averch et al. 1972). Further, where consistency is found, no systematic relationship is found between the variables of interest (Monk 1989), particularly those pertaining to teaching and learning. These studies may be based on the mistaken assumption that there is only one production function, when in fact there may be many (Rossmiller 1987), each depending on the characteristics of the learner.

Frustration with the failure of early production function studies to provide guidance in improving educational productiv-ity led to the development of the "more inductive effective-schools research strategy" (Monk 1989, p. 37). Inspired by the finding that teachers and schools differ in their effectiveness (Murnane 1975), these investigations adopted inductive ap-proaches "based on intensive case studies of unusually effective or ineffective" schools (Monk 1989, p. 37). Effective-schools research and the production function studies share a focus on student achievement as the measure of educators' effectiveness. In the former, lists of school factors associated with higher achievement are commonly derived (Edmonds 1981; Good and Brophy 1986; Purkey and Smith 1985). Like the inconsistent production function specifications, these lists have been diverse and inconsistent. Assessments of the effective-schools approach point to a number of weaknesses, such as the bias produced by focusing on small samples of "outlier" schools, the lack of generalizability from common case-study methodology, the limitations of adopting mean achievement on standardized tests as the measure of achievement, and the masking of within-school variation by the school-level focus (Witte and Walsh 1990). As a result, like the assessments of production function studies, the effective-schools research has received mixed reviews (Rowan, Bossert, and Dwyer 1983).

Cunningham (1967) correctly foresaw the powerful potential for administrative rationality resulting from the estimation of the education production function. Although theorists continue to recognize this potential, inconsistent and insignificant findings of both production function studies and the effective-schools research have illustrated the difficulties associated with searching for consistently significant input-output relationships in education. Recognition of the failure to adequately specify the parameters of these relationships has spurred further efforts to improve the specification of production function models and to refine the factors related to effectiveness (Monk 1989), but these efforts remain problematic because "analysts continue to lack independent knowledge of how adequate their specification is" (p. 36). Therefore, while analyses of input-output relationships are potentially powerful tools for the rational management of school systems, they represent a "high-risk research strategy" (p. 43). The lack of robustness of these studies has been called a problem of "omitted variables" (Benson 1988, p. 366). The promise of achieving efficiency in school management through the use of rational tools (i.e., the education production function) remains unfulfilled due to lack of knowledge of the variables associated with educational productivity and the nature of their interrelationships. Common output variables, such as student achievement, may be weakly linked to the ambiguous and conflicting goals of an educational organization, and the linkage between input variables such as teacher characteristics and outcomes may be uncertain and unknown. The rationality promised by input-output analyses is compromised to the extent that knowledge about the variables specified by the education production function is weak or nonexistent.

Knowledge of the Teaching-Learning Process

The difficulty of specifying a relationship between teacher characteristics and student outcomes in production function studies underscores basic problems in applying the kind of rationality that held such hope for Cunningham in 1967 to the management of the technical core of education, the teaching-learning process. The rational model assumes that clear goals are articulated within a tightly integrated hierarchy producing an efficient fulfillment of those goals (Estler 1988). Goals are therefore perceived as the primary unit of control over the technical core of schooling (Sykes 1990). Decisions made at the apex of the hierarchy are translated into outcomes through explicitly defined steps undertaken in the technical core. Applied to the teaching process, rational models assume that once instructional goals have been identified, efficient and effective means for achieving them can be specified and followed by teachers. The models propose that links between policymaking and teaching, and teaching and learning, allow the accomplishment of goals (Patterson, Purkey, and Parker 1986). In this rational perspective, educators can manage the technology of education in ways that will achieve greater productivity. However, the findings of production function studies during the past quarter-century contradict this assertion of increased efficiency. Despite numerous efforts to identify educational inputs and outcomes and their relationships, the technology of education remains underspecified. It remains unclear how school achievement comes about, or even whether it is produced in any consistent way across classes, schools, and regions.

At the center of this contested domain in research lie differing conceptions of the nature of the teaching-learning process based on differing perceptions of the teacher's stance toward students and the student's stance toward the task of learning (Devaney and Sykes 1988). One common conception reflects a rational model of educational technology in which instructional activities are "rationally planned, programmatically organized, and carried out on the basis of standard operating procedures" (p. 5). Although this model anticipates that teachers will be closely managed, it also recognizes that they are more than functionaries carrying out orders. Teachers must learn to decide what and how to teach. However, these decisions are drawn from standardized knowledge and "the essential encounter between teacher and student is often described as delivery" (p. 6). Cunningham (1967) described this model of teaching in his prediction that teacher training would undergo "substantial redesign," to ensure that teachers possessed the information-processing skills required to "enhance their client service performance records" (p. 16). In this rational model, teachers become client service workers, and learning is a passive act of consumption that occurs within a hierarchical bureaucracy. Although this conception of the teaching-learning process is commonly held by the public and by many politicians, it is currently being contradicted by trends in society and the economy which have transformed the organization of work in many American corporations, thus leading organizational theorists to question the utility of the rational bureaucratic model.

Foremost among these trends has been a declining need for blue-collar workers concurrent with the emergence of a knowledge-based economy which requires educated, sophisticated workers to perform complex intellectual tasks in an environment where the work of managers and workers often overlaps (Griffiths 1988). Although understanding of the requirements for such work is far from complete, it is evident that new perspectives on organizing education will be required to support our emerging understanding of the nature of the teaching-learning process. Such perspectives will challenge a key assumption of rational models of organization, that of goals as the fundamental unit of control (Sykes 1990). Instead the focus will shift to the core technology, the tasks of teaching and learning, and the guiding principle will be that "core technology drives structure" (Sykes and Elmore 1988, p. 84). Rather than reinforce the rationally designed educational structures that have failed to serve the needs of the core activities of education, the new perspectives advocate "unfreezing" conventional patterns of structure and technology (p. 81). The central problem will become finding structures to "reflect and reinforce competing theories of good teaching and learning" (p. 84). To address problems of institutional design, new ways of aligning external incentives and internal structures with our emerging knowledge of effective educational practice (including the practice of administrative leadership) must be found (Clune 1987; Gormley 1987; Sykes and Elmore 1988).

The Study of Administrative Leadership and the Rational Tradition

Nowhere have the problems posed by these assumptions about the knowledge base of educational administration been more significant than in the study of administrative leadership. The field of educational administration theory has relied heavily on research generated in other disciplines for its understanding of leadership. Two major reviews of the leadership literature in educational administration (Immegart 1988; Slater et al. 1994) draw extensively on the work of organizational theorists, sociologists, industrial psychologists, and others in fields outside of educational administration. It must be said, however, that while studies of leadership have been conducted by people from many areas, by and large the work has been dominated by psychologists with a strong behavioral orientation grounded in the assumptions of structural functionalism. In his review Slater acknowledges that while structural models still dominate the field, instead of a single paradigm for studying leadership in the field there exist at least four competing perspectives nested in broader theories of social organization. This multiparadigmatic argument was first made by Bolman and Deal (1984, 1991), who reasoned that failure to supplement a structural (rational) perspective on leadership seriously impairs organizational research and administrative practice. They suggest three other perspectives: a human resource view focusing on the needs of individuals who work in the organization; a political perspective treating organizations as arenas for group competition for power and scarce resources; and a symbolic perspective, seeing organizations as cultures driven by rituals, ceremonies, heroes, and myths, as distinct from formal rules, policies, and authority. As if to symbolize how rapidly this dissensus in the field has taken hold, one need only turn to the excellent but far narrower treatment of the topic in Immegart's review conducted five years earlier, in 1988. What Slater subsequently described as the "structural-functional" approach to the study of leadership was virtually the only perspective examined in Immegart's review. Bolman and Deal's challenge to it did not warrant any mention.

To be sure, Immegart (1988) found much wanting in this leadership literature, even working from within the rational decision-making model. For example, much of the recent literature has emphasized the situational nature of leadership and its dependence on such factors as the nature of the work technology under scrutiny, the maturity of the workers, and so on (Fiedler 1967; Fiedler and Chemers 1974; House and Baetz 1979). Yet the literature on leadership traits, style, and behavior tends to ignore organizational goals and motivations of leaders, not to mention the cultural and environmental aspects of situations (Immegart 1988, p. 271). Such omissions are doubly problematic: on the one hand, the literature fails to incorporate the goal dimension so critical to rational theory; on the other hand, it can be faulted for its failure to understand culture and environment, which is the soft underbelly of rational theory and which has contributed to its unpopularity recently. It is not particularly helpful, except in the most general theoretical sense, to know that effective leaders exhibit a repertoire of styles which in turn reflect situational contingencies such as context and task, unless one has more specifics. From both a theoretical and a training perspective, this is but an empty shell into which the content of the leadership actions must be poured.

One of the content areas lamentably absent when these theories are applied to education is knowledge of teaching and learning. Cunningham's memorable picture of the administrator effortlessly guiding pupils' progress working from some scientific manual borders on the comic (or tragic). As pointed out previously, such detailed knowledge has yet to materialize. Even at a more proximate level of knowledge—one which attends to issues of instructional grouping, classroom organization, grading, curriculum, and other components of instructional management—the field of educational administration is largely silent, despite exhortations by some scholars that it move in this direction (Bossert 1988; Erickson 1978). The effective-schools literature attempts to specify elements of an instructional management strategy for administrators, but this literature was developed largely outside the field of educational administration. The problems and limitations of the effective-schools research are, however, well-known and need not be reviewed in detail here (for a summary see Bossert 1988, pp. 346–347).

To be sure, much that is located specifically in the educational administration literature deals with instructional leadership, a concept dating back many decades (Cubberley 1924). The central idea of these studies is that school administrators should be more than managers who procure, organize, and coordinate resources to reach organizational goals. Management is confined, much of this literature holds, to maintaining the existing order and keeping things running smoothly, while leadership, particularly instructional leadership, attends to change which can improve learning. Yet the concept of instructional leadership, while widely accepted by school principals, remains vaguely defined (Gorton and Schneider 1991). In general, it targets the improvement of teaching performance through instructional supervision. While laudable, the models generally applied to guide administrators in this literature lean heavily on the process of improving teaching performance rather than on the broad range of strategies encompassed by instructional management. Further, the literature virtually ignores school and community influences on learning. Not only is such a conception of leadership a prisoner of the rational assumptions of structural-functional theory but it is a very weak application of that perspective to the problems of educational administration.

In broad outline, it can be said that major developments in the education knowledge base since the late 1960s pose a severe challenge to the assumptions of rationality and progress that guided most thinking in that period. While promising areas of new knowledge are emerging and have been alluded to, it would be a vast exaggeration to say that the pieces of the "knowledge puzzle" fit together in any coherent way now. Much of the new knowledge which has emerged has either undercut the rational model or has failed to establish key dimensions upon which rationalization depends, such as the development of undisputed production functions. This reality—the unraveling of the faith in scientific rationality as a basis for educational administration and policymaking that prevailed when Cunningham wrote a quarter-century ago—should greatly temper any assumption that new knowledge, in and of itself, will be the primary lever of progress in education. Clearly, a realignment of values and interests must be part of this process, which necessitates a clear understanding of how interests are embedded within the problem of reform and progress.

Political Interests and Values in Administration

As we have suggested, the rational model of educational administration and governance has been under repeated assault in the last quarter-century, its credibility sharply undercut by the existence of several types of knowledge that are in short supply or are estimated to be of limited importance to administrators working within a rational model of organization. Another set of forces exists whose impact on administration is equally problematic for structural-functional models. For convenience, it is useful to consider them together under the label of "interests and values," a grouping useful to the degree that both interests and values embody a subjective dimension of individual behavior. Of course, like all classifications, this one is at some level arbitrary in that interests and values arguably have a rational component and involve an element of calculation and awareness on the part of persons who exhibit them. The point here is that the presumption of technical neutrality upon which rational theory is based—the basic premise that it is possible and desirable to separate facts and values, as Hume argued—is challenged by the complementary influence upon organizational behavior of interests and values. Further, treating interests and values as a separate category from knowledge makes sense for another reason. Comprehension of political forces operating in schools or the role which values play would aid educators immensely in administration. Unlike the four kinds of knowledge reviewed previously (goals, social forces, production function, and the teaching-learning process), which are inherently in short supply, knowledge of interests and values is attainable to a much greater degree. The challenge this information poses to a rational model, then, is not its limited access as an informational problem but rather the limited awareness of its importance and the failure to build models of leadership around the important role which these factors play in shaping organizational behavior.

At the time that Cunningham wrote, the tendency to view schooling as a political enterprise was in its infancy in the United States. Progressive reformers early in the twentieth century had successfully cast educational administration, like other types of public administration, as a domain of technical expertise to be removed from partisan politics and run according to businesslike corporate principles. This meant sharply reducing the influence of lay persons, particularly those without education and status, on school affairs, making school administration an autonomous sphere for experts. This governance model comports well with the rational-theoretical model of decision making.

Cunningham was of course well aware of the political nature of educational decision making. He correctly predicted further political pressures in the form of demands for new governance mechanisms and the further collective organization of employee interests intended to limit managerial authority. That the model of organization reflected in his analysis remained a rational one illustrated the coexistence of and indeed, if MacIntyre (1989) is right, the definitional quality of interest-group politics and technical rationality in the liberal state. A number of explanations of the coexistence of pluralism and technocracy have been offered. Some argue that organizations cope with discordance, such as the contradiction between the incrementalist decision making required by pluralist politics and the calculated rationality of scientific management models, by decoupling them from each other (Meyer and Rowan 1977).

Sternberg (1989) identifies strategies in which techniques of technical rationality have been used as political weapons. Despite the proclaimed objectivity of rational methodologies, some researchers have observed the opportunistic use of the technical tools of decision making by advocacy groups (Feldman and Milch 1982). Methods such as cost-benefit analysis, for example, are malleable enough to have been used as a justification for political decision making. Analysis is also used as an ex post facto justification for administrative decisions (Pressman and Wildavsky 1973). Others have documented the symbolic or semiotic adoption of rational methodologies such as PERT by organizations wishing to present a picture of rational management to the outside world while maintaining a political and partisan model of decision making in practice (Sapolsky 1972).

In addition to discussion of the role of political interests in educational administration, an ongoing debate has emerged about the role of values in administration. The core of that question, briefly stated, is whether rationality or values should be the final grounding of administrative work. At opposite ends of the spectrum of opinion regarding the nature of administrative work are two diametrically opposed visions of the administrator. On the one hand, the founding literature in management science and educational administration is rooted in a view of the administrator as a rational decision maker, as a system optimizer whose choosing among alternative courses of institutional action can and ought to have the attributes of traditional engineering informed by positivist science. The other view is that administration is the arbitration of conflicting values about the most important issues of institutional and social purpose—in Hodgkinson's (1978) terms, "philosophy in action." Herbert Simon, who sent management science down the path of rational technocracy in 1945 with the publication of *Administrative Behavior* (1957), also ironically fired one of the first critical shots at its underlying assumptions of value-neutral rationality two decades later in the book *Organizations* (March and Simon 1966).

In the two-and-a-half decades since, the debate which this questioning spawned in the broader literature on administration divided the educational administration community. Following the lead of their management-science mentors, Halpin (1958, 1966), Griffiths (1957, 1977, 1979), and others first introduced the assumptions, worldview, and methods of positivist social science to the field of educational administration. Dissenting voices, however, led by T. Barr Greenfield, have found these underpinnings wanting in their power to contribute to any useful understanding of administrative work, especially in education. For Greenfield, educational administration, far from being a matter of algorithmically rational decision making, is about "the wielding of power and the making of decisions when much is on the line" (1986, p. 77). Greenfield and others have argued that as North American society becomes increasingly pluralistic, tensions and conflict over the content, structure, and value commitments of publicly funded education seem more likely to escalate than to abate. Accordingly, they suggest that the failure of research in educational administration to converge on any truly generalizable laws or principles is ultimately the result of, in the first instance, the nature of administrative work as the arbitration of conflicting values and, in the second, the particularly value-laden nature of strategic decision making in education (Greenfield 1986).

In the last quarter-century, then, the recognition that educational decision making is political and value laden has sharply undermined the technical, nonpartisan model. Several major challenges to this model, represented by the pluralist, radical, and public-choice models, have moved the concept of political interests to the forefront of educational decision making. According to these political models, educational decisions should be understood as a by-product of dominant or competing interests, not as an attempt to optimize a rational decision outcome; thus they represent a basic challenge to the rational model of decision making and leadership.

Pluralist Perspectives

One of the first serious examinations of educational politics was presented in a landmark article by Thomas Eliot, a political scientist outside the educational establishment, in a 1958 edition of the *American Political Science Review*. By the mid-1960s many leading university graduate programs in educational administration had established specialties in the politics of education, although even today this area remains a peripheral interest in educational administration. Open-systems models such as David Easton's *Systems Analysis of Political Life* (1965) were coming to rival the old closed-system organizational models which had dominated the field. The behavioral science movement, which had swept aside traditional studies in public administration within political science, found its way into the study of the politics of education. The first major textbook in the field, authored by political scientists Frederick Wirt and Michael Kirst (1972), reflected this behavioral perspective. Broadly speaking, they endorsed a pluralist model which portrayed educational policymaking as a contested arena among competing groups. Although some studies (e.g., Zeigler, Jennings, and Peak 1974) portrayed how truly closed and dominated by professionals education policy has been, pluralist theory remains the most influential model in the field. In this model, no one set of interests is said to dominate all issues, and the political system is capable of functioning despite incomplete public participation and group mobilization. A good example of this pluralist logic is Iannaccone and Lutz's (1978) theory of school board elections. Most of this literature has taken a black-box approach to the inside of the organization. One exception is Peterson's (1974) study of school board and bureaucratic decision making in Chicago.

Implementation studies were some of the first strands of empirical research to suggest that the promise of progress through rational decision making outlined by Cunningham had not been met. Much of the research focused on problems of implementation of educational reforms. Beginning with the classic studies showing how the intentions of the U.S. government Elementary and Secondary Education Act were modified at the local level (Murphy 1971), the studies went on to show how "street level bureaucrats" reshape policy (Weatherley and Lipsky 1977; Mann 1978), how policy implementation involves a process of mutual adaptation by local sites and innovations (Berman and McLaughlin 1976), and how the making and implementing of policy continues throughout the implementation process (Weatherley and Lipsky 1977). Recent implementation studies have produced more optimistic evaluations of reform progress (McLaughlin 1987; Murphy 1989).

Critics charge that past research on implementation has provided limited guidance for policymakers because of its focus on relatively narrow programs and has not systematically specified the "relationships among the problems being addressed, the basic design features of the policies, the implementing organizations, or the political and organizational context in which policy targets must respond" (McDonnell and Elmore 1987, p. v). It is this argument that has led to calls for more comprehensive information about approaches to policy design (Boyd 1988; Linder and Peters 1989; McDonnell and Elmore 1987; Schneider and Ingram 1989).

When Cunningham wrote in 1967, he predicted further dissatisfaction with educational government and further employee organization within school systems. Yet the thrust of his analysis reflected a rational paradigm which cannot adequately account for, or cope with, political demands which even then were overwhelming the administration and governance of our school systems. In subsequent decades, the problem of politicization of educational decision making has grown to the point where some critics (e.g., Chubb and Moe 1990) see school systems as largely unmanageable under political rule.

Radical Critiques of Class, Race, and Gender

A second line of political models comes from radical political economy. This research tradition has been directed not simply, or even principally, at traditional rational organizational models but rather at the entire mainstream of research in education. (Of course, similar models have emerged in organizational theory generally; for a review, see Morgan 1986.) Perhaps the first of these critiques in educational policy in the United States was provided by Bowles and Gintis (1976). Many of these studies are rooted, in a disciplinary sense, more in educational sociology than in politics, and some have only the loosest connection to political studies in the mainstream of American political science. Again, because of the potentially vast terrain here, it is not possible to do more than scratch the surface to illustrate how important this line of analysis has proven to be in undermining the rational model.

Guiding Cunningham's optimism for a rationalized system of education, where specialized diagnosticians would provide teachers with detailed student assessments, is a model of the school as an "information-processing factory." In this metaphor, schools are busy factories actively engaged in processing the material, i.e., students. Through the application of "advanced machine assistance," "client-serving personnel" in such factories would determine the best methods and tools for producing educated students and thereby improving the quality of American life (Cunningham 1967, p. 11). The goal would be to maximize efficiency through specialization and a system of top-down decision making by "educational data managers" (p. 14).

Efficiency is the fundamental goal of such factory models (Oakes 1986). Cunningham's information-processing factory represents a variation on the scientific-management model which continues to dominate school administration in North America. This rational-bureaucratic model, based on the division of labor and specialization, has been adopted as the best way to manage the diverse population served by schools. Its industrial efficiency assumptions have shaped the form education has taken and have defined the central mission of schools as the preparation for work. The guiding assumptions of such a model, according to Oakes (1986, p. 62) are that schools are fair and meritocratic places able to determine who is best suited to learn various kinds of technical knowledge and skills, and that schools are capable of impartially certifying individuals for work roles on the basis of this learning. This rationale assumes that work roles require not only different kinds of skills but also different levels of preparation. Translated into patterns of organization and control in schools, the assumptions support differentiation of schooling experiences through mechanisms such as tracking students by ability levels. Consistent with American democratic principles, this industrial model of schooling views education as a neutral process in which the ability and effort of students determine their academic track. In this model, educational opportunity is determined by the merit of each student, and the economic rewards that accrue are fairly obtained (Oakes 1986).

In practice, however, it has become clear that schools have not succeeded in uniformly "credentialing members of society" (Ogbu 1990, p. 149). Poor and minority families, often discriminated against in employment, are relegated to menial jobs and low pay. Their children, channeled into inferior schools and placed in vocational tracks, learn that school credentials do not carry weight in obtaining employment. The persistent underachievement of minority and poor students, already well documented when Cunningham made his predictions (see Coleman et al. 1966), continues today despite reform efforts (Jencks et al. 1972; Ogbu 1974, 1978, 1987; Erickson 1984; Trueba 1987, 1988). The recognition of inequities led in the 1960s to efforts to equalize educational opportunities through various compensatory programs geared to altering characteristics of individual students. Efforts to equalize education by changing individual students largely ignored the patterns of organization and control in schools (Bates 1983) and the eventual social and economic returns for educational credentials commonly obtained by poor and minority groups (Oakes 1986). Compensatory programs for minorities, for example, were often supported by the findings of sophisticated research focusing on the linguistic aspects of underachievement (see Cummins 1983). However, the emphasis on language issues fails to address the social and cultural knowledge which is required in order for students to participate fully in school life (Trueba 1988). Many of the compensatory efforts directed to improving the school performance of minority students by focusing on the internal workings of the school or classroom have ignored the larger context and history of the structural position of minority groups in society (Ogbu 1990).

Yet a focus on the prevalent underachievement of minorities makes us recognize that economic and historical factors often lead to racial exploitation and discrimination (De Vos 1983). The sociohistorical school of psychology (Vygotsky 1978; Trueba 1988) argues that academic underachievement "is not an attribute of the individual, but a sociocultural phenomenon related to social factors that isolate minorities" (Trueba 1988, p. 202). Cultural isolation, it is argued, prevents minorities from obtaining the requisite knowledge and skills to succeed in school. Critics argue that compensatory programs that focus on the individual characteristics of students have rarely addressed structural properties of schooling that support and reinforce the dominant patterns of inequality in the wider society (Bates 1983). For example, although formalized segregation has been abolished, educational practices for Blacks continue to remain unequal to those for most White students (Ogbu 1990).

Reform efforts have generally not questioned the concept of the differentiated school. Nor has the assumption of neutrality in schooling been widely contested. Continued discriminatory practices are largely ignored in the current wave of reforms aimed at achieving educational excellence in order to ensure "national prosperity." The value of education is reduced to economic utility (Apple 1987, 1990), and education becomes merely a "medium of economic exchange." In the pursuit of a single standard of excellence, provisions for supporting student differences are viewed as a threat (Twentieth Century Fund 1983). For instance, reform initiatives ignore the impact of cultural differences between the cultures of ethnic minorities and the mainstream public schools (Erickson 1987). Current reforms assume that all schools and students are fundamentally more alike than different and that formal bureaucratic characteristics define what constitutes "Real School" (Metz 1990). Real School occurs in similar time frames and in "egg crate" settings, where similar subjects are offered using the same textbooks despite the needs of culturally different minorities and the disadvantaged. Reforms have not touched "the fact that the behavioral and academic rituals of Real School seem to connect poorly with these students" (p. 145). In fact, current reforms, driven as they are by the economic crisis and the resulting perceptions of resource scarcity, have stripped away what many view as cosmetic compensatory programs, to reveal what Oakes (1986, p. 72) refers to as the "fundamentally unequal structure of schooling." The only counterpoint to this trend is the current concern about children in poverty and the urban underclass. It is argued that attention should be given to these students as a matter of national investment (Committee for Economic Development, 1987).

Critical theorists argue that this unequal structure is supported by dominant patterns of organization and control based on a rationalization of service delivery through a bureaucratic hierarchy of dominance and submission (Foster 1987) and charge that rational-bureaucratic models of school organization and management lack a "fundamental commitment to the ideas of community and to the mutuality of social concerns" (Bates 1983, p. 39). Bureaucratized schools imitate patterns of dominance in the workforce by structuring knowledge in ways that imitate the various patterns of hierarchy and status in society as a whole. The kind of knowledge required for human capital development that will lead to the largest economic payoff is valued above cultural knowledge, and this knowledge is generally transmitted in the academic tracks closed to minorities. Further, critics point out that these patterns of dominance are embedded in the larger context of the durable racism of a society sharply stratified by class (Molnar 1983–1984).

A related but distinct feminist critique of the dominant rational-bureaucratic model of school organization and management has emerged during the past two decades. Feminist poststructural theories, for example, examine the interactions and contradictions among subjectivity, power, language, and unquestioned underlying assumptions that are used to examine the exercise of power (Capper 1992, p. 3). Feminist critiques often highlight patterns of dominance and control by men in the educational hierarchy, a hierarchy which has produced an educational system where "many women teach and a few men supervise, evaluate, and manage" (Ortiz and Marshall 1988, p. 123). Critics charge that during the formative years of the organization and development of North American educational systems, administration became separated from teaching. Supported by the practice of sponsorship, men retained power through control over the administration of schools, while women, shut out of the network of sponsored support, were denied access to administrative positions (Marshall 1979; Ortiz 1982). Recent analyses confirm that this pattern remains virtually unchanged; women continue to occupy the lowest positions in the educational hierarchy, while White males occupy the more powerful administrative positions (Shakeshaft 1987). Theories of administration derived from the rational management models and research conducted with virtually all male samples continue to dominate the academic training programs for educational administrators and further compound the structured inequality of this hierarchy (Shakeshaft 1987). As a result, the perspectives and contributions of women are ignored or devalued in most organizational theory. The scientific management model of administration that dominates education in North America emphasizes control and competition rather than the kind of cooperation and collaboration commonly practiced in the female domain of instructional practice (Ortiz and Marshall 1988). Critics conclude that such perspectives continue to structure the inequality of access for women to positions of power.

In recent years some models of micropolitics at the school level have also emerged (Ball 1987; Blase 1991), supplementing the pluralistic models which already have been developed to explain organizational politics (Morgan 1986). Microtheorists expose the operation of politics at the school level (see Townsend 1990 for a critique); for example, teacher-administrator relationships are portrayed as dominated by power considerations. This line of analysis focuses not merely on social reproduction as it affects students but also on the structure of inequality in role relations affecting producers of schooling, with teachers portrayed as a disadvantaged group.

Public Choice Critiques of Educational Administration

Neoconservative political economy models represent another revision of rational theories of educational administration. Unlike radical political economy, with its roots in sociology and its interest in equality, this line of political inquiry comes to education principally from economics, where analyses center on problems of efficiency. Because traditional microeconomic models had no adequate theory of the firm, the field of organizational economics emerged to explain such things as why organization hierarchies emerge to compensate for market failures (for a discussion, see Moe 1984; and Barney and Ouchi 1986).

One branch of this emerging field of organizational economics, public choice theory, strives to explain the failures of government. Working from rational choice models of human behavior, public choice posits that bureaucrats, like other utility-maximizing individuals, strive to achieve personal benefits from their work. The benefits include large salaries, luxurious offices, and other amenities which have little to do with achieving the organization's goals. Because of an asymmetry of information between the owner (i.e., the public) and the managers and employees, it is possible for the owner's interests to be displaced by those of the managers and workers, a process facilitated by the conditions within government. Michaelsen (1980, 1981) argues that the larger and more heterogeneous the community, the more difficult it is for a board of education to interpret public wants and demands clearly, and thus the board is unable to hold administrators clearly accountable. Under such conditions of autonomy, the private interests of administrators and teachers prevail.

Private interests are the centerpiece of this critique. Because these interests operate in public agencies and shape governmental outcomes, they are political interests. The underlying premise of most public choice analyses is that bureaucracies are less efficient means of meeting consumer preferences than markets; this is the implicit argument in Chubb and Moe's (1990) recent analysis of effective American schools. While some critics of this line of work (e.g., Wilson 1989) point out that it has yet to prove its hypotheses, the critique has appeal at a time when the size and effectiveness of government are under increasing public scrutiny.

Since the time that Cunningham wrote, then, a sobering body of knowledge has developed which tempers any optimism about an inexorable link between education and the reduction of social inequality, yet much reform, and indeed much literature in educational administration, ignores these findings on inequality. Efforts to incorporate these findings about inequality into reform efforts confront the reality that there is a conflict between the interests of dominant groups and the interests of the disadvantaged (Bates 1980).

Political Conceptions of Leadership

There is just as wide a range of political models of leadership as there is variety in political models of decision making, some closely tied to pluralism. By contrast, radical political-conflict theories of leadership (e.g., Bates 1980) focus on the relationship between knowledge and social control. Educational administrators, for example, have an important role in defining who gets into schools and who has access to the knowledge taught in schools. (See Slater et al. 1994, for a more complete discussion.)

Despite the difference of perspective on how political concerns shape leadership, much of the literature focusing on this issue tends to share one attribute: it is very macropolitical in focus, tending not to be concerned with problems of human agency. The reader will have difficulty in gaining insight from the literature into how an administrator is to accomplish goals and objectives effectively. Given this problem, until the recent emergence of micropolitics as a domain of inquiry into school administration, political conceptions of administration have had little impact in the training of educational administrators, even when professors accept the premise that acts of leadership are political in nature. The emerging study of the micropolitics of administration offers more specific understanding of the micropolitics of school leadership (Greenfield 1991) and political issues such as ideological control in schools (Anderson 1991).

To recap, several different political models of organizational behavior have emerged to challenge the once-dominant rational paradigm. Pluralist, radical political economy, and public choice critiques differ as much from one another as from traditional rational organizational models; nonetheless, their cumulative impact has been to further erode the legitimacy of rational models. The various political models are problematic for traditional approaches to the teaching of school administration. Although most textbooks now acknowledge that there is a political side to decisions, most often the tension created by this recognition is resolved by falling back on Hume's classic distinction between facts and values. The general view is that although educational decision making may be political and value laden, decisions ought to be made using a rational model. New challenges continue to erode this assumption, and a discussion of challenges to the rational model and their impact on our understanding of leadership would not be complete without at least a brief treatment of the growing popularity of the critique now found in the cultural perspectives current in the study of educational organizations.

Organizational Culture's Challenge to the Rational Model

The predecessor of a cultural view of organizational behavior was what Bolman and Deal (1984, 1991) refer to as the "human resource frame" which first challenged rational models by emphasizing the human side of organizations, claiming that they are inhabited by people who bring to their official roles personal needs, wants, values, skills, and so on. The long tradition of research on "organizational climate" (e.g., Halpin and Croft 1962) grew out of this perspective.

Subsequently, this frame evolved into still another frame for understanding organizations, the "symbolic" one (Bolman and Deal 1992). Formal structures can be viewed as myth and ceremony (Meyer and Rowan 1977), and organizations as cultures driven by rituals, ceremonies, heroes, and myths.

Constructivism, or symbolic interaction theory, provides an important philosophical foundation for cultural views of organizations, which assert that society and reality exist largely in the mind. Those who place a strong emphasis on the necessity of changing society are often called "critical humanists." Many of them share with constructivists an emphasis on the nominalist, antipositivist, voluntarist, and idiographic aspects of society.

Because cultural views of organizations as natural systems have so many and such diverse adherents, they attribute quite different meanings to organizational cultures. Some, like the earlier human relations view of organizations, see culture as an inevitable but potentially negative force which must be harnessed in service of rational ends. Others view organizational cultures negatively because of their role in reproducing the inequities of the existing social structure; still others see organizational culture as a positive force to be celebrated.

Cultural Views of Leadership

This same diversity characterizes the cultural approach to leadership. From one subjectivist angle, much of the importance we attribute to leaders is mistaken; attribution theory says that leadership is a social construction and that leaders do not really solve problems, instead fulfilling a largely symbolic role resulting in what Slater et al. (1994) call a kind of "anti-leadership" position. Less radical is the approach which sees the leader as one who is part of an organizational culture working both within it and outside it to accomplish goals. Leadership actions are important only insofar as they convey appropriate meaning to the recipients of the leaders' actions. The rational model of leadership, which sees leadership as a series of tasks and specific functions, is at a polar extreme from this interpretivist view. There is, nonetheless, some promise that this broad perspective on leadership as essentially a problem of values may have some impact on our understanding of administrative leadership. For example, Starratt's (1991) ethical perspective argues that school principals ought to be committed to three ethics: the ethic of critique, the ethic of caring, and the ethic of justice. While not a theory of leadership per se, it is a step in that direction. Sergiovanni (1992) has also argued for a conception of educational leadership which incorporates this moral vision.

Conclusion

Challenges to rational theories of educational administration have continued to grow since the late 1960s, when Cunningham predicted what educational policy would be like in 1991. His optimism that by 1991 rationality would transform the educational system has proven to be mistaken. We have progressed in our accumulated understanding of the constraints to real change in schooling, however, and now have a much better knowledge base about the role which interests and values play in educational policy. We also recognize the knowledge limitations that persist about teaching and learning. This understanding highlights the limitations of the kind of technical rationality that held such promise in the 1960s and that has continued to guide reform efforts since that time. The failure of rationality to drive progress in reforming North American schooling is reflected in the intellectual disarray currently to be found in the field of educational administration, particularly in the study of leadership.

Despite the discrediting of the rational model of administration and leadership, much of the training of educational administrators proceeds as if this intellectual revolution had never occurred. Greatly overshadowing any other recent change in university training programs for administrators is a focus on internships and more extensive field-based experiences. As a result of the recommendations of numerous study groups, often heavily represented by practitioner organizations, this hands-on approach has emerged as a new orthodoxy. Several discouraging decades of education reform suggest that field-based training will not significantly improve matters. Properly framed, more exposure to the problems of changing schools could not help but have a salutary effect on the quality of administrative leadership. But there is little ground for optimism that such exposure will be accompanied by the kind of critical reflection and problem-based methodology (Robinson 1993) that would effect the real paradigm shift so desperately needed.

Answers which will propel such a radical change of outlook in the field of educational administration remain to be formulated. Any progress in the direction of a new approach to leadership in the field first requires the recognition that current reform paradigms are based on problematic assumptions rooted in the now discredited rational theory.

Cunningham was accurate in anticipating the pressure to rationalize education, to revise educational government, and to increase participation in educational decision making that have dominated education during the past quarter-century. His vision failed, however, because of his faith that each of these trends would produce the educational reform he predicted. After several decades of frustration in school reform, it has become clearer that rationality alone cannot drive progress and that political interests and values are fundamental components in the calculus of educational change. To be sure, technology, the handmaiden of the rational paradigm and the great hope of the 1960s, continues to hold promise and hope in the 1990s. Voices of caution tell us, however, that technology alone cannot change fundamental constraints such as inequality of learning opportunities. In fact, administrators and teachers face issues of inequality and ineffectiveness in education in 1994 just as they did in 1967.

However incomplete our knowledge, we have nevertheless learned much in recent decades. The urgent task before us is to build on this knowledge to construct better theories of how education should be administered and governed. The task is difficult, for as Thomas Kuhn warned, paradigms survive long after they are discredited. Despite lessons on the limitations of technical rationality learned from failed reforms, and despite the current rhetoric about restructuring, the rational-technical paradigm remains alive and well. If educational administration is to play a major role in reshaping schools for the coming century, reformers must take care not to replicate the errors of recent decades. The challenge for today's administrators and teachers is to learn from those mistakes while maintaining the kind of optimistic vision of education for human development that Cunningham expressed.

NOTES

The authors acknowledge the contribution of Richard G. Townsend, who drew from his files Cunningham's unpublished lecture and who first suggested its use as a vehicle for reflection.

Research for this chapter by Hanne B. Mawhinney was originally supported by a Canadian Social Sciences and Humanities Research Council Doctoral Fellowship.

REFERENCES

Allison, G.T. 1971. *The Essence of Decision*. Boston: Little, Brown.

Anderson, G. 1991. Cognitive Politics of Principals and Teachers. In *The Politics of Life in Schools: Power, Conflict, and Cooperation*, ed. Joseph Blase, 120–138. Newbury Park, CA: Corwin.

Apple, M.W. 1987. Producing Inequality: Ideology and Economy in the National Reports on Education. *Educational Studies* 18: 195–220.

———. 1990. What Reform Talk Does: Creating New Inequalities in Education. In *Education Reform: Making Sense of it All*, ed. Samuel B. Bacharach, 155–164. Boston: Allyn Bacon.

Averch, H.A., S.J. Carroll, T.S. Donaldson, H.J. Kiesling, and J. Pincus. 1972. *How Effective Is Schooling? A Critical Review and Synthesis of Research Findings*. Santa Monica, CA: Rand Corporation.

Bacharach, S.B., and E.J. Lawler. 1980. *Power and Politics in Organizations.* San Francisco: Jossey-Bass.

Bacharach, S.B., and S.M. Mitchell. 1987. The Generation of Practical Theory: Schools as Political Organizations. In *Handbook of Organizational Behavior*, ed. Jay W. Lorsch, 405–418. Englewood Cliffs, NJ: Prentice-Hall.

Ball, S.J. 1987. *The Micro-Politics of the School: Towards a Theory of School Organization*. New York, NY: Methuen.

Barney, J.B., and W.G. Ouchi. 1986. *Organizational Economics*. San Francisco: Jossey-Bass.

Bates, R.J. 1980. Educational Administration, the Sociology of Science, and Management of Knowledge. *Educational Administration Quarterly* 16: 1–10.

————. 1983. *Educational Administration and the Management of Knowledge.* Geelong, Australia: Deakin University.

Bell, D. 1973. *The Coming of Post-Industrial Society.* New York: Basic Books.

Benson, C.S. 1988. Economics of Education: The U.S. Experience. In *Handbook of Research on Educational Administration,* ed. Norman J. Boyan, 355–372. New York: Longman.

Berman, P., and M.W. McLaughlin. 1976. Implementation of Educational Innovation. *Educational Forum* 40: 345–370.

Blase, J. 1991. *The Politics of Life in Schools: Power, Conflict, and Cooperation.* Newbury Park, CA: Corwin.

Bolman, L.G., and T.E. Deal. 1984. *Modern Approaches to Understanding and Managing Organizations.* San Francisco: Jossey-Bass.

————. 1991. *Artistry, Choice, and Leadership: Reframing Organizations.* San Francisco: Jossey-Bass.

————. 1992. Leading and Managing: Effects of Context, Culture, and Gender. *Educational Administration Quarterly* 28: 314–329.

Bossert, S.T. 1988. School Effects. In *Handbook of Research on Educational Administration,* ed. Norman J. Boyan, 341–352. New York: Longman.

Bowles, S., and H. Gintis. 1976. *Schooling in Capitalist America.* New York: Basic Books.

Boyd, W.L. 1988. Policy Analysis, Educational Policy, and Management: Through a Glass Darkly. In *Handbook of Research on Educational Administration,* ed. Norman J. Boyan, 501–522. New York: Longman.

Boyd, W.L., and W.T. Hartman. 1988. The Politics of Educational Productivity. In *Microlevel School Finance: Issues and Implications for Policy,* ed. David H. Monk and Julie Underwood, 271–308. Cambridge, MA: Ballinger.

Capper, C.A. 1992. And Justice for All—Secondary School Restructuring and Nondominant Groups: A Poststructural Analysis. Paper presented at the American Educational Research Association Annual Meeting, San Francisco, CA.

Chubb, J.E., and T.M. Moe. 1990. *Politics, Markets, and America's Schools.* Washington, DC: Brookings Institution.

Clark, D.L. 1985. Emerging Paradigms in Organizational Theory and Research. In *Organizational Theory and Inquiry: The Paradigm Revolution,* ed. Yvonne S. Lincoln, 43–78. Beverly Hills, CA: Sage.

Clune, W. 1987. Institutional Choice as a Theoretical Framework for Research on Educational Policy. *Educational Evaluation and Policy Analysis* 9: 117–132.

Cohen, M.D., J.G. March, and J.P. Olsen. 1972. A Garbage Can Model of Organizational Choice. *Administrative Science Quarterly* 17: 1–25.

Coleman, J., E. Campbell, C. Hobson, J. Partland, A. Mood, F. Wenfield, and R. York. 1966. *Equality of Education Opportunity*. Washington, DC: U.S. Department of Health, Education, and Welfare.

Committee for Economic Development. 1987. *Children in Need: Investment Strategies for the Educationally Disadvantaged*. New York, NY: Committee for Economic Development, Research and Policy Committee.

Cubberley, E.P. 1924. Public School Administration. In *Twenty-Five Years of American Education*, ed. Isaac L. Kandel. New York: Macmillan.

Cummins, J. 1983. The Role of Primary Language Development in Promoting Educational Success for Language Minority Students. In *Schooling and Language Minority Students: A Theoretical Framework*, 3–49. Sacramento: Bilingual Education Office, California State Department of Education. See *Harvard Educational Review* 56 (1986): 18–36.

Cunningham, L. 1967. *The Administrator and the Teacher*. Paper presented at the University of Chicago Graduate School of Education Seventy-fifth Anniversary Lecture Series, "Teaching and Learning 1991."

Devaney, K., and G. Sykes. 1988. Making the Case For Professionalism. In *Building a Professional Culture in Schools*, ed. Ann Lieberman, 3–22. New York: Teachers College Press.

De Vos, G. 1983. Ethnic Identity and Minority Status: Some Psycho-Cultural Considerations. In *Identity: Personal and Socio-Cultural*, ed. A. Jacobson-Widding. Uppsala: Almqvist and Wiksell.

Easton, D. 1965. *A Systems Analysis of Political Life*. New York: Wiley.

Edmonds, R.R. 1981. Making Public Schools Effective. *Social Policy* 12: 28–32.

Eliot, T.H. 1959. Toward an Understanding of Public School Politics. *American Political Science Review* 52: 1032–51.

Erickson, D.A. 1978. Research on Educational Administration: The State-of-the-Art. *Educational Researcher* 8: 9–14.

Erickson, F.D. 1984. School Literacy, Reasoning, and Civility: An Anthropologist's Perspective. *Review of Educational Research* 54: 525– 544.

———. 1987. Transformation and School Success: The Politics and Culture of Educational Achievement. *Anthropology and Education Quarterly* 18: 335–356.

Estler, S. 1988. Decision Making. In *Handbook of Research on Educational Administration,* ed. Norman J. Boyan, 305–319. New York: Longman.

Feldman, E.J., and J.J. Milch. 1982. *Technocracy vs. Democracy: The Comparative Politics of International Airports.* Boston: Auburn House.

Fiedler, F. 1967. *A Theory of Leadership Effectiveness.* New York: McGraw-Hill.

Fiedler, F., and M.M. Chemers. 1974. *Leadership and Effective Management.* Glenview, IL: Scott, Foresman.

Firestone, W.A., and R.E. Herriott. 1982. *An Empirical Study of the Applicability of Images of Organizations to Schools.* Philadelphia: Research for Better Schools.

Foster, W. 1987. *Paradigms and Promises.* New York: Falmer.

Good, T.L., and J.E. Brophy. 1986. School Effects. In *Handbook of Research on Teaching,* ed. Merlin C. Wittrock, 328–375. New York: Macmillan.

Gormley, W.T. 1987. Institutional Policy Analysis: A Critical Review. *Journal of Policy Analysis and Management* 6: 153–169.

Gorton, R.A., and G.T. Schneider. 1991. *School-Based Leadership: Challenges and Opportunities.* 3rd ed. Dubuque, IA: William C. Brown.

Greenfield, T.B. 1986. The Decline and Fall of Science in Educational Administration. *Interchange* 17: 57–80.

Greenfield, W.D., Jr. 1991. The Micropolitics of Leadership in an Urban Elementary School. In *The Politics of Life in Schools: Power, Conflict, and Cooperation,* ed. Joseph Blase, 161–184. Newbury Park, CA: Corwin.

Griffiths, D.E. 1957. Toward a Theory of Administrative Behavior. In *Administrative Behavior in Education,* ed. Roald F. Campbell and Russell T. Gregg, 354–390. New York: Harper.

———. 1959. *Administrative Theory.* New York: Appleton.

————. 1977. The Individual in Organizations: A Theoretical Perspective. *Educational Administration Quarterly* 13:1–18.

————. 1979. Intellectual Turmoil in Educational Administration. *Educational Administration Quarterly* 15: 43–65.

————. 1988. Administrative Theory. In *Handbook of Research on Educational Administration*, ed. Norman J. Boyan, 27–52. New York: Longman.

Halpin, A.W. 1958. *Administrative Theory in Education*. Chicago: Midwest Administration Center, University of Chicago.

————. 1966. *Theory and Research in Administration*. New York: Macmillan.

Halpin, A.W., and D.B. Croft. 1962. *The Organizational Climate of Schools*. U.S. Office of Education, Research Project Contract no. SAE 543–8639, August.

Hanushek, E.A. 1989. The Impact of Differential Expenditures on School Performance. *Educational Researcher* 18: 45–51.

Hodgkinson, C. 1978. *Towards a Philosophy of Administration*. Oxford: Basil Blackwell.

House, R.J., and M.L. Baetz. 1979. Leadership: Some Empirical Generalizations and New Research Directions. In *Research in Organizational Behavior*. Vol. 1, 341–423. Greenwich, CT: JAI.

Iannaccone, L., and F.W. Lutz. 1978. *Public Participation in Local School Districts*. Lexington, MA: Lexington Books.

Immegart, G.L. 1988. Leadership and Leader Behavior. In *Handbook of Research on Educational Administration*, ed. Norman J. Boyan, 259–277. New York: Longman.

Jencks, C., M. Smith, H. Aclard, J. Bane, D. Cohen, H. Gintins, B. Heyrs, and S. Michaelson. 1972. *Inequality: A Reassessment of the Effects of Family and Schooling in America*. New York: Basic Books.

Kirst, M.W. 1989. Who Should Control the Schools? Reassessing Current Policies. In *Schooling for Tomorrow: Directing Reforms to Issues That Count*, ed. Thomas J. Sergiovanni and J.H. Moore. Boston: Allyn and Bacon.

Lawrence, P.R., and J.W. Lorsch. 1967. *Organization and Environment: Managing Differentiation and Integration*. With the research assistance of James S. Garrison. Boston: Division of Research, Graduate School of Business Administration. Harvard University.

Linder, S.H., and G.B. Peters. 1988. The Analysis of Design or the Design of Analysis? *Policy Studies Review* 7: 738–750.

Lortie, D.C. 1975. *Schoolteacher.* Chicago: University of Chicago Press.

Lowi, T.J. 1979. *The End of Liberalism.* 2d ed. New York: W.W. Norton.

MacIntyre, A. 1988. *Whose Justice? Which Rationality?* Notre Dame: University of Notre Dame Press.

Mann, D. 1978. *Making Change Happen.* New York: Teachers College Press.

March, J.G., and J.P. Olsen. 1976. *Ambiguity and Choice in Organizations.* Bergen, Norway: Universitetsforlaget.

March, J.G., and H. Simon. 1966. *Organizations.* New York: John Wiley and Sons.

Marshall, C. 1979. Career Socialization of Women in School Administration. Ph.D. diss., University of California, Santa Barbara.

McDonnell, L.M., and R.F. Elmore. 1987. *Alternative Policy Instruments.* JNE-03. Center for Education Research in Education, RAND Corp.

McLaughlin, M.W. 1987. Learning from Experience: Lessons from Policy Implementation. *Educational Evaluation and Policy Analysis* 9: 171–178.

Metz, M.H. 1990. Some Missing Elements in the Educational Reform Movement. In *Education Reform: Making Sense of it All,* ed. Samuel B. Bacharach, 141–154. Boston: Allyn and Bacon.

Meyer, J.W., and B. Rowan. 1977. Institutionalized Organizations: Formal Structure as Myth and Ceremony. *American Journal of Sociology* 83: 340–363.

Michaelsen, J.B. 1980. The Political Economy of School District Administration. *Educational Administration Quarterly* 17: 98–113.

———. 1981. A Theory of Decision Making in the Public Schools: A Public Choice Approach. In *Organizational Behavior in Schools and School Districts,* ed. Samuel B. Bacharach. New York: Praeger.

Moe, T. 1984. The New Economics of Organization. *American Journal of Political Science* 28: 739–777.

Molnar, A. 1983–1984. School Desegregation: Moving the Debate Forward. *Educational Leadership* 41: 90–91.

Monk, D.H. 1989. The Education Production Function: Its Evolving Role in Policy Analysis. *Educational Evaluation and Policy Analysis* 11: 31–45.

Morgan, G. 1986. *Images of Organizations*. Berkeley, CA: Sage.

Murnane, R.J. 1975. *The Impact of School Resources on the Learning of Inner City Children*. Cambridge, MA: Ballinger.

Murphy, J. 1971. Title 1 of ESEA: The Politics of Implementing Federal Education Reform. *Harvard Educational Review* 41: 36–63.

———. 1989. Educational Reform in the 1980s: Explaining Some Surprising Success. *Educational Evaluation and Policy Analysis* 11: 209–221.

Oakes, J. 1986. Tracking, Inequality, and the Rhetoric of Reform: Why Schools Change. *Journal of Education* 168: 60–80.

Ogbu, J.U. 1974. *The Next Generation: An Ethnography of Education in an Urban Neighborhood*. New York: Academic Press.

———. 1978. *Minority Education and Caste: The American System in Cross-Cultural Perspective*. New York: Academic Press.

———. 1987. Variability in Minority Responses to Schooling: Nonimmigrants vs. Immigrants. In *Interpretive Ethnography of Education: At Home and Abroad*, ed. G. Spindler and L. Spindler, 255–280. Hillsdale, NJ: Lawrence Erlbaum Associates.

———. 1990. Minority Status and Literacy in Comparative Perspective. *Daedalus* 119: 141–165.

Ortiz, F.I. 1982. *Career Patterns in Educational Administration: Women, Men, and Minorities in Educational Administration*. New York: Praeger.

Ortiz, F.I., and C. Marshall. 1988. Women in Educational Administration. In *Handbook of Research on Educational Administration*, ed. Norman J. Boyan, 123–141. New York: Longman.

Patterson, J.L., S.C. Purkey, and J.V. Parker. 1986. *Productive School Systems for a Nonrational World*. Alexandria, VA: Association for Supervision and Curriculum Development.

Perrow, C. 1982. Disintegrating Social Sciences. *Phi Delta Kappan* 63: 684–688.

Peterson, P. 1974. The Politics of American Education. In *Review of Research in Education II*, ed. Fred Kerlinger and John Carroll, 348–398. Itasca, IL: Peacock.

Pfeffer, J. 1982. *Organizations and Organizational Theory*. Boston: Pitman.

Pressman, J.L., and A. Wildavsky. 1973. *Implementation*. Berkeley: University of California Press.

Purkey, S.C., and M.S. Smith. 1985. School Reform: The District Policy Implications of the Effective Schools Literature. *The Elementary School Journal* 85: 353–389.

Robinson, V. 1993. *Problem-Based Methology: Research for the Improvement of Practice.* New York: Pergamon.

Rossmiller, R.A. 1986. *Resource Utilization in Schools and Classrooms: Final Report.* Madison: University of Wisconsin-Madison, School of Education, Wisconsin Center for Education.

————. 1987. Achieving Equity and Effectiveness in Schooling. *Journal of Education Finance* 12: 561–577.

Rowan, B., S.T. Bossert, and D.C. Dwyer. 1983. Research on Effective Schools: A Cautionary Note. *Educational Researcher* 12: 24–31.

Sapolsky, H.M. 1972. *The Polaris Missile Development.* Cambridge: Harvard University Press.

Sarason, S. 1990. *The Predictable Failure of Educational Reform: Can We Change Course before It's Too Late?* San Francisco: Jossey-Bass.

Schneider, A., and H. Ingram. 1989. Systematically Pinching Ideas: A Comparative Approach to Policy Design. *Journal of Public Policy* 8: 61–80.

Schön, D.A. 1982. *The Reflective Practitioner: How Professionals Think in Action.* New York: Basic Books.

Sergiovanni, T.J. 1992. *Moral Leadership: Getting to the Heart of School Improvement.* San Francisco: Jossey-Bass.

Shakeshaft, C. 1987. *Women in Educational Administration.* Newbury Park: Sage.

Simon, H.A. 1957. *Administrative Behavior: A Study of Decision-Making Process in Administrative Organization.* 2d. ed. New York: Free Press.

Slater, R.O., L. Bolman, G.M. Crow, E. Goldring, and P.E. Thurston. 1994. *Domain IV: Leadership and Management. Processes: Taxonomy and Overview.* New York: McGraw-Hill PRIMIS Textbook System.

Starratt, R.J. 1991. Building an Ethical School: A Theory For Practice in Educational Leadership. *Educational Administration Quarterly* 27: 185–202.

Sternberg, E. 1989. Incremental versus Methodological Policymaking in the Liberal State. *Administration and Society* 21: 54–77.

Straussman, J.D. 1978. *The Limits of Technocratic Politics.* New Brunswick, NJ: Transaction.

Sykes, G. 1990. Organizing Policy into Practice: Reactions to the Cases. *Educational Evaluation and Policy Analysis* 12: 349–353.

Sykes, G., and R.F. Elmore. 1988. Making Schools Manageable: Policy and Administration for Tomorrow's Schools. In *The Politics of Reforming School Administration*, ed. Jane Hannaway and Robert Crowson, 77–94. New York: Falmer.

Thomas, J.A. 1968. *The Productive School.* New York: John Wiley and Sons.

Townsend, R.G. 1990. Toward a Broader Micropolitics of Schools. *Curriculum Inquiry* 20: 205–235.

Trueba, H.T. 1987. *Success or Failure.* New York: Newbury House/ Harper & Row.

————. 1988. Peer Socialization Among Minority Students: A High School Prevention Program. In *School and Society: Learning Content Through Culture*, ed. Henry T. Trueba and Concha Delgado-Gaitan, 201–217. New York: Praeger.

Twentieth Century Fund. 1983. *Making the Grade: Report of the Task Force on Federal Elementary and Secondary Education Policy.* New York: Author.

Vygotsky, L.S. 1978. *Mind in Society: The Development of Higher Psychological Processes.* Cambridge: Harvard University Press.

Weatherley, R., and M. Lipsky. 1977. Street-Level Bureaucrats and Institutional Innovation: Implementing Special Education Reform. *Harvard Educational Review* 47: 171–197.

Weick, K.E. 1976. Educational Organizations as Loosely Coupled Systems. *Administrative Science Quarterly* 21: 1–19.

Wilson, J.Q. 1989. *Bureaucracy: What Government Agencies Do and Why They Do It.* New York: Basic Books.

Wirt, F.M., and M.W. Kirst. 1972. *Political and Social Foundations of Education.* Berkeley, CA: McCutchan.

————. 1989. *Schools in Conflict.* Berkeley, CA: McCutchan.

Witte, J.F., and D.J. Walsh. 1990. A Systematic Test of the Effective Schools Model. *Educational Evaluation and Policy Analysis* 12: 188–212.

Zeigler, L.H., M.K. Jennings, and G.W. Peak. 1974. *Governing American Schools: Political Interaction in Local School Districts.* North Scituate, MA: Duxbury Press.

18

Privatization: Integrating Private Services in Public Schools

Ellen B. Goldring
Anna V. Shaw Sullivan

Introduction

Privatization, the use of private services to replace part or all of specific educational services in public schools, is a growing trend in education. It assumes a multitude of forms, from private management corporations that run entire public school systems to private practice teachers who teach selected courses. School officials often view privatization as a means to allay increasing public criticism while coping with shrinking budgets.

The term privatization in education often denotes choosing between the public and private sectors (see Chubb and Moe 1990). Thus, analysis and discussion has focused on vouchers and tuition tax credits as choice options. Our discussion of privatization in this chapter is about the public sector only. We define privatization as the "transfer of activities from the public sector to the private sector" (De Alessi 1987, p. 24). According to this definition, school officials "disaggregate" the educational system into individual components and put those components up for competitive bid (Rist 1991a). These efforts do not force individuals to choose between the public and private sectors. Instead, school officials overlay private services on an existing public system. This, in turn, encourages private providers to offer a growing variety of educational services (McLaughlin 1992). Some business analysts believe the result is a new growth industry spurred by the current political and economic climate (Huemer 1992). In many areas of government privatization is not particularly radical or new. For years municipalities have been contracting out, a process in which parts of public services are transferred outright to the private sector, to save money. What is new is the application of this concept to public schools. The change leads to a variety of questions and considerations that extend beyond cost saving. We examine the role of privatization in the public school sector, give specific examples of privatization measures now being advanced, and connect them to critical concerns.

We do this in six parts: (1) we survey the scope of privatization in the public education sector; (2) we establish the climate for the growth of privatization in public education; (3) we discuss potential benefits of privatization in public education; (4) we discuss its hazards; (5) we explicate the two areas of health care and prisons; (6) we delineate key issues surrounding privatization efforts in education.

Privatization in the Public Education Sector

Educators faced with rapid social change and fluctuating economies at the federal, state, and local levels seek new methods for developing needed resources. Privatizing services such as maintenance, food service, transportation, and supplies is one fairly widespread method for developing these resources (Drucker 1985). School leaders choose among service providers to obtain the one that best fits their school system's needs (Kolderie 1984, p. 20). In addition, school leaders can invest savings from one area, such as transportation, in other areas, such as computers (Natale 1993). Privatization thus enables school systems to reap the benefits of greater efficiency and greater savings.

These privatization efforts reflect a historic emphasis on privatizing areas related to peripheral services within educational systems. Pack (1987) terms these peripheral services, such as maintenance, "intermediate goods." Savas (1987) labels them "physical, commercial" and further distinguishes them from "protective, human services," those areas that focus more upon human service programs and outcomes. The success of privatization efforts in "intermediate" areas encourages educators to consider similar changes in the "protective, human services" areas. For example, educators in some states have privatized drug treatment and educational testing.

The trend toward privatizing client services also extends to the core technology of schools: teaching and learning. School leaders are exploring privatized options for teaching special classes and for providing services that directly impact students' achievement in the classroom. The shift can be seen in three distinct areas: contracts with private firms, business and foundation partnerships, and private practice teachers.

Contracting with Private Firms

One form of privatization is contracting with private firms to provide specific services and/or to manage entire systems. By contracting, school leaders tailor specialized services to an individual school setting. Such specialized services often require unique training, personnel, and materials that are not included on an ongoing basis in the educational system's budget. In many cases it would not prove cost-effective to develop and maintain these resources continuously in the district. For example, national legislation requires equal provision of education to all groups, from the disabled to the gifted, but does not provide enough resources for those services. To obtain such services some schools turn to external providers. The contracts allow the school leaders to negotiate for services as needed. Since the provider furnishes the professional staff and expertise, the school leader eliminates the necessity for continuously funding operations but gains the advantage of providing the services required by law. In this way, contracts provide a distinct advantage for schools.

Contracting with private management firms is another area where school districts provide needed services while conserving resources. For example, Minnesota-based Educational Alternatives, Inc. (EAI), has managed public schools and school districts in Minnesota, Maryland, and Florida. EAI supports charter schools, in which the school board contracts with an independent entity to manage the entire school district. Although a private firm manages the school, state laws governing the delivery of educational services apply. The benefits of public schools are maintained while costs associated with the administration of those schools are saved.

The widely publicized Edison Project provides another example of contracting. The for-profit school program undertook to develop a nationwide chain of schools (Rist 1991b), but financial difficulties forced the project's originators to alter initial projections of owning and operating as many as one thousand schools. Company officials announced in mid-1993 that they will focus on managing public schools until they secure financing for their original goals (Walsh 1993), thus competing directly with other private firms for management contracts. Although it has been scaled back, the Edison Project remains significant both as a challenge to the educational status quo and as an alternative to the traditional management of public schools.

Contracting with private firms can offer important advantages, but educators must also consider potential limitations of contracting. This form of privatization may provide innovative methods of reducing administrative overhead and educational costs while providing flexibility in offering specialized services. However, because these contracts apply to human service areas, the systems often fail to offer clear evaluation measures. In intermediate areas, such as bus service, school leaders evaluate a contract on the basis of whether the company followed the letter of the contract, e.g., whether the buses ran on schedule. Bennett (1992) suggests that school leaders must establish a similar evaluation tool in human services areas. He recommends "quantifiable student performance outcomes" (p. 31) as part of the contract or service agreement to evaluate the effectiveness of the service provider. Such clear evaluative measures would enable the school leader to retain the benefit of contracts and private management while ensuring that the best interests of the students take precedence.

Business and Private Foundation Partnerships

A second form of privatization in the public sector is the development of partnerships with businesses and private foundations. Businesses and private foundations enter into partnerships with schools by providing equipment, personnel, expertise, and money. Financial and service cutbacks at all levels of government contribute to public school officials' interest in developing partnerships with businesses for goods and services (Taylor 1992). Such arrangements benefit schools by providing needed resources and help corporations by ensuring their involvement in developing a well-educated workforce for the future (King and Swanson 1990). Corporations such as IBM, RJR Nabisco, and BellSouth support schools through either direct corporate contributions or private foundations. A 1992 survey estimates that almost half of all public schools participate in such partnerships (Saving, 1992). During 1992, corporations and corporate foundations gave away approximately six billion dollars, with about one-third specified for education-related projects (American Association of Fundraising Counsel 1993). These figures indicate significant involvement of both schools and businesses in establishing partnerships.

Business and corporate involvement also extends beyond providing funds for schools. For example, the Business Roundtable and the National Alliance of Businesses serve as resources for corporate and business leaders who are concerned about the current educational system (National Governors' Association 1993). The state and local divisions of these groups work to influence state educational policy. By getting involved beyond a specific school site, these organizations help shape the governing policies that encourage change and, ultimately, benefit corporate and business interests.

Further evidence of the participation of business and private foundations in public education is the New American Schools Development Corporation (NASDC) (Blount 1992). NASDC, which grew out of President Bush's America 2000 initiative, is funded by American corporations. The independent nonprofit organization exists to fund the design of schools that would spur new strategies for educators. The organization selected eleven projects out of 686 proposals during its first year.

NASDC has raised approximately fifty-five million dollars of a projected two hundred million dollars needed to accomplish its goals (Mecklenburger 1992). The organization is significant because it highlights the growing interest by corporations in public education. It also indicates a high level of governmental encouragement for such endeavors.

Private foundations support school partnerships by changing their funding guidelines to support educational partnerships (Lieberman 1992). For example, private foundations played a significant role in funding the reports of the early 1980s that helped to bring about current educational reforms (Leonard 1992). Another more direct example is the recent announcement by the John S. and James L. Knight Foundation, established by the Knight Newspapers' founders, that it would support such partnerships. This places the foundation "among a growing number of foundations that are paying more attention—and shifting their resources—to precollegiate education" (Knight Fund 1993).

Like contracts with private firms, partnerships provide a means for school leaders to serve more students with fewer resources. A corporate donation to furnish a computer laboratory, for example, releases money in the school budget for other needs. The students receive the immediate benefit from learning using current technology. Partnerships are unlike contracts with private firms, however, in that no immediate profit returns to the corporation or foundation. The benefit accrues over a long period and may not be immediately evident.

Educators raise concerns over the increased reliance on corporate-school partnerships. They suggest that value conflicts can emerge when corporate resources replace public commitment to education. McLaughlin (1992) claims that corporate-initiated programs to support schools signify that public educators have failed to deliver "basic educational services" (p. 26). When school leaders turn to "corporate America" for services, they may be allowing the corporation to define what is best for the school and the community, which may serve only the narrowest corporate interests. The broader agenda of public education, defined as serving the best interests of all students and their communities, takes second place to narrower interests. When value conflicts arise, school leaders often become mediators between narrowly defined corporate interests and more broadly defined educational goals.

Private Practice Teachers

A third form of privatization is the hiring of private practice teachers. Private practice teachers offer school leaders yet another option for providing specific teaching services to schools. Randall (1992) explains that private practice teaching involves "sole practitioner educators, teacher partnerships, educational service corporations, and charter schools formed by teachers" (p. 3). School leaders hire private practice teachers and enter into agreements with them to teach in specific academic areas, such as biology or French. School districts typically hire private practice teachers when they cannot hire full-time teachers or when they need services in areas in which there are few teachers (Lochhead 1990). For example, North Carolina legislation requires all children in grades K-5 to study a foreign language. Since the Wake County, North Carolina, district does not have enough full-time foreign language teachers at the elementary level, the school board has opted for more than nine years to hire private practice teachers to offer the instruction (Private-practice 1990). By using private practice teachers, schools in similar situations provide needed and mandated services in specific areas while maintaining system flexibility.

Sufficient numbers of private practice teachers now exist to support a national organization. The American Association of Educators in Private Practice, a Milwaukee-based group formed in June, 1990, represents these teachers (Lochhead 1990). The organization operates much like other self-regulating professions, such as college faculty or medical professionals, who police themselves and have professional autonomy to establish standards.

Proponents of private practice teaching believe that this system of privatization provides more flexibility for schools and teachers alike (Sneider 1991). Critics question how schools can assure teacher standards, although ostensibly the teacher must meet standards set forth by the individual schools. Critics believe that conflicts may arise when the teachers' own professional standards conflict with the expectations of the contracting schools.

Contracts with private firms, business and foundation partnerships, and private practice teaching encompass alternatives to traditional educational service delivery. School leaders use these privatized options to cope with changing social and economic pressures. Each option provides critically needed resources and publicly applauded innovations for improving education. However, school leaders face a continuing challenge to balance the benefits and the drawbacks of these arrangements in a highly charged political and economic climate. We next discuss the parameters of this climate and relate it to the changes in education.

The Climate for Privatization

The political and economic environment surrounding governmental service delivery in general and education in particular provides support for change toward greater privatization. As social problems remain intractable, an eroding confidence in public enterprises leads to increasing demands for change. The past decade witnessed growing and widespread dissatisfaction with government. For many, government-run enterprises were characterized by waste, poor performance, and negative bureaucracy (Lieberman 1989; Osborne and Gaebler 1992). Given this climate, some city governments felt the need to expand the possible routes for service delivery. Simply raising taxes was no longer a viable option, but citizens' increasing demand for services forced officials to consider alternatives. By linking private and public enterprises, local and state governments became facilitators rather than providers of key services. Officials "learned how to bring community groups and foundations together to build low-income housing; how to bring business, labor, and academia together to stimulate economic innovation and job creation; how to bring neighborhood groups and police departments together to solve problems that underlay crimes" (Osborne and Gaebler 1992, p. 28). Local and state governments thus discovered the benefits of privatizing services to improve delivery.

An increasing national debt spurred similar shifts at the federal level. Federal officials dismantled some services to allow for privately delivered components (thus shifting responsibility and costs out of the federal sector). Proponents touted these efforts as providing needed services while cutting bureaucratic structures, streamlining service delivery systems, and enhancing market response to public demand. Widespread public demand and political support thus culminated in transformed service delivery at all governmental levels (Walsh 1992; Whitty 1984). These changes provided the added benefit of revitalizing the private companies that provided the services.

This climate, coupled with numerous negative reports about children's test performance and the state of education in the United States, encouraged educators and policymakers to support similar radical changes in public education (Cooper 1988). As public and political support for alternatives in public service delivery expanded, proponents of privatization viewed education as one arena for growth. The combination of public outrage over continuing social problems and the successes of privatization in other areas of government created a positive climate for the change in education. In addition, economic challenges to educational budgets encouraged school leaders to explore new options for providing services to students. Proponents cite specific advantages of privatization in the educational setting.

Why Privatization?

Supporters of private service provision within public organizational frameworks cite two predominant benefits: effectiveness and efficiency (Butler 1990). In addition to these two benefits, however, Gormley (1991) suggests several other reasons for choosing privatized options: equity, reliability, quality, accountability, empowerment, and legitimacy. Equity focuses on the dual concepts of treating those in similar circumstances in similar fashion and of working to reduce or eliminate income disparities. Reliability pertains to uninterrupted provision of services, while quality identifies components that ensure superior service delivery. Accountability includes methods for periodic review, and empowerment provides for clients' control over the selection process. Finally, legitimacy involves citizens' overall perceptions of the process, the service, and the outcomes (for a more complete discussion of these concepts see Gormley 1991).

Advocates of privatization in public education emphasize the expected benefits for schools. For example, efficiency is often a benefit of privatization. Educational Alternatives, Inc., claims that by charging the same per-pupil costs as their partner school districts, they reduce operating and administration spending by 25 percent (David 1992). Administrative overhead and other associated costs can be reduced and the profits returned to the school system. Kolderie suggests that "the school board retains the public policy role of determining who gets taught what, at what cost, when and where; it is up to the school board to design the contractual arrangement it wants" (Rist 1991a, p. 26). In an economic climate marked by reduced budgets and increasing demands, school leaders must consider the savings that privatized services bring to the system as a whole.

Effectiveness, reliability, and accountability are also expected benefits of privatization in schools. For instance, the Corporate/Community School of America (C/CSA), a nonprofit coalition of businesses managing an inner-city school in Chicago, reports that their students show higher standardized achievement test scores than students with similar socioeconomic backgrounds in the Chicago public schools (David 1992). School leaders can utilize similar measures to determine whether private firms are effective and whether they should renew individual management contracts. Similarly, private practice teachers indicate that they are held accountable for their services, since tenure and union contracts cannot protect their jobs if students do not demonstrate acceptable performance levels on tests (Lochhead 1990). Student performance objectives also bind charter schools since school leaders can revoke a charter at any time if students do not meet performance objectives (Kolderie 1992).

Proponents assume that privatization generally leads to higher-quality programs, not only in terms of outcomes. They suggest that educational entrepreneurs offer more innovative, creative programs to meet the needs of a wider array of students. For example, private practice teachers, who must compete for the clients they serve, "may achieve levels of professionalism that have eluded them as salaried employees governed by collective bargaining contracts" (Lieberman, 1986 p. 734). In other words, competitive professionalism and the open market may encourage outstanding performers.

Proponents also advocate privatization as an empowering tool for educators and school boards, one that allows for flexibility and diversity. For example, charter schools hire and fire employees, devise budgets, and develop curriculum, but they are accountable to the school board. School boards are empowered to make difficult educational decisions that they would not make if their own permanent school personnel were involved (Lieberman 1986). Contracting enables school boards to acknowledge that innovations have failed and pursue creative alternatives based on contract performance standards.

Proponents of privatization also mention equity as a benefit. Perhaps most notable is the involvement of private foundations and businesses in the direct financing of educational programs to ensure equity. Schools often use such money to fund extracurricular activities, recreation facilities, and elective courses, which are often cut during budget crises. Thus, quality services may be available to populations that do not otherwise have access to them (Rubin 1983). In addition, districts may contract out services for special students' needs so that all students receive programs uniquely tailored to their needs.

Proponents of privatization enumerate the benefits of efficiency, effectiveness, reliability, accountability, and equity when school leaders overlay public education with private services. Proponents relate these benefits to progress in educational service delivery. But just as privatization includes proponents, it also has opponents.

Why NOT Privatization?

Despite the stated positive benefits of privatization, critics question its virtues. They stress that public service delivery and private management comprise inherently different structures and goals. One aims to provide services for broad social benefit while the other focuses on bottom-line outcomes. Goodman (1987) says, "It is generally assumed that the government provides socially desirable services that the private sector will not or cannot perform" (p. 37). Critics of privatization point to funding, accountability, competition, and community-building as important reasons for opposing privatization.

Funding

Opponents of privatization raise numerous concerns regarding corporate funding of private initiatives for public schools. First, private financial support is not guaranteed indefinitely. As foundations choose new areas of emphasis, funding may be directed away from educational endeavors. Second, schools may confront difficult questions relating to expectations and obligations resulting from the financial support (Taylor 1992). For instance, will schools comply with the unwritten expectation that they will support the grantmaker's values? Third, funding is often linked to a specific time frame. When funding reaches its conclusion, school leaders must seek and obtain new funding in order to continue offering the program or service (King and Swanson 1990). This may encourage educators to assume a shortsighted view of specific programs in case foundations and corporations alter direction rather than consider the long-term needs of the entire school. In addition, educators may focus on programs that are "fundable" rather than on programs that are essential. Schools may utilize private funds to gain greater latitude in providing educational services, but they should develop long-range plans that address these concerns.

Competition

Opponents of privatization also believe that foundation and private funding may create competition between schools that ultimately proves detrimental (King and Swanson 1990). The wealthier, more prestigious schools may be better positioned to obtain funding than schools with fewer resources and perhaps greater needs. In California after Proposition 13 was passed, the wealthier districts succeeded in raising substantially more money from private foundations than did the poorer districts (Rubin 1983). Wood (1990) states that "to allow public school districts to pursue outside sources of fiscal support, however noble in the intent to support public education, is to allow the districts to engage in laissez-faire self interest. This agenda is indifferent to local resources or lack thereof, the educational or fiscal needs and the allocation of resources to this goal" (p. 60). A related concern is the possible negative impact on permanent public budget allocations to education if schools rely on private sources of funds. As legislators perceive that public education needs can be met with private money through competition, they may be less likely to support public education initiatives.

In addition, service providers may not furnish services at the same level of quality or availability for all types of students. Without equal opportunities to acquire such services, decisions about whether to pursue those opportunities are made for the schools. This creates a system uneven in quality or even in the number of services available. Hurl (1986, p. 11) writes, "Competition may exacerbate interest group activity, fragmentation, poor coordination, and imbalance in the service system." For example, how will schools guarantee balance if competition creates a "bidding war" for highly talented teachers? Salaries and class sizes could become issues in such disputes, with benefits accruing more heavily to those schools that already enjoy advantages in amounts of flexible resources. In a worst case scenario, the self-employed teacher emerges as the main beneficiary of the system, not the school and the children served by the school. These difficulties may offset the benefits of privatization. School leaders must grapple with the issue of uneven advantages in competition. This helps to ensure that schools with broadly different concentrations of students from differing economic, social, racial, and ethnic backgrounds will have the same opportunities to acquire services.

Accountability

Opponents of privatization also question the assertion that privatization increases accountability. A central question is, accountability to whom? To the individual school, to the organization with which the teacher has a contract, or to the school board? As private educational programs operate in a competitive market, school leaders must develop the necessary checks and balances for system-wide accountability. Starr (1988) believes that individuals serving in privatized programs that represent social values must place programmatic interests above their own more narrow self-interests.

Mecklenburger (1986) recalls efforts during the late 1960s and early 1970s, much like current proposals, to link teacher compensation to measurable student results. He warns of the pitfalls of this type of accountability system, including narrowly focused teaching strategies and the exclusion of key components of the curriculum. He urges school leaders to develop appropriate safeguards and to begin discussions to resolve the lingering questions associated with accountability and contracting.

Motives

Opponents of privatization believe that public education is an inappropriate setting for private profit. Parents and children have little recourse if private companies cannot fulfill their contractual obligations. Financial difficulties and the contracted company's lack of long-range commitment to educational projects pose significant challenges to school leaders. In one example in Milwaukee, a privately run school encountered financial difficulties and was forced to close. As a result, the children attending the school were unable to be reimbursed for the voucher funds that would enable them to make other educational choices. School leaders made no provisions for such a situation (Rist 1991a).

Arnold Fege of the national PTA believes that many school boards rush into contractual agreements, attracted solely by the motive of providing education at a lower cost. He believes that the motivations of profit-oriented service providers and public service providers are irreconcilable. "The market doesn't care about providing public services, it cares about making money," Fege states (Rist 1991a, p. 28). If profit overrides all other motives, school systems may find that contracts with private service providers lead to reduced, rather than enhanced, educational services.

Community Building

Opponents of privatization also believe that privatized services may destroy the ideal of school community. School community arises from "commonly shared values, an agenda that brings students and teachers together, and a supportive pattern of collegial interaction among the adults in the institution" (Driscoll 1993, p. 6). Research on school effectiveness and improvement indicates the positive impact of school community on teacher efficacy and effectiveness (Bryk and Driscoll 1988; Louis 1992). School leaders do not know how private practice teachers will impact school improvement efforts that hinge on a cohesive school community, teacher empowerment, and participation in decision making. Private, part-time teachers face a difficult challenge in becoming an integral part of the school community if they spend little time at the school.

Full-time teachers may view private practice teachers as specialized experts in a narrow field. The specialization may contribute to isolation and fragmentation of the teaching force (Hurl 1986). This trend bears similarities to higher education's use of adjunct faculty members. Organizational and social structures often exclude adjunct faculty members from the institutional community, resulting in alienation and charges of a "two-tier" teaching system (Katz and Tuckman 1984; Mortimer, Bagshaw, and Masland 1985; Tuckman and Caldwell 1979). School leaders must create strong support networks and clear guidance systems for private teaching professionals in the school.

Opponents of privatization in education cite concerns relating to funding, competition, accountability, motives, and community building. In each case they have viable objections to the addition of privatized services to the public education system.

Lessons from Other Industries

There has been little empirical study of privatization in public schools. However, the health care and corrections industries provide some insights into the complexities which emerge when private services are provided in public sectors. The moves toward privatization of health care and prisons used different means but the fundamental reasons for them were the expected benefits accruing from increased effectiveness and efficiency.

Health Care

Health care, like education, has fallen under increasingly intense scrutiny during recent years. Also like education, health care is an intensely human issue. Privatized health agencies include psychiatric hospitals, substance abuse centers, nursing homes, and general hospitals. The move to privatization in health care occurred because many individuals believed it would create heightened efficiency and quality at a lower cost (Demone and Gibelman 1987, p. 50). As investor-owned, for-profit hospitals became more common, industry analysts criticized them on the grounds that health care should be viewed as a public good and therefore an entitlement of all citizens (Relman 1980). Others argued that for-profit ventures discriminated against the poor and minorities and perhaps limited access to care.

In contrast, Demone and Gibelman (1987) point to several studies that, while highlighting differences in for-profit and not-for-profit health care ventures, contradict charges of inequity. They note that studies show no significant differences in patient mix or in patient care costs per case when public and private health care are compared. These authors conclude that emphasis on efficiency to the exclusion of other considerations perhaps creates significant conflicts in values but does not necessarily impact the effectiveness of health care.

Corrections

Proponents of the privatization of prisons, while acknowledging conflicts in values and efficiency, suggest that privatization may offer imaginative options for a seemingly unsolvable problem (Geis 1987). Unlike health care clients, prisoners have no choice over the options offered by a private provider. Individuals do, however, have certain legal and moral rights that must be protected even while they are incarcerated; for example, they have the right not to be subjected to "cruel and unusual" punishment as part of their sentence. Society, by means of our legal system, has established parameters for determining acceptable standards for this principle.

Privately owned or run prisons do not *replace* the existing system; they *complement* it by providing additional options. They provide one possible solution to the ongoing problem that the public wants to feel safe from criminals but does not want to pay a high price for their safety (Geis 1987). Privately owned prison facilities are deemed successful in that they have provided new and expanded forms of such correction facilities as treatment programs, new technologies for surveillance and control, and low custodial programs (Feeley 1991).

Privatized corrections facilities may carry greater potential for success when "private enterprise . . . is scrupulously monitored by independent public agencies" (Geis 1987, p. 80). Although prisoners may be held at a privately owned facility, the system itself remains subject to broader public policies and standards for governance. This arrangement maintains the link between public good and private interest.

In school settings, maintaining this link means that students receive the benefits of public education while also benefiting from the innovations arising from private involvement. Federal and state governments do not abandon education. They do, however, seek to provide those services in alternative modes.

Lessons for Education

The most compelling similarity between hospitals, prisons, and schools is their orientation toward human issues. All are necessary components of a society that values the individual worth of its citizens. All three share problems of cost, equity, and reform. As was true of privatization of health care, sharp criticisms may be leveled against educational systems if they are perceived to sacrifice quality, increase costs exponentially, or decrease global service delivery. As with prisons, the maintenance of individuals' rights and privileges remains paramount. Critics of the privatization of prisons have suggested that these privately owned facilities will not want to parole inmates because they would lose money (Geis 1987). These concerns highlight the possible conflicts between the motives of privately owned corporations and public values. The public is critical if schools are seen as sacrificing commonly held values in the interest of profits and efficiency. As the lines between public and private enterprise blur, school leaders cannot easily predict that schools will receive the full benefits of one while escaping the negative aspects of the other.

Issues Surrounding Privatization Efforts in Education

Increasing privatization poses crucial questions that educators and educational policy must face. Gormley (1991) emphasizes that the privatization of human services creates new problems that have not yet been considered, much less addressed. He lists four key issues. First, human services require complex, long-range systems for evaluation of success. As schools invest in contracts and other privatized endeavors, establishing criteria for success may not be enough. Numerous external social factors interfere with those efforts. School systems must consider their own commitment, in terms not only of immediate results but also of long-range impacts, both negative and positive.

Second, the provision of human services involves multiple levels of governmental and private control. On the one hand, Gormley notes, this creates increased opportunity for innovation. On the other hand, it also increases the possibilities for gridlock.

School leaders must consider standards and methods of negotiating through all of these levels. They also must establish protocols to ensure that schools are protected in such negotiations.

Third, Gormley suggests that privatization forces new conceptions of the role of nonprofit organizations such as foundations. As independently funded foundations and corporate-funded foundations exert greater influence in school decision making, we must address questions of whether those foundations provide equitable opportunities, whether they exert undue influence on political or organizational decision making, and whether they offer the best solutions to educational challenges.

Fourth, school leaders must consider legal, ethical, and even sociological implications far more carefully in human ser-vice delivery than in product delivery. For instance, in certain situations, police departments may be liable for the off-duty ac-tions of their officers working privately (Reiss 1991). Would school systems have such liabilities for teachers who pursue ad-ditional private practice opportunities? Another consideration relates to the empowerment of schools to exercise greater lati-tude in establishing contracts: does this empowerment also open the school and decision makers to lawsuits if the arrangements fail to produce the anticipated outcomes? Safeguards must be es-tablished to protect children as well as schools, so that children do not become the victims of failed social experiments begun without clear ethical and moral guidelines. School leaders must address the legal and ethical dilemmas before embarking upon privatized ventures.

If there is universal agreement that our schools require fundamental change, the real question about privatization becomes whether its effects are positive or negative. Downs and Larkey (1986) claim that private sector contributions to reforms in other areas encouraged "the widespread .belief" that "problems can be solved by making government more like business" (p. 55). However, government agencies such as schools express the core values and beliefs of our society. These "expressive functions" serve as important benchmarks in our society (Heymann 1988). Critical change occurs when the expressive functions present an accurate picture of how we want our social programs to operate. School leaders are charged with restructuring our educational programs so that they coincide with commonly held values and conserve resources while still offering high-quality products and services. This is the challenge that lies behind the move toward privatization.

REFERENCES

American Association of Fundraising Counsel. 1993. *Giving U.S.A.* New York: American Association of Fundraising Counsel Trust for Philanthropy.

Bennett, D. 1992. Will Public/Private Control Reinvent School System Governance? *Education Digest* 58 (November): 30–32.

Blount, F. 1992. Creating the New American School. *Vocational Education Journal* 67 (January): 22–23.

Bryk, A.S., and M.E. Driscoll. 1988. *The High School as Community: Contextual Influences and Consequences for Students and Teachers.* Madison, WI: National Center for Effective Secondary Schools.

Butler, S. 1990. Privatization for Public Services. In *Privatization and Its Alternatives*, ed. W. Gormley, Jr., 17–24. Madison: University of Wisconsin Press.

Chubb, J., and T. Moe. 1990. *Politics, Markets, and America's Schools.* Washington, DC: Brookings Institution.

Cooper, B. 1988. School Reform in the 1980s: The New Right's Legacy. *Educational Administration Quarterly* 24: 282–298.

David, A. 1992. Public-Private Partnerships: The Private Sector and Innovation in Education. *Policy Insight*, no. 142.

De Alessi, L. 1987. Property Rights and Privatization. In *Prospects for Privatization*, ed. S. Hanke, 24–35. New York: Academy of Political Science.

Demone, H., Jr., and M. Gibelman. 1987. Privatizing the Acute Care General Hospital. In *Private Means, Public Ends*, ed. B. Carroll, R. Conant, and T. Easton, 50–75. New York: Praeger.

Downs, G., and P. Larkey. 1986. *The Search for Government Efficiency.* Philadelphia: Temple University Press.

Driscoll, M.E. 1993. The Conditions of Work for Beginning Teachers: An Urban Portrait. Paper presented at the annual meeting of the American Educational Research Association, Atlanta.

Drucker, P. 1985. *Innovation and Entrepreneurship.* New York: Harper & Row.

Feeley, M.M. 1991. The Privatization of Punishment in Historical Perspective. In *Privatization and Its Alternatives*, ed. W.T. Gormley, Jr., 199–225. Madison: University of Wisconsin Press.

Geis, G. 1987. The Privatization of Prisons: Panacea or Placebo? In *Private Means, Public Ends*, ed. B. Carroll, R. Conant, and T. Easton, 50–75. New York: Praeger.

Goodman, J. 1987. Privatizing the Welfare State. In *Prospects for Privatization*, ed. S. Hanke. New York: Academy of Political Science.

Gormley, W., Jr. 1991. The Privatization Controversy. In *Privatization and Its Alternatives*, ed. W. Gormley, Jr., 3–16. Madison: University of Wisconsin Press.

Heymann, P. 1988. How Government Expresses Public Ideas. In *The Power of Public Ideas*, ed. R. Reich, 85–107. Cambridge, MA: Ballinger.

Huemer, J. 1992. Education Opens Its Doors. *Venture Capital Journal* (April): 24–27.

Hurl, L. 1986. Keeping on Top of Government Contracting: The Challenge to Social Work Educators. *Journal of Social Work Education* 22: 6–18.

Katz, D., and H. Tuckman. 1984. Displacement of Full-timers by Part-timers: A Model for Projection. *Economics of Education Review* (summer): 85–90.

King, R., and A. Swanson. 1990. Resources for Restructured Schools: Partnerships, Foundations, and Volunteerism. *Planning and Changing* 21 (summer): 94–107.

Knight Fund Turns to Partnerships. 1993. *Chronicle of Higher Education* 34 (23): A29.

Kolderie, T. 1984. The Puzzle of the Public Sector and the Strategy of Service Redesign. In *An Equitable and Competitive Public Sector*, ed. T. Kolderie. Minneapolis: University of Minnesota Press.

———. 1992. *Public Services Redesign Project.* St. Paul, MN: Center for Policy Studies.

Leonard, M. 1992. The Response of the Private Sector: Foundations and Entrepreneurs. *Teachers College Record* 93: 376–381.

Levin, H. 1983. Education Choice and Pains of Democracy. In *Public Dollars for Private Schools*, ed. T. James and H. Levin, 17–38. Philadelphia: Temple University Press.

Lieberman, A. 1992. School/University Collaboration: A View from the Outside. *Phi Delta Kappan* 74 (October): 147–156.

Lieberman, M. 1986. Privatization and Public Education. *Phi Delta Kappan* 67 (June): 731–734.

———. 1989. *Privatization and Educational Choice.* New York: St. Martin's.

Lochhead, C. 1990. A Lesson from Private Practitioners. *Insight* (December 24, 1990–January 7, 1991): 34–36.

Louis, K.S. 1992. Social and Community Values and the Quality of Teachers' Work Life. In *The Contexts of Teaching in Secondary School*, ed. M. McLaughlin, J. Talbert, and N. Bascia, 17–39. New York: Teachers College Press.

McLaughlin, J. 1992. Schooling for Profit: Capitalism's New Frontier. *Educational Horizons* 71 (fall): 23–30.

Mecklenburger, J. 1986. A Diamond in the Rough? *Phi Delta Kappan* 67 (June): 735–737.

———. 1992. The Braking of the "Break the Mold" Express. *Phi Delta Kappan* 74 (December): 280–289.

Mortimer, K., M. Bagshaw, and A. Masland. 1985. *Flexibility in Academic Staffing: Effective Policies and Practices.* ASHE-ERIC Higher Education Report No. 1. Washington, DC: Association for the Study of Higher Education.

Natale, J. 1993. Education Is His Business. *The Executive Educator* 15 (May): 20–25.

National Governors' Association. 1993. Business Involvement in Ohio's Education Reform. *In Brief* (August): 1–4.

Osborne, D., and T. Gaebler. 1992. *Reinventing Government.* Reading, MA: Addison-Wesley.

Pack, J. 1987. Privatization of Public Sector Services in Theory and Practice. *Journal of Policy Analysis and Management* 6: 523–540.

Private-practice Teachers Offer Boards New Staffing Options. 1990. *School Board News* (September 25).

Randall, R. 1992. What Follows School Choice: Teachers as Entrepreneurs and Charter Schools? Paper presented at the annual meeting of the American Association of School

Administrators, San Diego, CA. ERIC Document Reproduction Service No. ED 343 237.

Reiss, J. 1991. Private Employment of Public Police. In *Privatization and Its Alternatives*, ed. W. Gormley, Jr., 226–240. Madison: University of Wisconsin Press.

Relman, A. 1980. The New Medical-Industrial Complex. *New England Journal of Medicine* 303: 963–970.

Rist, M. 1991a. Education, Inc. *The American School Board Journal* 178: 24–29.

———. 1991b. Whittling Away at Public Education. *The Executive Educator* 13: 22–23, 25–28.

Rubin, V. 1983. Responses to Local Fiscal Stress: Privatization and Coproduction of Children's Services in California. *Children's Time Study*. Berkeley: University of California. ERIC Document Reproduction Service No. ED 311 098.

Savas, E. 1987. *Privatization: The Key to Better Government*. Chatham, NJ: Chatham House.

Saving Our Schools. 1992. *Businessweek Magazine* (September 14).

Sneider, J. 1991. Legislative Proposals Could Push Private Practice Issue to Front Burner. *The Business Journal Magazine* (April): 6–7.

Starr, P. 1988. *The Limits of Privatization*. Washington, DC: Economic Policy Institute. ERIC Document Reproduction Service No. ED 311 243.

Taylor, J. 1992. Desperate for Dollars. *The American School Board Journal* 178 (September): 19–25.

Tuckman, H., and J. Caldwell. 1979. The Reward Structure for Part-timers in Academe. *Journal of Higher Education* 50: 745–760.

Walsh, M. 1992. Think-tank Proposals Mirror Clinton Education Agenda. *Education Week* 12 (December): 23.

———. 1993. Scaled-Back Edison Plan Focuses on Managing Schools. *Education Week* 13 (September) (1): 14.

Whitty, G. 1984. The "Privatization" of Education. *Educational Leadership* 41 (April): 51–54.

Wood, R.C. 1990. New Revenues for Education at the Local Level. In *The Impacts of Litigation and Legislation on Public School Finance: Adequacy, Equity, and Excellence*, ed. J.E. Underwood and D.A. Verstegen, 59–74. New York: Harper & Row.

19

Why School Choice?
A Question of Values

Peter W. Cookson, Jr.
Barbara Schneider

Introduction

Few school reform movements have aroused such deep public passions as school choice. On the face of it, this is somewhat surprising, because school governance issues have seldom electrified educators or the public at large. How schools are organized normally does not seem as important as curriculum, pedagogical practices, or academic values. Today, however, the issue of school choice has become a national debate. Sides are being taken, and lines are being drawn. Clearly, there is a political and educational context for this debate, but there is also a very deep philosophical and moral subtext. The political and educational context is about school improvement, but the philosophical subtext is about values, identity, and freedom. Undoubtedly, school choice has become infused with emotion because it is an educational reform that goes directly to the heart of several American dilemmas. What is the correct balance between individual and family freedom and the rights of the community? How can public education be improved? Are markets an efficient and fair way of creating a more innovative and responsive educational system? Will choice lead to educational variety or educational anarchy? Clearly, the answers to these questions are difficult to determine, but the struggle to arrive at the answers will shape American education for a long time, whatever the eventual policy outcomes.

The idea that parents and students should be allowed and encouraged to attend the schools they wish to is not revolutionary. Throughout American history, individuals and groups have challenged the authority of the state when it required students to attend state-controlled schools. But since the 1920s, the United States Supreme Court has consistently protected the rights of families and religious groups to educate their children outside the public school system, although public authorities are prohibited from funding religious schools. These legal and structural characteristics have created a system of education where there is a strong boundary between the private sector and the public sector. Until the 1980s, few Americans questioned the status quo in terms of school governance. During Reagan's presidency, however, the public school system was challenged at a very basic level. As the leader of a powerful conservative coalition, Ronald Reagan legitimized a political ideology that was essentially antigovernment and probusiness.

With the rise of the conservative coalition, the school choice movement gained national recognition and credibility. Alternative school advocates and libertarians, who had been marginal to the educational establishment, now found a voice in the White House. The strength of this voice has been magnified severalfold by the Roman Catholic Church, which finds itself in the paradoxical situation of having declining enrollments in its schools at the same time that the research community has been claiming that the Catholic schools are superior to public schools. At the local, state, and national levels, the choice forces have gathered into a potent political coalition. If the coalition successfully implements its policies, American education will be profoundly changed. But before the assumptions of the school choice movement are accepted, scholars must ask the hard questions that need to be asked before the public school system is radically changed by choice policies. The issues are equity, feasibility, and constitutionality. At the root of these issues is the unresolved question of whether school choice leads to greater achievement by students.

We begin exploring these issues by examining the historical and philosophical origins of the choice movement. We then provide a brief overview of choice legislation, followed by an examination of the outcomes of choice in terms of student achievement, school outcomes, equity, and community. We conclude by offering a few speculations on how choice will evolve in the current political and reform climate. Data for this chapter are drawn from three major studies of choice. Cookson recently completed a national study of choice that was based on site observations, in-depth interviews, and a review of previous research (Cookson 1994). Schneider has examined in two major studies how choice affects student learning and educational opportunities (Plank et al. 1993; Slaughter and Schneider 1986). Extended discussions of sample methodology and results can be found in these studies.

The Rise of the School Choice Movement

Since the 1980s Americans have experienced what amounts to a national panic attack about the condition of their children and their schools. Squeezed by inadequate resources and waves of poor immigrant children, public school systems in virtually every large American city are collapsing: dropout rates are well above 50 percent, truancy is the norm rather than the exception, violence is common, and students struggle for basic literacy, often without success. The condition of American children is so serious that at the very basic level it could be said that all American children are at risk. To cite but a few examples: one-fourth of all pre-school-age children in the United States live in poverty; each year roughly 350,000 children are born to mothers who were addicted to cocaine during pregnancy; 15 million children are being reared by single mothers whose incomes average a little over eleven thousand dollars a year; on any given night approximately 100,000 American children have no home; each year child protection agencies receive over two million reports of child abuse and neglect.

To compound this social and educational malaise, since the 1960s public education has become increasingly politicized and culturally fragmented. Civil rights leaders have been divided as to whether public schools should be a mechanism for integrating different cultures and races or whether they should serve particular communities that may or may not wish to associate with different racial or ethnic groups. Racial conflict has created a virtual state of educational apartheid, drawing public schools into the ongoing controversy over racial integration. Moreover, the banishment of prayer from the public schools offended many religious Americans and outraged Protestant fundamentalists. To make matters worse in the eyes of fundamentalists, many of the public educators who banished prayer endorsed sex education. Some religious families began to withdraw their children from the public schools and started their own private schools. The dream of a vibrant public school system that could mitigate the divisive effects of race and class and educate young people for productive lives has become tarnished in the public mind.

The fragility of the public school system has provided a window of opportunity for those reformers who believe that there can be no educational transformation without changing the very structure of American public education. In the 1980s these reformers were carried into the mainstream of educational policymaking by a rising tide of conservatism that swept up from the Southwest, where free enterprise and antigovernment sentiments dominated public discourse. There was a loss of faith in public institutions, which were often pictured by conservatives as being expensive, self-interested, and incompetent. Some conservative critics argued that liberal social welfare policies actually created more inequality rather than less. The loss of faith in public institutions paved the way for a new belief that drew its inspiration, not from the democratic social metaphor of community and cooperation, but from the market social metaphor of individual interest and competition. In the 1980s the market metaphor gained new credibility and moved from the wings of the social theater to take center stage. Because of the ascendancy of the market faith, by the early 1990s privatizing public education became a credible policy in the eyes of certain reformers, newspaper reporters, and educational policymakers.

Public opinion polls generally show that Americans support the idea of school choice. When, for instance, a poll conducted by *Phi Delta Kappan* (Elam 1990) asked parents whether they favored or opposed allowing students and their parents to choose among public schools regardless of where they live, roughly 62 percent of all respondents were in favor of public school choice regardless of residence. The poll found that men and women held similar views about school choice, but that non-Whites were more in favor of school choice than Whites. We know, however, that public opinion is highly volatile and that the results of polls can often be attributed to the way questions are asked. A recent study by the Carnegie Foundation for the Advancement of Teaching (1992), for instance, calls into question the degree to which the American people are in favor of school choice. In a survey of parents of children attending public school, 70 percent answered no to the following question: "Is there some other school to which you would like to send your child?" The respondents were offered the choice of a public or a private school, within or outside the respondent's district. Moreover, 62 percent of the parents surveyed in the Carnegie study were against issuing private school vouchers funded at the public expense. And surprisingly, 87 percent of these parents were either very satisfied or somewhat satisfied with the quality of the education their children received in 1991. These findings suggest that there is still strong support for the neighborhood school among American parents. Yet studies find that the school choice movement is far more than an artifact of questionnaire design or a media campaign.

Scholars have disagreed about why school choice has become the dominant reform idea of the present time. Sociologist Kevin Dougherty and educator Lizabeth Sostre have attempted to explain the rise of the school choice movement through the "state-relative-autonomy" theory of political power and the "garbage-can theory of organizational decision-making" (Dougherty and Sostre 1992, p. 160). The former theory hypothesizes that the state is a neutral arbiter, weighing and directing interest-group pressure; the latter theory makes the commonsensical point that people choose policies for conflicting reasons and because different options are available.

Organizational leaders have short-term objectives and do not actually know what the consequences of their decisions will be. Our conclusion from studying school choice, however, is that this idea symbolizes something intrinsic to American society. The ideals of individualism, autonomy, and competition run deep in the American character. We believe that we are in the midst of a profound cultural transition; the core consensus that united public opinion since the Great Depression has all but evaporated. An essential element of this consensus is the firm belief that public schools are the mediators of merit and the cradles of democracy. With the weakening of the consensus, however, traditional methods of educational reform appear inadequate and seemingly serve the self-interests of the public school establishment.

During the 1980s the United States underwent a political, intellectual, economic, and cultural revolution of great magnitude. The social consensus forged by Franklin D. Roosevelt during the New Deal had run its course and came to a dramatic end on the killing fields of Southeast Asia and with the collapse of the Great Society. The economic foundation of the country shifted from east to west, from agriculture and industry to new technologies and multinational corporations. The cultural revolution of the 1960s had anticipated, if not created, a different kind of society. Consumption and personal fulfillment replaced the older values of family, savings, and personal denial. The very definition of community shifted from its traditional anchors of family, neighborhood, church, lodge, and school to race, gender, occupation, and sexual preference. The new culture of self fulfillment and acquisition was made possible partly because of the withdrawal of the middle and upper-middle classes from public spaces and public commitments. Forced desegregation by busing solidified suburban enclaves, which remain self-contained and cut off from the cities they surround. In sum, traditional loyalties have been replaced by what might be called lifestyle loyalties. These loyalties are based not on group affiliations but on individual preferences.

At the same time that the United States was undergoing a profound cultural and economic transformation, the exchange value of educational credentials was considerably deflated. A high school degree could no longer guarantee employment, and a college degree was no longer an automatic ticket to the good life. The power of education to lift the disadvantaged out of poverty into the mainstream almost evaporated. Education lost its luster, and even its intrinsic value was open to destruction. Many Americans were caught in the credentials crunch, in which their degrees and diplomas had little effect on their social mobility.

In sum, the social, economic, and educational context from which the school choice movement arose was unlike any other period in American history. A patina of wealth masked serious economic problems. The rootlessness of much of American life became apparent in lifestyles which valued consumption and status, and lacked social commitment to public institutions. The middle and upper-middle classes led increasingly privatized lives and millions of Americans fell into poverty. The condition of children became increasingly problematic. It was under these circumstances that the school choice movement emerged from the margins of American education.

The Scope of School Choice

The term "school choice" covers a multitude of student assignment plans that vary significantly in their underlying assumptions and operational procedures, although all choice plans encourage or require students and their families to become actively engaged in choosing schools. Although the variety of school choice plans makes it difficult to summarize them, a few major types can be identified. Some choice plans partially restrict the educational choices families can make, while others have virtually no restrictions. The former type of plan is often referred to as "controlled-choice" and the latter as "open-enrollment." Most choice plans fall near the middle of the continuum between the two types. Virtually every state in the Union has either enacted or is considering a choice plan that is uniquely configured by its political environment and educational problems. Here are some definitions of choice plans:

Intradistrict choice. A plan that allows students to choose schools within one public school district. Depending on the specific plan, the range of choice may include anything from a few schools to all schools in a district.

Interdistrict choice. A plan in which students may cross district lines to attend school. Tuition funds from the state follow the student, and transportation costs are usually provided. Unlimited interdistrict choice is equivalent to statewide open enrollment.

Intrasectional choice. A plan that is limited to public schools.

Intersectional choice. A plan that includes both public and private schools.

Controlled choice. A student assignment plan that requires families to choose a school within a community, with choices possibly restricted to ensure the racial, gender, and socioeconomic balance of each school. Often such plans reflect a strategy to comply with court-ordered desegregation.

Voucher plans. Any system of certificate or cash payments by the government that enables public school students to attend schools of their choice, public or private. Vouchers have a fixed value and are redeemed at the time of enrollment.

As we can see from these definitions, tailoring a choice plan is itself a creative endeavor. Choice can be limited to one district and thus have minimal educational design consequences, or it can be statewide and intersectional and thus completely alter the way schools are organized within a state. Nobody has yet proposed an interstate choice plan, and as far as we know, nobody has seriously suggested a classroom choice plan. Thus, choice plans tend to fit within the traditional structure of American education. However, if the movement toward privatization of education accelerates, there may be new types of schools that do not fit within the traditional structure of American education. For now, however, most choice plans have been developed and implemented within the parameters established by state constitutions and by traditional conceptions of a public school district.

How widespread is school choice in terms of legislation, and what does it look like where it has been implemented? There is little doubt that the idea of choice has become increasingly popular. In 1988 Minnesota, which has traditionally been in the forefront of the alternative-school movement, initiated a groundbreaking statewide choice program. In 1989, Arkansas, Iowa, Nebraska, and Ohio also adopted choice plans; by 1991 ten states had approved some form of choice legislation. By late 1992, some kind of choice legislation had been introduced in thirty-seven states. The most common forms of legislation are voucher proposals and interdistrict open-enrollment proposals. Choice is extremely popular in the Midwest.

There is very little school choice in the South, which is ironic because the South originated the concept of freedom of choice in education. The northeastern United States has not been a hotbed of school choice legislation, although many local plans are quite successful. Most recently, a choice initiative was defeated in the Pennsylvania House of Representatives. Choice has not had a great impact in the West either, although there are strong movements in Colorado and Utah. In states that are thinly populated and where towns are separated by great distances, there are obvious practical limitations to how much choice parents and students can exercise. The West Coast, on the other hand, has been very active in the choice movement; in Oregon and California in particular, voucher proposals have aroused a great deal of public controversy. There are no choice plans in Hawaii or Alaska.

School choice movements are quite individual; each state's choice coalition is drawn together by grassroots choice movements, which are often backed by major businesses. In Illinois, for instance, the choice coalition is called TEACH (Taxpayers for Education Accountability and Choice); in Pennsylvania, the coalition is REACH (Road to Educational Achievement through Choice); in Arizona, the coalition is called PACE (Parents Advocating Choice in Education). Other groups include Floridians for Educational Choice, Oregonians for Educational Choice, and the Tennessee Parent Power Program. During George Bush's administration, these groups came regularly to Washington, D.C., where the Center for Choice in

Education sponsored brown-bag lunch seminars. As governor of Arkansas, President Clinton was a strong supporter of public school choice, there is little likelihood that his administration will support private school choice.

During the 1980s, the Department of Education shifted its emphasis away from public education and tilted distinctly toward private education and school choice. Virtually all Republican secretaries of education were conservative supporters of school choice, and the most recent one, Lamar Alexander, publicly championed choice without reservation. The Department of Education is only one of many Washington-based public policy centers and institutes. Some of these centers have created what amounts to a conservative infrastructure which promotes market solutions to public problems. The Washington lobbying infrastructure includes a variety of private school organizations that are strong advocates of school choice. Prominent among them are the National Association of Independent Schools (NAIS) and the Council for American Private Education. These groups have forged a collaboration with a number of religious and other private education groups, called the National Coalition for the Improvement and Reform of American Education. The school choice coalition also has been aided by think tanks, interest groups, and individuals who are not based in Washington and do not approach school choice from a religious or private school perspective. One of the most prominent and intellectually respected of these advocacy groups is the Manhattan Institute. It has released several studies about the benefits of school choice for poor, inner-city minority children. The Manhattan Institute continues to advocate school choice and is led by some of the country's most prominent banking and corporate executives, university professors, and Republican politicians, as well as a sprinkling of public school administrators and labor leaders.

Choice initiatives have touched off intense political debates. In Pennsylvania, for instance, the battle for a choice bill was led by the Road to Educational Achievement through Choice (REACH), a coalition headed by the Pennsylvania Catholic Conference. Pitted against the 1991 choice bill was a coalition of twenty organizations led by the state teachers unions, the League of Women Voters, and the American Civil Liberties Union. Observers said that the school choice debate in Pennsylvania was even more vitriolic than the controversy that surrounded the legislature's passage of a restrictive abortion law. Threats and counterthreats were exchanged, and according to one observer, "it was very hardball" (Diegmueller 1992).

Even when choice bills are defeated in state legislatures, the political drive for choice does not seem to diminish. In some ways choice has won the moral, if not the political, high ground. Choice has caught the imagination of educational reporters and politicians, many of whom see choice as a way of reforming education without spending much money.

What Is the Evidence?

One of the major questions regarding school choice is, how effective is it for improving education? This question has been investigated from two distinct yet complementary perspectives. First, there are studies that compare the culture of private or public schools of choice, most notably magnet schools, with that of public comprehensive schools. Focusing on process, these studies examine constancy of attitudes and values among school community members, parental involvement, administrative practices, faculty morale, and pedagogical techniques (Bryk, Lee, and Holland 1993; Cibulka, O'Brien, and Zewe 1982; Cookson and Persell 1985; Chubb and Moe 1990; Driscoll 1989; Erickson and Nault 1980; Slaughter and Schneider 1986). Second, there are studies which have looked at more proximate outcomes, such as student achievement, student educational aspirations, and high school graduation rates (Coleman, Hoffer, and Kilgore 1982; Coleman and Hoffer 1987). As in most social science research, these distinctions are not entirely dichotomous; among the first set are studies in which student academic performance is examined in detail. Moreover, among the second set are studies that also examine how school community characteristics influence student academic performance and social development.

These studies rely on a variety of methodological techniques, such as qualitative in-depth cases, quantitative analyses of large-scale data bases, or some combination of the two (Bryk, Lee, and Holland 1993 provide an example of combining such methodologies). However, it is not the variations in methodological approaches that are of interest here but rather the underlying quest to substantiate or refute commonly held beliefs about differences between the two sectors of schooling.

Clearly, amassing undisputable evidence to prove or disprove the benefits of private or public schools of choice requires an unusually high degree of scientific rigor to meet the intense scrutiny of competing political interests. Meeting such a standard with social science data would indeed be difficult. Unquestionably, making distinctions between the environment of one type of school in contrast to that of another is hardly controversial if student outcomes, that is, academic performance and expectations, are not at issue. Scientific work that suggests being in one type of school rather than another has distinct academic consequences and invites controversy, rebuttal, and reanalyses.

Although researchers have examined the differences between public and private schools (comprehensively reviewed in Erickson 1986; Erickson and Bauch 1992), these studies, with their relatively small sampled populations, have not drawn the attention of scholars or policymakers that the release of Public and Private Schools (Coleman, Hoffer, and Kilgore 1982) received. The Coleman, Hoffer, and Kilgore analysis of the 1980 initial wave of the High School and Beyond survey (HS&B) of more than 58,000 sophomore and senior students from 894 public, 84 Catholic, and 27 nonreligious private schools concluded that private high schools enhanced academic achievement more than public schools. Comparing the average test scores of public and private school sophomores and seniors, they found that there was not one subject in which public school students scored higher. This major finding launched more than a decade of continued academic debate (see Report Analysis 1981; Special two-volume series 1982; Series of papers 1983; Third special issue 1985) and public attention.

Essentially, the major controversy around the Coleman et al. findings centered primarily on "magnitude," that is, on how much better the test scores were for private school students and how much private schools reduced the inequities between advantaged and disadvantaged students, at least with respect to their achievement scores (Haertel 1984). Subsequent reanalyses of the data failed to produce results that could conclusively refute the academic effects of Catholic schools as reported by Coleman, Hoffer, and Kilgore (1982). Moreover, further analyses of the first follow-up survey of High School and Beyond provided additional evidence that substantiated the earlier findings of Coleman et al. (1982).

The controversy about test score differences overshadowed other findings that pointed to the ability of private schools to produce a more equitable schooling environment for poor and minority children. For example, Coleman et al. found that Catholic schools seem to be more effective in maximizing the social opportunities of poor and minority students by helping them stay in school. Graduates of private high schools were also more likely to enroll in post-secondary institutions (Coleman and Hoffer 1987). Coleman's (1987) findings suggested that school policies concerning academic order, demands, and discipline played a major role in how private and public schools differed. The most important factor was that students in Catholic schools were much more likely to follow an academic program of studies. These findings were substantiated by Greeley (1985) who, using the same data set, highlighted the organizational structure of the schools and the quality of their instruction.

In 1988 the National Center for Education Statistics began a new longitudinal study, the National Education Longitudinal Study of 1988 (NELS:88), which attempted to replicate the design and some of the same questions used in the High School and Beyond study. Beginning with a national random sample of 26,000 eighth-graders and their parents, teachers, and administrators, the study was designed to examine student achievement over time. Its focus was on family, community, school, and classroom factors that may promote or inhibit educational success. The sampling design for NELS:88 was purposefully developed to include a substantial number of private religious and nonreligious schools.

The effects of NELS:88 school types on educational outcomes was recently examined by Plank et al. (1993). Looking at test score performance on four cognitive tests from eighth to tenth grade, they found that private school students on the average had the highest test scores in eighth grade and gained the most in tenth grade. While the gain in test scores was higher for private school students, the magnitude of that gain was considerably smaller than the gain found for private school students in HS&B. But making a direct comparison to HS&B using NELS:88 is clearly suspect, for the gains in academic performance among NELS:88 private school students occurred from eighth to tenth grade, whereas the gain in HS&B private school students occurred from tenth to twelfth grade.

However, recent work comparing academic growth in mathematics from tenth to twelfth grade among NELS:88 students shows findings nearly identical to those of HS&B, controlling on student background characteristics, prior achievement, and educational aspirations (Schiller 1994). Employing the same analysis as Coleman and Hoffer (1987), Schiller asked how much an average student in public school learned in two years and then how much more that student would have learned if he or she had been in a Catholic school. This analysis, which uses mathematics growth from tenth to twelfth grade among NELS:88 students, produces results nearly identical to those of HS&B (Schiller 1994).

Moving beyond test score differences between the two sectors, ongoing analyses of NELS:88 continue to replicate some of Coleman's other findings regarding private schools. Schiller (1994) also finds higher educational aspirations among twelfth-graders in private schools compared to those in public schools Studies of dropout rates using the NELS:88 data set also demonstrate that Catholic schools are more effective in keeping students in school (Schneider, Stevenson, and Link 1994).

Coleman and Hoffer (1987) suggest that these differences in school types, particularly among public and Catholic schools, are the consequence of functional communities which are more likely to exist in private schools. Functional communities are formed in environments where close relations among students, teachers, and families forge shared norms and goals toward academic achievement. Regardless of how much of a difference exists between the academic performance of students in public and private schools, several studies tried to discover what it is about private schools that raises educational expectations and reduces dropout rates.

The Culture of Private Schools

At the elementary school level, Cibulka, O'Brien, and Zewe (1982) examined inner-city Catholic schools. They found that these schools had strong institutional leaders and that parents and staff had shared values concerning the mission and goals of the schools. Similar findings were reported by Slaughter and Schneider (1986), who also studied private elementary schools. They found that the organizational structure of private schools helps them accomplish their goals with minimum interference and misuse of resources. Slaughter and Schneider attribute the success of private schools to such characteristics as autonomy and accountability, matched expectations and communication policies, and goal clarity and consensus.

Looking into the culture of private high schools using the HS&B data set, Bryk and Driscoll (1988) developed a series of measures which have shown that a system of shared values, a common agenda of activities, and a distinctive pattern of social relations embodying an ethos of caring are more likely to occur in private high schools than in public ones. They find that schools with these characteristics tend to have teachers who report more work satisfaction and exhibit higher morale and are absent less frequently. The students demonstrate similar positive behaviors and attitudes; they misbehave less often, drop out less, and learn more mathematics between their sophomore and senior years.

Investigating these issues in somewhat greater detail, Bryk, Lee, and Holland (1993), in a quantitative analysis of HS&B that relies on qualitative case materials, found, first, that Catholic high schools manage to achieve relatively high levels of student learning by limiting the content and number of elective courses, thus requiring students to take a more focused academic curriculum. Second, there are many school activities that provide opportunities for students and teachers to interact in nonacademic environments, affording extensive opportunities for expressions of individual concern and interest. Third, the small size of Catholic schools facilitates personalism and social intimacy, which strengthen mutual trust and respect between staff and administrators. Finally, membership, ownership, and high degrees of autonomy in managing school operations help to promote an institution that functions as a voluntary community.

The voluntary nature of private schools, that is, the ability and opportunity to choose a school, might lead one to suspect that school choice may be a major contributor to the creation of functional school communities. A family that chooses its child's school may have a greater sense of commitment in the school's goals simply because the family selected it. Communicating student admission policies may be the first step in socializing families into buying the philosophy and programs of the school. A family's willingness to keep their child in the school depends on how comfortable they are with the actual work of the school in relation to its expressed values and goals.

School Choice

The direct evidence that school choice in itself leads to greater achievement is unclear. Evidence for the indirect effects of voluntary ownership and compatibility of goals is perhaps more straightforward. However, it is important to examine who uses schools of choice and what effect choice has (for a review of parental choice of school, see Maddaus 1990). The first instance of school choice that was seriously studied by social scientists was the Alum Rock experiment, in which parents of elementary school students could choose among school programs for their children in any of fourteen public schools. The Alum Rock experiment indicated that initially, families with high incomes and educational levels had greater knowledge of school program alternatives. However, over time, informational differences between family groups were reduced. Regardless of their social and economic backgrounds, most of the parents chose their child's school because of its proximity and the racial and social composition rather than because of its instructional program (Bridge and Blackman 1978).

Slaughter and Schneider (1986) also found that most families, regardless of their socioeconomic or minority status, did not make school choices on the basis of programs or teaching styles. However, in contrast to Bridge and Blackman (1978), they found that choices of private schools were often made on the basis of the family's beliefs about the type of schooling environment that best suited its own educational philosophies and the needs of its children. Poor and minority families, like other families in the study, articulated distinguishable values about what constitutes quality education, and these beliefs guided their selections of specific private elementary schools. The process by which disadvantaged families selected a private school reflected their personal ideologies about education. Although middle- and higher-income families had the financial and social resources to consider more private school options, their decisions were firmly based in their educational philosophy about who should have primary responsibility for the education of the child and about the activities the school would use to promote the child's intellectual and social development.

More recently, for the past three years John Witte has been studying Milwaukee's experimental Parental Choice Program (Witte 1993). It is the first government-subsidized voucher program in the United States that, unlike the Alum Rock experiment, involves private schools. The families who seek to get into the program are poor but are more educated, more involved in school activities, and have higher educational expectations than comparison public school families. In terms of outcomes, the results are mixed. In the first year, reading scores increased, but they declined in years two and three. In terms of mathematics performance, the results are slightly more positive. For the first two years of the program, mathematics performance for school choice students was essentially the same but it significantly increased in the third year. Witte attributes the fluctuations in achievement test results for choice students to attrition from the program (Witte 1993). Overall, Witte maintains that while the choice schools seem to have the same problems as public schools in the inner city in raising achievement scores and coping with high proportions of student mobility, they do allow poor parents to send their children to alternative programs which they could not otherwise afford.

Coleman, Schiller, and Schneider (1993) investigated responsiveness to opportunity for choice using the NELS:88 database. In many ways their findings mirror those of Witte (1993). Students from families with somewhat lower incomes and less-educated parents are the most likely to enroll in public schools of choice. African-American and Hispanic students are more likely to enroll in those schools than White or Asian-American students. The highest tenth-grade enrollments in public schools of choice are among students who scored in the lowest eighth-grade test quartile compared with students who scored in higher eighth-grade quartiles. With respect to achievement, students in chosen public schools do not experience higher gains in achievement than students in assigned or private schools.

The findings of Witte (1993) and Plank et al. (1993) concerning public school choice raise questions about the value of choice, at least in the public sector, as the key to massively improving public education. Chubb and Moe (1990) argue on the basis of HS&B data that the privatization of schools ultimately holds the answer to school improvement. Critics Cookson (1991), and Lee and Bryk (1993) have methodologically attacked the evidence Chubb and Moe use to frame their conclusions. But it would be foolhardy not to recognize that there are some characteristics of school privatization—autonomy, accountability, and social participation—that do contribute to some of the uniqueness of private schools.

Cookson (1993) defines choice as a form of empowerment that gives a person a sense of dignity that is hard to achieve when a family feels compelled to send their child to a particular school. He argues that managed school choice can be the mechanism that requires schools to open their doors to families, thus breaking down the barriers that have isolated schools from their communities and parents from schools. Research clearly indicates that parental involvement in schooling is beneficial to students' cognitive and affective growth. School choice can be thought of as perhaps the most overt form of parental involvement. Schools are social organizations, and if they influence families to be more participatory, then school choice can be considered one way to help create a viable school community. However, there is no evidence that choice in itself and the resulting greater parental participation lead to school improvement or the transformation of public education. Nor can we reasonably suspect that privatization in itself holds the key.

REFERENCES

Bridge, G., and J. Blackman. 1978. *A Study of Alternatives in American Education*. Vol. 4, *Family Choice in Schooling*. Washington, DC: National Institute of Education.

Bryk, A.S., and M.E. Driscoll. 1988. *The High School as Community: Contextual Influences and Consequences for Students and Teachers*. Madison: National Center for Effective Secondary Schools.

Bryk, A., V. Lee, and P.B. Holland. 1993. *Catholic Schools and the Common Good*. Cambridge: Harvard University Press.

Carnegie Foundation for the Advancement of Teaching. 1992. *School Choice*. Princeton: Carnegie Foundation for the Advancement of Teaching.

Chubb, J.E., and T.M. Moe. 1990. *Politics, Markets, and America's Schools*. Washington, DC: Brookings Institution.

Cibulka, J., T. O'Brien, and D. Zewe. 1982. *Inner City Private Elementary Schools: A Study*. Milwaukee, WI: Marquette University Press.

Coleman, J.S., and T. Hoffer. 1987. *Public and Private High Schools: The Impact of Communities*. New York: Basic Books.

Coleman, J.S., T. Hoffer, and S.B. Kilgore. 1982. *High School Achievement: Public, Catholic, and Private Schools Compared*. New York: Basic Books.

Coleman, J.S., K. Schiller, and B. Schneider. 1993. Parent Choice and Inequality. In *Parents, Their Children, and Schools*, ed. Barbara

Schneider and James S. Coleman, 147–186. Boulder, CO: Westview.

Cookson, P.W., Jr. 1991. Politics, Markets, and America's Schools: A Review. *Teachers' College Record* 93: 156–160.

———. 1993. Assessing Private School Effects: Implications for School Choice. In *School Choice: Examining the Evidence*, ed. E. Rasell and R. Rothstein, 173–184. Washington, DC: Economic Policy Institute.

———. 1994. *School Choice: The Struggle for the Soul of American Education.* New Haven: Yale University Press.

Cookson, P.W., Jr., and C.H. Persell. 1985. *Preparing for Power: America's Elite Boarding Schools.* New York: Basic Books.

Diegmueller, K. 1992. Despite Defeat, Choice Still Likely to Resurface in PA. *Education Week* 31.

Dougherty, K., and L. Sostre. 1992. Minerva and the Market: The Sources for the Movement of School Choice. *Education Policy* 6 (2): 160–179.

Driscoll, M.E. 1989. The School as Community. Ph.D. diss., Department of Education, University of Chicago.

Elam, S. 1990. Trends and Support for Parent Choice. *Phi Delta Kappan* (September): 43–44.

Erickson, D. 1986. Research on Private Schools: The State of the Art. Paper presented at the conference on Research on Private Education: Private Schools and Public Concerns: What We Know and What We Need to Know. Catholic University of America, Washington, DC.

Erickson, D., and P.A. Bauch. 1992. Catholic Schools. *Encyclopedia of Educational Research.* 6th ed.

Erickson, D., and R. Nault. 1980. *Effects of Public Money on Catholic Schools in Western Canada.* San Francisco: Center for Research on Private Education.

Greeley, A.M. 1985. The Catholic School. In *American Catholics since the Council: An Unauthorized Report.* Chicago: Thom Mac.

Haertel, E. 1984. The Question of School Outcomes: A Synthesis of Competing Arguments. Paper presented at the conference on Comparing Public and Private Schools, Institute for Research on Educational Finance and Governance, Stanford University, Stanford, California.

Why School Choice? A Question of Values 577

Lee, V.E., and A.S. Bryk. 1993. Science or Policy Argument? A Review of the Quantitative Evidence in Chubb and Moe's *Politics, Markets, and America's Schools*. In *School Choice: Examining the Evidence*, ed. E. Rasell and R. Rothstein, 185–208. Washington, DC: Economic Policy Institute.

Maddaus, J. 1990. Parental Choice of School: What Parents Think and Do. *Review of Research Education* 16: 267–296.

Plank, S., K. Schiller, B. Schneider, and J.S. Coleman. 1993. Effects of Choice in Education. In *School Choice: Examining the Evidence*, ed. E. Rasell and R. Rothstein, 111–134. Washington, DC: Economic Policy Institute.

Report Analysis: Public and Private Schools. 1981. *Harvard Educational Review* 51: 481–545.

Schiller, K. 1994. Private and Public Schools in Two Decades: Sophomore Classes of 1980 and 1990 Compared. Paper presented at the annual meeting of the American Educational Research Association, New Orleans, Louisiana.

Schneider, B., D. Stevenson, and J. Link. 1994. Social and Cultural Capital and Early School Leavers. Paper presented at the annual meeting of the American Educational Research Association, New Orleans, Louisiana.

Series of papers on the Public and Private School Debate. 1983. *Sociology of Education* 56 (October): 170–234.

Slaughter, D., and B. Schneider. 1986. *Newcomers: Blacks in Public Schools*. Final Report to the National Institute of Education. Vols. 1 and 2. Contract no. NIE-G-82–0040. Northwestern University. ERIC documents ED 274 768 and ED 274 769.

Special two-volume series on the debate surrounding Public and Private Schools (1981). 1982. *Sociology of Education* 55 (April–July).

Third special issue devoted to Public and Private School debate. 1985. *Sociology of Education* 58 (April).

Witte, J. 1993. The Milwaukee Parental Choice Program. In *School Choice: Examining the Evidence*, ed. E. Rasell and R. Rothstein, 69–110. Washington, DC: Economic Policy Institute.

Contributors

Michael W. Apple is the John Bascom Professor at the University of Wisconsin–Madison with joint appointments in the Departments of Curriculum and Instruction and Educational Policy Studies. His research interests center on critical social thought and ideology and curriculum.

Kathryn M. Borman is Professor and Director of Research Initiatives at the University of South Florida's David C. Anchin Center. Her current interests include the school-to-work transition and education reform policy in the United States.

Louis Castenell is Professor and Dean of the College of Education at the University of Cincinnati. His areas of research interest include the career trajectories of women and minorities in higher education administration.

James G. Cibulka is Professor of Administrative Leadership and Director of the Ph.D. program in Urban Education at the University of Wisconsin–Milwaukee. His areas of specialization are educational politics and policy, education finance, private schools, and urban education.

Judith H. Cohen is Associate Professor of Education at Adelphi University, a practicing attorney in New York State, and a member of the Law Guardian panel on Long Island. Her interests include both teacher education in literacy and child advocacy.

Peter W. Cookson, Jr. is Associate Provost, Adelphi University. His interests are school choice and educational policy.

Mary Erina Driscoll is Assistant Professor of Educational Administration in the School of Education at New York

University. Her research interests encompass social organization of schools with particular focus on issues of school community.

Karen Gallagher is Dean of Education, University of Kansas. She has done research on the role of business in education reform.

Ellen B. Goldring is Professor of Educational Leadership and Associate Dean for Academic Affairs at Peabody College, Vanderbilt University. Her areas of interest are the organization and control of schools and their impact on educational leadership and parents.

Ivor F. Goodson is a Professor at the University of Western Ontario, where he is a member of the Faculties of Graduate Studies, Education, Sociology and the Center for Theory and Criticism. He is also the Frederica Warner Scholar in the Graduate School of Education and Human Development at the University of Rochester. He is the author of a range of books on curriculum and life history studies, including such titles as *School Subjects and Curriculum Change* and *Studying Curriculum: Cases and Methods.*

Maureen T. Hallinan is the White Professor of Arts and Letters at the University of Notre Dame, Department of Sociology, and President-Elect of the American Sociological Association. Her research interests are school organization and its effects on student achievement and, in particular, tracking and its effects on student achievement. She is also interested in school choice and in school effects on student social relations.

Thomas B. Hoffer is Senior Study Director at NORC. His research interests center on the sociology of education policy analysis.

Sally B. Kilgore is Senior Social Scientist at the Hudson Institute in Indianapolis, where her research focuses on organizational dilemmas in changing school culture.

Mindy Kornhaber is Research Coordinator of Project Zero, the Graduate School of Education at Harvard University. Her research centers on the question of how institutions enhance or impede a development of individual potential.

Mara Krechevsky is Project Director of Project Spectrum, Harvard University Graduate School of Education. She is interested in alternative forms of student assessment and issues surrounding school reform.

Hanne B. Mawhinney is Director of the Professional Development Program, Education Department at the University of Ottawa, Ontario. She is the principal investigator for SACA (School and Community Agency) study, a three-year, four-province study of the structures and strategies evident in high school interagency collaboration.

Debra A. Martinson is a consultant with SPSS, Chicago.

Roslyn Arlin Mickelson is Associate Professor of Sociology and Adjunct Associate Professor of Women's Studies at the University of North Carolina at Charlotte. Her research examines the political economy of schooling, in particular the ways that race, class, and gender shape the educational processes and outcomes.

Chandra Muller is Assistant Professor of Sociology at the University of Texas at Austin. Her current research interests are in parent involvement and the interface of families, peers, and schools in the life of adolescents.

Gary Natriello is Associate Professor of Sociology and Education at Teachers College, Columbia University. His areas of interest include student assessment and school organization.

Sumie Okazaki is a postdoctoral scholar at UCLA, Department of Psychology. Her research interests include culture and psychopathology, family factors in serious mental illness, and academic achievement in Asian Americans.

Aaron M. Pallas is Associate Professor of Educational Administration and Adjunct Associate Professor of Sociology at Michigan State University. His primary areas of interest are educational stratification, school organization, and the life course.

Rolland G. Paulston is Professor of Administrative and Policy Studies at the University of Pittsburgh and past President of the Comparative and International Education Society. His current research examines implications of the postmodern turn for educational reform studies/pragmatics.

Thomas S. Popkewitz is Professor of Curriculum and Instruction, the University of Wisconsin–Madison. His work centers on a political sociology of educational reform, educational sciences, and professionalization.

Barbara Schneider is a Senior Social Scientist at NORC and The University of Chicago. Her areas of interest are schools as organizations and student school careers.

David Lee Stevenson is Senior Policy Adviser, Office of the Under Secretary, U.S. Department of Education. His main fields of interest are the organization of schools, educational policy, and comparative study of education.

Anna V. Shaw Sullivan is a doctoral candidate in the Department of Education at Vanderbilt University.

Kenneth K. Wong is Associate Professor in the Department of Education and the College at The University of Chicago. He is Principal Investigator of a research project, "Systemwide Governance in the Chicago Public Schools." He is coeditor of *Rethinking Policy for At-Risk Students* (McCutchan, 1994).

Dunchun Zheng is a Research Associate at the National Research Center of Asian-American Mental Health at UCLA and a children's social worker in Los Angeles County, Department of Children's Services. His research interests are Asian-American mental health and Asian family culture.

Index

C/CSA (Corporate/Community
School of America), 542
Cain, D. P., 86
Caldwell, B. M., 59
Caldwell, J., 547
Callaghan, J., 324
Calvin, J., 308
Campbell, B., 378
Campbell, C., 338
Campbell, E., 215
Campbell, R., 222
Caplan, N., 81, 83, 85, 87
Capper, C. A., 516
Carlson, D., 422, 446
Carnegie Foundation for the
Advancement of Teaching,
561
Carnoy, M., 146, 154, 168, 171
cartography, social, 162
Case, C., 472, 477
Castel, R., 436, 438
Castenell, L., 134–135, 238, 241
Catholic high schools, 571–572
Catholic schools, 464–465, 558,
569
Caudill, W., 87
Celis, W., 278, 279
central-city school systems; *see*
big-city school systems
CETA (Comprehensive
Employment and Training
Act of 1973), 28
Chapter 1 of the Elementary and
Secondary Education Act
of 1965, 286–287
charismatic principals, 330
Charner, I., 123
Chemers, M. M., 505
Chen, Q., 84

Cherryholms, C., 169, 172
Chicago teachers union, 481–482
child abuse and neglect, 267–270,
280–285
child advocacy as educational
responsibility, 267–294
child protective proceedings,
280–285
child services, educational equity
and, 271–273
Children's Defense Fund, 117
Chira, S., 288, 289
choice, school; *see* school choice
Choy, M. H., 81, 83, 85, 87
Christian-Smith, L., 348, 358, 359,
365
Chubb, J. E., 247, 331, 465, 473,
474, 490, 512, 518
Chun, M. B. J., 87
Chung, N., 483
Cibulka, J., 407–408, 479, 567, 571
Cippolone, A., 250
Clark, D. L., 496
Clarke, J., 446
class, 423
class differences in education, 81–
101
classroom system, 315, 316
Clifford, J., 169, 174, 416
Clignet, R., 149, 150, 159, 166, 168
clinics, 287–288
Clinton, B., 286, 566
closed-system organizational
models, 511
closed systems, 25
Clune, W., 483, 504
Coalition of Essential Schools,
183–184, 330
cognitive mapping, 162